The first book-length study of Dean Rusk, Secretary of State for John F. Kennedy and Lyndon B. Johnson, provides new explanations of the part he played at critical times in American history.

Dean Rusk served as Secretary of State for eight years, second in length of office only to Cordell Hull. The story of his years as Secretary touches upon every major event in world affairs from 1961 to 1969: the Bay of Pigs invasion, the Cuban missile crisis, problems with the Soviet Union, China, Great Britain and France, war in the Middle East, and most of all the war in Vietnam.

By examining Rusk's earlier career as well, especially the years he served under George Marshall and Dean Acheson in Harry Truman's State Department, Professor Cohen is able to penetrate Rusk's reserve, to determine the pattern of his thought, to illuminate the course he followed in the 1960s.

Cohen's analysis is based on extensive interviews with Rusk and the men who worked with him to shape American policy in the sixties, and on documentary evidence obtained under the provisions of the Freedom of Information Act.

Warren I. Cohen is Professor of History and Director of the Asian Studies Center at Michigan State University. His other books include *The American Revisionists: The Lessons of Intervention* (1967) and *America's Response to China* (1971).

Dean Rusk

The American Secretaries of State and Their Diplomacy

SAMUEL FLAGG BEMIS, Founding Editor
ROBERT H. FERRELL, Editor

VOLUME XIX

Dean Rusk

WARREN I. COHEN

COOPER SQUARE PUBLISHERS
Totowa, New Jersey

Copyright © 1980 by Cooper Square Publishers

First published in the United States of America, 1980, by
Cooper Square Publishers, 81 Adams Drive, Totowa, New Jersey.

Library of Congress Cataloging in Publication Data

Cohen, Warren I
    Dean Rusk.

    (The American Secretaries of State and their
diplomacy ; 19)
    Bibliography: p.
    Includes index.
    1. Rusk, Dean, 1909-   2. United States—
Foreign relations—1961-1963. 3. United States—
Foreign relations—1963-1969. 4. Statesmen—United
States—Biography. I. Series: Bemis, Samuel Flagg,
1891-1973, ed. American Secretaries of State and their
diplomacy ; 19.
E183.7.B462   vol. 19   [E748.R94]   973s
ISBN 0-8154-0519-7   [973.92′092′4] [B]   80-10943

Printed in the United States of America

For Fay Cohen
   (in lieu of a Mother's Day card)
and James A. Prichard
   (in lieu of interest)

Contents

Preface

I undertook this study because Dean Rusk intrigued me. I have always been fascinated by able men who won sinister reputations, eager to find patterns in their thought. Readers may remember my portrait of Harry Elmer Barnes in *The American Revisionists* or of George E. Sokolsky in *The Chinese Connection*. I think I understand Rusk now, and I write to explain, not to praise him.

Research in the recent past has advantages that compensate for missing official documents. I enjoyed interviews with participants immensely. Confidence in my ability to judge character is one of my conceits. More important, I could determine each man's perspective: what mattered to him and, as in the old Indian fable about the blind men describing an elephant, I could tell what part of my elephant each man had felt.

My arrangement with Rusk must be noted. He allowed no access to his personal papers: there are none. His files were left with the Department of State. He agreed to read the manuscript and call attention to errors of fact, to mistakes that would embarrass me when the official record became available. We spent two days together during which he commented at length on the manuscript and answered my questions. We rarely touched matters of interpretation. Neither of us sought a convert.

I read several oral histories that I was not allowed to cite. Similarly some of my interviews were on a "not-for-attribution" basis. I am not satisfied with such arrangements and have avoided dependence on these sources—except for a bit of gossip in Chapter One.

Acknowledgments

I have always been fortunate to have friends who read my manuscripts critically. Robert H. Ferrell, who doubled as editor, gave this book his usual treatment—some of which I undid when he was not looking. Donald Lammers spent many hours listening to my ideas and carefully corrected the manuscript. William B. Hixson read the entire volume and provided a thoughtful and detailed critique. Dorothy Borg, Philip C. Jessup, Madison Kuhn, Peter Levine, Robert M. Slusser, Paul Sweet, and Allen S. Whiting each commented on a part. I benefitted from discussions with Norman Pollack about the overview I presented to the annual meeting of the Organization of American Historians in New York in April, 1978, and from the comments on that paper by Walter LaFeber, Ronald Steel, and Richard White.

William P. Bundy was notably supportive of my work and allowed access to his lengthy manuscript on policy toward East Asia, particularly Vietnam. Like most of my readers, he took exception to some of my conclusions. My sessions with Lucius D. Battle, McGeorge Bundy, Roswell Gilpatric, Ernest A. Gross, and Philip C. Jessup were especially rewarding. Chester Bowles kindly talked with me under extraordinarily difficult conditions.

Senator John Sparkman and members of the staff of the Committee on Foreign Relations fought mightily on my behalf, wielding the Freedom of Information Act to force declassification of Executive Sessions of the 1960s. My friend Robert Blum helped begin the process, generous as always with his special knowledge. Beverly Zweiben-Slany contributed her experience to my FOI approaches to the Department of State.

More mundane needs—eating, travel, typing—were met with

help from Michigan State University which granted me sabbatic leave and the Ford Foundation which provided the funds that allowed me to spend the academic year 1976-1977 on this project. My cousins, the Phillips family, provided food, shelter, love, office space, and the secretarial assistance of Elizabeth Robinson during much of my stay in Washington.

Dean Rusk
from the painting by Gardner Cox
in the collection of
the Department of State

CHAPTER ONE

The American Dream

In 1961 the well-known journalist Richard Rovere revealed his discovery of the American Establishment and announced his suspicion that Dean Rusk was its president.[1] Rovere's satire underlined the fact that David Dean Rusk, born on a small farm in Cherokee County, Georgia, February 9, 1909, erstwhile wearer of floursack drawers, now sat at the head table during the blacktie dinners of the Council on Foreign Relations.

The poverty of Rusk's antecedents and the story of his rise is the stuff of which the American Dream is made. His was not the genteel poverty of the northeastern clergy—the Achesons, Dulleses, Lamonts—who eked out a living sufficient to send their sons to elite boarding schools preparatory to matriculating at Harvard, Princeton, or Yale. His father, Robert Hugh Rusk, was an ordained Presbyterian minister, but a throat ailment forced him to leave the ministry. The elder Rusk worked a forty acre rented farm, built the house that Dean was born in, and sold not quite $100 worth of cotton annually—with some of the money used to buy the books that he and his wife, a former schoolteacher, treasured. The Rusk children went barefoot, in homemade clothes and hand-me-downs to ramshackle schools, but all were serious, God-fearing students who found in education a key to upward mobility in American society.[2]

The Rusks moved to Atlanta in 1913 and Dean was educated in the Atlanta public school system. An extremely able student, good athlete and outstanding ROTC cadet, co-winner of the cup for best all-around boy, he graduated from high school in 1925 at the age of

1

sixteen. Unfortunately, he had no money for college, and scholarships were rare and inadequate. Two years of work in a one-man law
office convinced him that he could never save enough to pay for four
years of school, so he took what he had and enrolled at Davidson—a
good North Carolina college that his father had attended before
entering a seminary. His performance at Davidson equaled his high
school record. He excelled in his studies, in athletics, and in the
ROTC. Scholarships and part-time jobs supplemented his savings
and allowed him to graduate in four years.

In 1931, his senior year at Davidson, Rusk won an extraordinary
opportunity: a Rhodes Scholarship that permitted three years at
Oxford University in England. As a sixth grader Rusk had been sent
home from school with a demand that his parents provide him with
shoes. At 22, he had "digs" and "a man" at Oxford. Strict Calvinist
upbringing and youthful thoughts of serving God did not prevent
young Rusk from learning the pleasures of being a gentleman. He
played tennis for the "Penguins" and more than his share of
billiards. In the fall of his third year he received permission to study
in Germany and was soon ensconced in an "opulent Neubabelsberg
mansion," enjoying a regimen that might have proven attractive to a
blue-blooded hedonist.[3]

The joys of Neubabelsberg ended when a friend reminded Rusk
that the deadline in the competition for the Cecil Peace Prize was
approaching. It was time to write and Rusk went to a Berlin hotel
where he quickly pounded out the prize-winning essay, a study of
the relationship between the British Commonwealth and the
League of Nations. To his comrades at Oxford, the story of the Cecil
Prize epitomized Rusk. They recognized in him someone of quicker
mind and greater ability. Without taking his studies more seriously
than a gentleman should, he always performed well. Perceived as
neither scholar nor playboy, he attracted friends and followers
easily.[4]

If the years as Rhodes Scholar were as close to idyllic as anything
Rusk might have imagined, the prospect of returning to the United
States to seek employment in 1934 must have been sobering. He
was fortunate to come to the attention of Aurelia Reinhardt,
President of Mills College in California, who collected Rhodes
Scholars. She invited him to join her faculty to teach government

and international relations. In addition to teaching, Rusk served as Dean of the Faculty and studied law at the University of California. Despite so demanding a schedule, he found time to court Virginia Foisie of Seattle, one of his students, whom he married.

When war broke out in Europe in 1939, Rusk, then 30 years old, had at last achieved genteel poverty, a condition faculty members at women's schools could share with the clergy. Teaching, small college administration, and presiding over a family promised a full life—and an easier one than seemed possible from the perspective of Cherokee County, Georgia. But Rusk's interest in world affairs was more than academic. In high school he had evidenced a strong commitment to the League of Nations, as was common among Southern Democrats, awakened to foreign policy issues by Woodrow Wilson. Politics and world affairs dominated his programs at Davidson and Oxford. While in Germany, neither his frolics nor his writing prevented him from recognizing the menace of Nazism. After his return to the United States, he participated in the American peace movement. Although his ideas about international organization and preparedness approximated those of the collective security wing of the peace movement, he retained contacts with the pacifist wing—specifically with Ray Newton of the American Friends Service Committee. With eight years of ROTC training and a reserve commission, Rusk was an unlikely pacifist, but he had great respect for the Quakers.[5]

In December, 1940, as war enveloped Europe, the Army called in its note. Captain Rusk was ordered to active duty, as an infantry officer. Just prior to the Japanese attack on Pearl Harbor, he was transferred from the the the Third Infantry Division to Military Intelligence and sent to Washington. Rusk met the War Department's need for someone with a knowledge of the British Empire, but his assignment to concentrate on South, Southeast Asia, and the Western Pacific led him along unfamiliar paths. In 1943, Major Rusk was sent to New Delhi, to join the staff of General Joseph W. Stilwell in the China-Burma-India Theater. By December, 1944, he was deputy chief of staff for the entire theater—and received his first mention in the *New York Times*.[6]

On active duty Rusk once again compiled a superb record. He was a brilliant staff officer who won the respect and admiration of peers and superiors alike. He had the ability to do almost everything better than anyone else—and to be liked in the process. In particular, Rusk's ability to write, to prepare lucid and succinct reports and cables, was widely recognized and won favorable attention for him in Washington. Also of note is the fact that the rough crowd of Stilwell loyalists headquartered in New Delhi, especially Frank Merrill of Merrill's Marauders, evidenced a warm affection for him. He was reported to have a marvelous sense of humor, to be a great sport at the card table, and, although rather more difficult to verify, something of a ladies' man.[7]

In Washington, Brigadier General George ("Abe") Lincoln, a Rhodes Scholar upon whom General George C. Marshall depended for finding first-rate men, was assembling a staff to provide Marshall and Secretary of War Henry L. Stimson with long-range planning on political-military affairs. Studying Rusk's reports, checking with men who had known him at Oxford, in Washington, and in New Delhi, Lincoln concluded that the army had no one better suited for the task. No one in the army wrote as well. In April, 1945, Rusk was recalled to Washington and assigned to the "Lincoln Brigade," the Operations Division (OPD) of the General Staff. On Lincoln's staff, Colonel Rusk renewed his acquaintance with Colonel Charles H. Bonesteel, a fellow member of the Oxford "Penguins." Together, in August, 1945, they chose the 38th parallel as the dividing line between American and Russian responsibilities in the liberation of Korea—a line chosen in haste, under great pressure, and without any awareness of its historic significance as the divider between Japanese and Tsarist spheres of influence in Korea.[8]

On Lincoln's staff Rusk focused his attention on the security aspects of the United Nations, especially the arrangements envisaged under Chapter VII of the UN Charter. When the war ended, he was working on implementation of Article 43, to provide military forces for the Security Council. Demobilized in February, 1946, he was immediately offered and accepted a position in the Department of State as Assistant Director of the Division of International Security Affairs. For State he served as principal liaison officer with the Military Staff Committee described in Article 47 of the Charter, doing much the same work as before.[9]

But Rusk had enjoyed his years with the Army, especially the heady experience of working with the talent that Lincoln had assembled in OPD. When, after a few months with State, Secretary of War Robert P. Patterson invited him to return to the Pentagon as special assistant to the Secretary, Rusk accepted the position with alacrity. He decided to become a career officer, confident that the stars would come without a West Point degree. For Patterson, Rusk worked on problems of political as well as military significance and had responsibilities for liaison with State. But the work proved to be disappointing. In 1946 the Pentagon could not attract men of the quality of those with whom Rusk had worked during the war. Patterson was not in Lincoln's league and Rusk's new colleagues were not like Bonesteel or Ernest Gross, the latter a bright young lawyer who had moved over to State.

One day in February, 1947, shortly before Rusk was to sign the papers that would commit him to a career in the army, he encountered Gross at a meeting of the State-War-Navy Coordinating Committee (SWNCC). Rusk indicated his disappointment with War Department work and his apprehension about making the army a career. Gross mentioned that Alger Hiss, Director of the Office of Special Political Affairs, had resigned to accept the presidency of the Carnegie Endowment for International Peace. Would Rusk be interested in the job? In January, Marshall had become Secretary of State and Foggy Bottom suddenly looked more exciting. Rusk was interested and Gross called his availability to the attention of the Under Secretary, Dean Acheson. Marshall soon asked Rusk to succeed Hiss. The United States Army had lost an exceptional officer and on March 5, 1947, Rusk began his rapid rise through the bureaucracy of the Department of State.[10]

CHAPTER TWO

United Nations Affairs

The Office of Special Political Affairs (SPA) had been created in January, 1944, with responsibility for overseeing American involvement in the United Nations. When Rusk replaced Hiss in March, 1947, the Office had three divisions: International Organization (General Assembly), International Security (Security Council), and Dependent Areas (Trusteeship Council, non-self-governing territories generally). He informed his staff that he would personally assume the usual responsibilities for running the office, for relations with the secretary, undersecretary, and assistant secretaries, and for relations with Congress and other officials. He would also represent SPA on the State-War-Navy Coordinating Committee. In addition, Rusk called attention to his particular concern with the security functions of the United Nations—matters under Chapter VII of the Charter with which he had worked for well over a year.[1]

On virtually every issue with which SPA dealt, a potential for conflict with other offices within the Department existed. If the issue involved any other country directly or indirectly, as when its cooperation was sought, Rusk might have to negotiate with the country desk officer or with the regional assistant secretary. His responsibilities cut across all regional and functional divisions. With exception of the director of the Policy Planning Staff, no officer below the undersecretary had to range as widely as the director of SPA. When two or more countries were involved in a dispute at the UN, Rusk had to perform a function not unlike that of the undersecretary, of working out compromises between desk officers or regional assistant secretaries unable to reconcile their views.

SPA had one additional problem that made its task unique. Within the career foreign service and among high level presidential appointees in the Department, there was great skepticism about the efficacy of the United Nations. Men like George F. Kennan, director of the Policy Planning Staff, styling themselves "realists", preferred to keep major issues out of the United Nations. They had no faith in concepts of world government and were contemptuous of the "idealists" and "moralists" who expected international organization and international law to replace traditional diplomacy. When issues like colonialism or racism emerged in the UN, the so-called realists were troubled by a process in which a majority of small and weak regimes might outvote the great European powers. SPA was especially taxed on colonial issues, when the Europeanists who dominated the Department generally chose to side with the imperialist power. The arguments for retaining French or British or Dutch good will and the tangible support of those powers were familiar and long accepted in the Department. The argument for jeopardizing that good will and support on behalf of the principles of the United Nations Charter, however American those principles seemed, was relatively new and less convincing to men like Dean Acheson and Robert Lovett who settled most such disputes during George Marshall's years as secretary.

Rusk's attitude toward the United Nations has been a matter of some dispute. Kennan, frequently appalled by views emerging from SPA, thought Rusk a moralist who supported UN activities even when they were contrary to the interests of the United States. On a number of occasions, when the Department was formulating the Truman Doctrine, Marshall Plan, and American response to the outbreak of war in Korea, Rusk pressed for a UN role that Kennan thought unnecessary, perhaps even harmful. On Rusk's staff, however, a different view of the boss prevailed. Several of his subordinates were ideologues, committed to making world government work, to a new morality in world affairs. They had the greatest respect for Rusk who broke lances on their behalf and brought back more than they had imagined the Europeanists would yield. They were convinced, however, that he was not one of them. He was a moral man, but not a moralist, not an ideologue. He was not committed, would not fight for ideas.[2]

Rusk did have a deep philosophical commitment to the United Nations, but the idealists on his staff were not entirely wrong. His approach was expressed most clearly in a dispute between Policy Planning and SPA over policy toward Israel in August, 1948. Policy Planning took an unusually solicitous approach toward the future of the UN, arguing against a particular policy on the ground that it might lead to circumstances that would hurt the organization's prestige. Rusk argued that it was wrong to deal with matters in terms of UN prestige. If disputes could be settled and peace maintained, the prestige of the UN would take care of itself. The UN, he remarked, "is not an end in itself but a means to an end."[3] Rusk believed in the principles of the Charter and believed that the UN could play a major role in keeping the peace. But he was flexible, pragmatic, prepared to work around the organization when it malfunctioned, when some other means of settling a dispute appeared more sensible.

On a spectrum between men like Kennan and Acheson, generally contemptuous of the UN, more attuned to traditional power politics, and the idealists of SPA, Rusk was closer to the latter. On issues involving colonialism or racism, he was very close to the ideologues, though more prepared than they were to achieve his goals piecemeal. His intense hostility to imperialism never overcame his conviction that few problems could be solved with one majestic stroke. On the handling of the Palestine question, or more specifically support for the United Nations in the face of Israeli intransigence in October, 1948, the idealists found more to fault. The ease with which Rusk followed the incredibly sinuating White House course, as President Harry S. Truman tried to hold the Jewish vote, appalled many of his admirers. Herein Rusk revealed another conviction: that the President of the United States alone had the constitutional right to make policy. He could argue his case up to the point when the President decided. Thereafter his job was to execute. George Marshall, whom Rusk chose as his model, had been so angry at Truman's pandering to the Jewish vote that he told Truman in the presence of White House and State Department staffers that if the President continued to favor Israel he would vote against him in the election. Nonetheless, Marshall would not resign on the issue. Disagreement over policy was not ground for resignation.

On one matter Rusk encountered little argument within the Department. Even Kennan conceded the value of appearing to strengthen or support the UN. Often Rusk would argue that for the sake of "appearances" it was important for the United States to work through the UN or to support a UN activity. Whether his concern was in fact limited to appearances or he coated his profound concern for the UN with language palatable to Kennan and Acheson is not clear. The latter is more likely, but either way, he was arguing for a larger role for the organization—and for SPA—than Kennan or Acheson would have considered on their own.

2

The immediate postwar years were dominated by the emerging Soviet-American conflict. Rusk had had nothing to do with European or Soviet affairs during the war, but immediately afterward encountered frustration trying to work with the Russians on the implementation of Chapter VII of the UN Charter. In the spring of 1946, the United States was eager to negotiate the agreements prerequisite to providing the Security Council with the forces it might need to maintain "international peace and security." China, France, Great Britain, and the United States had submitted their statements of general principles to the appropriate subcommittee, but the Russians had not. The Russian statement was one month overdue and Rusk was anxious, considering a complaint to Moscow. But, he reported, the American military delegates "do not yet attach sinister implications to the Russian delay." Old Russian hands thought a three-month delay would be normal procedure for the Soviet bureaucracy. The American delegates to the Military Staff Committee assured Rusk they had found the Russians cooperative and had developed a good working relationship with them. Rusk recommended giving the American delegation its head for a while, but he remained suspicious of the Russians, warning that at some point the Soviet delay would have political ramifications.[4]

Russian behavior at the working levels of the United Nations continued to arouse Rusk's suspicions throughout the year. In February, 1947, he had the Secretary of War forward to the Secretary of State a memorandum by General Matthew B. Ridgway outlining the Soviets' tactics and purpose as revealed in their UN maneuvers.[5] Ridgway warned that the Russians were aiming at the unilateral disarmament of the United States by creating agreements which world opinion and the conscience of the American people would require the United States to observe, while the Soviet Union blocked the creation of safeguards against clandestine manufacture of atomic weapons. The mistrust exhibited by Rusk and Ridgway permeated Washington by the beginning of 1947. When Rusk moved across the river to State in March, his assessment of Soviet behavior was very much in accord with that of Kennan and Acheson.

On March 5, Rusk was named Director, Special Political Affairs. The night before, the first draft of the speech later known as the Truman Doctrine was produced. On the sixth Rusk and Kennan, the newly appointed director of Marshall's as yet nonexistent Policy Planning Staff, saw the speech. Kennan objected strongly to both the tone of the message, which he considered provocative, and to some of the actions contemplated. He took his complaints to Acheson and was told it was too late: the decisions had been made. On the eighth Rusk objected and won minor changes of language but not of substance. Members of his staff had been angered by the President's willingness to bypass the United Nations. Rusk could not persuade Acheson to rely on the United Nations to cope with the problem of Greece—nor is there evidence that he thought the United States should have left the problem to the United Nations. On the contrary, Rusk asked for a more explicit statement of American confidence in the UN and of the reasons why the United States had decided to act unilaterally. Acheson agreed to amplify the reference to the UN in the speech, but the White House staff cut out half of Rusk's contribution. More was said about the UN than would have been said without Rusk's intercession, but not as much as he wanted.[6]

Truman delivered the speech on March 12 and subsequent public opinion polls indicated majority support for economic aid to Greece and Turkey. The proposals for military assistance, about which Kennan had been unhappy, failed to win the approval of a majority. The largest outcry against the Truman Doctrine focused on the administration's failure to work through the United Nations. In 1947 public support for the UN was intense and even that segment of American society that accepted the need for direct aid to Greece regretted the neglect of the UN. On March 18, Walter Lippmann published a column arguing that the United States had an obligation to consult with the United Nations. He urged that the damage be repaired by offering a full explanation of American intentions to the Secretary General of the UN and by having the American representative explain the American proposals to the Security Council before the Russian delegate attacked them. On the same day, Rusk argued the case for a letter from the President to the Secretary General with Acheson. Acheson remained adamant, insisting it was time Americans faced the fact "that it is impossible for the UN to intervene in cases involving subversive movements."[7]

Dismay over the administration's approach did not disappear and Congressional leaders succeeded where Rusk had failed. On March 28 the American representative on the Security Council spelled out his country's view of the situation in Greece and contended that UN and United States actions there were complementary. He promised that the United States would work toward equipping the UN to assume full responsibility itself. Several days later the Senate Committee on Foreign Relations approved an amendment to the Greece-Turkey aid bill directing the President to terminate aid if the UN determined that it was unnecessary or undesirable.

Rusk remained troubled on two counts. First, he recognized the validity of Acheson's argument about the difficulty of the UN meeting threats posed by subversion or "indirect aggression" as opposed to overt, direct aggression. Second, he was not satisfied that his government was giving adequate consideration to the possibility of achieving its ends through the UN. Consequently he began a campaign to find ways for the UN to stop indirect aggression and to persuade his superiors not to bypass the UN with their plans for European economic recovery and international control of atomic energy.

Rusk's plan for transforming the UN into an instrument for preventing or stopping indirect aggression involved two steps presented separately to his superiors. Initially he called for establishment by the General Assembly of a 21-nation commission to study indirect aggression, such as "infiltration and Fifth Column activity, the subversive actions of minority groups, illegal traffic in arms, the abuse of economic concessions, the machinations of international communism, or other measures falling short of outright armed aggression across frontiers." He conceded that the Russians could prevent such a commission from acting, but at minimum the United States could get a spotlight on indirect aggression for six months. UN attention to the problems, he contended, would help the Department educate the American public to the dangers and responsibilities faced by the United States. Kennan, at best skeptical of anything that came out of SPA, conceded that there was merit in this idea and advised that Rusk be allowed to proceed along these lines. He also wanted Rusk to prepare for possible use a record of American efforts to strengthen the UN and a thorough indictment, "dispassionate but vigorous," of Soviet obstructionism. But subsequent objections by Charles Bohlen and John Foster Dulles, serving with the American delegation to the UN, deflected this approach.[8]

The second step in Rusk's plan was implementation of Article 43 of the UN Charter. Throughout 1947 and 1948, Rusk argued that the article obligated the United States to have military forces available to the Security Council. He rejected arguments that such forces could never be used, given the Soviet proclivity for using the veto, and was angered by suggestions that he was perpetrating a cynical farce to appease public aspirations for the UN. He contended that the political situation might change and that there were situations such as existed in Indonesia and Palestine in which such forces might readily be used. In January, 1948, he offered a series of disingenuous supporting arguments: 1) that obligations of Article 43 allowed the government to ask the people to maintain a military establishment as large as believed necessary in the absence of a universal security system; 2) Congressional ratification of an offer of armed forces to the Security Council would increase Congressional support for preparedness; 3) existence of UN forces would lessen the likelihood that the Russians would withdraw from the UN. They would want to stay to veto the deployment of UN forces—which in turn would reveal Soviet obstructiveness. This battle, too, Rusk lost, but he persisted in his belief that the lack of forces at the disposal of the Security Council hampered its peace-keeping ability—a view widely held in the American liberal community.[9]

Rusk's efforts to preserve the UN role in European recovery and the control of atomic energy were no more successful. He argued that if the administration bypassed the UN on European recovery it might provoke a groundswell of public opinion that could wreck the program. Acheson recalled the miscalculation with the Truman Doctrine and was responsive to Rusk's argument, but Undersecretary William L. Clayton, the principal architect of the Marshall Plan, was not. Rusk called for working through the UN's newly created Economic Commission for Europe. Although the Commission had been created in response to an American initiative, Clayton was convinced it was unusable, even to begin the process he planned.[10]

Fighting to keep open the possibility of the UN Atomic Energy Commission's reaching an agreement on international controls, Rusk was overruled by Acheson's successor, Robert Lovett. Initially, Rusk's contention prevailed: the United States should keep trying for an agreement to focus world attention on Soviet responsibility for failure. He won Marshall's support against opponents within the Department of State and against the misgivings of the Secretary of War and the Secretary of the Navy, and won approval of the UN-AEC report in September, 1947. But his time ran out in April, 1948. At a meeting with Lovett, he argued tenaciously, countering every objection posed by Lovett. He quoted an earlier Lovett memo, a joint agreement of the Secretaries of State, War, and Navy, a statement by Marshall—all to no avail. The minutes of the meeting suggest that Lovett was irritated by Rusk's persistence, indicating an inability to comprehend continued doubt that the end had been reached, declaring that "the time had come to be frank . . . the time had come to stop." Still Rusk argued on—and tried to retain language in the document instructing the American delegation that would allow continued negotiations. Lovett's special assistant, Edmund Gullion, feared that Rusk's words might be read as meaning the United States wanted to continue the negotiations. Rusk replied doggedly that the United States should "never want to close and lock the door". Lovett insisted that negotiations be terminated.[11]

When the UN met to discuss the atomic energy question on September 30, Benjamin V. Cohen, a senior American delegate, indicated an interest in retaining the possibility of further negotiations. Without apparent reference to his argument with Lovett, Rusk—the good soldier—advised Cohen that the National Security Council and a special Senate subcommittee had decided it would be inappropriate for the United States to ask for further negotiations. When Dulles, also a delegate, asked if the American position on controls was so tough that it could not be proposed without giving the Russians a tremendous propaganda advantage, "Mr. Rusk indicated that this was a correct view."[12]

Much of what Rusk argued for at the time of the Truman Doctrine, at the formative stages of the Marshall Plan, and on atomic energy might be explained in terms of the bureaucratic principle, "where you sit determines what you say." As director of the Office of Special Political Affairs, responsible primarily for UN affairs, he would be expected to argue for a greater role for the UN. The UN was his client. His constituents were the believers in international organization in his own office and all over the country. But his stubbornness on the control of atomic energy suggests profound convictions. In April, 1947, he indicated to Lovett his dissatisfaction with American rigidity on controls. Rusk saw time running against the United States. If agreement on international controls was not reached before the Soviet Union perfected its atomic weapons, the interests of the United States would be threatened. To him, agreement was of greater importance to the United States than it was to the Soviet Union. His views were heard—and rejected. He then followed orders, leading some of his subordinates to suggest that his military experience had left him susceptible to discipline. They went on to other careers and Rusk won the respect of his superiors. He was a man who argued forcefully for what he believed to be right and he accepted defeat with good grace.

3

One issue on which Rusk met some success was colonialism. Perhaps because he was a liberal Southerner, perhaps because of his experiences in the China-Burma-India Theater, he was very sensitive to the aspirations of colonial peoples. He differed significantly from many of his colleagues and from many other Americans in that he did not restrict his anti-imperialism to the British and French empires. On an issue much closer to home, he was responsive in 1947 to Panamanian opposition to US bases. He tried to draw a parallel between British insistence on treaty rights in Egypt and American insistence on similar rights in Panama. He argued that to insist upon stationing troops in a country contrary to the wishes of the country was a mistake, that the United States could give up its bases and fall back on the Canal Zone. Rusk was ahead of his time and the Panamanian issue ticked on.[13]

The major success of the campaign against imperialism in the late 1940s came in the struggle of the people of Indonesia for independence. Within the Department of State, the Europeanists worked to protect Dutch interests and *amour-propre*. When Acheson returned to the Department as Secretary of State in January, 1949, the Europeanists were strengthened by his support. Acheson did not brood about oppressed peoples and could not easily imagine any advantages that would accrue to the United States should it support the Indonesians and in the process alienate the Dutch. But the Europeanists were outmaneuvered by Rusk's troops supported by Far Eastern Affairs and Acheson was effectively neutralized by Philip C. Jessup's commitment to self-determination. Jessup, perhaps Acheson's closest friend during this era, served with the American delegation to the UN and through much of the debate over Indonesia was acting American representative. Jessup led the fight at the United Nations and Rusk provided the essential support, both at the UN and in Washington.[14]

Italy's former colonies in Africa posed the same kind of problem for Rusk, but in this instance the intradepartmental complications were compounded by pressures from the Joint Chiefs of Staff. The principal point of contention was Libya, which had been administered by the British since the Italian surrender. The Italians were bold enough to ask for an Italian trusteeship, at very least for the Tripolitanian division of Libya as well as what had been known as Italian Somaliland. The Truman Administration appeared united in its determination not to allow Italy back into Libya, partly out of fear of antagonizing the Arab world, already sufficiently alienated by American behavior in the Palestine affair. In addition, the American government was apprehensive about Communist strength in Italy. If the Italians were returned to Libya, then joined the Communist camp, the Russians would have access to an area of presumed strategic importance to the United States. But as he chased the Jewish vote all over the Palestine question, Truman did not want a confrontation with the Italians in 1948.[15]

The General Assembly postponed consideration of the Italian colonies until the spring of 1949, but the American delegation still could not get a clear mandate. Rusk argued for a UN trusteeship for at least part of Libya, posing his argument in terms of an arrangement that might receive support in the General Assembly. The Joint Chiefs were unyielding. Despite Rusk's contention that a British trusteeship would not be approved, the military prevailed. When the issue arose before the Assembly, the United States and Great Britain supported a British trusteeship. The American-supported resolution was overwhelmingly defeated by a coalition of Arab, Asian, Latin American and Soviet bloc states. It was the Russians who called for and eventually won support for a plan for direct UN administration of Libya. Rusk had no reason to regret the outcome.[16]

4

Of all the UN questions with which Rusk was involved, the most complex, the most revealing of the man—and the issue with which he won the admiration and gratitude of his superiors—was Palestine. In its simplest outlines, the American response in 1948 to the inevitable termination of the British mandate in Palestine resulted from a struggle between officials of the national security bureaucracy whose estimates of American interests led them to brush aside Jewish aspirations and a President sympathetic to Jewish aspirations—and very responsive to the demands of liberal and Jewish voters in an election year. Rusk's views and role illustrate how much more complicated the internal debate was.

After World War II there was a tremendous surge of sympathy in the United States for those European Jews who had escaped Hitler's gas chambers. The desire of many of those Jews to migrate to Palestine also relieved those Americans who were hardly more inclined in the 1940s than they had been in the 1930s to invite the victims of Nazi oppression to the United States. The British were pressed between Zionist hopes and American pressures on the one hand and intense Arab resistance to Jewish immigration on the other. In 1946 an Anglo-American Committee of Inquiry recommended admission of 100,000 Jewish immigrants to Palestine, transfer of the British mandate to the United Nations, and the ultimate creation of a single state in which the rights of Arabs and Jews would be protected. Leaders of both Arab and Jewish communities rejected the recommendations as did the British government. In 1947, the British took the problem to the UN, where Rusk had to wrestle with it.

The dominant officials within the Departments of State and Defense discounted Jewish claims to American support. State Department specialists in Middle East affairs argued that support for a Jewish state in Palestine would alienate the Arabs and compromise vital American interests in the area. Europeanists were anxious lest the United States damage its relationship with Britain or jeopardize the flow of Arab oil so important to European economic recovery. The Pentagon feared Soviet penetration of the area—and the Secretary of Defense seemed unnerved by images of a Jewish state as a Soviet Trojan Horse. These men believed that the strategic and economic concerns of the United States and its allies had to be given priority over humanitarian concern for the plight of European Jewry. If the Jews could be kept quiet, forced to settle for the constitutionally guaranteed rights of a minority within an Arab state, the interests of the United States would be well served. If the Jews persisted in their demand for a separate Jewish state, there would be violence. If the United States supported the Jewish demand, it might become involved in military operations that would not only inflame the Arab world against the United States but deplete strategic reserves essential for the Cold War confrontation developing with the Soviet Union.

President Truman considered these arguments and found them wanting. His closest advisers, many American political leaders, and most liberals did not share the assessment that prevailed in the Departments of State and War. They urged the President to support the partition of Palestine and the creation of an independent Jewish state that would immediately receive the approximately 100,000 survivors of the holocaust who remained in camps for "displaced persons." The Department of State was ordered to work for partition, and to this end, Rusk directed his efforts at the United Nations.

By November, 1947, a plan for partition appeared to have sufficient support to win adoption by the General Assembly. Rusk and Loy Henderson, who was generally considered to be the arch enemy of the partition plan, negotiated a document they were both able to sign as a recommendation to the Secretary of State. They recommended that the American delegation vote for partition and against the plan for a unitary state. Henderson had grudgingly yielded to the insistence of the White House. The recommendation included, however, a clear warning that acceptance of the partition plan by the General Assembly would probably mean immediate violence in Palestine, likely to lead to a demand for action by the Security Council to implement the plan. Should this happen, the United States would be morally bound, as a protagonist of partition, to do its share to implement it. The Soviet Union would very likely suggest introducing its own forces. The question they posed for Marshall—and ultimately for the President—was whether American forces should be used or whether the United States should oppose the use of force to keep the Russians out and to avoid irreparable damage to American relations with the Arabs.[17]

Clearly, Henderson had been relieved of none of his reservations about partition. Support the plan, but be ready to fight to implement it—and recognize the likelihood of wrecking hopes for friendship with the Arabs and of bringing Soviet military power into the area. Implicit in Henderson's assumptions was the expectation that the Jewish state could not withstand the expected Arab onslaught and that the same Zionist pressures that led the White

House to partition would then demand UN or American protection. The President directed the American delegation to vote for partition and the plan was adopted by the General Assembly on November 29, 1947.

Until the partition plan was adopted by the General Assembly, Rusk's principal activities were directed toward creating a fair plan. Partition was the President's policy when Rusk came on the scene. Rusk was aware of the debate that had preceded the decision, understood the basis for the decision, and accepted it. His job was to get the best possible plan and most of the obstacles he found were posed by the unreasonable demands of the Palestinian Jewish organization, the "Jewish Agency," and its tremendous influence with the White House. The illegal landing of Jewish immigrants in Palestine and the complicity of American citizens in some of these operations troubled Rusk. He seemed less panicky than some of his colleagues about the number of Soviet agents being infiltrated among the refugees, more sensitive to the plight of these displaced persons, but nonetheless firm in warnings to the Jewish Agency about the importance of preventing further landings. Rusk concluded that the Assembly subcommittee defining the borders of the proposed partition states had been overwhelmed by the Jewish Agency. He intended to have the American delegation urge the subcommittee to transfer part of the Negev to the Arabs, but a Zionist alert led to White House intervention. Rusk argued his case with Lovett—and followed the wishes of the President. Henderson made an independent effort to hold the line, but again the White House was informed and Henderson's order countermanded by Lovett. Understandably it was Henderson and not Rusk who became the bete noir of the White House staff.[18]

In the months that followed the vote for partition, Rusk concentrated on making the American-supported UN policy of partition work. Henderson and Kennan worked frenetically to win a reversal of American policy. In Palestine, there was violence but it was limited by the British presence. On December 11, however, the British announced that they would withdraw their troops and renounce their mandate on May 15, 1948. Violence increased as both sides maneuvered into position for an all-out struggle.

As Kennan, Henderson, and Secretary of Defense Forrestal

fought a rearguard action to destroy the partition plan, Rusk countered them. He argued that a change in policy toward Palestine required approval of the President and leading members of Congress. He denied that opponents of partition had presented a case requiring reconsideration. He claimed that he did not consider the partition decision sacrosanct but that the mere revival of old objections did not constitute a "new situation." The plan was worth a try for a few months to see if both sides could be calmed down and work out an arrangement to accept partition. Rusk was much more critical of the Arabs than Policy Planning had been and compared the assistance Arab states were giving to Palestinian Arabs to the situation in Greece. He thought the United States had a responsibility as a permanent member of the Security Council to act "within the limits of the Charter" to prevent Arab aggression. He also expressed anger with what he deemed to be the irresponsible attitude of the British. For the American government, "it would appear obligatory" to determine what steps could be taken to implement the UN decision.[19]

In considering alternatives, Rusk warned that a decision to turn Palestine into a single Arab-dominated state was no more likely to bring peace than was partition. If peaceful partition proved to be impossible, and the UN reopened the question, he thought a UN trusteeship worth considering, with the United States taking a fair share of responsibility. In conclusion he agreed with the opponents of partition that the United States had substantial obligations under the plan, but he insisted that "if an alternative plan is considered, it would be frivolous not to suppose that the United States must play a leading role in the execution of such an alternative."

Kennan and Henderson were deeply troubled by Rusk's memorandum. In a long reply for the undersecretary Kennan denied that armed interference by the Arab states would constitute aggression requiring action by the United States. He blamed the Jews for the violence in Palestine because they sought objectives that could only lead to violence. Rusk's attitude toward the British also irritated Kennan, who contended that the United States should do nothing to jeopardize Anglo-American collaboration in world affairs. In a separate memorandum Henderson also opposed Rusk's arguments. Within the Department, at least, the issue was fairly joined.[20]

A meeting of the National Security Council was scheduled to attempt to iron out disagreements over partition. A Policy Planning Staff memorandum posed three alternatives, of which the only acceptable one called for a change of policy: support a trusteeship or a federal state. PPS saw only one disadvantage to this policy. The Zionists would not like it. The Arabs would ànd the policy would be good, therefore, for national security and other American interests in the area. Secretary Marshall, notoriously impatient with lower-level wrangling, presided over a meeting between Rusk and George Butler of PPS. He decided the PPS paper could be presented to the NSC meeting as a working paper, but not as State's position on the issue.[21]

At the NSC meeting, despite warm support for the Kennan-Henderson position from the Joint Chiefs and Secretary Forrestal, Rusk's argument, modified in one important respect, prevailed. The draft report, approved by the President, February 22, 1948, concluded that the United States should continue to support the UN partition plan by all means short of force. The military members of the Council asked that their unwillingness to concur be made a matter of record. The NSC concluded that if the General Assembly ever chose to reconsider the Palestine problem, the United States should propose trusteeship under the Trusteeship Council. On the question of American responsibility to provide forces to the Security Council to enforce partition, Rusk lost the argument. The NSC concluded that the United States should oppose the dispatch of armed forces to impose partition. The best Rusk could get was a statement that the United States should urge the Arab states to refrain from aggression. Truman's approval of the report included the statement that "nothing should be presented to the Security Council that could be interpreted as a recession on our part from the position we took in the General Assembly."[22]

Henderson stubbornly continued the fight. On 27 February, however, Rusk was informed by his deputy that "Mr. Lovett set Loy Henderson straight on the future alternatives which confront the UN in the Palestine case."[23] Nonetheless, apprehension mounted in

Washington about what would happen in Palestine when the British withdrew in May.

At the White House, Clark M. Clifford, the President's counsel and key adviser on election strategy, insisted that the United States could and should jam partition down the throats of the Arabs and the British. He contended that the Arabs needed the United States more than Americans needed the Arabs; that the Arabs could not turn to the Soviet Union. Those who claimed partition would not work were the same people who never wanted partition and "have been determined to sabotage it." Although the Democrats had just two weeks earlier suffered a shocking defeat in a special congressional election in New York City, a defeat generally attributed to the victorious American Labor Party candidate's strong support for the Palestinian Jews, Clifford's memorandum contained no reference to domestic political considerations. On the contrary, he argued that national interests, strategic and economic—including bolstering the United Nations—demanded implementation of the UN decision on partition.[24]

At State and in the United Nations, the conviction grew that violence in Palestine was out of hand, beyond the capacity of the British to control, and likely to worsen if an attempt to impose partition was made in May. As the Security Council studied means of coping with the situation, the idea of a temporary trusteeship—such as Rusk had proposed earlier—took hold. To Rusk, the critical point about the trusteeship idea was that it would allow the United Nations to send a peace-keeping force to Palestine which could effect a truce and then guarantee whatever arrangements—presumably partition—that the Palestinian Arabs and Jews could work out without outside interference. For Henderson and Kennan, the trusteeship may have been seen as requisite to a reversal of support for partition, but to Rusk it was a step to create a stronger legal basis for UN action—action that would deter aggression by neighboring Arab states.

On March 19, when it was clear that the Security Council had given up hope of peaceful partition, Warren Austin, the American representative, spoke in favor of a temporary trusteeship. The Jewish Agency and American Zionists responded with rage, fearing a reversal of American policy, a victory for the opponents of a Jewish state within the American government. The timing of Austin's speech greatly embarrassed President Truman who on the previous evening had assured Chaim Weizmann, the Jewish leader, that there would be no slackening of American support for the creation of a Jewish state. Truman apparently believed, as Clifford had suggested, that elements in the State Department were trying to sabotage his policy, but there remains no doubt that Truman had seen and approved the plan for proposing trusteeship. He apparently understood that trusteeship would be offered after the Security Council *voted* to indicate its loss of faith in partition, so that the record would be clear. Austin spoke when it was obvious that the Security Council had given up on partition, without first allowing the vote. The difference was of little importance to the Department of State, but it was of tremendous importance to Truman politically—and in terms of his honor and integrity with the Jews.[25]

Immediately after the tempest over Austin's speech, a direct, mandatory channel was set up between the State Department and the White House to guarantee presidential approval of every step taken on Palestine. Rusk and Clifford were designated to control this channel and a close working relationship developed between the two men. On March 22, in a memorandum addressed to Marshall, but sent to the White House as well, Rusk outlined the situation succinctly. The UN had reached an impasse and large-scale fighting would break out when the British withdrew—unless emergency action was taken. The American proposal for a temporary trusteeship was conceived as emergency action directed solely toward the maintenance of peace pending a political settlement. In the matter of a trusteeship, Rusk contended, the UN was not restricted to making recommendations. It was empowered to act as a government and would find no obstacles in the Charter to enforcing law and order in Palestine. On March 25, Truman issued a statement on Palestine drafted by Rusk, Clifford, and Bohlen, incorporating Rusk's position.[26]

Immediately an issue arose over a matter on which Rusk had strong convictions. Austin wanted to know how to respond if asked whether the United States would contribute armed force for the maintenance of law and order in Palestine under a trusteeship. Rusk answered "Yes, if troops became necessary, along with other United

Nations members." He had always argued that the United Nations required an enforcement capability, that Chapter VII of the Charter was of vital importance. But the White House said "no," American forces would not be available. This time Rusk was not prepared to back down without a fight. His target, however, was not the White House, but rather the Pentagon. Forrestal and the Joint Chiefs had consistently opposed the use of American forces in Palestine contending, among other reasons, that it would require the commitment of the entire strategic reserve and leave the United States vulnerable to Soviet probes. The coup in Czechoslovakia in February, 1948, was fresh in everyone's mind and there was considerable uneasiness about Soviet intentions in Yugoslavia and Germany. On April 4, Forrestal, supported by the Joint Chiefs and their planners, met with Rusk and other State Department officials to discuss the policing of a possible trusteeship. Having won the right to discuss the question, Rusk then demonstrated that he knew the way to Forrestal's heart: the Russians were coming. If the United States did nothing, the Russians "could and would" take steps to gain control in Palestine by infiltrating specially trained immigrants or capitalizing in some other way on the civil war that was likely to break out in the absence of UN forces. Turning to the Chiefs, he argued that the presence of American forces in Palestine might have strategic advantages. Outrageously disingenuous, he suggested that the United States might gain an opportunity to construct bomber fields in the Middle East. However much he may have stirred his audience, his views on the use of American forces won only partial acceptance, in a very different context, some months later.[27]

By late April, Rusk was concentrating his efforts on personal diplomacy to bring about a truce between Jews and Arabs. He met informally with Mahmoud Fawzi Bey of the Egyptian delegation and won his interest in informal truce talks. He found Moshe Shertok, principal negotiator for the Jewish Agency, receptive. Fawzi Bey reported that the Saudis were willing to participate. For almost three weeks, Rusk immersed himself tirelessly in these truce negotiations, drafting articles of agreement, isolating points of contention, probing for flexibility. He found the immigration issue unnegotiable because both sides feared their constituents would explode over any compromise. He detected evidence they might be receptive to an arrangement presumably "imposed" on them—a solution that would keep their records clear, establish no precedent, and leave both sides free for further negotiation. Truman met with Rusk to discuss the progress of his efforts. Rusk warned Truman that the Arabs might accept the truce arrangements but not the Jews. Truman replied that if the Jews refused a reasonable truce offer, they could not expect any help from the United States. He promised Rusk his support.[28]

As late as May 8, a week before the British mandate was to end, Rusk thought he was very close to reaching an agreement for a truce. A split within the Jewish Agency indicated some strong support among Jews and one Jewish leader, Nahum Goldmann, led Rusk to believe that American pressure on Shertok might succeed. Rusk recommended that Marshall speak bluntly to Shertok and be equally firm with the Arabs on the immigration issue. But when Marshall met with Shertok May 8, he concluded that there was no chance of winning Jewish acceptance of the truce. The game was over because the Arabs had been betrayed. Britain's protege, King Abdullah of Transjordan, had sent word to the Palestine Jews that he would accept partition; that upon the departure of British forces, his troops would invade Palestine, but only that part allotted to the Arabs under the UN's partition plan. The Jews could have the rest. As Marshall deduced correctly, Abdullah's proposal undermined the position of those Jews receptive to a truce. The Jews would now gamble on their ability to hold off the other Arab forces and to establish their own state.[29]

The new conditions in Palestine ended any hope for a trusteeship. Rusk thought there was still a chance for a truce and perceived a large majority in the General Assembly willing to support American truce proposals. But Clifford and Truman were already focusing on the question of when to recognize the Jewish state. On May 12, Marshall and his staff met with Truman and the White House staff to discuss American actions after the British terminated the mandate at midnight on the fourteenth. Clifford proposed immediate recognition. Rusk, he said, had estimated that he needed two weeks to get a truce and had been unable to get one in six. The Jewish state would come into existence and be recognized. Clifford wanted an immediate announcement that the United States would extend recognition—to steal a march on the Russians, he suggested. Lovett and Marshall argued that immediate recognition would be a transparent dodge to win votes; that the UN was still working on a truce at American initiative and could not be undermined. Lovett countered Clifford's "beat the Russians" ploy by warning against buying a pig in a poke—a singularly inept way of expressing an occasional fear that the new Jewish state would be Soviet-dominated. This was the situation in which Marshall was angered enough to warn Truman that if he followed Clifford's advice he, Marshall, would vote against him in the election—if he voted.[30]

If Marshall and his staff thought they had carried the day, Clifford outmaneuvered them. Armed with their objections, he arranged for the Washington representative of the Jewish Agency to request recognition and to issue assurances on Jewish willingness to accept the borders of the UN partition plan. He then persuaded Truman to recognize the State of Israel as soon as it was proclaimed. To Lovett he conceded the persuasiveness of State's arguments. The President, however, was under unbearable pressure to recognize Israel and timing was of the utmost importance from the domestic point of view. If recognition was inevitable, why not now?[31]

Midnight in Jerusalem came at 6:00 PM in Washington. At 5:45 PM on the evening May 14, while the United Nations was meeting to approve the American truce proposal, Rusk received a telephone call from Clifford. He was informed that at 6:00 the State of Israel would be proclaimed and that President Truman would recognize it immediately. Rusk objected. Such an action would undermine and humiliate the American delegation. Clifford informed him the President had made his decision. So be it. Rusk called Austin at the UN, and Austin was so distraught that he went directly home without informing the rest of the American delegation. Marshall then asked Rusk to go to New York to stave off the resignation of the US mission.[32]

A week later, Kennan felt obliged to record once more his distaste for American policy toward Palestine and for the limits imposed on the Department by the White House and public opinion. He argued that Palestine was so important a question that decisions should be reached only on the advice of the National Security Council. Policy Planning believed that the United States should take no action that would lead to conflict with Britain over Palestine. Kennan insisted that the United States was heading in the wrong direction, threatening to jeopardize vital national interests, undermine policy toward the Soviet Union, and destroy the United Nations. But both Lovett and Marshall endorsed Rusk's position on two major points. Lovett contended, and Marshall agreed, that the United States would cooperate with Britain whenever it could, but not when the British behaved irresponsibly. It was equally as important to respect obligations undertaken as a member of the UN. Lovett also professed himself unable to understand how UN action to maintain peace and security would lead to a collapse of the UN.[33]

In addition to their differences on policy, Kennan and Rusk displayed very different styles in the Palestinian brouhaha. Kennan had little patience for the political process and complained bitterly whenever domestic political considerations affected policy. Rusk shared his commitment to "rational" (*i.e.*, expert) policy, but shared Marshall's sense that the Constitution gave the President responsibility for making policy. Rusk was more tolerant of the imperfect world in which he functioned, much less of a hothouse flower than was Kennan. When Acheson became Secretary of State in 1949, this difference in style had much to do with Kennan's decline and Rusk's increasing importance. Acheson, much given to quoting his father on the subject, found complainers and whiners unbearable. What cannot be changed must be borne. Complaints about what cannot be remedied are at best a bore and quickly make life intolerable. Rusk did not complain. He worked energetically, courageously for the goals of his country, and he allowed his superiors to set those goals.

With the recognition question settled, Marshall and Rusk moved to head off another Clifford project: lifting of the American arms embargo to allow the Israelis to obtain arms from the United States. Together they went to Truman and tried to impress upon him the importance of the arms embargo and of the proceedings at the UN. It was urgent, they warned, not to disrupt UN efforts again. The President understood. The Department sent Truman a memorandum on the subject that was very likely intended for the White House staff. Should the Security Council order a cease-fire in Palestine and there were a failure to comply, the United States would be obliged to adjust its embargo policy to support the Security Council. Implicit was the question of whether the President could resist pressures if it were necessary to turn the screw on the Jews. With a degree of righteousness perhaps not unfitting for the occasion, the Department of State wished "particularly to invite the attention of the President to the fact that the policy proposed . . . engages the most solemn powers and responsibilities of the Security Council and involves a major political commitment on the part of the United States." If the policy was to work it would have to be "pursued with vigor and singleness of purpose" or the Security Council "will be demoralized." Not many secretaries of state would have had the courage to send such a lecture to the President; nor would many Presidents have had the humility to swallow it.[34]

Marshall went into the hospital at the end of May, 1948, and Rusk took off for a rest in June. In the months that followed, the White House continued to be deeply concerned with the exigencies of the election campaign. Rusk was occasionally displeased by Israeli actions, but was responsive to Truman's needs. He yielded nothing on points he deemed important, but managed not to upset the White House staff—which continued to focus on Henderson as the man to be contained.

Rusk believed that maintaining the truce to which both sides had agreed in June was the highest priority in Palestine. At the same time he wanted to give the utmost support to Count Folke Bernadotte, the UN-appointed mediator who had taken over Rusk's task of trying to reach an agreement between Jews and Arabs—after the fact of the proclamation and recognition of a Jewish state. To this end Rusk returned to one of his persistent ideas: to provide the Security Council with the forces necessary to carry out its mission. Bernadotte needed equipment and personnel to maintain the truce during his mediation effort, but Forrestal and the JCS remained opposed. With the Pentagon, Rusk negotiated as tactfully as if he were dealing with a foreign and perhaps not too friendly country. He appealed to the pride and fears of the military. He understood the "heavy demand already being made on the National Military Establishment," presumably by the crisis in Berlin, but stressed the importance of the truce to national security—especially the danger of Soviet exploitation of continued violence to take over Israel. To Marshall he spelled out his views more frankly, taking a position he maintained long afterward. He contended that American security would be "severely prejudiced" by large–scale fighting anywhere in the Middle East, particularly in Palestine. He suspected the Russians of stirring trouble and feared that "continued warfare between Jewish and Arab forces would undermine the gains which have been made in Greece, Turkey, and Iran." The Arab world, Rusk feared, might be permanently alienated from Western influence. Marshall endorsed Rusk's call for support for Bernadotte and prevailed against the intense opposition of the JCS.[35]

In the effort to support Bernadotte and, after he was assassinated, his successor, Ralph Bunche, in their attempts to arrange a settlement, the Department of State was handicapped by two manifestations of the domestic political situation in the United States. First, Clifford had persuaded Truman to bypass the Department in appointing a diplomatic representative in Israel. Lovett and Marshall were irritated by having an outsider imposed on them, without consultation. Rusk and other officials working on the Palestine problem were deeply troubled by the obvious bias of the appointee, James G. McDonald of the Foreign Policy Association, in favor of Israel. McDonald's machinations with the government to which he was accredited, the fact that he shared Clifford's view of the State Department as "the enemy", and his direct communications with the White House created serious problems for Rusk. Whenever his telephone rang, there was a possibility that Clifford would be on the line to report that he and McDonald had persuaded the President to reverse the policy for which the American delegation to the UN had just lobbied or voted. At one point Rusk, attending the General Assembly meeting in Paris, cabled Lovett, warning him to reserve a wing for the delegation at the local mental institution.[36]

The other problem Rusk worked on was the muzzling of Thomas E. Dewey, Truman's opponent in the election of 1948. Rusk was eager to minimize discussion of Palestine in the campaign, well aware that the imbalance between Jewish and Arab voters would lead to constant bidding for Jewish favor. Working with Rusk on the American delegation was Dulles, commonly known to be Dewey's choice for Secretary of State. Rusk and Dulles had worked well together and developed an enduring mutual respect. In October, 1948, they tried to eliminate the Palestine question from the campaign. Rusk informed Lovett: "Speaking as a non-political civil servant, I told Dulles I thought the leadership of two parties had unnecessarily exposed themselves to Jewish pressure by failure to arrive at bipartisan agreement." Dulles then contacted Dewey whose response allowed Dulles to inform Rusk of Dewey's "very strong intention" not to stir up the Palestine issue in the remaining weeks before the election. Rusk passed the information on to Lovett who passed it on to Clifford, in an effort to ease anxieties in the White House—and to win a free hand for the Department to do what it thought best. The arrangement almost worked. Unfortunately Dewey was persuaded to imply that Truman had not met the promises of the Democratic platform toward Israel and Clifford and Truman concluded that they were freed from the informal agreement.[37]

In August, 1948, Rusk began to focus his attention and that of his superiors on another Palestinian question he thought might ultimately be transcendent: how to provide for the relief, rehabilitation and return of Arab refugees. He feared tragedy for the refugees, "with consequent repercussions not only in terms of human suffering but also in terms of the political and security interests of the United States." And he quickly realized that the Israelis were unsympathetic to the plight of Palestinian Arabs who had fled or been driven from their homes. During the election campaign he understood that he could not expect Truman to press the Israelis, but he experimented with package deals, with "sweeteners." He proposed, for example, a loan to Israel for the purpose of the rehabilitation of Haifa, contingent upon the return of Arab refugees to their homes in that city and an Iraqi agreement to resume the flow of oil to the port.[38]

After the election and after an armistice between Israel and the Arab states, Rusk continued to work on the refugee question. In March, 1949, he argued that a final settlement of the Palestinian question was not possible until the refugee problem was resolved and insisted again that the national interest of the United States was "heavily involved." With Undersecretary James E. Webb, Rusk worked out arrangements for an American mission to deal with refugee matters, under the direction of George McGhee. Israeli intransigence continued to be the major obstacle. In 1949 the American government was free to apply more pressure—although perhaps not too much more. Several times in the spring of 1949, Rusk urged Acheson to berate the Israeli foreign minister or ambassador. Rusk was himself unrelenting in a meeting with an Israeli diplomatic mission in June, calling Israel to account for its treatment of refugees and for its refusal to surrender territories conquered in 1948 in excess of the boundaries assigned by the UN resolution of November, 1947. But foresight was not sufficient. Israeli determination to retain the territory and to exclude the refugees was far greater than the determination of the Truman administration to win justice for the Arabs.[39]

5

By the spring of 1949, Rusk had been elevated to deputy-undersecretary of state. In a departmental reorganization, based in part on a report of the Hoover Commission, in part on the needs of Acheson, the new secretary, Rusk was appointed assistant secretary in February, 1949, but designated deputy-undersecretary. As the new position evolved, Rusk became one of a triumvirate who had de facto control of American policy. He was initially supposed to help the undersecretary on policy matters and serve as chief liaison officer between State and Defense—a role for which he was uniquely qualified. As Acheson ran the Department, Rusk's role became far more than that. Like other secretaries before and since, Acheson wanted his subordinates to work out their problems and to come to him with recommendations he could endorse and take to the President. All too often, however, the conflicts between geographical divisions could not be worked out at the assistant secretary level. Here, in Acheson's organizational plan, Rusk took over. Working with the assistant secretaries, he would solve the problem, informing Acheson that the problem had arisen and how he had worked it out. Familiarity with all the geographic and functional divisions and an awareness of which of the various satrapies would be affected by a given problem or decision—derived from his role as head of UN affairs—made Rusk the obvious choice for the new position. In his two years of handling UN affairs for the Department he had, of course, exhibited other qualities that called him to Acheson's attention.

CHAPTER THREE

Deputy-Undersecretary 1949–1950

No one who worked with Rusk prior to 1949 was surprised at the speed with which he was drawn to the top of the Department. He had a quick mind, a first-rate mind and he worked very hard, tirelessly. Clearly, he was ambitious, but neither his peers nor his subordinates saw him as a man driven by "cold" ambition. Nonetheless, they saw him as a comer, a man who would surely rise to the top of the bureaucracy and might well some day be secretary of state.[1]

Rusk's subordinates liked working for him. They liked the way he ran meetings, the way he drew out all views and fashioned a consensus. They were pleased by the ease of communication up and down the line. They were delighted by his willingness to delegate authority and by the gentleness of his reproaches when they failed him. His peers, too, found much to praise. They found him strikingly able, a brilliant technician, extraordinarily well-organized, lucid, balanced. He was unsurpassed as an "explainer." No one could match his ability to explain American policy to a skeptical audience—and win its confidence. His superiors were aware of many of these attributes and were also favorably impressed by his ability to grasp complex issues and to carry out assignments diligently and effectively. And the canniest of his fellow toilers at Foggy Bottom were aware of his excellent antennae—as finely tuned as any in Washington.

Several people who worked closely with Rusk on UN affairs noted another quality that became increasingly apparent as his responsibilities grew. He was something of a loner. He played his hand close to the vest. He had a way of nodding, of saying "uh-huh" that left most people thinking he was agreeing with them. He avoided disagreement, avoided argument. Once in 1948 Dulles began to rant in his presence about "liberating" Eastern Europe. Rusk disagreed, but said nothing, allowing a friend—a relatively junior official—to explain the absurdity of the idea to Dulles. As time passed, fewer and fewer people knew what Rusk thought, what Rusk was telling Acheson.

Other qualities endeared him to Acheson. With the exception of Jessup, Acheson's alter ego, Rusk emerged as the man closest to the secretary. Rusk was the man who volunteered for the sticky problems and tried to settle them before they entrapped the secretary. Palestine was such a problem and Rusk offered to accept personal responsibility for looking after the White House concerns while negotiating over Palestine. Cardinal Spellman got fidgety about Jews in Jerusalem and Rusk told Acheson he would see the Cardinal and take care of things. Jewish groups got fidgety about Catholic groups trying to influence the situation in Jerusalem and Rusk advised Acheson that he would meet with the White House staffers who looked after Jewish and Catholic interests and take care of things. Rusk was politically astute, sensitive to the currents of domestic and bureaucratic politics. Without moaning about the intrusion of politics, he took the situations and worked out the best solutions possible.[2]

In the course of the two years with UN affairs, Rusk had worked closely with two key figures and won the admiration of both: Jessup and Dulles. Jessup, an internationally prominent Columbia law professor, was one of the few men Acheson considered his intellectual equal. The families of Acheson and Jessup also enjoyed a close social relationship. Jessup in turn admired Rusk and succeeded in bringing him into the professional relationship (socially, Rusk's limited means kept him at a distance). In Jessup and Rusk, Acheson had two associates of the highest ability whose loyalty to him he never had any reason to question. They challenged him to keep his mind honed and they balanced his most outrageous views, as for example on colonial questions. As best they could, they repaired the damage Acheson often did when his quick tongue outraced his quick mind. Rusk's most precious quality was his ability to soothe Congressmen—the fools Acheson tried in vain to suffer.[3]

Rusk's relationship with Dulles was of comparable importance. Dulles was the Republican Party's spokesman on foreign policy, but Acheson could barely tolerate him. Senator Arthur H. Vandenberg was the leading Republican on the Senate Foreign Relations Committee and generally viewed as the keystone of bipartisanship on foreign policy. Acheson was contemptuous of him. Dr. Walter H. Judd was the most articulate Republican supporter of Truman's containment policy in the House, but he and Acheson were at war over policy toward China. It was Rusk who served as the instrument of bipartisanship. Rusk and Dulles could talk, could meet informally to iron out partisan differences. It was Dulles who informed Vandenberg and Judd that Rusk was reliable and responsive. When Rusk was nominated to be assistant secretary in February, 1949, Vandenberg assured his colleagues privately and stated for the record later that Rusk was "one of the most hopeful additions" to the Department.[4] And when policy toward China became an acutely sensitive political issue in 1950, perhaps the only inevitable step that followed was Rusk's appointment—his voluntary demotion—to Assistant Secretary for Far Eastern Affairs.

2

Rusk's position as deputy-undersecretary involved him in everything of importance that came before the Department. He participated in the drafting of the North Atlantic Treaty and in the efforts to lift the Berlin Blockade. Jessup credits Rusk, along with Bohlen, with noticing the key omission in a statement by Stalin that led to the Berlin settlement in 1949.[5] When the British ambassador to the United Nations thought a chance remark by the Soviet ambassador might lead to a settlement of the conflict in Greece, Acheson sent Rusk to New York for "informal and personal" negotiations.[6] As the Communist victory in China penetrated the public consciousness, Rusk was given additional responsibilities for East Asian affairs, of little interest to Acheson. As deputy-undersecretary, Rusk found himself required to make more public appearances. He could not be a faceless bureaucrat, but had to represent the Department before Congressional committees and world affairs clubs. And he did it all so well that before the year was over, he was sharing responsibility for policy planning with Kennan and was designated as the Department's National Security Council consultant.

In his appearances before Congressional committees and before nongovernmental groups, Rusk's personal views were rarely discernible from the administration's policy line. On occasion, as when he played down the damage to the UN caused by the failure of the Security Council to obtain armed forces as envisaged under Chapter VII, he was clearly arguing a position not his own. His efforts within the government and his private correspondence leave no doubt that he thought much had been lost. With Congress he was direct, informative, and firm. The transcripts of Congressional hearings, public and executive sessions provide ample evidence of his success. With the public his strokes were much broader, the canvas impressionistic. His approach is revealed most readily in a note to Acheson after the latter's press conference on March 18, 1949. Rusk told Acheson he had erred in using certain language in response to a question and urged him to be more general in his answers.[7]

Many of his public appearances lent themselves to discussions of the United Nations. He opposed changing the organization, arguing that its failures had been due not to flaws in the Charter but to the conduct of the Soviet Union. A UN police force would not be a panacea because a Soviet veto could prevent its use, he contended—when Milton Eisenhower claimed the absence of such a force was a fatal flaw. Eisenhower thought the UN was threatened by its inability to act in Palestine and Indonesia. Rusk, characteristically less given to apocalyptic visions, assured his audience that the UN would survive, that it had effective machinery for settling international disputes. At a confidential round table with eminent "consultants" including Reinhold Niebuhr, Hamilton Fish Armstrong, Clark Eichelberger, and Harold Urey, Rusk did admit to concern about the impact of new members on the organization. The new states were from Asia, Africa, and the Middle East and were possessed of very different value systems. What would this mean for the future?[8]

In late 1949 and early 1950, Rusk spoke often about the Soviet Union and the nature of its threat. He was emphatic about distinguishing between Communism and Russian imperialism, singling out the latter as the source of America's problems. How the Russians organized their own society was their concern. He condemned international Communism not as an economic system but as a counter-revolutionary and reactionary device for subjecting other peoples to the interests of Russia. He called his audience's attention to the fact of Moscow's intolerance of Yugoslavia, a Communist state that would not submit to Stalin's control. Deploring Soviet tyranny in Eastern Europe, underlining the resentment of Western Communists at being compelled to serve Russian interests, he wondered aloud about the Chinese. How long would it take them to feel "the impact of the same bitter truth?"[9]

At the round table, in November, 1949, Urey asked Rusk if the Russians were preparing to attack. Rusk thought not: "We don't believe that they will mount armies and move across Europe and Asia." But he did expect them to "try to the fullest extent possible other techniques with which we are all familiar"—presumably subversion. In most of his appearances, Rusk stressed Soviet obstructionism in the UN, charging the Russians with failing to abide by the provisions of the Charter. New agreements were not necessary, if only the Russians would abide by their existing agreements.[10]

Displeased as he was by Soviet behavior in the UN, Rusk categorically opposed efforts to drive the Russians out. On the contrary, he argued that Soviet participation in the United Nations was important and that it was highly desirable to draw them in further, involve them in the activities of the specialized agencies.[11] One of his most cherished themes, perhaps central to his conception of world affairs, was the idea that small acts of cooperation over the years would reduce mistrust and bring about solidarity behind the principles of the UN Charter. He often emphasized the hundreds of daily international meetings that escaped the eye of a public awakened only by crisis. He generally thought great breakthroughs unlikely and urged patience as small steps were taken to create a sound foundation for international amity.

Rusk was aware that some Americans were debating the sources of Soviet conduct, stirred in part by Kennan's "Mr. X" article of 1947. It was characteristic of him to be impatient with such controversy. His insistence that the real problem was Soviet behavior, not its source, was hardly defensible.[12] Apparently, Rusk was manifesting his conviction that aggression must be stopped; one did not study the aggressor's behavior to find excuses for him or ways to appease him. If the Soviet Union had legitimate grievances, these could be redressed peacefully. All the Russians had to do was to abide by the principles of the Charter.

Rusk and Kennan also approached atomic weapons differently. Both men unquestionably hoped they would never be used again and dreaded the prospect of nuclear war. But in August, 1949, as the Russians prepared to explode their first nuclear device and the Pentagon demanded expanded bomb production for the United States, they found themselves on opposing sides in the discussion of State's response. Kennan thought the Pentagon program excessive and suggested that it might be best if a decision were reached never to use the atomic bomb. Rusk, supported by Acheson, rejected Kennan's proposal. They argued that self-denial could not be justified, particularly if the failure to use atomic weapons meant a great loss of lives—presumably American—or defeat. At that time and in later discussions on arms control, Rusk appeared concerned with the relationship of the bomb to conventional weapons, eager to arrange limits on both as necessary to prevent any nation from starting an aggressive war.[13]

One of the sticky issues Rusk took on was the reversal of American policy toward Franco's Spain—anathema to American liberals and to the Left. In March, 1949, Rusk indicated publicly that the United States no longer considered Spain a threat to the peace and was prepared to drop sanctions, restore diplomatic relations, and accept Spain in the United Nations and related agencies. He suggested that sanctions strengthened rather than undermined Franco's dictatorship and that outside the UN, Spain benefitted from its work without sharing in the responsibilities. Only two years earlier the United States had joined in a UN condemnation of Spain and withdrawn its ambassador, but by 1949 Pentagon pressures for bases in Spain pointed toward rapprochement. The issue remained dormant until the end of the year when Rusk endorsed a call for renewed contact with Spain, suggesting advantages for the United States and possible strengthening of democratic forces in Spanish society. For Acheson, Rusk prepared a very shrewd approach through Congressional leaders of both parties and senior delegates to the UN, specifically Eleanor Roosevelt, Cohen, and Dulles (temporarily appointed Senator from New York). This approach succeeded and Congress agreed to financial assistance for Spain in 1950. Despite Truman's intense distaste for Franco, diplomatic relations were restored in 1951. Liberal ideologues were not making policy in the Cold War.[14]

3

In Dean Acheson's memoir, *Present at the Creation,* he complained of the misfortune of having China collapse on him shortly after taking office. Acheson was intensely concerned with the Atlantic community and its Soviet adversary. Saving, burying, or resurrecting Chiang Kai-shek were not the choices with which he expected or cared to be confronted. Neither he nor Truman, nor Jessup, nor Rusk thought Chiang worthy of saving, even if he could be saved. But most importantly, none of these men thought the job could be done, given the enormity of the task, the limits of American power and the European priorities upon which they were agreed. To comfort themselves in a situation in which they felt little else could be done, they stressed evidence that the Chinese Communists were also nationalists who came to power on their own and would refuse to serve as instruments of Soviet policy.[15]

In the summer, 1949, as the People's Liberation Army began to mop up remnants of Kuomintang forces on the Chinese mainland, Acheson decided it would be necessary to answer critics of American policy with a full statement of what that policy had been and why the United States was not responsible for Chiang's failure. He was determined to end American involvement in the Chinese civil war, to quash in advance any new onslaught by Chiang's American friends, to drive in the last nail. Jessup agreed to oversee the collection and editing of documents and Rusk was among the half-dozen other members of the Department who participated in preparing what became the White Paper. The first draft of Acheson's oft-quoted letter of transmittal was based on a memorandum prepared by Rusk and Undersecretary Webb. [16]

When the People's Republic of China was proclaimed, Acheson met with all the principal officers of the Department, including Rusk and Kennan, and with a panel of outside consultants. A consensus was reached against immediate recognition and also against any maneuvers to detach Formosa, the island to which Chiang had fled, from the mainland. On the contrary, the principal aim of American policy toward China was to detach the Peking regime from Stalin's control, to encourage the development of a Sino-Soviet split. Nothing was to be done that might drive the Chinese into the Russian embrace. A "Titoist" China was the unstated goal. [17]

At the confidential round table in November, 1949, one participant contended that American policy was overweighted toward Europe while the Russians were really after the Far East. Rusk was tactful, as always, but rejected the argument, claiming that the situation in the Far East had come about without much Soviet effort. He explained that the Chinese had never been in the orbit of the United States and "I am sure they will probably never be in anybody's orbit." Later in the discussion he argued against dealing with China "as simply a fence to the Russian problem." Of particular interest was his contention that Chinese expansionism into Burma and Indochina would exist independently of the Cold War confrontation with the Soviet Union. Presumably such expansion was a Chinese national aspiration. [18]

As the reactions to Mao's victory in China and to the Department's China White Paper thundered around Washington in the last months of 1949 and early 1950, Rusk served as a lightning rod. He met frequently with Wellington Koo, China's ambassador, and with representatives of Congressmen and private groups sympathetic to Chiang and eager to obtain aid for the forces on Formosa. He listened, questioned, and deflected their demands. He had a marvelous facility for embarrassing Koo with gentle questions that pinpointed opposition to Chiang on Formosa, the disunity among anti-Communist Chinese leaders, the waste of resources already available on the island. When Koo advised him that China wanted to take its case to the UN to accuse the Russians of interfering in China's affairs, Rusk was sympathetic, but pressed him for evidence, warning that in the absence of evidence American support would be very limited. When Koo sought assurance that the United States would not recognize the People's Republic of China, Rusk refused, leaving the Chinese Ambassador without any doubt that the United States would extend recognition at the first propitious moment.[19]

In much of Rusk's work, Dulles helped. Koo would see Rusk and then go to Dulles to look for an opening. Invariably, if Koo's diary and memoranda for his own government are to be trusted, Dulles assured him that Rusk and Jessup were doing all they could for the Republic of China. Dulles played a similar role with Republican Congressmen, although there was no way he could restrain the notorious "Senator from Formosa," William Knowland.[20]

The question of what to do about Formosa elicited tense debates in the National Security Council and, perhaps inevitably, leaked into public print. No one in the Truman Administration wanted to "give" Formosa to the Chinese Communists. While Mao's regime appeared unfriendly there was no interest in its aggrandizement. State Department participants in the debate agreed with the JCS contention that Formosa was important as a base should China attack aggressively elsewhere in East Asia, either as an instrument of Soviet imperialism or in a quest for Chinese hegemony in the region. Acheson, Rusk, and Walton Butterworth, Assistant Secretary for Far Eastern Affairs, pressed the Joint Chiefs on two counts: 1) how important was control of Formosa? where did it rank among JCS priorities?; 2) what would it take to deny control of the island to the People's Republic? The military leaders were unwilling to be explicit about priorities, but conceded that they could not spare American forces needed to guarantee the repelling of a Communist invasion. On the other hand, in December, 1949, they argued that a lower-level operation, the extension of military assistance to the Republic of China, was feasible and might very well serve the security interests of the United States.[21]

The skepticism exhibited by Rusk's colleagues reflected in part their contempt for Chiang. Fundamentally, it rested upon their assumption that the People's Republic showed tendencies toward independence, that encouraging this independence was more important for American security than control of Formosa. To assist Chiang's regime on Formosa would reinsert the United States in the Chinese civil war, enrage Mao, drive the latter closer to Stalin, and increase the likelihood of aggressive Chinese action. If the Chinese Communist regime were not antagonized, there might not be any need for a base. Military assistance to Chiang, rather than strengthening American security, would create the need for a base. Moreover, to extend assistance at a level that was not assured of success, seemed hardly worth the risk, given the stakes involved. In addition, Rusk asked General J. Lawton Collins, Army chief of staff, about the strategic importance of Korea, from which the Army had insisted upon withdrawing. Collins admitted that Korea would be more important than Formosa for a Communist attack on Japan and that, indeed, Formosa was not much more valuable to the Chinese than bases they already had on the mainland.[22]

Within the government the State Department position prevailed, but Republican political leaders picked up the JCS position and called for aid to Formosa. Undoubtedly much of the attack was partisan in intent, Republicans in desperate quest of an issue with which to end Democratic dominance of American politics. Some of the attackers were also guided by an affinity, sometimes sincere, sometimes purchased, for the cause of Chiang Kai-shek. But some of those angered by the administration's refusal to aid Chiang simply did not share its fundamental assumption about Chinese independence. They were persuaded that Stalin and Mao were brothers, that the Chinese Communists took orders from Moscow, and that it was futile to attempt to encourage Chinese independence. If, as they assumed, the Chinese Communists were inexorably allied to the Russians in a world-wide confrontation with America and its friends, Chiang as their enemy was entitled to whatever help possible.

The critical issue was the relationship between the Chinese Communist movement and the Soviet Union. If China proved to be independent, the administration would be vindicated. But if China proved to be a Soviet satellite, Truman and Acheson would be excruciatingly vulnerable. It was a risk Acheson was prepared to take not only because of the estimates of his subordinates about the nature of Mao's regime, or because he abhorred Chiang, but perhaps primarily because he believed American priorities were in Europe. Rusk was uneasy about the gamble on Mao's independence, urged more attention to the affairs of the Orient, and emerged as the Department's leading proponent of containment in East Asia—including schemes for denying Formosa to the Communists.

A comparable problem existed in Southeast Asia where French efforts to retain some vestige of their empire in Indochina were being thwarted by nationalist resistance led by Communists. The State Department, as well as the Pentagon, was apprehensive about the role the People's Republic of China would play in Southeast Asia. If the People's Liberation Army intervened in the south, the French would likely be defeated. Communist control of Southeast Asia would be politically embarrassing for the United States and more immediately, for the Truman Administration. In addition, the resources of the area were considered to be of some importance. Because France, a NATO ally, was involved in Indochina, Acheson's interest was more readily engaged there than in Formosa, and he proved willing to extend some support to the French. Here again the Joint Chiefs yielded to none in the importance they would attach to keeping the region out of Communist hands, but they insisted that American military resources were already committed to the utmost. Additional military responsibilities were unacceptable.

In early March, 1950, Rusk drew the lines sharply for the Secretary of Defense. The State Department, he wrote, "believes that within the limitations imposed by existing commitments and strategic priorities, the resources of the United States should be deployed to reserve Indochina and Southeast Asia from further Communist encroachment." The State Department viewed Indochina as "the most strategically important area" of Southeast Asia. It had engaged all political resources, and was searching for additional economic resources. What was the military prepared to do?[23] The military, in fact, was prepared to do nothing. The State Department, however, came up with a scheme that must have delighted Acheson. Chiang's friends in Congress had demanded aid to Formosa under threat of blocking foreign aid legislation deemed vital by the administration. A compromise had been worked out that resulted in an appropriation for "the general area of China." In May, 1950, a large part of those funds were diverted to the French in Indochina. At the time it seemed a remarkably clever device for frustrating Chiang and his China bloc by demonstrating the administration's willingness to contain Communism in China without getting involved in anything as fraught with danger as the Chinese civil war.

4

In the spring of 1950, Rusk stepped down from his post as deputy-undersecretary to take the most dangerous job in the Department, Assistant Secretary for Far Eastern Affairs. Butterworth had fallen victim to what Acheson called "the attack of the primitives." Chiang's friends were relentless in their attack on the administration's policy toward China and State Department officials associated with that policy were harassed mercilessly. In February, Senator Joseph R. McCarthy had launched his career with a scurrilous attack on the Department. Acheson decided to send Butterworth to Sweden. Rusk volunteered to step into the breach. His qualifications for the job were evident. If anyone could take the pressure and quiet the opposition, it was Rusk. He alone of the Acheson loyalists had any influence with the Republican leadership in Congress. Acheson was apparently moved by the offer, never forgot it, and never regretted Rusk's role. In December, 1960, he told the story to President-elect John F. Kennedy and recommended Rusk for Kennedy's consideration as Secretary of State.[24]

CHAPTER FOUR

The Cold War Comes to East Asia

On March 28, 1950, the *New York Times* reported that Rusk was replacing Butterworth at Far Eastern Affairs. With classic understatement, "informed sources" represented the transfer as an effort to strengthen the Department's relations with Congress, "some segments of which have been sharply critical of the Far Eastern policy."[1]

For the next three months Rusk spent a tremendous amount of time testifying before Congressional committees, defending Acheson's priorities. He was called upon again and again to justify the administration's unwillingness to aid Chiang Kai-shek's forces on Formosa. Rusk also met frequently with Wellington Koo, finding ways to deny Koo's importunities without further enraging American friends of China with whom Koo was in constant contact. His task was complicated enormously in a way he may well have suspected but probably did not know. Paul Griffith, an assistant secretary of defense, was meeting privately with Koo, helping Koo to plot strategy with which to embarrass the Department of State. Griffith provided Koo with information that was never intended for foreign ears. Apparently Louis Johnson, the Secretary of Defense, was determined to reverse policy toward China and Griffith reported their hope that Acheson would be driven from the government by McCarthy's clamor.[2]

Rusk was not without help. He quickly persuaded Acheson to bring Dulles, whose short reign as Senator from New York was over, back into the Department. Appointed ambassador-at-large, Dulles was expected to restore some semblance of bipartisanship, particularly on issues related to China. Dulles worked tirelessly, although with limited success, at the task of reining in some of his party's wild jackasses. He was much more successful at persuading Koo and friends to give Rusk a chance, that Rusk was receptive to their needs.

Rusk was unquestionably more sympathetic than Acheson to the plight of mainland Chinese on Formosa. He thought the United States had "let China down" before 1941 and claimed to understand better than his colleagues the reasons why Chiang's regime was exhausted and corrupt. Accepting Acheson's priorities he nonetheless thought the United States should be more assertive in East Asia. He shared Kennan's view that Formosa was too important strategically to allow a Communist takeover and that the United States had the means to act successfully there. Rejecting Kennan's bizarre suggestion that American forces throw Chiang's army out of Formosa and the Pescadores, Rusk devised plans aimed toward the same goal: a regime independent of mainland control, without pretension to being the government of China. Acheson had always been receptive to the possibility of an independent Formosa emerging as a showcase of liberal democracy.[3]

In May, 1950, Rusk favored a UN trusteeship for Formosa, a solution to which Chiang was intensely hostile. He wanted Dulles to visit the Kuomintang leader and tell him the fall of the island was inevitable. The United States would not come to the rescue. Chiang's only recourse was to appeal to the UN for a trusteeship. If he did, the United States would support him in the UN and protect the island while action on the trusteeship was pending. Aware of the possibility of Chiang's continued recalcitrance, Rusk expressed interest in covert operations to strengthen Formosan defenses, an American demand for neutralization of the island, the voluntary or involuntary termination of Chiang's leadership, and, if all else failed, a place of refuge for Chiang.[4]

In June, Dulles explained to Koo that Rusk was coming around and seemed better disposed toward the Kuomintang regime. He then proceeded to tell Koo that Formosa had to do more for itself, echoing Rusk's theme. Koo's informants also reported that Dulles told a closed meeting of Republican Senators that Rusk's attitude toward China was "less adamant" than that of Truman and Acheson.[5]

Koo accepted Dulles' puffery of Rusk, but personally found Rusk inscrutable. He liked him better than Butterworth, but seemed to long for the simplicity and directness of Butterworth's approach. Rusk was less prejudiced, but so very deliberate and careful that Koo confided to his diary that he had difficulty grasping the implications of Rusk's words.[6]

On most issues, Rusk's messages to Koo were clear enough. Koo wanted American support in the UN for an effort to deny moral and material support to the People's Republic. Rusk explained that other delegations had views of their own. Koo asked for military aid for the Kuomintang, arguing that its armies were fighting to contain Communism in Asia. Rusk asked innocently if there was evidence of troop movements that implied Communist expansion—and left no doubt that the administration was not prepared to reconsider its refusal to send military aid to Formosa. Koo pressed for more economic aid and Rusk found a welter of technical reasons why more would not be possible.[7]

On one issue Rusk was more guarded with Koo and his associate, Hollington K. Tong. Early in June, Tong spoke to both Rusk and Dulles and came away with the idea that they might be more disposed to aid Formosa if Chiang "would be a little humble." As Koo and Tong reflected on this message and other statements by Rusk, they concluded that Chiang was the obstacle to aid. Maybe, they thought, Rusk and Dulles were saying that Chiang should step aside.[8]

Rusk's strategy before Congressional committees was to testify to the Department's great concern about the efforts of the "Politburo" to use Asian Communists for its own ends and to explain the need to act—in the Philippines, in Indonesia, in Indochina—almost anywhere but Formosa. The opposition, whether sincere or opportunist, could not easily charge him with failing to appreciate the dangers of international Communism or with unwillingness to act against Communist expansion in Asia. Congressman Judd was thoroughly disarmed and facilitated Rusk's efforts. Early in a long and difficult hearing on the Mutual Defense Assistance Act of 1950,

Judd praised Rusk: "more has happened since you took over the Far Eastern desk than has happened in the preceding five years. In fact longer than that. Since Alger Hiss first moved into it in 1939, there was nothing but negativism and defeatism until you took it over." Rusk never endorsed Judd's position on the past, yielded nothing on China and, indeed, offered a very spirited defense of the reporting from Formosa that implied a defense of early reporting from China to which Judd and his cohorts had objected. Worse than biased reporting was the refusal to accept unpalatable facts. "We must not," Rusk asserted, "just because these people report facts we don't like to hear, assume they are reporting them for biased or unpatriotic motives." In a dozen less critical situations, Rusk found ways to soothe and flatter Judd, deferring to him for example on the psychology of overseas Chinese.[9]

Rusk had less success with Senator Knowland, who could not be put off with demonstrations of assistance to noncommunist countries other than Formosa. Knowland argued there would have been nothing available for Southeast Asia but for the efforts of those like himself who felt that Formosa should not be overlooked. When they had accepted the flexible language of "the general area of China" they had not expected the Republic of China to be ignored. Rusk agreed that Chiang's administration of the island had improved, that there was less likelihood of a revolution there than in 1949, but there were still doubts about the loyalty of some of the troops. Knowland claimed that Sun Li-jen, a VMI-educated general popular with Americans, was running Formosa, but Rusk indicated reservations about how much power Chiang had in fact relinquished. Knowland kept pressing and Rusk indicated that he was looking into things, moving some programs along that had been jammed in the bureaucracy. Another friend of the Republic of China, Senator H. Alexander Smith (R-NJ), accepted Rusk's statement and expressed appreciation of his efforts, implying that at last the Republic of China would cease to be victimized by the State Department. The pattern held: Knowland attacked, Rusk explained, Smith supported Rusk. Emboldened by his success in isolating Knowland, Rusk suggested that Chiang's reported shortages were not real, that his government had supplies stored all over the island and could not find them, that there was a parallel with Chiang's practice of blaming the United States for his own inaction during the war.[10]

Although the administration persisted in its determination to hold the line against Chiang, Rusk indicated clearly that it was drawing another, very different line elsewhere in Asia. Funds were sought to strengthen the Philippine and Indonesian governments against Communist guerrillas, and the administration had committed two-thirds of the money for "the general area of China" to help the French in Indochina. Slowly, with the allocation of minimal resources, Truman and his advisers were moving to extend the policy of containment to Asia. In the spring, 1950, however, most of the effort was rhetorical. The $50 million committed to Indochina, following the recognition of Ho Chi Minh's regime by Moscow and Peking in January, involved the expenditure of funds the administration had not wanted. The money had to be used before there was pressure to give it to Chiang. Indeed, the subsidy presumably strengthened France, the better to play its role in Europe—perhaps the decision's greatest appeal for Acheson.

So Rusk gave Congress words instead of substance. There was no question but that the Truman Administration continued to be oriented overwhelmingly toward Europe. Pressed by Congresswoman Frances Bolton, Rusk answered characteristically: "There is no question, Mrs. Bolton, I think, about the importance of Formosa, nor, as a matter of fact, the importance of any other area now being directly threatened by communism. The problem is how far, under all of our world commitments and all the situations with which we are faced, how far we should go in trying to ourselves meet the situation, and with what we can work." Rusk could not be hectored into conceding that he or Acheson thought Asia or specifically Formosa unimportant, but, he explained patiently, "a country can be important and not be within our unlimited commitments at any given time."[11]

Rusk did, however, make some verbal concessions of considerable importance. He defended American support of the French in Indochina, despite reservations about French policy, on the ground that the war there was no ordinary civil war against colonialism. It was not analogous to the risings in India, Burma, and Indonesia where the United States had supported the rebels. He argued that the war in Indochina had been transformed into "a tool of the Politburo." He described it as "part of an international war" that could not be viewed as a "liberal democratic revolution." Asked to compare events in Indochina with those in China, he argued that "the leadership of both revolutions fell into the hands of the Politburo."[12]

Rusk also returned to an earlier concern about indirect aggression. Questioned specifically about a request for funds to strengthen the Indonesian constabulary, he conceded that the domestic affairs of Indonesia were involved, but he qualified that distinction to the point of being meaningless. He explained that there were armed bands in areas not under control of the Indonesian government; that these bands were subject to Communist penetration, which could lead to guerrilla operations against the government, resulting in its overthrow, bringing Indonesia under Politburo control "which is not a domestic matter." He insisted that it was not a matter of defending the regime against internal revolutionaries but rather a matter of "internal security against an external threat through international communism."[13]

Throughout the hearings in the spring of 1950, Rusk's statements on the relationship between Asian Communists and Moscow were at variance with his public and private statements during the year he served as deputy-undersecretary. Most likely he had changed his mind. There were few signs of Titoism emanating from Peking and the Department seemed resigned to a long wait before the Sino-Soviet split came. There were also tactical reasons for his posture. First, the McCarthyite attack on Acheson's policy toward China had begun. Rusk sought to disarm critics and to protect the administration if various Asians did prove to be instruments of the Kremlin. Second, he was responding to advice from Policy Planning that it would be useful to accuse the Chinese Communists of being Russian puppets as a device for strengthening nationalist elements, by shaming them into behaving like nationalists.[14] Regardless of purpose, Rusk's analysis contributed to the undermining of those who persisted in arguing that Mao was no one's puppet. If the administration yielded the point to its critics, who was left to argue it? The dangers inherent in Rusk's claim that internal revolutionaries who happened to be Communists constituted an *external* threat was not readily apparent in 1950.

Another country on which Rusk touched was Korea. In May, 1949, he had been disturbed by the reduction in appropriations for Korea, referring to a "scuttle and run" attitude which he warned would be resented by friends and exploited by the Soviet Union. He insisted that the United States had an "implied commitment" to the United Nations to leave "southern Korea" as a going concern. He had reservations about the withdrawal of American troops. But his argument made no appreciable difference at that time. On June 20, 1950, he spoke on behalf of South Korea. He conceded that its government was not democratic but claimed substantial progress for the Rhee regime. South Koreans had a morale problem because the United States did not acknowledge responsibilities for their defense comparable to those accepted for Japan and the Philippines, but Rusk claimed they had demonstrated the will to resist incursions from the north. He did not think they could protect themselves in a major war in which the North Koreans received large–scale support from the Russians, but, he assured the House Committee on Foreign Affairs, "we see no present indication that the people across the border have any intention of fighting a major war." Approximately five days later North Korean forces launched a massive attack across the 38th parallel. Despite evidence of large shipments of Russian equipment to North Korea, Rusk—and the intelligence community upon which he relied—had grossly miscalculated the intentions of the Soviet Union.[15]

2

Warnings of increased activity in North Korea were ignored in large part because Acheson, Rusk, and their colleagues simply did not want to see the Cold War extended to Asia and minimized the possibility of a major Soviet move in that part of the world. Pressure for the Truman Administration to raise its priorities in East Asia was centered in anti-administration circles and viewed as being directed toward the fall election. The criticism was often partisan, it was generally uninformed and irresponsible, and in the process of defending itself, the Truman Administration underestimated the seriousness of the situation in Korea.

Rusk was the first senior State Department official to learn of the attack. Joined by Secretary of the Army Frank Pace, with whom he had been at dinner when the initial report reached him, and John D. Hickerson, Assistant Secretary for UN Affairs, he informed Acheson, who was at his farm in Maryland. The President was in Independence. Rusk and Hickerson recommended that the issue be brought before the Security Council, that the Secretary General be alerted immediately, while the Department continued to gather information. Acheson approved and notified the President.

Thoughtful scholars have suggested that if Rusk had not been the first senior officer involved, the United States might have bypassed the United Nations. Given his commitment to the United Nations, he immediately called Hickerson, whose position predisposed him to turn to the UN. Had Kennan been present, his opposition to UN involvement might have reinforced Acheson's own skepticism about the efficacy of that organization. These were days, however, when Rusk's currency was valued much more highly by the secretary. Additionally, Jessup, one of the first people to whom Acheson turned in the crisis, was equally committed to the United Nations. And Acheson was quick enough to appreciate the value of a UN sanction for any action the United States chose to take.[16]

Rusk was one of the central figures in the framing of the administration's response. There was never any doubt in his mind that the United States would have to respond to an act of aggression. He had a faint hope that the North Koreans might be induced to halt their attack by a Security Council resolution, but he had dealt with the Russians in the UN too long and too closely to be optimistic about words sufficing.

In the discussions that followed the return to Washington of President Truman, questions were raised about Formosa.[17] Secretary of Defense Johnson, who had just returned from Japan, was more concerned with Formosa than with Korea. It was Acheson, however, who proposed that in addition to steps to repel the North Korean attack, the United States order its Seventh Fleet to prevent the People's Republic from invading Formosa—and the Republic of China from attacking the Chinese mainland. Until the North Korean attack, Acheson had been prepared to allow Chiang to fend for himself and anticipated a Communist conquest of Formosa. Despite his acceptance of the idea that Formosa was important, he did not think it important enough to divert scarce resources to defend it. But if Korea, which he had placed outside the defensive perimeter of the United States in the same speech which located Formosa beyond the pale, was to be defended, Acheson would be hard-pressed to justify inaction on Formosa. Ordering the Fleet to the Formosa Straits was an action that would mute criticism in the short run and could be reversed later without committing the United States to Chiang.

President Truman indicated an interest in getting Chiang's forces to do some of the fighting in Korea, but Acheson expressed reservations about getting mixed up with Chiang's regime. Truman declared his own contempt, insisting the United States would not give the Chinese a nickel for any purpose whatever, claiming that all the money Americans had given them was invested in real estate in the United States. But the President was clearly eager to find a way to do something about Formosa as a valuable territory to be denied to the Communists—without helping Chiang. Rusk reinforced Truman's concern by noting Kennan's estimate that Formosa would be the next likely Communist target.[18]

The problem of Formosa—how to turn it into an asset without being contaminated by Chiang, without becoming reinvolved in the Chinese civil war—demanded much of Rusk's attention during the summer of 1950, while the battle raged in Korea. His task was complicated enormously by the machinations of Johnson and General Douglas MacArthur, both eager to ally the United States to the Kuomintang regime. Rusk met frequently with Koo, brushing aside Koo's offer of Chinese troops for Korea or a coordinated landing on the Chinese mainland. The United States was not interested in offensive operations by Chiang's troops. Acheson, Rusk, and the Joint Chiefs were skeptical of their ability and of their will to fight. Indeed, they wanted to be rid of existing Kuomintang troops on the mainland and pressed Koo to have troops that had fled to Burma surrender to Burmese authorities to preclude giving the People's Liberation Army an excuse for invading Burma. Occasionally impatient, Rusk pointedly reminded Koo that his government had claimed its forces were inadequate to defend Formosa. With what later revelations indicated to be marked understatement, Rusk warned that the commitments of the Seventh Fleet were too extensive to assure the defense of Formosa.[19]

Koo had been informed by Johnson that the administration had changed its policy on aid to Formosa. In fact, Johnson asked Koo to inform Madame Chiang and her brother-in-law, H. H. Kung, that he had kept his promise to win a policy reversal. But Rusk and Acheson were determined to win concessions before opening the spigot. They wanted the Republic of China to be restricted to the island of Formosa and to forget about the mainland and they wanted Chiang to step aside. Clearly, the administration was backing away from its earlier willingness to tolerate a Communist victory on Formosa. Amidst war in Korea, the island's strategic importance seemed much greater in late June than Acheson would have conceded at the beginning of the month. Acheson and Rusk were prepared to help the Chinese on Formosa to defend themselves, but not to resume the civil war. They were prepared to give aid to the Republic of China, but they still hoped to see it converted into a liberal democracy, sans Chiang. On July 24, Rusk met for two hours with Hu Shih, the well-known Columbia-educated philosopher and one-time ambassador to the United States, trying to persuade Hu to lead a liberal anti-Chiang movement. Koo met with Rusk shortly afterward and flew to Taipei to be sure that his government understood American terms for military aid.[20]

When Koo returned from Formosa he informed Rusk that he had found progress in Taipei, but admitted that Chiang still ran the show. He spoke of a tension between the Japanese-educated military and Anglo-Saxon-educated civilians, in which he predicted victory for the civilians. Rusk did not press him on this point but rather focused on the difficulty the United States would have supporting Formosa in or out of the UN, so long as the Communists retained control of the Chinese mainland. Stressing also the importance of not provoking the People's Republic, Rusk appeared intent on maneuvering Koo toward a "two China"—or one China, one Formosa—policy. The hostile attitude of America's friends would make it difficult for the United States to help the Republic of China maintain its international position, its claim to be China. Yet

Rusk conceded that Chiang's regime on Formosa had a restraining influence on the Chinese Communists. Apparently the administration had despaired of ridding the Chinese of Chiang's baneful influence and was preparing to provide aid on the basis of promises of democratic reforms and restraint in operations against the mainland.[21]

On September 9, 1950, as MacArthur's forces drove the North Koreans out of South Korea, Rusk made a speech in which he outlined American policy in East Asia. After preliminary reference to traditional American values and purposes, he called for a free and united Korea—a proposal that received warm support from liberals. Against the opposition of Kennan and his successor at Policy Planning, Paul Nitze, Rusk had persuaded Acheson to retain the option of sending American forces across the 38th parallel and to reopen the possibility of creating a united, democratic—*i.e.*, noncommunist—Korea. The United States intended to get UN sanction for this effort and hoped also to get the UN to call for the cessation of hostilities between Formosa and the Chinese mainland. Rusk announced to his audience that he welcomed UN consideration of the Formosa question, but that in any event the United States would continue its economic assistance and "furnish selected military assistance" to enable Formosa to defend itself.[22]

In the same speech Rusk continued the administration's efforts to convey to Peking the absence of any aggressive intent toward the People's Republic. But he also warned vaguely against "acts of aggression which might be set in motion in mainland China on behalf of a Communist conspiracy." Presumably he was vague so as to leave Mao uncertain as to whether the United States was threatening to retaliate against action in Southeast Asia, against Formosa, or in Korea. In keeping with the Department's effort to strengthen independent nationalists among the Chinese Communists, Rusk warned that the United States would "not accept the right of any clique in China to preside over the dismemberment of China for the benefit of Soviet imperialism." Rusk had privately told Koo that he could not believe that "men like Mao Tse-tung would be willing to carry out the orders of the Kremlin rather than work for the welfare of the Chinese people." Koo conceded the point, but argued that the Communists were split and that some of them were

Soviet stooges. American analysts concurred and Rusk's tactic was to try to strengthen Mao.[23]

In his speech Rusk declared that the time had come for a peace settlement with Japan and that the United States would be providing military assistance to Indochina and the Philippines and economic assistance to Southeast Asia. The containment line in Asia was being brought into sharp focus.

Rusk indicated to Koo that the American commitment to Formosa was very tentative. Truman had announced that as soon as the war was over in Korea, the Seventh Fleet would be withdrawn from the Straits. Rusk admitted that Truman had spoken hastily, and that the administration was uncertain what it would do in the long run. Koo asked if the United States was playing for time until Soviet intentions were clarified—and recorded that Rusk blushed! For the moment the status quo on Formosa was mutually beneficial to the United States and to the Republic of China, but a longer-range commitment was not yet contemplated.[24]

On October 1, South Korean forces crossed the 38th parallel, driving north. A week later, despite sharp warnings that the People's Republic would be forced to respond in kind, American troops marched into North Korea. Aggression had been resisted. The aggressor had been defeated and driven back. The integrity of the UN had been demonstrated. But although its initial war aims had been accomplished, the United States continued to fight. Rapid success brought greater ambition and Rusk, as much as anyone else, was responsible—and accepted responsibility for what followed.

The Americans had been confident that the Chinese Communists would not intervene in Korea. Truman, Acheson, and Rusk had indicated that the United States harbored no aggressive designs against the People's Republic. They were persuaded that the Chinese had all they could handle with their internal pacification campaign, that they were deterred by fear of an attack from Formosa, and by an awareness of the enormous punitive power of the United States. The Americans were aware that North Korea was a Russian satellite and that Peking's principal concern since the outbreak of the war was manifestly Formosa. Nonetheless, Chinese signals aroused some uneasiness in Washington and Truman decided to meet with MacArthur to discuss various aspects of the war.

He asked Acheson to allow Rusk and Jessup to accompany him.[25] Acheson was dubious about the meeting but consented. At Wake Island, MacArthur assured the President and his companions that the Chinese would not dare to intervene and that if they did, it could not be in sufficient force to make much difference. There was no need for concern. The boys would be home for Christmas.

Initial contact with Chinese forces annoyed but did not deter MacArthur. On November 21, Acheson, Jessup, Rusk, Nitze, and H. Freeman Matthews met alone, then with Marshall and Lovett representing the Department of Defense.[26] They decided to press on to the Yalu with only slight modification of MacArthur's orders. On November 24, MacArthur announced his "end the war" offensive. On November 26, the Chinese counterattacked with approximately 200,000 men and MacArthur's forces were shattered and driven back. In just a few weeks, as UN forces reeled back across the 38th parallel and seemed once more in danger of being driven off the Korean peninsula, MacArthur, shrouded in gloom, was predicting defeat unless he was allowed to bomb China.

Massive Chinese intervention in Korea shook Acheson, Rusk and their colleagues badly. It was, as MacArthur said, a new war. Chiang Kai-shek may have welcomed that new war. There were doubtless a few Americans spoiling for a chance to fight and destroy Chinese Communism. But Truman, Acheson, and Rusk had imagined the war in Korea to be almost over. They had demonstrated the will of the United States and of the United Nations to resist aggression and had run the North Korean invaders out of the south. They had seen an opportunity to end some of their frustrations, to go on the offensive and liberate the rest of Korea, to roll back Communism for the first time since the Cold War had begun. For several weeks the decision to cross the 38th parallel to unite Korea looked as brilliant as the gamble MacArthur took at Inchon. In Korea, MacArthur's forces rolled north with slight opposition. The Chinese noised about but dared not act. At home, critics of the administration had been silenced. These were heady moments, but the reverie was shattered by the offensive of the People's Liberation Army (PLA).

Acheson and Rusk questioned their own assumptions about the People's Republic and concluded that there had been greater

Chinese involvement in the North Korean aggression than they had realized. They feared, too, that the Chinese were as hostile to the United States as were the Russians. Although Rusk briefly considered the possibility that the Chinese were responding to the march of American troops toward their borders, neither he nor Acheson dwelled long on the thought that the United States had provoked Chinese intervention.

Rusk made much of the fact that in the months preceding the outbreak of war, the Chinese had transferred 12,000 Korean soldiers from the PLA to North Korea. These were Koreans who had fought with the Chinese during the war against Japan and again during the civil war. Rusk claimed, however, that they were *Chinese* of Korean origin and that their movements were evidence of Chinese complicity in the earlier stages of the war. Subsequent studies of the troops and the timing of their return to Korea have not supported Rusk's analysis.[27]

Rusk indicted the Chinese on several minor counts of aiding aggression, but he was most disturbed by the offensive of November 26 and the subsequent loss of American lives at Chinese hands. However much he looked elsewhere for explanations of what had gone wrong he could not have escaped a sense of his own responsibility. None of the men who shared in the decision to send American forces across the 38th parallel could relieve himself of that burden. In mitigation, he could explain to his family, his god, and his fellow Americans that he had acted in ways consistent with both the ideals and the self-interest of the American people. In a television appearance Rusk spoke of fighting in Korea to prevent world war, to demonstrate that aggression did not pay, that the world would not again tread the path that led from Manchuria to Ethiopia to Munich to Poland to Pearl Harbor. Twenty million gallant Koreans could not be abandoned to Communism, and America's friends in the Philippines and in Japan had to be assured that the United States would meet its commitments.[28] He never explained why these goals, however admirable, had required crossing the 38th parallel.

If men like Rusk had to bear the burden of having sent thousands of their countrymen to their deaths, at least they could believe the cause had been worthy, that Americans could be proud of what they were trying to do. They sought nothing more than peace for themselves and their neighbors, near and far. On November 28, however, Wu Hsiu-ch'uan, representing the People's Republic of China, delivered a vituperative attack at the UN on the role of the United States in Korea and on America's historic policy in China, branding the United States an imperialist aggressor. Rusk was profoundly offended by the charges and sufficiently troubled to ask Koo to have the Republic of China's ambassador to the UN, T. F. Tsiang, rebut them and to stress the historic friendship between the American and Chinese peoples, the absence of any aggressive designs on China by Americans.[29]

As the Chinese advanced, the panic MacArthur evidenced in Korea began to infect Washington. Rusk tried to focus attention on American objectives in Korea. When MacArthur's defeatism had both the Departments of Defense and State considering the need to abandon operations in Korea rather than attack China and risk starting World War III, Rusk and Kennan joined forces to stiffen first Acheson, then Marshall and Lovett. They argued that MacArthur was giving up too easily, that the United States had to show the kind of spirit the British had shown in 1940. Rusk contended that the United States had sufficient forces in Korea to exact a terrible toll from the Chinese, to punish them severely for intervening. He thought American forces could dig in, hold a line, and force a tolerable cease-fire on the Chinese. Rusk went so far as to suggest that Truman send General Collins to assume command in Korea, "allowing" MacArthur to concentrate on his duties in Japan. The moment of fear passed, American forces eventually regrouped and held.[30]

When Clement Attlee, British Prime Minister, came to Washington during this crucial time, he argued for seating the People's Republic in the United Nations as a course that might lead to peace. Rusk opposed. He saw no need to seat the "Chinese Reds" to demonstrate American good will. There would be no rewards for aggression, no concessions under the gun. But the administration may not have been rigid on the issue. Dulles told Koo that if a formula which saved face for everybody were devised, it would probably be approved by a majority of UN members and be acceptable to the United States. He assured Koo, however, that the

United States would neither recognize the People's Republic nor turn Formosa over to it.[31]

With the war in Korea transformed into a war between the People's Republic and the United States, questions about policy toward China, toward the rival Peking and Taipei regimes, vied with events on the battlefield for attention of the Truman Administration. At the front MacArthur eventually had to be relieved of his command for insubordination. General Ridgway replaced him and restored the morale of American forces. Without nuclear weapons or attacks on China, Ridgway succeeded in reversing the course of the war and driving the Chinese back across the 38th parallel. This time the United States was prepared to rest its case there and seek peace without the unification of Korea. In Washington, Rusk and colleagues had to reevaluate their premises about the People's Republic and calculate anew the best strategy for coping with it. Once the fighting stabilized, Acheson took two weeks' vacation in February, 1951, leaving East Asia to Rusk.

Perhaps surprisingly, Chinese intervention in Korea did not lead to a change in one fundamental premise of the State Department's leaders. They continued to assume—rightly—that the Chinese Communists were strongly nationalistic and that some day it would be possible to separate them from the Soviet Union. Appeals to Chinese nationalism continued to enter into most public statements, but in the form recommended by John P. Davies of accusing them of selling out Chinese interests and serving as Soviet puppets. As Davies perceived Chinese psychology, to "ma" the Chinese, to shame them, would force them to demonstrate their nationalism. In a Voice of America broadcast on December 29, 1950, Rusk said of the Chinese Communists: "They seem willing to dismember China to suit the Kremlin's interest." It was unmistakable that "while the acts staged by Peiping are Chinese, the puppet master is Soviet." Still smarting over Wu's attack at the UN, Rusk referred to the Chinese Communists, "faithfully echoing the voice of their masters." Let them prove they were independent—presumably by behaving more appreciatively toward their historic benefactors, the American people.[32]

A second premise on which American policy had been based, that by washing its hands of Chiang and Formosa the administration could mute Mao's hostility toward the United States and keep him from Stalin's embrace, was abandoned. Chinese actions indicated that Peking expected the worst from the United States and Mao's sensibilities were no longer a central concern. Nonetheless, Acheson and Rusk had a difficult time developing a friendlier policy toward Formosa. Rusk never gave up the hope of getting rid of Chiang Kai-shek and his sons. Judd, Koo and several special Chinese missions to Washington came away from Rusk's office struck by Rusk's interest in political figures who might serve as alternatives to Chiang. At one point the American government was preparing to assist anti-Communist guerrilla operations on the mainland and even as CIA operatives moved across the Pacific with their supplies, Rusk was rigidly refusing to accept Chiang's leadership. Similarly, Rusk consistently rejected offers of military assistance from Formosa, continuing to deprecate the ability of Kuomintang forces to defend the island or their will to fight elsewhere. A little aid to strengthen the Republic of China's defenses on Formosa would be forthcoming, but nothing more. Nothing for the recovery of the mainland. In late March, 1951, Koo found Rusk surprisingly cold and abrupt. Additional aid would not be forthcoming. The accelerating rearmament of the United States would require cuts in foreign aid. New expenses were lowering the standard of living of the American people. Formosa would have to lower its standards. Koo concluded that Rusk was not satisfied with alleged progress away from a Chiang dictatorship.[33]

The controversy over MacArthur absorbed much of Rusk's energies in April. Like his superiors, he appeared publicly and before Congress to justify the administration's concept of limited war. Korea could not be abandoned without returning to the trail that led from Manchuria to Pearl Harbor. China could not be attacked without risk of general war. Inability to end the war, continued loss of American life, the recall of MacArthur—all fed the plague McCarthy was spreading in the country. The administration was under tremendous pressure and in mid-May, amidst the Congressional hearings on the "Situation in the Far East", the National Security Council prepared a new statement of American policy in East Asia that won the approval of the President.

NSC 48/4 conceded one opposition point that was no longer

arguable: the most immediate threat to American interests was in Asia. The Russians appeared to be attempting to gain control of the mainland of East Asia, Japan, and other principal offshore islands. They were working "primarily through Soviet exploitation of the resources of communist China." In the long run the United States had to eliminate or reduce Soviet power in the region and secure its resources for the free world. The more immediate objectives of the United States seemed restatements of the goals of the past year: "detach China as an effective ally of the USSR and support the development of an independent China which has renounced aggression." Avoid extension of the Korean War to a general war. Continue to recognize the Republic of China while punishing the forces of the People's Republic of China in Korea. Try to expand noncommunist leadership in China and try to get people to reorient or replace the Communist regime. Stimulate differences between Peiping and Moscow and create cleavages within the Peiping regime itself by every means possible. Consistent with earlier military planning it was agreed that if a major war with the Soviet Union developed, the United States would withdraw from Korea and deploy its forces elsewhere. One point, relating to Formosa, was modified: Formosa was to be denied to any Chinese regime tied to the Soviet Union, and the strengthening of its defensive capabilities was to be expedited. Peking's opportunity to conquer Formosa without American interference had passed.[34]

On May 18, the day after President Truman approved NSC 48/4, and less than two weeks before Acheson's ordeal by Senate investigation began, Rusk delivered an address before the China Institute of New York City that created a furor. Borrowing phrases from earlier speeches, he continued his criticism of the Communist leaders "who seem to love China less than they do their foreign masters." He charged that the independence of China was being threatened and implied that the Russians were in the process of separating Manchuria, Outer Mongolia, and Sinkiang from China. The Chinese had intervened in Korea because they had been "driven by foreign masters." After declaring that the job of retaining their independence was a job "only the Chinese can do" with "tremendous support from free peoples in other parts of the world," he declined to promise anything from the United States but a refusal to recognize Mao's regime. To drive home his point, Rusk used a rhetorical flourish that plagued him for many years afterward: "The Peiping regime may be a colonial Russian government—a Slavic Manchukuo on a larger scale. It is not the Government of China. It will not pass the first test. It is not Chinese." The hyperbole was outrageous—a sublimely ridiculous extension of the idea of shaming the Chinese into demonstrating their independence. But the times were not funny. Henry Luce, presiding at the meeting, was greatly moved. Here, as Dulles had promised, was a man of good sense, a rare patriot in the Department of State. And when Rusk went on to indicate that the United States recognized the Republic of China which would continue to receive "important aid and assistance" from the United States, he pleased Chiang's friends in the audience, while promising nothing.[35]

What did Rusk's "Slavic Manchukuo" speech mean? The press generally interpreted Rusk's comments to mean that the Department of State was announcing a radical reversal of American policy toward China. The next morning's *New York Times* headlined the story "Rusk Hints U.S. Aid to Revolt in China." Arthur Krock of the *Times* later claimed that it was widely inferred from Rusk's remarks that after the Korean War the United States would try to restore Chiang to power on the Chinese mainland. Krock thought Rusk had mistakenly implied that the United States would not negotiate with the People's Republic at precisely the time when negotiations to end the war were being sought. Other commentators believed Rusk was indicating American willingness to help in efforts to overthrow the People's Republic; that the Truman Administration had fired MacArthur, then adopted MacArthur's policy. There were reports that the British embassy panicked and that the British government was deeply disturbed by the speech.[36]

In the days that followed, clarifications flowed from the Department and the *New York Times* tried to present a correct interpretation of Rusk's remarks. Officially, the Department insisted there had been no change of policy. Unofficially, word was leaked to the press that Rusk's speech had not been cleared by Acheson, that some of what he had said was out of line, and that he had been "roundly scolded." Acheson stated categorically that the United States was willing to negotiate with the People's Republic to end the war in Korea and the *Times* agreed editorially that it was wrong to think Rusk had indicated anything to the contrary.[37]

The mass circulation periodicals, *Time, Newsweek,* and *U.S. News and World Report* all interpreted Rusk's speech as evidence of a stiffening of American policy in Asia. *US News and World Report* emphasized the domestic political consequences of the speech, calling it a coup by the Department to quiet its critics. *Time* and *Newsweek* focused on Acheson's denials, which the Luce publication brushed aside as efforts to reassure the British.[38]

Koo and his associates were not in agreement on some elements of the speech but were inclined to believe that it meant additional aid for Formosa. Their Republican friends warned that the State Department had not really changed and would sell Formosa out in the end. One of Koo's aides reminded Koo that the Department was unrelenting in its hostility toward Chiang, but Ch'en Chih-mai, his principal counselor, rejected Republican warnings. Parts of the event—its timing and the denial that it meant anything new— puzzled Ch'en, but he was much more impressed by the fact that "we could look forward to substantial assistance from the United States." Wise in the ways of American politicians, he thought the Republican line on Rusk's speech reflected the "highly political nature of their position." Not love of China, but rather a desire to undo Democrats moved them. He advised Koo to be cautious, but not cynical.[39]

One other person of note who was puzzled and disturbed by Rusk's speech was President Truman. The furor in the press reached his attention as did the cries of anguish from Congressional supporters of administration policy who thought they'd been left defending an unpopular policy that the administration had abandoned without warning. Acheson was called to the White House where he went over the speech with the President, "pointing out to him in detail that Mr. Rusk had not suggested or in any way made any change in policy, but had merely repeated what had been said by both the President and me many times in the past. The attention given to this speech and the implications sought to be drawn from it were the product of the present investigation on the Hill."[40]

Although Acheson was not quite candid with the President, he was unquestionably correct in contending that Rusk had said nothing inconsistent with government policy. Certainly there was nothing in the speech that was not in NSC 48/4, signed by the President on the day preceding the speech. But NSC 48/4 had articulated policy developments during the months subsequent to the outbreak of the Korean War—and especially since China intervened in that war—that did represent a reversal of administration policy. In particular, the administration had announced the popular decision to reinvolve the United States in the Chinese civil war. Recognition of the People's Republic was no longer pending. The People's Republic might still be shamed away from Moscow's strings, but it would not be wooed by the United States. And most important, Formosa would not be abandoned. Holding his nose, Acheson would funnel aid to Chiang's regime, enemy of our enemy.

Rusk had tried out much of what he had to say about the People's Republic in earlier speeches, given in quieter moments in remote places like Philadelphia. No one had noticed. On May 18 he spoke in New York, with Henry Luce presiding and the rest of the media well represented. The recall of MacArthur had focused national attention on all of the issues of East Asian policy and Rusk's appearance was a major "event." The Department seized the opportunity. He shared the dais with Dulles as well as Luce, and his role was to blunt criticism of the administration which was running before the McCarthyite terror. Together, he and Dulles sought to reestablish a basis for bipartisan policy in East Asia. They spoke for Acheson, to protect him and the administration, repudiating policies on which Acheson months earlier had given up, but which he had defended too bitterly to renounce publicly.

After the event, Acheson could refine and qualify, as the responses from various quarters necessitated. He and Rusk were aware, most likely, that the British would not be pleased by the tone or content of the speech, but they had been irritated by British simpering throughout the Korean War. They had determined that they would do what they could to carry the British along, but would not let the British prevent them from doing what had to be done. When the speech worried the British, Acheson gave them the necessary assurances. Thoughtful people who feared the administration was contemplating backing Chiang in an assault on the main-land might be assured by other administration spokesmen, like Senator Brien McMahon, who called attention to Rusk's point that the job to be done in China had to be done by the Chinese.[41]

In one important respect, Rusk's hyperbole—his "Slavic Manchukuo"—was harmful and reinforced an undesirable ten-dency in American society. By using language originally intended to shame the Chinese Communists into behaving more like nationalists, intended to strengthen Mao against presumably Russian-controlled Chinese leaders, Rusk was misleading the American public about the nature of the People's Republic. Con-ceivably, he could not recognize genuinely Chinese reasons for China's actions in Korea. More likely, given views he expressed at other times, he was well aware that although China was hostile to a degree not anticipated, China was not a Russian puppet. But he did not perceive any functional consequence to distinguishing between a China independently hostile to the United States and a China hostile at Moscow's direction. He and Acheson, though they clearly would have preferred a noncommunist regime in Peking, had, in their fashion, wooed the Chinese Communists. They hoped to assure them that American good will was a better guarantee of Chinese interests and aspirations than anything that Stalin, the treacherous imperialist, might offer. Ideology had prevailed and Mao had chosen to stress Communist internationalism. At the policy level, it hardly mattered whether Communism was monolithic, if all Communists would be suspicious of and hostile toward the United States.

Seeking a consensus with administration critics hostile to Mao's regime, Rusk supported the belief in monolithic Communism that so plagued American attitudes on world affairs for the next decade. His words fanned a public hatred toward the People's Republic that delayed a rapprochement for two decades. Certainly he did not produce these evils himself. In a milieu in which any call for understanding of the People's Republic was dangerous, he could not likely have prevailed over administration critics had he chosen to fight them on the question of the nature of Mao's regime. But with his speech the administration had conceded the debate and one generation of Americans never again heard a sane public voice on the issue.

3

When the stir over Rusk's speech passed and Acheson had survived his ordeal on the Hill, the administration revived efforts to obtain a cease-fire in Korea. Rusk and Dulles also devoted an increasing amount of attention to a peace treaty with Japan. Southeast Asia, especially Indochina, also won an occasional moment of Rusk's time. Having resigned itself to the conclusion that the containment of Soviet—or was it Communist—expansion would be required in Asia, the administration set about its task dutifully.

On June 23, 1951, in response to a query from Kennan, the Soviet representative at the UN, Jacob Malik, indicated interest in a cease-fire. Kennan went to New York to talk privately with Malik, and Gromyko was questioned in Washington. Acheson and Rusk quickly concluded that the Russians were serious and signaled their willingness to begin negotiations. On July 2, Rusk appeared before the Senate Foreign Relations Committee to explain what had happened, what it meant, and what would follow.

At the outset of the hearing, Senator Connally needled Rusk about his "Slavic Manchukuo" speech, eliciting Rusk's promise to be discreet on this occasion. One point on which he dwelled rendered absurd the whole conception of his notorious phrase. He explained that the Department was puzzled by the apparent lack of communication or cooperation between Moscow and "Peiping": "although on theory we would think the two capitals were acting very closely together, their propaganda does not reflect it." He did not think they were trying to deceive the United States. Several weeks later, in a different context, he corrected Congresswoman Bolton's reference to China having the largest number of people "under the control of the Kremlin." He offered instead the phrase "under Communist control," distinguishing between indigenous Communist control and Soviet control. For Connally and colleagues, Rusk manifested his central theme: that lack of coordination between Russian and Chinese Communists, even the absence of puppetry, "does not mean there is any difference in their basic policy."[42]

Rusk and Acheson were persuaded that the Russians were sincere in their desire for a cease-fire without settling political and territorial questions. The Truman Administration was delighted to be able to limit the talks to the battlefield where the focus could be kept on Korea and away from a broader Pacific settlement that might involve Formosa and the seating of the People's Republic in the United Nations. On the latter issues, of greater concern to the Chinese than to the Russians, the United States feared isolation from its allies, most obviously the British. And the atmosphere on the Hill was too explosive for any compromises relating to the Chinese civil war.

There were two tactical matters that Rusk explained to the Senators with great care. First, the United States could not make public its conditions for a cease-fire. If the United States revealed its minimum position, the other party would immediately chip away at that and make it appear that the United States was fighting for an inconsequential point. If the Americans announced their opening bargaining position, there would be trouble with allies. General agreement among the allies could probably be found only on the minimum position. In addition, to announce a bargaining position to the public would commit American prestige to it, making the intended retreat difficult. Indeed, it might appear to be appeasement.[43] Rusk's professional opposition to public negotiations was obvious, apparently sensible—and long-lived.

The second matter, on which he requested Congressional assistance, was the need to explain to the American people that the shooting could not stop until there was an armistice. He did not want public pressure to force a cessation of hostilities before an agreement was negotiated. If the United States agreed to a cease-fire prior to arranging a formal truce, it would be difficult for the United States to take the initiative to resume shooting if the other side obstructed a complete end to the war. In particular Rusk seemed concerned about a continued Chinese buildup. Some kind of agreement on behind-the-lines inspection would probably be necessary to protect UN forces against sudden violations of the truce.[44]

Several years later, when a group of Truman Administration

stalwarts met to reconstruct the events of the Korean War, they were asked why it took two years to conclude a truce when the Russians seemed so eager in June, 1951. Kennan suggested it was because the United States eased the military pressure on the Chinese so that their needs were reduced and they demanded less of the Russians. Rusk, supported by Acheson and Nitze, explained that the administration could not ask men to take the heavy casualties necessary to maintain pressure if a truce seemed around the corner. He argued that there was no change in Russian desire for a truce; that there remained a matter of matching Russian conditions with American. Referring to American insistence on the military line rather than the 38th parallel as a basis for the truce and the later interjection of the POW question, he suggested that the United States, posing unanticipated questions for the Soviet Union, was responsible for the long-drawn-out negotiations.[45]

Rusk was long out of the Department before the truce was finally signed in Korea, but he did have the satisfaction of consummating the arrangements for peace with Japan and the basis of a new Japanese-American relationship that was of enduring importance. Dulles played the central role in negotiating the peace treaty with Japan after the Department—and General MacArthur—had agreed that the time had come to end the occupation, that Japanese consent was not likely to endure much longer. After Rusk had persuaded Acheson and Truman to bring Dulles, "a notorious leaker to the press," back into the Department, Acheson sought something safe for Dulles to do—something he would not use against the administration in the election of 1950. Rusk wanted him in Far East, along with Jessup, in his quest for bipartisan support. Acheson agreed that putting Dulles to work on the Japanese peace treaty might keep Japan out of the storm that raged over everything Acheson himself touched in East Asia. Dulles immediately scrapped a massive Departmental draft treaty, too detailed to negotiate with forty-odd countries and substituted a general "short form." Months of difficult bilateral negotiations followed, with wide-ranging disagreement over reparations in particular among Japan's World War II enemies. Dulles talked to the Japanese and to the other prospective signatories while Rusk protected him at home, especially from a Pentagon willing to yield little of its occupation privileges.[46]

On the domestic front, Dulles and Rusk were remarkably successful. They worked closely with the Democratic leadership in Congress and Dulles was able to win the approval of Republican leaders for his efforts despite their rage over the recall of MacArthur. Internationally, little cooperation was expected or received from the Russians, but British approval was critical and not easily attained. The British raised the question of whether Taipei or Peking would sign for China. The British would not accept Chiang's participation in the proposed peace conference or his signature on the treaty. The United States could not, in the spring of 1951, accept the People's Republic as the Chinese participant. Eventually, a compromise was worked out. Neither Taipei nor Peking would be invited to participate. Satisfactory to the Truman Administration and to the British government, the compromise quite naturally outraged Chiang and created tensions among his American friends that required all of the skill Dulles and Rusk could muster.

In response to Koo's protests, Rusk and Dulles warned him separately and together that if the treaty failed because of Chiang's obstruction, Formosa would suffer. It would pain them greatly if some formula were not reached to prevent such suffering on the island. Then they offered him a consolation prize. As a result of great effort by Dulles, the British had agreed to allow the Republic of China to sign a separate treaty. Koo protested that they were threatening a separate peace, in violation of the Declaration of the United Nations in January, 1942. Dulles and Rusk brushed aside his legalism, arguing that victory ended the obligation. In Taipei, Chiang's diplomats could not contain his anger, and he attacked the separate treaty formula publicly. Dulles and Rusk informed Koo that they had no choice but to announce the formula publicly to the American people. Koo protested vigorously, but Rusk handled him bruskly. Rusk contended that such international standing as the Republic of China still enjoyed was the result of American pressures on its behalf. He declared bluntly that other governments who objected to Taipei's participation had reason to: the signature of Chiang's representatives *did not commit China*. More soothingly, Dulles reminded Koo that he and Rusk had demonstrated their support for the Republic of China in May, with their speeches before the China Institute. And suddenly it appeared that Rusk's "Slavic Manchukuo" speech had another purpose. Determined to get a peace treaty with Japan despite Taipei's objection, Dulles and Rusk had indulged in rhetorical excesses as a means of softening the blow for Chiang and his friends.[47]

Outmaneuvered, Chiang was forced to accept exclusion from the peace conference. Koo fought hard to have the separate treaty between Taipei and the Japanese signed at the same time, but failed. Efforts to work through friends in Congress failed. Judd was persuaded by Rusk that there would be good news for the Republic of China after the conference and took Rusk at his word.[48] Early in September 1951, a conference was held in San Francisco to ratify the peace treaty and the combined skills of Dulles, Rusk, and Acheson overcame Russian obstruction. The treaty was signed on September 8.

The promised good news for Taipei was slow in coming. Koo worried that the Japanese, once freed of the occupation, would turn to Peking. Rusk told him that all would be well if Chiang would be calm and *quiet*. In December, after Rusk flew to Tokyo to talk with Japanese leaders, Prime Minister Yoshida Shigeru wrote to Dulles to assure him and through him the United States Senate and the Republic of China that his government would normalize relations with Chiang's regime as soon as the peace treaty was ratified and Japan regained its sovereignty. Yoshida also gave assurances that his government had no intention of entering into bilateral relations with the People's Republic of China. Such were the rewards for Chiang's patience.[49]

Rusk had one major task remaining in Japan. On September 8, the Japanese signed a mutual security treaty with the United States. Acheson asked Rusk to negotiate as necessary with the Pentagon and with Japanese leaders to determine the administrative arrangements under which American forces remaining in Japan would operate. Even after countless trips across the Potomac, Rusk needed five weeks in Tokyo to win the American military over to conditions with which the Japanese government could live. Rusk was convinced that "it was short-sighted from the military point of view to think that you could maintain bases in the middle of 90 million people who were resistant to the idea."[50] Japanese consent, critical to success of the occupation, was equally important for the security arrangements that were to follow. He had come to a comparable conclusion years before regarding Panama, but he understood the concerns of General Ridgway and other military men responsible for American security. His forte was to convey that understanding without allowing the military to maximize its posture. Indeed, his greatest asset generally seemed to be an ability to persuade the disaffected that he was their friend and that all was well—without giving away anything of substance.

4

For all Acheson's indifference to Asia and the administration consensus on the primacy of Europe among American interests, Rusk's activities in 1950 and 1951 left no doubt that he and Dulles and Jessup were building a little containment line across the Pacific. Rusk labored unendingly to change Acheson's mind about the defense of Formosa and to create a Formosa the secretary might find attractive. In January, 1950, when Acheson spoke of the defensive perimeter of the United States, he excluded the entire Asian mainland and Formosa. The Korean War led to changes. By May, 1951, Acheson had been won over to much of Rusk's program for a strong American stand against Communist expansion in Asia: the line was extended to include Korea, Formosa, and more ambiguously, Southeast Asia.

The Truman Administration had been infected by French apprehensions of a Chinese Communist attack through much of 1949. Early in 1950, funds appropriated for the "general area of China" had been directed toward Indochina. After the war began in Korea, fears that the Chinese would move south increased and the administration tried to find a way to deter such an attack without committing the United States to defend Indochina. Rusk and Jessup stressed the need for outbidding the Communists in meeting the nationalist aspirations of the people of Indochina. In August, 1950, the United States began Voice of America broadcasts to Indochina. In the first of these, Rusk, joined by Jessup and President Truman, contrasted American economic, military, and political support to the governments of the three states of Indochina with the threat of Communist imperialism and pledged American aid in the achievement of "true" nationalism. Rusk had no illusions about French imperialism or Ho Chi Minh's appeal to his people. Somehow the United States had to support nationalist alternatives to Ho, had to overcome the stigma of French colonialism. With General Frank Merrill, a comrade in the China-Burma-India Theater, he sought ways to build a strong native army in Vietnam that might some day be able to hold off Ho and deter Chinese intervention. He nudged the French toward granting independence in public statements, and within the bureaucracy maneuvered as best he could to strengthen noncommunist nationalists in Indochina. On one occasion, when the Asian desk at ECA was prevented by the European desk at State from giving aid directly to the governments of Indochina, Rusk interceded and insisted that the French be by-passed.[51]

Indochina posed a difficult problem for the administration. During all the years it had been part of the French Empire, the United States had demonstrated slight concern for the territory. The State Department had conceded the strategic value of Southeast Asia under pressure from the Joint Chiefs and Congressional critics of its policy toward East Asia. Even then the concession was grudging. *All* areas endangered by Communism were important, but there had to be priorities and Acheson's speech in January, 1950, left no doubt as to how he ranked Southeast Asia—as well as Korea and Formosa. Just as the Korean War drove the administration back into the arms of Rhee and Chiang, so it eventually enmeshed the United States in Indochina. One lesson drawn from the North Korean attack of June, 1950, was that the United States had invited the attack by failing to indicate its determination to resist aggression. Acheson's speech had apparently indicated that the United States was not committed to the defense of Korea, so the Communists attacked. To prevent Chinese intervention in Indochina, there had to be signals that the United States would not stand by idly if the People's Liberation Army invaded. Somehow the United States had to signal a credible commitment to defend an area in which it had little interest—in any sense of the word.

Rusk faced the same problem with Congress. Seeking appropriations for aid to Indochina, he had to explain why Southeast Asia was important. Interests had to be found to justify an effort to deter an attack in a peripheral area. For both Congress and the Communists these interests had to be overstated. Both had to be persuaded that the administration had suddenly gotten religion. With Congress, Rusk never claimed a direct American interest. He argued instead that Southeast Asia was a Communist target; that its resources were important, particularly to Japan. Moreover, he told a joint meeting of the Senate Committees on Foreign Relations and the Armed Services that Communist China, "reinforced with the breadbasket of Southeast Asia, would be an ever more formidable problem."[52] The region had to be denied to the Communists and its raw materials, strategic position, and manpower preserved for the free world. As interests were found to justify involvement, involvement deepened and interests grew, like Topsy, until the process hardened into the sacred concept of commitment.

Rusk was well aware of the problems of trying to extend a program that had been successful in Europe to Asia. To members of the House Foreign Affairs Committee, eager for better results in Asia, he explained that the institutions of Asia were not developed to the point where the most effective use of aid was possible. There was, he thought, a need to go slowly in the face of intense and sensitive nationalism. Unlike Europe where the Marshall Plan was a key element in containment, Asian countries did not have war-devastated industrial societies that merely required restoration. In Asia, small sums, used as "seed-corn," were more efficient to get pre-industrial societies started. But he was not optimistic, frequently arguing that helping to build new institutions in new nations was far more difficult than the Communist objective of tearing down such fragile structures.[53]

Asked if American efforts to help might not be seen by the people of Southeast Asia as an attempt by the United States to impose American values on them, Rusk replied with one of his deepest convictions:

I believe that we can come to a common ground with most of these peoples and the governments of Asia on the basis of the principles written into the Charter of the United Nations . . . I think that if we could look at the preamble in [sic] articles 1 and 2 of the Charter, we would find there a number of broad propositions about the kind of world we thought we were moving toward at the end of World War II, which would be entirely agreeable to the people of Asia as well as to us, and which would, in fact, represent our basic common interests.[54]

In November, 1951, a month before his resignation from the Department of State was announced, Rusk gave his valedictory address, a summary of "The Underlying Principles of Far Eastern Policy."[55] He declared the American people had reached a consensus on all of the major questions: the Japanese peace treaty, the need to fight in Korea without risking a general war, support for the Republic of China on Formosa, and assistance to the "free" nations of Asia. He saw disagreements based largely on the extent of American aid to Asia and explained that there had to be limits posed by the limitation on American resources and the paucity of people qualified to go into the field in Asia. But, he insisted, "our policy and action in Asia are by no means to be considered as crumbs from the European table." A little less certain of the consensus on Indochina, Rusk argued that the issue there was not French colonialism but whether the people "will be subjected to a Communist reign of terror and be absorbed by force into the new colonialism of a Soviet Communist empire." Given his frequent testimony that Ho Chi Minh was a nationalist, it would appear that the response to his "Slavic Manchukuo" speech had encouraged further rhetorical excess. Designed to win support for aid to the anti-Communist effort, Rusk's speech was another stroke in the portrayal of an international Communist monolith, directed from Moscow.

5

On November 30, 1951, the *New York Times* carried a story of Rusk's impending resignation. On December 7, Truman's acceptance of his resignation and his appointment as President of the Rockefeller Foundation, effective June 30, 1952, were reported. In the interim he remained with the Department as a consultant, completing his work on the arrangements with Japan. Editorially the *Times* commended the Rockefeller Foundation for its choice: "Regarded as possessing one of the keenest minds in the State

Department, where in mid-1950 he undertook the difficult task of supervising our Far Eastern Affairs, his record of courageous action and willingness to tackle difficult assignments has acquired fresh luster."[56]

The judgment of the editorial writer for the *Times* was widely shared in the top echelons of the Department, by Congressional Republicans as well as Democrats—and by the President of the United States. In May, 1952, Major General Harry H. Vaughan, the White House military aide, indicated to the President that Davidson College wanted a statement from him for a testimonial to Rusk. Vaughan indicated there was no need for the President to respond, but Truman, in a handwritten note, replied that he wanted to, because "This Dean Rusk is tops in my book."[57]

CHAPTER FIVE

Rockefeller Foundation

In January, 1948, John Foster Dulles invited Dean Rusk to dinner with Raymond Fosdick, President of the Rockefeller Foundation, Walter Stewart, Chairman of the Board of Trustees of the Foundation, and John D. Rockefeller III. Rusk was then responsible for United Nations affairs and the gentlemen from the foundation were eager to explore ways in which they could cooperate with the UN. Dinner apparently went well, for Rusk became a trustee shortly afterward. Later in the year Robert Lovett mentioned the possibility of the presidency of the foundation. It was, after all, a not uncommon pattern. Alger Hiss, Rusk's predecessor at State, had resigned to become President of the Carnegie Endowment for International Peace. But Rusk, who was rising rapidly within the Department, still had too many worlds to conquer before repairing to the relatively staid world of the foundations.[1]

By the autumn of 1951 the auspices were quite different. McCarthyism was rampant in the land and the future in Washington looked anything but bright for a Truman appointee. Rusk assumed, quite correctly, that the campaign of 1952 would end as soon as General Eisenhower announced his willingness to accept the Republican nomination. If new employment would have to be found the next year, why not now? Talks were underway in Korea; the Japanese peace treaty had been signed and needed only a few months' careful handling to be secured. There was nothing much he could do to save either Acheson or the Republic. Dulles now informed him that the committee to select a new President of the Rockefeller Foundation had unanimously recommended him. Would he accept if elected by the board? He said yes.[2]

Rusk's admission to a pinnacle of the establishment was not to be that easy. In November, 1951, someone on the selection committee panicked. Struck by the parallel with Alger Hiss, troubled by Rusk's association with Acheson, one member feared that the appointment of Rusk would provoke an attack by McCarthy and his Democratic compatriot Senator Pat McCarran that might destroy the foundation. Working with Dulles, Rusk was forced to contrive a defense. He declared that his record for loyalty and security was unimpeachable. Even McCarthy and McCarran had given up trying to find something on him. He would defend the foundation, if as expected, McCarran attacked it, but the trustees should be reminded that McCarran's interest derived from twenty-five years of foundation support for the Institute of Pacific Relations, rather than from overtures to Dean Rusk. He vigorously denied the parallel with Hiss and left no doubt that he would consider it a grave injustice and an extraordinary penalty for having served in the State Department if timidity stemming from the Hiss case cost him the position.[3]

On one issue, most likely policy toward China, Rusk offered an oblique defense that obscured his views on policy issues while underlining his conception of his constitutional role. Once again he referred to Marshall's concept of duty and responsibility, with which he clearly concurred: a public official did not resign on an issue merely because of disagreement with those who are constitutionally responsible for making decisions. Fed to James Reston's Uniquack machine, the statement might have been translated to say that continued service with the Department did not mean Rusk agreed with Truman and Acheson in their handling of China. Indeed, had one sought such an implication, it was possible to conclude that Rusk had been unsympathetic to that policy. With the help of Rusk's letter Dulles saved the day and Rusk went on to become President of the Rockefeller Foundation.

In December, 1951, when the appointment was settled and announced, Rusk indicated to friends some additional reasons for taking the position. To Herbert Feis he denied reports that he was exhausted by the job at State. He was not, he insisted, a victim of the diminishing returns of public service. He was "just tempted mightily." Writing to Jessup on New Year's Eve, he was a little more reflective, unusually revealing of himself. "For one who decided as a very young man to stay out of politics and competitive business," he thought the Rockefeller presidency a post of "peculiar challenge and attraction." The reference to "competitive" business offered a particularly useful insight. Rusk was able and he was ambitious, but he did not enjoy and tried to avoid competition. Unlike so many of the lawyers among his colleagues in Washington, he hated the rough and tumble exchanges, the Darwinian contests to determine truth and ability. There was, after all, a difference between the traditions of the South and those of the Harvard Law School. [4]

2

As President of the Rockefeller Foundation, Rusk had a freer hand at running an organization than he had enjoyed at Mills or at the State Department. He liked his role, and the warmth and light touch that had been so notable in New Delhi and the early years in Washington were evident once again. His staff liked him. They found him to be a good listener and readily accessible. He was modest, encouraged discussion, and welcomed disagreement. Consistent with the role he had enjoyed most at State, he showed more interest in policy and program than in administrative matters. Quite naturally, he received better marks for policy than for administration. [5]

Rusk's problems with administration at the Rockefeller Foundation were also revealing. First, he did as little as possible, trying to keep administrative problems at the lowest possible levels, away from his program officers and away from himself. He delegated responsibility happily to his executive vice president, a man with direct ties to the Rockefeller family. He tried, with little success, to break down barriers between divisions of the foundation, to get programs interrelated. There was some criticism of his handling of appointments, of his failure to consult widely. Conceivably, the Rockefellers were interfering from behind the scenes through the executive vice president. If so, Rusk was unaware. The only serious complaint his staff had at the conclusion of his tour would not have astonished his subordinates at State. He played things "too close to the vest," they claimed. They did not know what he thought, did not know what to expect, and the result was "too many surprises." But they liked and respected him.[6]

A minor problem, which Rusk overcame, may have derived from Southern chivalry, which appeared sexist. One high ranking officer of the foundation was a woman and she was disturbed to find Rusk treating her with warmth and courtesy, but very much as if she were a particularly able clerk-typist. At meetings, he apparently expected her to take notes, but did not look to her when canvassing opinion. Sure of herself, she forced a confrontation that resulted in an enduring mutual respect.[7]

One source of his staff's admiration was the great skill with which Rusk handled the Congressional investigations of the foundation that absorbed most of his energies in his first year as president. First came the Cox Committee investigation of tax-exempt foundations, an apparently serious study of how the foundations functioned, with an eye to legislating an end to abuses of tax-exempt status. No stranger to hearings, Rusk was lucid and dignified in his defense of his organization. His staff was tremendously impressed by his preparations and his performance during the two days that he testified. They were still more impressed by his courage in responding to the "investigation" of the Reece Committee in 1953. The committee functioned in the best McCarthyite tradition and Rusk did not hesitate to denounce the committee staff as incompetent and its procedures as "shockingly unfair." Denied an opportunity to respond to charges against the foundation at the hearings, Rusk took his case to the public. This was a period in which Rusk defended not only the Rockefeller Foundation, but also an old friend, John Davies, from McCarthyism. He had better luck saving the foundation than he had protecting Davies' career.[8]

Serving as president of the foundation allowed other public activities, much pleasanter in nature. Rusk had become what political scientists call a "nongovernmental opinion leader." The views of the leader of so prestigious an organization were widely sought and readily publicized, especially given his experience in the realm of international affairs. He gave public addresses to elite groups like the English-Speaking Union and the Fifth Avenue Association and to the usual assortment of local world affairs councils and institutes.

He helped Walter Judd's Committee to Aid Refugee Chinese Intellectuals raise funds and chaired the Amvets International Affairs Division. He participated in study groups sponsored by the Council on Foreign Relations and shouldered the Rockefeller Brothers Fund effort to study problems of American foreign policy in the late 1950s. He was in frequent contact with the Democratic shadow cabinet—Acheson, Bowles, Harriman, Nitze, and Stevenson—and with the Republican Secretary of State, Dulles. Internationally, he served as co-chairman of the American participants in the Bilderberg Group—about ninety leading American and European figures meeting to discuss transatlantic frictions and the solidarity of the Western community, under the aegis of Prince Bernhard of the Netherlands. It was a heady life for a poor boy from rural Georgia. And it was a comfortable and meaningful life.

Rusk's principal contribution to the Rockefeller Foundation program, his particular stamp on the foundation's work, came in the area of aid to underdeveloped countries. The foundation and the Rockefellers had long been involved in good works abroad, particularly in the field of public health. Rusk concluded that responsibility for the public health programs should be passed on to the recipient countries, like India, and that more fundamental problems had to be faced. Early in the 1950s he argued that Africa and Asia would not much longer tolerate the unequal distribution of the world's wealth. Just as he believed that all men sought the guarantees of peace and freedom of the UN Charter, so he believed that they aspired to the same standard of living enjoyed by peoples of the wealthy industrial states of the West. He was fond of citing population figures, noting the tiny percentage of Europeans and Americans who consumed so much of the world's resources. In time there would be a vast redistribution of wealth and knowledge and he was eager to place the foundation in position to facilitate the process. His ideas approximated those of Truman's "Point Four"—the vision of aid to underdeveloped countries to which American liberals had been so responsive in 1949.[9]

After several years of meeting with leaders of underdeveloped countries and discussions with members of his staff and with John D. Rockefeller III, Rusk presented the trustees with a proposal for what came to be known as his "expanded program." He asked for and received permission to go into the foundation's capital for $5 million per year for a period of five to ten years to finance additional technical assistance programs. The primary aim of the program would be to train the peoples of Africa and Asia in the exploitation of their own resources for their own ends. Rusk was very careful to distinguish between the kind of program he envisaged and the program of the government. He was determined to work outside of the Cold War, outside of foreign policy. On at least one occasion, he warned the trustees that the ends of the government and those of the foundation were not congruent, that the foundation had to be careful not to be used.[10]

Rusk was particularly interested in East Asia, Africa, and the Middle East. The foundation's work in Latin America, long a Rockefeller priority, required less attention. Despite his hopes to the contrary, focus on underdeveloped countries meant a gradual withdrawal of support from programs in Europe and Japan. He had hoped to finance programs in industrial countries that would encourage scholars to study the problems of developing countries, that would bring some of the best minds of Europe and Japan to bear on his concerns. In the program for which he won approval Rusk's first priority was leadership training, with considerable emphasis on fellowships and aid to American universities offering the training. He was also much concerned with developing techniques for the exchange of scientific information. He knew progress would be slow and became increasingly troubled by the growing gap between expectations and reality in Asia and Africa. Gradually, he became persuaded that population control was critical and toward the end of the 1950s, his thoughts dwelled increasingly on birth control and food production programs.[11]

3

Despite the foundation's focus on development problems, Rusk could not escape the political issues between the West and the less developed countries of the world. Early in 1956 Dulles asked him to undertake a study of the "colonial question" to seek ways to improve relations with the non-Western nations. Dulles was also interested

in a kind of "reverse Bandung", a conference "aimed at a demonstration of a community of interest across racial lines and a slowing down
of the racially conscious antipathy now developing in non-white
areas." In the autumn, as the Suez crisis simmered, Rusk met Paul
Henri Spaak, then Foreign Minister of Belgium, at a World
Brotherhood meeting. To his astonishment he found Spaak also
calling for a conference to deal with the wounds of colonialism, to
discuss "The Liquidation of Colonialism." Rusk shared the concern
of Dulles and Spaak, and brooded about the anti-Western attitudes
of former colonial nations now members of the UN. But whatever
hopes Rusk may have had in early October for a plan to improve
relations between the West and its former colonies, were shattered
by the Anglo-French-Israeli attack on Egypt at the end of the
month. [12]

Throughout the years with the Rockefeller Foundation, Rusk's
views on a variety of foreign policy issues and processes were
solicited. He did not lack access to policy makers or to other opinion
leaders. Within the establishment, some of his ideas were well
known. In particular he was widely regarded as a leading authority
on UN affairs. The range of issues with which he had dealt during
his years with the Department of State led to his involvement in
virtually every question of significance in the 1950s. But Rusk
remained a private figure, unknown to the general public, never a
media hero, working in the establishment pattern.

When he talked about the United Nations, there was an interesting dichotomy between his approach to policy makers and his
approach to a world affairs club. When addressing himself to the
interested public, in person or in a rare article, he kept his claims for
the organization modest, trying to moderate his audience's expectations. He knew he was talking to the faithful, to men and women to
whom the organization did not have to be sold. They had to be told
of the limits of the UN. Debate in the UN was useful, but it was not
a substitute for traditional diplomacy. He argued that it was senseless to score points off friends or enemies in the UN if there would
be no substantive result. He warned against smothering the organization by giving it more than it could handle, more than it could do.
But when Rusk sat alone with men like Acheson, Nitze, and
Kennan—skeptical practitioners—he became the eloquent defen-

der of the United Nations. The organization was important and the principles of its Charter were important. At very least it served as an "icebox", taking the fever out of a crisis.

One theme to which Rusk constantly reverted featured his "little threads" concept. He argued that in the thousands of committee and subcommittee meetings each year, people from various countries were sitting down and finding broad common interests to pursue together. They were building a network of "little threads that bind you together," that will bring people together in time of crisis.

Rusk had more faith in UN agencies than Acheson, Kennan or Nitze ever had. He thought the agencies were more effective in inducing a desired response than the United States could be because it was politically safer for the leader of another country to act in accord with the UN than to appear moved by the desire to support the United States. Through the proper exercise of American leadership, more could be accomplished working through the UN than unilaterally or bilaterally. But Rusk's conception of proper leadership showed him to be critical of Acheson's approach to the UN. In a meeting of Acheson's aides at Princeton in 1954, he confronted Acheson with the charge that strategy in the UN was not planned systematically. The Assembly agenda might have 60-70 items and each staff officer, each delegate would try to win for the American position. At the end of the session, they would total up the score and determine America's batting average. But all issues were not equally important and Rusk argued that it was the responsibility of the Secretary of State to determine which issues were vital, which secondary. Then allow friends to have the satisfaction of modifying the American position on issues of minor importance, while supporting the United States on more important matters. He thought past performance at the UN provided evidence Americans were difficult to work with, trying to win on every issue. It was important to leave some prestige for friends. Acheson took the criticism gracefully, moved by Rusk's words and Jessup's concurrence.[13]

The range of Rusk's thinking about China in the 1950s is also clear. In March, 1952, Dulles asked him to read a draft of an article that was to be published the following month in *Life*. Rusk suggested changes based on "weaknesses in detail" and on the possibility that Dulles would soon be Secretary of State. One weakness in detail was Formosa. Rusk objected to the idea of declaring that the Seventh Fleet not only protected Formosa but was in the Straits to encourage Chiang to attack the mainland. Such a policy might force China to attack Formosa, posing a major military problem for the United States. Encouraging Chiang to attack would isolate the United States internationally. Rusk argued that neutralizing the Straits was the only chance of getting substantial international and domestic support for the defense of Formosa. He insisted that the idea of Chiang attacking the mainland without American participation was quixotic and might embarrass the nominee of the Republican convention.[14]

In the letter to Dulles, Rusk's position was clearly that of "two Chinas." The United States should offer protection to Formosa, preferably without a commitment. No effort should be made or even threatened to return Chiang to the mainland. Rusk hoped conditions on the mainland would change, as evidenced by a speech he gave a month later, but he was not optimistic and did not see the United States as an instrument of that change. When he spoke at a fund-raising dinner for Judd's Committee to Aid Refugee Chinese Intellectuals, he declared that "there are many of us who are not convinced that dictatorship has come to China to stay." He asked for contributions for the men who would lead China "when freedom returns to that unhappy land," mouthing the words appropriate to the occasion. They neither reflected his expectations nor contributed to the edification of his audience.[15]

Dulles, whose legendary intransigence toward the People's Republic was symbolized by his refusal to shake Chou En-lai's hand in 1954, eventually accepted Rusk's position. In 1956 he asked Rusk to explore with Senator Walter F. George, Democratic chairman of the Foreign Relations Committee, the possibility of bipartisan support for a new policy toward China, for recognition of the existence of two Chinas. George chose not to run for reelection, however, and the project was dropped.[16]

Three and a half years later, Chester Bowles, a leading liberal Democratic spokesman on foreign policy, perennially at war with the Cold Warriors in his own party, asked Rusk to read a draft of an article he had written on China. Rusk claimed to be in general agreement with Bowles, but offered several suggestions for change. He agreed that the recognition question could be put aside as fruitless "and, indeed, unimportant." But the question of China's representation in the UN could not be put aside so easily. Outlining a paragraph on the UN question, Rusk argued the United States did not have any responsibility for carrying "Peiping" into the United Nations. It should not give up one unrealistic position—the argument that Chiang's regime was China—for another, a substitution of Mao's regime as if Taipei did not exist. There were two Chinese governments and he contended that the UN membership had to come up with a solution to represent both of them. The United States did not have sole responsibility for the existing impasse.[17]

Rusk suggested that Bowles emphasize more "the importance of our assisting in building up the strength and viability of non-Communist nations in Asia," essentially a strengthening of the containment line. He also argued against isolation of the People's Republic. He thought it would be useful for the United States to trade with the mainland Chinese, perhaps through Hong Kong or Japan, to circumvent the complication of nonrecognition. He contended that it would be advantageous to create a situation in which the Chinese had a stake in normal relations with countries outside the Communist bloc, developing Chinese interests with other countries. In mid-1960, he made a similar point in another context. Deeply concerned about the dangers of biological warfare, he privately explored ideas for achieving an international ban. His plan involved the World Health Organization (WHO) as overseer and "Red China should not only be invited, but urged to participate."[18]

By 1960, Rusk had concluded that recognition was impossible because of the domestic political situation. He conceded that the Peking regime was entitled to representation in the United Nations, but not at the expense of the Republic of China. He sought some kind of two-China formula although very much aware of the difficulty of gaining acceptance for the idea in Peking, Taipei or other capitals. Perhaps most striking was the assumption that Mao's regime would be around for a very long time and that it would be best to develop contacts with it, to enmesh it in those "little threads" that might some day bind us all together and permit humanity to survive. In an era not known for enlightenment on questions related to the People's Republic of China, Rusk's ideas put him far in advance of leaders in both parties. Had they been widely known, his chances for public office in 1961 might have been diminished.

Rusk's thinking about the Soviet Union was a little more apparent in the 1950s than it had been when he was with the government. He left office persuaded that the Russians had to be contained because they would otherwise "take up all the slack they can," but he was convinced that Stalin's priorities were in Europe rather than Asia. When Dulles quoted Stalin to argue that the Russians were pursuing an Asia First policy, Rusk argued that Stalin saw Germany as the country of crucial importance.[19]

His ideas about coping with Russian expansionism were less consistent than a theorist might desire. He stressed the Russian element in the Soviet Union's policies, but could not put aside the Communist element. The Russians would have been equally expansionist without Communism—and yet Communism meant something. Just what, he remained vague about. In a speech in September, 1953, he argued that the United States had tempted aggression after World War II by abandoning armaments and leaving doubt in the minds of Communist leaders as to whether the United States could or would resist aggression. He saw the problem as continuous. Americans had to make the Kremlin and the Russian people understand that aggression had to be abandoned. Rusk did not play a central role in preparation of the Rockefeller Brothers Fund report "International Security—the Military Aspect," but its call for a major increase in defense spending was consistent with his views on the need for military preparedness to warn off potential aggressors.[20]

Rusk was highly receptive to nonmilitary competition with the Soviet Union. From 1953 to 1955 he participated in a study of Soviet-American relations sponsored by the Council on Foreign Relations and chaired by John McCloy. In addition to Rusk and McCloy, Harriman, Bowles, Arthur Dean, Hamilton Fish Armstrong, and Henry Wriston participated in the study, the results of which were published in Henry L. Roberts' *Russia and America: Dangers and Prospects*. A principal conclusion of the study was its insistence that the United States take more seriously the Soviet economic, political, and social challenge in the "struggle for freedom." The participants urged that the United States enter into economic and cultural exchanges with the Russians, place less emphasis on the military power of NATO, and provide NATO countries with more economic aid. If Rusk's hand was not evident in Roberts' summary, the ideas were those prevalent in establishment circles. Rusk had earlier responded with alacrity and great warmth to Eisenhower's "Chance for Peace" speech, a bid to end the Cold War upon the death of Stalin in March, 1953.[21]

For all his stiffness in the face of the aggressor, for all the ROTC speeches on preparedness, Rusk was always moved by indications that disarmament, some easing of tensions was possible, that an opportunity to ameliorate the world's miseries instead of adding to them existed. Perhaps for this reason, Adolf A. Berle and Henry Kissinger, occasional colleagues of the 1950s, suspected he was not tough enough to deal with the Russians.[22] What they saw in him and probably misread was a lifelong sense of the need to balance power with an appreciation that the end of power was not aggrandizement but the preservation of peace in an international community. He mistrusted the Russians, wanted a club close at hand, but would encourage them to draw closer, confident that apart from Stalin, the Russian people too shared the aspirations implicit in the UN Charter.

4

The Rockefeller Brothers report on "The Mid Century Challenge to U.S. Foreign Policy" appeared in December, 1959. Rusk chaired the panel that prepared the report, written by August Heckscher "under direction of the panel." The views and the language of the report were generally vintage Rusk. In particular the introduction was constructed around several of his favorite themes. The old imperial system had broken down irreparably. The forces of change were running throughout the world and brought with them "rising expectations" in the poorer nations. The United States should work toward a world in which freedom expanded and peace was normal.

The introduction stressed the limits on foreign policy. The United States could not do everything and certainly could not do much without sacrifice. After the war it had been necessary to explain to the American people that not everything that went on in the world was attributable to American policy. Americans had learned what appeared to be one of Rusk's favorite homilies: "To be patient, limited in one's hopes, prepared for one's share of disappointments and harassments." Now the time had come—in anticipation of a new administration in Washington—to assert the positive nature of foreign policy. [23]

These were days when many commentators worried about America's loss of purpose and many candidates offered to restore that purpose. Rusk was concerned about the importance of a foreign policy consistent with American ideals, especially the commitment to the idea of consent of the governed. In the report the problem of Indochina was offered as an example. The United States had attempted to be realistic in Indochina and supported a colonial power to contain Communism. That effort had faltered because Americans realized that aid to the French was contrary to their inherent respect for national independence. Earlier Rusk had expressed despair at the inability to find "liberal democratic" leaders and at being forced to work with the likes of Chiang Kai-shek and Syngman Rhee. A few months after the report was issued he argued explicitly that government "support of or indifference to dictatorial regimes tended to make the United States purpose obscure in the eyes of Americans as well as of other peoples."[24]

The panel report defined America's purpose as one of working toward a world organized to insure peace and freedom for all—a shorthand expression for Rusk's much beloved Articles I and II of the United Nations Charter. "The international community thus conceived" might include all states that did not insist on imposing their values, their way of life on others. Communist states would be welcome, obviously even the People's Republic of China, if they were "prepared to assume the responsibilities and self-restraints of international life."[25]

Written in the context of a crisis in Berlin, the report was not sanguine about Soviet intentions. The schizophrenic analysis of Soviet behavior may have reflected difficulty in reaching a consensus on the panel or, as likely, problems interpreting Nikita Khrushchev's words and actions. It was clear that Soviet tactics had changed. Khrushchev was not Stalin. But "the underlying objective of domination remains." The panel noted Khrushchev's speech in Peking in September, 1959, in which he stressed the need for peaceful settlement of outstanding questions and quoted with evident approval his statement that "even such a noble and progressive system as socialism cannot be imposed by force of arms against the will of the people." Could you trust him? Probably not: "the possibility cannot be ruled out that the Soviet leadership, if it secures a clear superiority in the arms race, will use this advantage to blackmail or to attack its major opponent without warning."[26]

The panel took consolation in another favorite Rusk observation: the future was ours. "Of the new nations created since the war, none, with the exception of North Vietnam and North Korea, has fallen to communism." Of course there was an old nation, China, whose "avowedly expansionist external aims" had to be countered. There seemed no creative possibilities at the moment for American overtures toward China, but the report echoed Rusk's private remarks about the value of recognition or a place in the UN. China's real power was not affected by exclusion from the UN and "the need for complete knowledge of what is going on in China is so paramount that lesser interests or concerns should give way to insure full reporting by Americans on the spot." Hope of a Sino-Soviet split still glowed. Strains were not likely to be revealed soon, but the United States should avoid actions that would drive China closer to the Soviets. A few lines later a contrary theme, pleasing to other ears, was offered. The Cold War was being waged by the Communists as a coordinated conflict.[27]

A quick tour d'horizon expressed concern over alleged Chinese efforts to cut off Japanese markets in Southeast Asia, and honored Bowles's favorite cause by calling for aid to nonaligned India. The new nations of Africa were found worthy of sympathy and encouragement, in keeping with Rusk's view that Africa should be left to the Europeans to support. The Middle East, too, was disposed of briefly in Ruskian terms. Be patient with the Arabs, keep plugging, stay with what will necessarily be a long, hard task. This was an approach much more reflective of Cherokee County than of the background of most of his establishment colleagues, more familiar with instant gratification.[28]

The Rusk panel report offered some interesting predictions. The bipolar world was not expected to last. Again, reflecting a major Rusk concern, fear of a new and more durable bipolarity, based on color rather than ideology, was expressed. It was urgent that the United States settle its race problem first. Then it would be necessary to assuage the grievances of nonwhites denied their share of the world's blessings.[29]

Clearly the report bore Rusk's stamp and it contained a vague blueprint for the next administration's foreign policy, depending of course on who the next President and Secretary of State were to be. In the report, and in a subsequent article in *Foreign Affairs*, Rusk discussed the two positions and how they would function best. He shared the professional diplomat's distaste for presidential summitry. Dean Acheson was reflecting on summit meetings one day and asked Jessup if it made sense for the President to engage in these "really idiotic conferences?" Rusk's language was rarely as direct, but his point was much the same. The President should not travel except in the rarest of cases. His responsibilities at home were too great to be left dangling until he returned to Washington. Like most professional diplomats, Rusk was skeptical about a President's ability to find time to master the details of the problem to be negotiated, but he characteristically offered the argument in positive terms. The President could master all the nuances necessary for skilled negotiations only by neglecting other duties. He hoped no American President would develop General deGaulle's "appetite for grandeur," presumably putting showmanship ahead of statesmanship.[30]

Rusk made two other points that were persuasive. Negotiation should be kept away from the court of last resort. Someone had to review the result of negotiation and that responsibility should belong to the President. It would be unwise for him to be both negotiator and judge of the result. Rusk also argued that the President could not really act decisively in negotiation. Reminding his audience of what he called the "Woodrow Wilson Effect," he referred to the problem of making good on commitments when the President returned home. If he stayed home it was much easier for him to keep in touch with Congress, the executive departments, and party leaders.

Rusk's conception of the role of the Secretary of State was well defined in the panel report. The job was impossible—too much was expected of one man. The secretary was expected to administer the Department, negotiate abroad, act as troubleshooter at the scene of crises, represent the United States at international conferences, appear as the nation's spokesman at the UN, and explain and justify policy to Congress and to the public. In addition Rusk was particularly troubled by the time a secretary spent on complex negotiations within the executive branch of government. The result of all these demands on the secretary's time did not allow him to "give to over-all policy that continuous thought and attention that diplomatic strategy requires in a world so essentially interrelated, where every problem touches every other." The panel report called for the Secretary of State to concentrate on policy at the highest level and to leave the rest to diplomatic representatives on the spot. Implicitly a criticism of the way Eisenhower used Dulles, the report and Rusk's conception of the secretary's role corresponded with Rusk's idea of the way Acheson and to a greater extent Marshall had worked.

5

Rusk's views on the process of foreign relations and on most of the policy issues of the late 1950s were well known to the elite group centered in the Council on Foreign Relations. These were not men who agreed on all issues and they were not unanimous in their views on tactics. On the Democratic side, Rusk appealed to the most determined Cold Warriors, led by Acheson, and to men like Bowles and Stevenson whom Acheson thought vague and fuzzy and of whose views he was contemptuous. No other Democrat had comparable standing with Republicans, like the late John Foster Dulles, Lovett, and Luce. Nitze may have been skeptical about Rusk's attachment to the United Nations and Berle, Kissinger, and McGeorge Bundy had some reservations, but after the election of 1960, Rusk was an obvious establishment candidate for Secretary of State. A young President, viewed as an upstart by many leaders of his own party, victor over his Republican rival by an extremely narrow margin, needed an appointment that would be reassuring both at home and abroad. With the possible exception of Lovett, who was offered the position, no one else provided comparable assurance. When the President-elect sought recommendations from the elite, Rusk's name constantly appeared. He was not everybody's first choice, but men as disparate as Acheson, Bowles, and Lovett pushed hard for him. On December 12, 1960, John F. Kennedy announced that he had offered and Rusk had accepted appointment as Secretary of State in the new administration.

CHAPTER SIX

John F. Kennedy's Secretary of State

In January, 1961, the President-elect met with George Kennan whose writings and lectures in the previous decade had won him international acclaim. Among their common interests, in addition to the quest for enlightened methods of saving the Republic from the Russians, was a desire to save the presidency from the likes of Dean Acheson. Kennedy and Kennan respected Acheson, but both had felt his lash when they had deviated from positions he felt critical to the well-being of the Atlantic Alliance. Kennedy explained to the diplomat-historian that "he did not want to be in the position of Mr. Truman, who had, in effect, only one foreign policy advisor, namely Mr. Acheson, and was entirely dependent on what advice the latter gave."[1] Deliberately he chose as his Secretary of State a man whose temperament and modesty precluded his ever becoming an Achesonian presence in the Kennedy Administration. The President-elect intended to dominate foreign policy. Before he decided policy, he wished to hear many voices. To achieve his ends he brought to Washington a number of men to be played off against each other, both for the intellectual purpose of encouraging the exchange of ideas and as a mechanism for controlling the process.

Kennedy's intentions were widely known and reflected in the public response to the Rusk appointment. Several commentators referred to Kennedy's desire to be his own Secretary of State. Congressional Democrats interviewed by a *New York Times* reporter also saw the choice of Rusk as evidence of an intention to reassert the presidential role in the conduct of foreign policy. There was some sympathy expressed for Rusk as a man who would be caught between an opinionated, strong President and opinionated, strong subordinates, including Bowles, Harriman, Stevenson, and G. Mennen "Soapy" Williams, former governor of Michigan—some of whom were appointed by Kennedy with little reference to Rusk or concern for his sensibilities. Although there was general agreement that Rusk would not dominate policy, he was expected to stand tall. He would not be a Dulles or an Acheson, but his character was presumed to contain enough steel to preclude his being used as badly as Stettinius or Hull.[2]

Rusk's appointment was seen by *Business Week* as calculated to assure conservatives, but the liberals knew he was one of their own. The *New Republic* would have preferred Bowles or Stevenson, but Rusk was acceptable—the only acceptable alternative. His liberal credentials were impeccable. Indeed, unlike Bowles, he had staunchly supported Stevenson for the Democratic Party's presidential nomination. He had headed the Westchester Democrats for Stevenson and on the eve of Kennedy's nomination had sent a telegram to Harriman, urging him to hold the New York delegation for Stevenson. Dag Hammarskjold, Secretary-General of the United Nations, endorsed Rusk's appointment, further assuring the liberals. The editors of the *New Republic* were pleased to note his concern with underdeveloped countries and, for the same reason, representatives of Afro-Asian countries at the United Nations were reportedly overjoyed by Kennedy's selection. Stories of heroic deeds popped up here and there, of Rusk as the principal influence in the Graham mission that led to Indonesian independence, the "only anti-colonialist diplomatic venture of the early postwar years." Ralph Bunche recalled that Rusk had taken him into the officers' mess at the Pentagon, ending de facto segregation there. Others recalled Rusk's early concern about the effect of racism on foreign policy.[3]

Tested by the litmus of liberalism in America, circa 1960, Rusk passed on every issue. He had supported Stevenson, openly opposed McCarthyism, supported civil rights, and opposed imperialism. There were even reports that he would be more flexible in dealing with the People's Republic of China. Doubt about his

association with Acheson's policy of supporting the French in Indochina was dispelled by confidence that Rusk had seen the situation differently, that he was aware that some people, including the
people of Indochina, saw the struggle as a colonial war.[4]

For liberals who still had doubts there was the fact that the *New
York Times* liked him. The editors of the *Times* praised Kennedy for
"an absolutely first-rate appointment" and called Rusk "a figure of
tremendous ability, character and intellect, an excellent choice."[5]

2

Rusk had outlined his conception of the role of the Secretary of
State in his writings, but his views became much clearer after he
settled into his office on the seventh floor. His teacher was George
Marshall, but there were lessons, sometimes negative, learned from
Acheson and Dulles as well.

Rusk saw himself, first and foremost, as the principal advisor to
the President, in whom the Constitution vested authority to formu-
late foreign policy. His advice would be offered to the President
confidentially, preferably after all other voices had been heard. He
would not attempt to influence the debate, but preside over it,
listening, drawing out arguments, judging, and then, alone with the
President, express his opinion. Regardless of whether his advice was
accepted, the President's decision would be Rusk's decision. Few, if
any, in the Department, certainly no one in the press, would ever
be aware of disagreement between the President and his Secretary
of State. And the surest way to prevent leaks about disagreement,
about the President overruling the secretary, was to keep the views
of the secretary secret.[6]

Secondly, Rusk understood that he had to direct the operations of
an enormous organization, with thousands of employees. He had
more experience with that organization than any secretary before
him and he had definite ideas of how to use it. He recognized that
morale within the Department was low, ostensibly because of the
scourge of McCarthyism and because of Dulles' tendency to convert
the process of formulating policy into a one-man operation. He
tried, with limited success, to rehabilitate the Old China hands,

delaying retirements and finding embassies for them. He tried, with still less success, to hold top-level positions for outstanding career officers. With the President's verbal support, he assured members of the Department that they were expected to take charge of foreign policy, that power would gravitate to "those who are willing to make decisions and live with the results."[7]

The day-to-day administration of the Department interested Rusk less and to explain his system he was fond of quoting Marshall or offering anecdotes about him. His primary concern, as at the Rockefeller Foundation, was to find some way for the organization to administer itself—or be administered by someone else. Citing Marshall he encouraged initiative from below, and desired to have problems solved before they required his attention. The secretary would do only those things that he alone could do. Anything that could be done at a lower level, should be done at that level. He liked to delegate authority.

The key to success of the system as used by Marshall had been Robert Lovett, the undersecretary—and the relationship between the two men. Lovett was a man of extraordinary administrative competence in whom Marshall reposed complete confidence. Rusk hoped to develop the same relationship with his own number-two, Chester Bowles, chosen by Kennedy, but admired by Rusk as well. Critical of Dulles' travels, Rusk intended to stay home. On those occasions on which he would have to be abroad, he intended for Bowles to be in command. When Rusk was in residence, Bowles was to keep the Departmental bureaucracy functioning, bringing Rusk completed staff papers and the proposed answers to questions raised. Rusk would be free to reflect and give the President the benefit of his reflections.

Rusk's ideas for handling overseas negotiations fitted neatly into the same pattern. The secretary could not be scurrying all over the globe—and need not, when he had competent ambassadors in the field. The career foreign service was filled with able men and women who, reinforced by political appointees holding the President's trust, could handle most negotiations. To facilitate their work, Rusk set up an Operations Center, modeled after that of the Strategic Air Command, for instantaneous communications with ambassadors around the world. In extraordinary circumstances, a special envoy could be used. Harriman, who delighted in such roles, was readily available. Again the Department would be strengthened and the secretary allowed to concentrate on his primary function.

As with every new administration there was much talk in 1961 about reorganizing the executive departments and especially, given Kennedy's interests, the Department of State. Rusk was skeptical about reorganization plans, persuaded that finding good people to do the jobs would be more productive than rearranging lines on an organizational chart. Nonetheless, he had ideas for streamlining operations. He was determined to eliminate what he called "layering," the accumulation of positions between the country director or desk officer and the assistant secretary. In modest terms, he was able to simplify the structure of the Department, to move affairs quickly from desk officer, through the assistant secretary, to the undersecretary or his own office. If economic matters were involved, he shunned them like the plague, deferring to George Ball, Undersecretary for Economic Affairs. Otherwise the "linchpin" of the movement of business was the Executive Secretary, Lucius D. Battle. Luke Battle had been Acheson's personal assistant, knew *that* secretary's modus operandi, and was expected to determine Rusk's needs—and when Rusk was needed. In addition, Battle was responsible for communications with the White House, particularly with the President's special assistant for national security affairs, McGeorge Bundy. Theoretically every major paper, every idea that passed between State and the White House, passed through the Battle-Bundy channel.[8]

Rusk also wanted to be accessible to his staff. The one criticism expressed by several men who had worked with Marshall was that he was too distant, that he had little contact with, disdained mixing with his assistant secretaries. Rusk left no doubt that he wanted to see his assistant secretaries and to know their views. He encouraged them, as well as his undersecretaries, to exchange ideas and express dissent. All had a free hand, all were expected to perform with minimum direction, and with a minimum of reassurance. Rusk was fond of telling how Marshall never indicated his appreciation of a man's work, contending that good work was expected—and of the pleasure of being told by Marshall on one occasion that he had earned his pay that day. Rarely exhibiting anger, rarely extending praise, Rusk was accessible, albeit to some opaque.

The Policy Planning Staff had been Marshall's idea and was continued by his successors with less appreciation. Rusk gave the staff freedom to range, but was skeptical of grand plans and brilliant ideas. He handled the Department's Bureau of Intelligence and Research in much the same way. He rarely posed problems for either group, allowed them to investigate questions of their own choosing, welcomed their often contrary views, but left both with a sense of being peripheral in his formulations of policy.[9]

Finally, Rusk made little effort to put his own stamp on the Department. Other than Battle, George McGhee, who began as head of Policy Planning, was the only man he brought back into the Department. Two colleagues at the Rockefeller Foundation, who ran afoul of his successor there, were sent off to embassies, but for the most part the major posts were filled by Kennedy or by Bowles. To some extent, Kennedy left Rusk little choice, but Rusk was generally satisfied with the Kennedy and Bowles selections, most of whom were men he knew and respected. Perhaps the man who was closest to him in the years that followed, whom he used when he could as Acheson had used him, was U. Alexis Johnson, a career foreign service officer. Johnson had served as Rusk's deputy during the Korean War and Rusk appointed him deputy-undersecretary. If anyone was expected to serve as Rusk's trusted eyes and ears in the Department, it was probably Johnson. Llewellyn E. Thompson, a senior specialist on Soviet affairs, was another career officer in whom Rusk had unusual confidence.[10]

3

In February, 1961, approximately a month after the Kennedy Administration took office, James Reston of the *New York Times* reported that the President had been caught and thwarted in an attempt to steal the Vietnamese cook of the French embassy in London. Reston was not deeply troubled because he thought the

Secretary of State could pick up a Vietnamese cook when he attended the SEATO meeting in March. For Rusk it would be "a glorious chance."

He has been trying to break into the White House ever since he arrived in Washington. The place, however, is studded with foreign policy experts, who are in easier reach of the President than Rusk himself, but if he had his own man in the kitchen, he'd have the way to the President's heart or at least know what's cooking. [11]

Lightly, Reston touched on a problem seemingly inherent in Kennedy's approach to foreign policy. At the White House, the President had assembled his own staff. Bundy, the brilliant young dean of Harvard College, recruited an outstanding team of bright, lively young men. They were able and focused on issues quickly. They were activists, eager to find new approaches that would solve old dilemmas. They were intolerant of dullness, impatient with bureaucratic routines. If a problem arose, the White House staff might have a proposed solution hours, days, weeks—even months—before the State Department presented the President with a recommendation. On occasion the Department might match Bundy's bunch in confidence or brilliance, but never in speed. So the President invariably had an answer before Rusk came to whisper in his ear.

In addition to battling with Bundy's staff for the President's attention, State had a variety of other competitors. In the White House, the historian Arthur M. Schlesinger, Jr., did more than testify that Kennedy was more liberal than Richard Nixon. Schlesinger ran his own lines to the State Department and to the United Nations. With the able assistance of Richard N. Goodwin, a gifted young speech writer, he dabbled in Latin-American affairs. Maxwell Taylor was in residence to provide Kennedy with military advice and Walt W. Rostow was available for long-range planning. The President, with Rusk's approval, set up task forces to deal with several pressing problems—and had them report directly to the White House. Robert F. Kennedy, the President's brother and Attorney General, often had strong opinions on foreign policy, and direct access, of course, to the Oval Office. Finally, there was

Robert S. McNamara, the extraordinary Secretary of Defense, whose intellect and power of persuasion overshadowed all others. At minimum, it was clear that Kennedy's Secretary of State shared influence with McNamara and Bundy. And, from other rooms, there were other voices.

The process Kennedy established in January, 1961, was complex—and it did not work. Some of the difficulties were routine problems of transition, as for example the fact that with all his skill and experience, Luke Battle needed four months to get the Executive Secretariat functioning.[12] New men in new positions frequently missed signals or lost the ball when it was handed to them. Decisions were made without having them cleared with officers, agencies or foreign governments.

But there were deeper problems for which the President and his Secretary of State were responsible. Kennedy wanted a particular model of bureaucratic tension to provide himself with information and opinion for decision-making. He wanted a particular kind of man, one who would allow him to pose as his own Secretary of State, to hold that office. But the kind of man he wanted and chose as secretary could not and did not function well in the system he established. Despite the deliberate deference of men like Bundy and McNamara, the system Kennedy established required an aggressive, assertive Secretary of State to penetrate the palace guard and make himself heard over the cacophony in which the President apparently delighted. But Kennedy had knowingly, purposefully chosen a "gentle, gracious" man who, wholly lacking in political power, despite his intellectual tenacity, would not challenge the President.[13] Given the kind of man Kennedy wanted, the balance he desired between State and the other agencies had to be provided by the President. A lack of presidential leadership was the principal deficiency of the foreign policy process in 1961.

Some of the failings of the Department of State itself can be attributed to the President. To the extent that he and some of his subordinates by-passed the secretary and communicated directly with assistant secretaries and desk officers, Kennedy created problems. Delegating less authority, less responsibility to this secretary than had Truman or Eisenhower, he prevented Rusk from delegating as much as he had in the Truman era or wanted to delegate in the 1960s. The President's use of direct, "back-channel" communications with allied leaders complicated the secretary's task.[14] He misused his secretary, sending him all over the world on precisely the kind of errands Rusk had argued the secretary should never perform. He surrounded Rusk with appointees who set themselves up as independent satraps—Acheson referred to the "Duke of New York" and the "Viscount of Africa."

Nonetheless, there were problems in the Department that derived directly from Rusk's style of management. Stated most simply, Rusk failed to communicate with his subordinates. Some of them never knew what he wanted or what he thought of their work. Others lacked information necessary to perform their duties. George Ball attacked the barriers and eventually established a good working relationship with Rusk, but the task took two years. One assistant secretary claimed to have developed a way of interpreting facial expressions and another found direction listening carefully to Rusk's interviews with foreign ambassadors. The mischief Kennedy wrought was obviously compounded by the way Rusk ran the Department.[15]

Many of Rusk's expectations for himself and the Department were frustrated. In the beginning he had little private access to the President.[16] Members of the White House staff were usually present and Rusk did not like to offer his views subject to academic comments by people like Theodore Sorensen or Carl Kaysen, men without institutional responsibilities. He did not like to get into discussions at meetings of the National Security Council or of the Cabinet when there were too many people around to give distorted versions to their favorite columnists. Rusk often refused to reveal his views in the presence of members of Bundy's staff and they complained, quite honestly, that they did not know his position on major issues. Kennedy occasionally indulged in witticisms at Rusk's expense, reporting that when they were alone, Rusk would whisper that there was still one too many persons present. Often he professed not to know what Rusk thought, but there seems little doubt that when the President wanted the secretary's opinion, he asked for and received it.

Rusk's hopes for ending the demoralization of the career foreign service were impeded by both the President and Robert Kennedy.

The President thought the foreign service was burdened by too many incompetent senior officers who had achieved rank through longevity. As Rusk tried to reserve major posts for career men, Kennedy demanded to have their ranks thinned by forced early retirements and was irritated by Rusk's resistance. The effort to rehabilitate the Old China hands was impeded by Robert Kennedy's unwillingness to burden the administration with political liabilities, by men of whose loyalty the Attorney General may not have been convinced. Despite these handicaps, morale within the Department, never easily measured, seemed improved in 1961.[17]

Most disappointing to Rusk, and perhaps most detrimental to the influence of the Department, was his failure to establish a Marshall-Lovett relationship with Bowles. The flaw was in the conception. He was not Marshall, Bowles was not Lovett. Rusk did not have the awesome presence of Marshall, and Bowles for all his virtues was even less interested in administering the Department than was Rusk. The two men genuinely liked and respected each other at the outset, but were quickly disappointed. Bowles was a dreamer, a visionary, a man who could capture the liberal imagination with impassioned programs for dealing with the problems the underprivileged sectors of the world would face over the next quarter of a century. Under great pressure from the White House for rapid decisions, constantly pressed for time, Rusk grew weary of Bowles' lengthy expositions. Known for his own lucid and succinct memos, the secretary became impatient with Bowles' wide-ranging, sometimes metaphysical essays. He needed a man who could run the Department for him, a man of sound judgment and assured loyalty to him, and Bowles, though he tried, was not that man.

Congress and the press quickly noted some of the problems and analyzed them with striking accuracy. The President was held responsible for failing to establish clear lines of authority between the White House staff and the Department of State. Rusk was taken to task for being too amiable, for allowing Bundy's bunch to run wild. Kennedy bore the brunt of the criticism in the spring of 1961, primarily because of the restricted channels in which the decision to launch the Bay of Pigs operation was reached. Kennedy's errors with Cuba, his decision to meet with Khrushchev despite Rusk's advice to the contrary, the travels of Rusk and the exuberant promises Vice President Johnson was issuing in Asia, were generally blamed on the President's reliance on an inexperienced White House staff. The greatest confusion was in Latin American affairs, where the White House crew was assumed to have seized the most authority. Kennedy was advised to be more patient, to rely more on the "old pros" at State, and to let Rusk stay home to run the Department and serve as his principal adviser. A New York Times reporter found experienced diplomats and Congressmen persuaded that Kennedy would eventually realize that Rusk was the man who could help most. When Kennedy came to his senses, "the direction of foreign policy will take on a much wanted firmness."[18]

In July there were indications that the White House staff was deflecting criticism toward Rusk. Bowles was under fire and rumored to be on the way out, but word that he had opposed the Bay of Pigs invasion was leaked. Rusk was held responsible by the New Republic for allegedly failing to forward to the President a Bowles memo opposing the operation. Reston reported, very sympathetically, that Rusk had been found wanting—although it was not altogether clear by whom. Unattributed reports that Kennedy was dissatisfied by Rusk's "unassertive, conventional behavior" appeared. The President was not getting the ideas, the policy alternatives he wanted from State. With gentle wit, Reston summed up the situation: Rusk had

not quite managed to organize his department effectively, serve as principal adviser to the President, shine in the presence of all the other foreign policy experts in the White House and the Pentagon, act as chief negotiator abroad, educate the public, console the Foreign Service, attend five State dinners a week, satisfy the curiosity of 2,500 Washington correspondents, testify brilliantly on Capitol Hill, tame Khrushchev, develop the underdeveloped, deflate the over-developed, and stamp out Castro.[19]

Moreover, Reston noted, Rusk was actually trying to do all these things—"a manifest impossibility"—and had left administration of the Department to Alexis Johnson. Worse, he had sat quietly at meetings in which other "more loquacious characters" dominated the discussion, and "left the White House with the impression that it was getting neither the ideas nor the drive, nor the service it wanted from the department."

The leaks infuriated Kennedy whose charm and good humor did not extend to aides who claimed to have been right when he had confessed himself to be wrong. Bowles would not be fired when it might appear that the President was purging the only one of his advisors who had been true to liberal principles, but he began traveling to Africa and Asia. Rusk informed Kennedy that Bowles' "personal interests and talents lie in such activities."[20] With Bowles out of Washington, and Bundy and Battle working smoothly, the apparatus of policy formulation seemed in good order. The press was informed that the State Department was responding more rapidly to the President's needs and that the President and his staff had come to appreciate the complexity of the process and the need for deliberation. He and Secretary Rusk were reported to be developing a much closer relationship. In November, a formal reorganization of the Department was carried out, the "Thanksgiving Day massacre" that ended with Bowles out of town permanently and George Ball moving into the number-two slot at State. Rusk had to swallow Walt Rostow as head of Policy Planning, an appointment he had resisted, but the two men managed to work together. Rusk's friend McGhee was moved up to undersecretary. But the key move was the elevation of Ball, who was well equipped to play the Lovett role to Rusk's Marshall. He soon won the Secretary's confidence by keeping him informed of all dealings with the White House staff.

By November, on the eve of Bowles' departure, Joseph Kraft was writing on "The Comeback of the State Department."[21] Rusk, once in eclipse, had emerged "beyond any doubt as the President's principal adviser on foreign policy." Kraft concluded that his competitors had eliminated themselves one by one and Rusk of the "terse and incisive" mind, irrepressible wit, and "cautious, undramatic approach" had come to the fore, in part the result of his hard work on the Berlin issue. Nonetheless, dissatisfaction with Rusk persisted among some of his subordinates and among some White House staffers. Rusk never became the kind of secretary that Acheson wanted him to be, but by Thanksgiving it was clear that he and Kennedy had established a satisfactory relationship. If it was not all that either man wanted, the tensions and frustrations of previous spring were gone. By December, 1961, the shakedown cruise was over and the country had survived.

4

Obviously, Dean Rusk as Secretary of State in 1961 was not as widely admired and respected as when he served with the Department in the Truman era. In most respects, Rusk had changed little. He was still the superb explainer, more popular on the Hill and with foreign diplomats than anyone else concerned with national security. Congressmen found the arrogance of the young men in the White House—and this included their former colleague, the President—no more bearable than the arrogance of Acheson or Dulles. Rusk was patient, he was kind, and they liked him. He tried to delegate responsibility and authority to his subordinates, but his system did not work as well as he thought it had in his earlier tour in the Department. Kennedy, unlike Truman and Rusk's other superiors, often involved himself deeply in the specifics of policy. If the President was interested in a question, the secretary had to master the details. The issue could not be left to subordinates. Even when he was free to delegate, there were problems. As before there were men who exulted in the freedom he gave them. But he had many more subordinates and some needed more direction, perhaps preferred less responsibility. Others required more praise than he was comfortable providing. And a few, especially among those with ties to the White House, thought themselves brighter, quicker and more influential.

Earlier, men like Acheson, Jessup, and Dulles had praised and respected the quality of Rusk's mind. These were proud men, intolerant of lesser intellects—and they admired Rusk. Yet in 1961, the intellectuals in the White House were often contemptuous. The difference seems explicable in terms of the difference in the style of decision-making in the Truman and Kennedy Administrations and the difference in the roles Rusk played in each. In 1949 or 1950, Acheson, Jessup and Rusk might meet to exchange ideas. Rusk and Dulles might talk over an issue. A few men who had been solving problems together for a period of years, performed on a foundation of mutual respect. In 1961, the number of actors was larger, few had any previous contact with Rusk. He was the outsider on the team Kennedy assembled. Many were bright young men, quick with answers, admiring quickness and brilliance. They had little appreciation of deliberateness and experience, the qualities Rusk brought. Quite rightly, they concluded that Rusk was not a bona fide New Frontiersman, that he would be more comfortable in an older style. But because he was different, they judged him to be second-rate, ridiculed him at Georgetown cocktail parties, and made it difficult for him to win the confidence of the President. The same extraordinary control that enabled Rusk to retain his composure in a variety of past crises, carried him through 1961 with a minimum of bitterness. Schlesinger noted that despite these problems the dominant characteristics revealed were "his decency, dignity, durability."[22] The principal casualty of 1961 appears to have been his "twinkly good humor," which appears to have been less irrepressible than early observers had anticipated.

The decline in esteem for Rusk was perhaps inevitable as he moved into a new post which required qualities in addition to those for which he had been praised. Under Truman and Acheson, Rusk had been able to focus on operations, on problem solving—especially as deputy-undersecretary—and he had excelled. As secretary, there were too many other roles. No one could perform them all well. Rusk lacked the time for some of the chores assigned and the skill for others. As Kennedy used him, he could not focus on the things he did best. Inevitably, there were inadequate performances and the luster tarnished. But by the end of the year, Rusk's star was ascending, at very least in the eyes of the President whose understanding of his secretary's attributes and deficiencies was greatly improved.

CHAPTER SEVEN

Initial Responses to the World as Found

Dean Rusk understood when he took office in January, 1961, that the vision toward which American policy would be directed was that of the President, John F. Kennedy. Rusk the constitutionalist had no reservations about allowing the President to determine national goals. His own hopes, as expressed to his associates, were characteristically modest. He hoped that his tour as Secretary of State would provide the world with a few more years of peace, a few more years without nuclear holocaust. He expected to solve few of the world's problems. Many problems had roots in centuries past and would remain unresolved long after he was gone. His job was to prevent those problems from exploding into wars and whenever possible, to find a way to take a few small steps, to nibble away at the dangers, to push war a little farther away.[1]

Rusk articulated other ideas in which far more ambitious goals were apparent. An embodiment of the American Dream, he was a nationalist and a patriot in the best sense of those words: he wanted to share the blessings of democracy—not just with his fellow Americans, but with Africans and Asians as well. He was profoundly convinced that all peoples wanted what Americans enjoyed: food, shelter, freedom. He was persuaded that Communism had denied freedom to the peoples it ruled. Privately as well as publicly he informed his listeners that no former colonial people had ever chosen Communism; that democracy was the most revolutionary and most attractive concept in the world. The Communists, he contended, were violating some of the "fundamental aspects of human nature." Rusk, remembering Croce, found History on the side of liberty and argued that mankind was moving toward the progressive realization of greater and greater freedom, toward the extension of human liberty. Communism was a retrograde force and could not prevail. Rusk was the consummate Wilsonian, still responding to Lenin with the precepts of American liberalism.[2]

Ideologically Rusk was committed to a Wilsonian goal of preserving opportunities for the spread of democracy, of keeping the world safe for freedom. The great task of his day was to contain Communism, to prevent nations from falling behind the iron curtain, to preserve options for liberty. Rusk was not a hypocrite. He had no illusions about human rights under Franco, Trujillo or Chiang Kai-shek. But he believed that these dictatorships might someday give way to democracy. Once the Communists gained control of a country it was too late. The opportunity to be free was lost forever.

These goals required more activism than inhered in his hope to maintain peace. Combatting Communism wherever it threatened, preserving opportunities for freedom all over Asia, Africa and perhaps Latin America, appeared far more formidable than the task Rusk had shared during the Truman era. Acheson's attention had focused on the Atlantic community, on Western Europe. Rusk saw himself as a universalist, a man who believed all peoples, not just Europeans, were entitled to share in the American dream. In the 1960s he and most liberals in the United States saw the new states of Africa and Asia as the new arena in the struggle between Communism and liberalism. Similarly, Khrushchev saw these former colonial peoples as the most promising target for his own crusade—and the battle of the 1960s was fairly joined.

The means to which Rusk was committed were fundamentally Wilsonian. Advocacy of collective security rang through his speeches and private conversations like a catechism. He, Stevenson, and Harlan Cleveland, Assistant Secretary for International Organization, were eager to work through the United Nations whenever possible. More readily than Stevenson, Rusk was prepared to have the United States act alone if the UN failed to carry out its obligations. He did not seek responsibility for the United States, but he was quick to accept it when no international organization would do the job. For this role the United States had to prepare militarily.

Unlike Wilson's day, in the 1960s the United States had power that could be directed toward protecting little countries around the world. Rusk often expressed the idea that American demobilization after World War II had invited the Cold War, had "tempted thieves." The Korean War had permitted the rearmament of the United States and Rusk was committed to maintaining American military power to an extent Woodrow Wilson could never have imagined—and to using it when necessary.

Rusk's thought flowed easily into the course plotted by Paul Nitze's National Security Policy Committee. This group, convened by Kennedy after he received the Democratic nomination, included Dean Acheson, Arthur Dean, William Foster, Robert Lovett and John McCloy. Its members, and Rusk and Kennedy, shared the premise that the Soviet Union and its allies continued to seek world revolution. Unable to agree on whether nuclear superiority for the United States was a feasible goal, the committee members stressed the need for improvement of conventional forces, for development of a limited war capability. In his inaugural address Kennedy warned of deficiencies in American military strength and indicated his determination to create the power necessary to meet the Communist challenge anywhere. He and Rusk hoped for improvement in relations with Moscow and Peking, but they were persuaded, as were the members of Nitze's group and Kennan, that a show of American strength and determination was essential. As Rusk frequently recalled, Stalin had not been responsive prior to the resurrection of American power. With Khrushchev the test would come in the Third World.

2

In his initial public appearances, Rusk stressed the themes Kennedy had sounded in his inaugural. Central to his first news conference was a warning against optimism about Soviet-American relations. Yes, the Russians had released some American fliers whose plane had been shot down over Soviet territory. But Rusk indicated concern over remarks Khrushchev had made on January 6—remarks which appear to have shaken the new administration and its experts on Soviet affairs. Khrushchev had expressed confidence in the ultimate triumph of "socialism" and his determination to support wars of national liberation. He was particularly threatening about Berlin. The struggle would continue and Rusk, appearing on the *Today* show, warned that those who sought peace "must themselves be strong . . . We must not offer temptations to those who would upset the peace by letting them feel that they can upset the peace with impunity."[3]

On February 28, Rusk appeared before the Senate Committee on Foreign Relations to give its members the administration's first top secret tour d'horizon. His focus and the interest of the Senators who questioned him was the underdeveloped nations. He described a world in which nationalist revolution was accelerating, especially in Africa. He noted an intense demand for improved economic and social conditions. He saw the Communists, more sophisticated than in the past, using more subtle means than Stalin had imagined, striving to extend their influence. Their foreign assistance programs reflected "a much enlarged effort which is their recognition that the contest is shifting, perhaps, from the military problem in Western Europe to a genuine contest for the underdeveloped countries." Yes, there was a certain civility in formal relations with the Soviet Union now, but Rusk saw no reason to believe that the central tension had disappeared. The Berlin problem persisted and the Russians were causing problems in Laos, the Congo, and Cuba.[4]

At one point in the ensuing discussion, Rusk referred to an "uneven struggle," particularly in Laos, where the United States was forced to work through the aristocracy while the Communists came in on the side of the peasants. Something had to be done to reestablish the United States as a beacon of nationalist revolution, to demonstrate the traditional American concern for economic and social development. He brooded aloud about constantly finding the United States tied to weak allies, presumably the ancien regime, and spoke of a need to determine in what circumstances "can you or should you invest in a regime when you know in your heart that that regime is not viable." Under pressure from a Senator more sympathetic to European colonial regimes, Rusk insisted that the

United States would have to demand some movement in European policy. Americans could not be put in the position of supporting colonialism.[5]

Rusk's themes were clear and simple and he developed them eloquently in a series of public appearances, most notably the Charter Day Address at the University of California on March 20. Americans lived in a world of change, nationalism, and rising expectations. The Communists were reaching for world domination and applying great resources and energy to extend their control over Latin America, Africa, the Middle East and Asia. The contest ahead would be formidable. The United States could not be passive. It could not defend the status quo. Rusk was determined to see the United States lead in helping oppressed peoples gain their freedom, rule by law, and economic and social improvement. In a BBC interview he was clearly irked by Khrushchev's claim to speak for nationalist revolution. It was the American people who were committed to the idea that governments derive their just powers from the consent of the governed.[6]

In a speech to the United States Chamber of Commerce, Rusk chose not to play hardheaded businessman when appealing for support of the foreign aid program. Referring to Vandenberg's advice to Marshall in 1947 to come in roaring if he wanted Congress to appropriate the money the administration sought for Greece and Turkey, Rusk said: "Roar we did, but the roaring was discordant; it confused our purposes, misrepresented our motives and impaired our execution." Soviet bloc assistance to underdeveloped countries made an American program essential, but Rusk chose not to stress anti-Communism as the basis for aid. Instead he insisted that aid would be necessary in the absence of any threat, that "social justice is an imperative of the 1960s." Yet he left no doubt that social justice was the Administration's answer to the Communist challenge in the Third World.[7]

3

Between Rusk's Charter Day call for aligning the United States with nationalist revolutions and the day he tried to interest the

Chamber of Commerce in social justice, the administration tried a more direct approach to the Communist challenge in Cuba. In January, 1961, Fidel Castro, Marxist-Leninist, had provoked the Eisenhower Administration into breaking relations with Cuba. In his struggle to power against the corrupt and repressive Batista dictatorship, Castro had elicited the sympathy of many Americans and of those Cubans who dreamt of liberal democracy for their own people. When it became apparent that he was a Communist, he alienated most American sympathizers and many of his erstwhile Cuban supporters. In 1960, the Central Intelligence Agency, which had undermined a potentially Communist regime in Guatemala in 1954, won Eisenhower's approval to train and equip Cuban expatriates for an invasion of Cuba. Candidate Kennedy advocated aid to anti-Castro exiles and in April, 1961, President Kennedy sent them ashore at the Bay of Pigs.

Kennedy and Rusk considered themselves to be supportive of social revolution in the underdeveloped world. Neither man had any brief for Batista or any interest in restoring him or anyone like him in Havana. But Castro was a Communist, with links to the Soviet Union. He was unacceptable. He had destroyed the dream of freedom that armed so many Cubans who had risen against Batista. He had chosen the Soviet model, the totalitarian model, rather than the democratic model. His connection with the Soviet Union, unclear as it was, threatened the security of the United States. A Communist solution to the problems of the Third World was not acceptable to them.

It was one thing to dislike the Castro regime and quite another to get rid of it. Kennedy and his national security advisers examined the invasion plans inherited from the Eisenhower Administration. Rusk was skeptical, much more comfortable with the idea of an economic boycott as a means of troubling Castro and encouraging resistance. If the United States supported an exile invasion, Rusk feared American involvement could not be kept secret. The political ramifications of such involvement could be disastrous. Rusk was not convinced by CIA estimates that the Cuban people would rise against Castro. As was his wont, he expressed his reservations to Kennedy privately. In the discussions with other top advisers he raised questions, tried to focus attention on weak points in the plans. Among men accustomed to forceful advocacy his views went unnoticed. Only Richard Bissell, the CIA man responsible for the operation, was aware of Rusk's feelings. He understood that Rusk was whittling away at the operation, cutting back on the air cover Bissell thought necessary, determined to spare the United States embarrassment if the landing itself could not be prevented. He thought afterward that if Rusk had realized that the United States could not escape responsibility for the invasion, he would have argued more tenaciously and might have prevented the whole operation.[8]

Landed on inhospitable terrain without air cover, pinned down by Castro's air force, 1,400 CIA-trained Cuban exiles were easily mopped up by the Cuban army. The Cuban people did not rise to rid themselves of the Communist tyrant. Quickly the CIA plan was revealed to be utterly deficient in conception, based on false premises. The Castro regime could not be overthrown by a handful of exiles. Only a major effort by the armed forces of the United States would suffice—and this Kennedy was determined to avoid.

Once the exiles were trapped on the beach and American complicity in the operation realized world-wide, CIA officials called for further military support—at least another air strike. Some observers suspect that the planners knew all along that the exiles could not succeed alone and that they expected to force the President to commit American planes, even troops, to the overthrow of Castro. But once it was clear that the operation was in trouble and the United States implicated, it was Rusk who argued forcefully and successfully against a second air strike.[9]

At the end, after the 1,400 Cuban exiles were doomed, after Adlai Stevenson had unwittingly lied in denying American involvement before his colleagues of the United Nations, after American adherence to the traditional principle of nonintervention had been brought into question once more, Rusk spoke forcefully. Until then he adhered to Kennedy's admonition to secrecy, kept his department uninformed, and chose not to generate pressure in opposition to the course upon which the President was drifting. He had accepted the idea that the CIA-trained Cubans presented a "disposal problem." They could not be turned loose in Central America or in Miami. He had concentrated his efforts on minimizing the

American presence and the likelihood of American involvement being recognized. At a critical meeting on April 4, Senator J. William Fulbright forthrightly opposed the plan, with minimal support from Rusk. Finally, Rusk gave his verbal assent to the operation.[10]

Here again was Rusk the good soldier. He opposed the operation, expressed his dissent to the President privately, and accepted the President's decision—trying as quietly and unobtrusively as he could to minimize the potential damage. Here was Rusk the constitutionalist, wanting the President to be in charge. And here was Rusk the outsider, wary of developing gaps between himself and a President he hardly knew. In this instance a familiar pattern of action, so successful and so admired by his superiors in the past, proved a disservice to his President and country.

4

In Rusk's first closed meeting with the Committee on Foreign Relations, it was the crisis in the Congo rather than Cuba that drew the most questions. The Republic of the Congo (Leopoldville) had been granted independence by Belgium on June 30, 1960. The Eisenhower Administration recognized no strategic interests in central Africa and anticipated no problems for American economic interests in the new state. Though it continued to defer to Belgium, its NATO ally, the United States had urged that Patrice Lumumba head the Congo government. Africanists in Washington were persuaded that he was the only national leader in a territory in which the pull of tribalism seemed threatening. Lumumba became first premier of the Republic and the few American officials concerned with central Africa rested. But not for long.[11]

Less than a week after independence, a mutiny in the Congolese Army and the rapid reinforcement of Belgian troops that had been allowed to remain in the Congo led Lumumba to suspect a Belgian plot to replace him with a more malleable leader. His fears were intensified a few days later when Katanga, the province in which most European investments were concentrated, declared its independence. Lumumba and the President of the Congo, Joseph

Kasavubu, flew to Katanga, but were prevented from landing by Belgian paratroopers. Lumumba raged publicly about Belgian actions and intentions, giving vent to his most apocalyptic apprehensions. In rapid succession he called upon the United States, the United Nations, and the Soviet Union for help.

The United States sought to avoid any major involvement in the affairs of the Congo, deferring to the United Nations. Supported by the United States and the Soviet Union, a resolution was passed by the Security Council calling for withdrawal of Belgian troops and for military assistance to the government of the Congo. Weeks passed without any progress toward reunification and Lumumba turned again to the Russians. By September, 1960, large quantities of Soviet equipment and a number of Russian and Czech technicians appeared in the Congo.

Despite the fact that Lumumba had appealed to the United States first, the Eisenhower Administration came to see him as unstable and dangerous—a potential conduit to Communist influence in central Africa. As the Russians manifested interest in the area, its strategic importance was greatly magnified in the minds of American policy makers. Should the Communists gain control over the Congo, they would be in position to dominate sub-Saharan Africa. Tomorrow the World.

The Eisenhower Administration did not want to see Soviet influence extended to the Congo and it did not want a confrontation with the Russians in Africa. The best hope for restoring order without American involvement seemed to be the United Nations force, supplemented by a CIA operation to assassinate Lumumba. The administration was reluctant to press for an end to the Katanga secession, by no means adverse to seeing that province, an important source of cobalt, copper, and industrial diamonds, isolated from the menacing virus of Communism. The leader of Katanga, Moise Tshombe, supported by European mining interests and the Belgian government, quickly developed a following in Europe and among American conservatives.

In September, President Kasavubu, troubled by Lumumba's overtures to the Russians and his autocratic ways, consulted with the American ambassador and Andrew W. Cordier, the UN representative in the Congo, and then fired Lumumba. Lumumba attempted to seize power but Cordier ordered UN forces to close the airports, preventing Russian planes from moving pro-Lumumba forces to the capital. Joseph Ileo became premier and the former premier was placed under house arrest, protected by UN forces. Joseph Mobutu, supported by the CIA, emerged as head of the army, the strong man in the new regime.

The activities of the UN force in the Congo, in supporting Kasavubu against Lumumba, infuriated Khrushchev and Afro-Asian radicals as much as they pleased American authorities. For the next few months the battlefield shifted to New York where the Soviet Union, led by Khrushchev personally, abused Secretary General Dag Hammarskjold. It was in the midst of this verbal warfare that Khrushchev conducted his long remembered shoe-pounding episode, expressing his displeasure at the remarks of another speaker. The situation in the Congo remained reasonably quiet, however, with but one ominous exception. In late November, Lumumba escaped from the protective custody of UN forces, only to be recaptured and imprisoned by Mobutu's troops.

When Kennedy and Rusk took office, the basic issues in the Congo remained unresolved. The central government of Kasavubu and Ileo, supported by Mobutu, was only one of three power blocs in the territory it claimed the right to rule. The Katangan secession had gone virtually unchallenged and Lumumbist forces, led by Antoine Gizenga, were unbowed, vying for control of the government. Within the United Nations the Afro-Asian bloc demanded elimination of the Belgian puppet Tshombe. America's NATO allies were not eager to support UN action against Katanga which would jeopardize European interests there.

The Kennedy Administration was no less determined than its predecessor to prevent the growth of Soviet influence in the Congo, but the new American leadership was publicly committed to the support of African nationalism. Afraid of Gizenga and Lumumba, Kennedy, Rusk, Bowles, Williams, and Stevenson were also hostile to the neo-colonial activities of the Belgians and Tshombe. The solution appeared obvious, albeit difficult. A way had to be found to strengthen the central government against the Left without alienating the Afro-Asian bloc. Simultaneously, the Katanga secession had to be terminated without alienating the European allies.

The quest for the liberal center, safe from communist or colonial taint, quickly became the hallmark of administration policy in the Congo—and the Third World generally.

The complexities of the situation in the Congo immobilized men with other priorities, men worried about Khrushchev's belligerent speech on January 6, about Eisenhower's legacy in Laos, about plans for invading Cuba. Dramatic events involving Lumumba, however, forced Rusk to give early attention to the Congo.

Only days before Kennedy's inaugural, Washington was stunned by the incredible news that Mobutu had turned Lumumba over to authorities in Katanga. There was little sympathy for Lumumba among Kennedy's advisers. Rusk advised the President to oppose Lumumba's return to power and to continue to support Ileo as premier.[12] But the Kennedy Administration does not appear to have favored Lumumba's murder, fearing rather that he would be more dangerous to American interests if martyred. Nonetheless, in mid-February, Lumumba's "escape" was announced and his death was quickly revealed. In the United Nations the Soviet Union blamed Hammarskjold, demanded his dismissal as Secretary General and the withdrawal of UN forces from the Congo. The Russians also threatened to give aid to Gizenga's forces. Over the next few days the Lumumbists under the leadership of Gizenga were recognized by the United Arab Republic, Ghana, Guinea, Mali, Morocco, the Algerian National Liberation Front and the Communist bloc. The UAR, Guinea, Morocco and Indonesia withdrew their men from the UN forces and an emergency was averted only by India's timely offer of troops.

The murder of Lumumba and the response of the Soviet Union and some of the Afro-Asian states worried Kennedy and his advisers. They feared that the Soviet Union and the UAR would support a war of "national liberation" against the Kasavubu-Ileo government. Kennedy warned outside powers against intervention, apparently most troubled by UAR efforts to supply Gizenga's forces. The administration called for continued support of the United Nations effort and before skeptical Senators, Rusk defended the UN role. In a top-secret briefing he argued that but for the UN presence, Lumumba would have been in control of most of the Congo. There might have been a prolonged civil war between Lumumba's followers and the Katanga secessionists in which the help Lumumba would have received "from the other side" would have presented the United States with a "very disagreeable situation in the Congo." In short, the UN had served American interests in the first phase of the Congo crisis and the administration hoped it would serve as well in the future.[13]

One problem for the Kennedy Administration was lack of agreement in the country and in the government about the appropriate course of action. Tshombe supporters had quickly created an effective lobby and rallied such conservative stalwarts as William F. Buckley, and Senators Thomas Dodd and Barry Goldwater. An image of Katanga as a bastion of free enterprise and a bulwark against Communism was offered to the nation and found considerable acceptance in all the usual places. Kennedy could not risk supporting the suppression of Tshombe's movement until he could be reasonably sure that he would not thereby clear the way for a Communist takeover. He could not get rid of a Congolese Batista to facilitate the rise of another Castro. As a result, an informal coalition of conservatives, State Department Europeanists responsive to Brussels, Lisbon, London and Paris, and military authorities prevailed for several months over the State Department Africanists and UN people who did not fear Gizenga, despised Tshombe and wanted stronger UN action, including sanctions if necessary.

Rusk's natural position was alongside Bowles, Stevenson, and the Africanists, but he was more responsive than they were to Kennedy's domestic political problems. Perhaps because he had felt the heat that consumed the China specialists accused of losing China just a few years earlier, he was more cautious than the other liberals, less willing to gamble on Gizenga, less willing to take responsibility for pushing aside another hero of the friends of Chiang Kai-shek. For several months, as efforts to settle the affairs of the Congo through negotiations were constantly thwarted by Tshombe, as Tshombe's power seemed to grow, Rusk held back. Among his misgivings was a fear about the reliability of UN troops, about whether troops from radical African states would follow UN directions or orders from their national leaders.[14] Rusk did not have to be persuaded, however, that it was important for the United States to identify itself with the forces of nationalism lest the Soviet Union appear as their only supporter, and the United States be linked to a moribund colonialism.

By the summer of 1961, Rusk was convinced that the danger from the Left had been contained and that a reconvening of the Congo's parliament, called for by the Afro-Asian states, might have a salutary effect. The United States supported UN moves for a parliamentary meeting which resulted in a Congolese Government of National Unity. In the absence of Tshombe's representatives, Cyrille Adoula, a friend of Lumumba's with AFL-CIO endorsement, was elected premier. Rusk reported gleefully to Kennedy that the almost unanimous vote of confidence Adoula received from the Congo parliament destroyed Gizenga's claim to be the legal government. The election was, Rusk claimed, a defeat for the Soviet Union.[15]

The most important part of that parliamentary meeting, however, had been the reconciliation between Kasavubu and Gizenga. Kasavubu retained his post as President in the new regime and Gizenga accepted election as vice premier. Gizenga agreed to terminate his opposition to the regime and to serve it loyally, providing Adoula took action to end the Katanga secession. The new Congolese central government, with strong support from the United Nations and the United States, now turned its attention to the reintegration of Katanga. Belgium, France, and Great Britain were prepared to accept the end of Katanga's separate existence, but were insistent that it be accomplished peacefully. The United States also remained leery of using force, fearful of a situation in which Gizenga would emerge on top. All hoped that a brief "show" of force would suffice.

On August 28, UN troops in Katanga seized control of the broadcasting station and began to arrest foreign officers. Belgian officers "seconded" to the Katanga gendarmerie were recalled by Brussels, but Tshombe's mercenaries—mainly South African and Rhodesian whites—stayed on and he refused to yield. Early in September, UN authorities in the Congo decided another show of force might drive out the mercenaries and bring Tshombe to heel. They were wrong, and tragically so. For eight days, the fighting went on in Elizabethville, capital of Katanga, and Tshombe's forces held, killing 20 UN soldiers.

The resort to force angered the Belgians, British and French and apparently caught Hammarskjold and the United States by surprise. Rusk "infuriated" Hammarskjold by urging him to bring Adoula and Tshombe together, warning that American support for UN action would evaporate if Gizenga's approach to the problem prevailed. The United States continued its public support of the UN, but called for a cease-fire and indicated that Washington would like to be consulted before major decisions were implemented. Hammarskjold interpreted the American position as virtual support for Tshombe and an attempt to control the organization. Through Ralph Bunche he sent word to Rusk that the UN was better off without American support. Hammarskjold was killed in the Congo, trying to arrange a cease-fire, before he and Rusk were reconciled.[16]

A few days after Hammarskjold's death, Rusk informed the Senate Foreign Relations Committee that the United States did not want the UN to use force. He contended that military means were not appropriate, that there should not be a sustained military campaign to pacify Katanga. At the urging of the United States and others, Tshombe and Adoula were talking. October passed without progress—and then November. Still the United States hoped for the peaceful integration of Katanga. On November 11, Rusk sent Kennedy a statement of policy that summarized American activities neatly: support Adoula, put pressure on Tshombe, prevent the UN from precipitating civil war. Bunche assured the United States that he and other responsible UN officials would give negotiations first priority. If force were necessary, the UN would apply only so much as was necessary to persuade Tshombe to negotiate.[17]

By early December, the UN was ready to fight again—and the United States was prepared to support the use of force. Turning the anti-Communist argument of the Tshombe supporters on its head, Rusk and the Africanists argued that unless Katanga was reintegrated, there could not be a strong central government and the Congo would be open to Communist penetration. Publicly, after the fighting began, Rusk stressed the need for the peaceful reintegration of Katanga, but unequivocally declared American support for the UN effort in the Congo, regretting Katanga's use of force.[18] And American support went beyond words and the financial contributions to the "peace-keeping" force. The United States provided UN forces with air transport, necessary to reinforce troops in Elizabethville.

As the anger of America's NATO allies roared around his ears, President Kennedy became apprehensive about the situation in the Congo. Tshombe's friends on the Hill also rumbled loudly and an American Committee for Aid to Katanga Freedom Fighters protested both UN action and American logistical support for it. Rusk had assured the President that he would try to prevent the UN military operation from becoming an all-out effort to occupy Katanga, but Kennedy did not long resist the pressure. On December 13, Kennedy and Ball spoke to Rusk who was in Paris at a meeting of the NATO Council. They realized that the Congo issue could topple the British government and Kennedy concluded that he could only allow the UN offensive to run a few days. On the 14th Tshombe sent a cable indicating his desire to negotiate with Adoula. The UN offensive began on the 15th and on the same day Kennedy instructed that preparations be made for Tshombe and Adoula to be brought together by the American ambassador. State Department officials who were convinced that Tshombe would eventually have to be defeated militarily had to settle for a three-day offensive. On December 18, a cease-fire went into effect and on the 21st Tshombe and Adoula signed the Kitona agreement, formally ending the Katanga secession. While the Congolese politicians talked, Harold Macmillan, the British Prime Minister, noted in his diary that he had some success in getting Kennedy and Rusk to exert themselves "instead of leaving the direction to the Adlai Stevensons and other half-baked 'liberals' whom they commonly employ (for internal political reasons) at the United Nations." Unfortunately for all concerned, Tshombe had little intention of honoring the agreement. [19]

On January 18, 1962, Rusk accompanied by Ball briefed the Subcommittee on African Affairs of the Foreign Relations Committee. Their approach left no doubt that the administration was poised to protect itself from domestic critics on the Right. Both men justified American support for UN intervention on anti-Communist grounds. Without the UN, Rusk reiterated, there would have been violence and chaos in the Congo, an opportunity for Soviet exploitation "which the United States would have been compelled to counter." The UN, he claimed, blocked "the Soviet take-over scheme." Forced to distinguish between UN intervention in the Congo and UN operations against Katanga, Rusk argued that Congolese nationalism was so strong that no government could survive unless it demonstrated progress toward reunification. Rather than criticize Tshombe and invite the wrath of the latter's friends in the Senate, Rusk insisted that the "moderate strength of Mr. Tshombe" and the wealth of Katanga were needed in the central government. He implied that the problem was not with Tshombe, but with foreigners who tried to persuade him to maintain his secession by force. Clearly the administration was prepared to appease American conservatives by urging Adoula to find a place in his government for Tshombe.[20]

The Baron of Katanga was not ready, however, to accept a subordinate position in the central government. Months passed and the Kitona agreement was not honored. No revenue flowed from Katanga to the Adoula regime. Tshombe was not ready to surrender. He still had strong vocal support in the United States. More importantly, he still had the financial backing of the powerful Union Minière du Haut Katanga—the Belgian company that controlled Katanga's mineral wealth. And nothing happened.

By the summer of 1962 Adoula's patience had run out, U Thant, Hammarskjold's successor, was exasperated, and the American ambassador had concluded that sanctions would probably be needed to move Tshombe. Working closely with U Thant, the Department of State worked out a plan for the reintegration of Katanga that proved acceptable to the British and Belgians. Tshombe agreed to the plan "tentatively," but it was clear that he was continuing to stall while he built up his own military power. By October, U Thant wanted to impose an economic blockade on Katanga to force Tshombe to act. But it was too close to election time in the United States. Decisive action would have to wait for a month or two and George McGhee went to the Congo in a last effort to see if words could work.

The situation immediately following the American congressional elections seemed critical. India had clashed with China and wanted the troops it had dispatched to the Congo for possible use at home.

Adoula barely survived a vote of censure in the Congolese parliament. There no longer seemed time to talk. The American ambassador called for unleashing UN forces against Katanga. In Washington, the White House staff was skeptical about the urgency of the situation and Kennedy had reservations about economic or military sanctions. Nonetheless, serious fighting commenced in December and the United States resumed its airlift operations for UN forces. Despite opposition to the use of force from the Defense Department, on December 17 the National Security Council decided to provide the UN with the equipment necessary for a military solution to the problem of Katangan secession. At last, in January, 1963, Tshombe's forces were defeated and Katanga was reunited with the rest of the Congo. It was not the last of Tshombe—or of unrest in the Congo—but John F. Kennedy was spared the sequel.

American policy toward the Congo reflected the consensus within the Kennedy Administration that the Third World was the new arena of the Cold War; that Khrushchev had made the challenge explicit in January, 1961; that the United States would do what was necessary to prevail over the Soviet Union. In the context of the crisis in the Congo, determination to prevent Communist expansion combined readily with a wish to align the United States with African nationalism and a desire to support the United Nations. By no means a necessary combination, these ends were obviously not mutually exclusive. After Tshombe's surrender, the administration's goals in the Congo appeared to have been achieved. The Republic of the Congo was economically viable, under the direction of the "liberal" Cyrille Adoula. Both Left and Right had been checked and the Congo was ready for a New Deal.

The United States was surely fortunate that the UN action sufficed, because Ball explicitly, others implicitly, had contended that all of southern Africa was at stake in the Congo. Had Gizenga been more successful in 1961 or 1962, the Kennedy Administration could not easily have acquiesced in his triumph. The activities in Cuba and Southeast Asia leave little reason to doubt that it would have intervened as necessary to prop up the "choice" domino. There is no evidence to indicate that Kennedy or any of his advisers doubted that Lumumba and Gizenga would bring Communism to the Congo.

Rusk's position in the debate over policy toward the Congo is not readily identifiable. Like Kennedy, he was often preoccupied with more pressing problems: the Bay of Pigs, Laos, Berlin and the missile crisis. Kennedy appeared to vacillate, to be skeptical about UN operations against Katanga and the alleged need to eliminate Tshombe's fiefdom as a means of containing Communism. He was clearly concerned about the domestic political implications, reluctant to antagonize the American Right. Rusk was responsive to Kennedy's needs and effective as always when soothing suspicious Congressmen and angry allies. Certainly he evidenced no more sympathy for Lumumba or Gizenga as genuine nationalists than did Kennedy or other national security leaders. If there was a difference between Rusk and Kennedy, it would appear to have been Rusk's greater receptivity to the arguments of the Department's Africanists and UN specialists. Without Rusk on their side the men urging the United States to support the UN effort to force Tshombe's surrender would not have prevailed over the contrary counsel of the NATO allies, American conservatives, the Pentagon, and the Europeanists of the Department of State. For Rusk, too, it was never enough to contain the Left, never more comforting than when a blow could be struck simultaneously against the Right.

5

On the eve of Kennedy's inauguration, President Eisenhower had talked to his successor about Laos, where the Communist Pathet Lao, supported by neutralist troops, threatened to defeat American-supported Rightists. Eisenhower stressed the importance of preserving the independence of Laos, warning that if the Communists triumphed there, South Vietnam, Cambodia, Thailand and Burma would soon fall to them. He and Christian Herter, his Secretary of State, favored a political settlement, but if that proved impossible, American intervention would be necessary, even if it had to be unilateral.[21]

The tenuous situation in Laos was largely the consequence of American interference in that tiny country. The Eisenhower Administration had refused to accept the neutralization of Laos required by the Geneva Agreements of 1954. Suspicious of the neutralist leader, Souvanna Phouma, half-brother of the Pathet Lao leader, Souphanouvong, the United States had attempted to give Laotian neutrality a pro-Western, anti-Communist cast. But American aid, military and economic, combined with a variety of clandestine CIA operations, backfired. In the closing months of 1960 the machinations of the American protege, General Phoumi Nosavan, had driven key neutralist forces over to the side of the Pathet Lao, and triggered increased aid from Hanoi and a deeper involvement in Laos by the Soviet Union. In January, 1961, in blatant disregard of the Geneva Agreements, Eisenhower provided Phoumi with six fighter-bombers, hoping to retrieve the advantage for pro-Western forces. Enter Kennedy, Rusk, and company.

The problems of Southeast Asia were not new to either Kennedy or Rusk. As Assistant Secretary for Far Eastern Affairs, Rusk had participated in the initial American decision in 1950 to support the French effort to contain Communism in Indochina. He had been dubious about French methods, sympathetic to the nationalist aspirations of the peoples of the region, and suspicious of French imperial pretensions. He had opposed American participation in a regional security organization, unlike John Foster Dulles who created SEATO. But Rusk had endorsed the conclusion that the independence of Indochina was vital to the security of the non-Communist world, that Communism had to be contained in Southeast Asia, as in Europe or Korea. Kennedy, in 1954, had been an outspoken critic of French policy in Indochina. He had argued that French determination to maintain vestiges of an empire there was detrimental to the interests of the local people, that French puppets could not stop Communist expansion. For his criticism of a NATO ally, Kennedy was sharply criticized by his own party's last Secretary of State, Dean Acheson. But the young Senator's views were actually very close to Rusk's. Both men saw Southeast Asia as important. Both thought the Communists had to be prevented from conquering the area—and both saw French imperialism, no matter how prettified, as the principal obstacle to success. They were confident that if the nationalists of Indochina were freed from French interference, they would reject Communism. And both

Rusk and Kennedy were prepared to see the United States offer direct aid to the non-Communist nationalist leaders of the area.

Less than two weeks after the Kennedy Administration took office, Winthrop G. Brown, ambassador to Laos, called to give the President his assessment. The situation was not good. The American-recognized regime was not widely representative and lacked broad international support. Government forces showed no will to fight and the Communists, amply supported by a Soviet airlift, held the strategic plateau in the battle area. Kennedy concluded that he had to act to demonstrate to the Soviet Union that the United States would not tolerate a Communist takeover of Laos. McNamara evidenced extraordinary faith in airpower, calling for arming Laotian jets with hundred-pound bombs. Rusk was far more skeptical, however, and deflected the proposal with recollections of the ineffectiveness of bombing in comparable terrain during World War II. The prognosis was poor, but the danger was not immediate, and the new administration sought to explore its options—to consult with Congress and the nation's allies. Perhaps this problem would go away.[22]

By the end of February the military situation in Laos had deteriorated and it was becoming clear that nothing short of American intervention would turn the tide. Neither Kennedy nor Rusk wanted to send American troops into Laos, but they were not eager for a negotiated settlement. As Rusk explained to the Senate Foreign Relations Committee, the Lao lacked national spirit and they lacked the will to fight. Laos, he said, was "something of a quagmire." Even so, he did not want to negotiate because the situation on the battlefield was "frankly, not very favorable as a base for a negotiating position." Rusk's remarks indicated that the Kennedy Administration was willing to settle for less in Laos than Eisenhower and the Dulles brothers had sought. Laos did not have to become an American ally, so long as it was not a Communist puppet. A neutral Laos would be acceptable. It would suffice as a buffer against Communist penetration into Vietnam, Cambodia, and Thailand.[23]

The problem Kennedy perceived was how to get the Russians to agree to a neutral Laos now that the balance, upset by American ambition, had shifted to the Communist side. A strong stand by SEATO might help, but Rusk revealed that neither the British nor the French were willing. A second possibility was implicit in Rusk's suggestion that Russian activity in Laos might be "an attempt to put some brake upon the Chinese." With reference to the growing Sino-Soviet dispute, he placed responsibility for Communist activities, especially those of the North Vietnamese, on the Russians. Perhaps a neutral Laos would serve equally well as a check on Chinese aspirations and be achieved at less risk for the Russians.[24]

Before Rusk left for Bangkok to attend a SEATO meeting, Laotian government forces suffered a major defeat and fled the battlefield in disarray. Time was running out. In Washington, the Joint Chiefs of Staff were wary of any limited war, wanting but not getting assurances that there would be no sanctuaries, no restraints on American military operations if the United States intervened in Laos. On March 23, Kennedy revealed his decision. The U.S.S. *Midway* left Hong Kong, heading for the Gulf of Siam, a Marine detachment moved to Thailand, forces on Okinawa were put on alert, supplies began to move to bases near Laos. The military moves were deliberately transparent, a warning to Khrushchev. The President spoke to the American people—and to his adversaries—calling for a peaceful settlement and a "truly neutral" Laos. Communist attacks would have to stop or the United States might have to fashion a different response, foreshadowed by the operations underway.

In Bangkok, Rusk spoke of the American commitment to the principle of collective security and of obligation to assist the peoples of Southeast Asia. In a calculated paraphrase of the Truman Doctrine he declared "We will . . . continue to assist free nations of this area who are struggling for their survival against armed minorities directed, supplied, and supported from without." The American "sense of responsibility to other freedom-loving nations," he insisted, "has no geographical barriers." To ensure the credibility of Kennedy's warning to the Russians, Rusk deliberately removed all the limits Acheson had once placed on the alleged universality of the Truman Doctrine.[25]

Less publicly, Rusk tried to get SEATO to resolve to use force in Laos if the Soviet Union refused to negotiate. The French were adamant in their refusal and British support was reluctant and might well have vanished if the French had been less rigid. Unable to get joint action, Rusk succeeded in getting a SEATO endorsement of "appropriate" American action. The SEATO ministers also resolved not to acquiesce in a Communist effort to take over South Vietnam. Painfully aware that a stand in Laos might come too late, the United States was preparing to fall back on Vietnam—where the people reportedly had the will to resist.[26]

At Bangkok, Rusk allowed it to be known that the United States was prepared to intervene unilaterally. Combined with fleet and troop movements, Rusk's words suggested that a major confrontation in Southeast Asia might be developing. Recognizing the risk, Khrushchev indicated that he did not want war in Laos. In late March and early April, Western analysts noted signals that they interpreted as evidence of Russian willingness to negotiate. Macmillan was eager to restrain Kennedy and by April 1 was persuaded that a conference could begin "if the Americans do not suddenly run amok."[27] Negotiations might have begun in April had not the highest American authorities been preoccupied with plans for the Bay of Pigs operation. Nonetheless, plans for a conference in Geneva moved ahead and a cease-fire in Laos was announced May 3. The meeting opened on the 16th.

As late as April 29 a major intervention in Laos by American forces was given careful consideration by Rusk, McNamara, Bundy, Robert Kennedy and the Joint Chiefs. Had the Chiefs not pressed for freedom to use nuclear weapons and to attack China, combat forces might have been introduced in Laos on the eve of the conference. Rusk, who dominated the discussion, opposed execution of contingency plans for large-scale operations, denying that the southward deployment of Chinese bombers constituted a major change in the situation in Southeast Asia. On the other hand, he expressed profound concern over the impact on other nations if the United States did not defend Laos. He referred to fears expressed to him by a Thai diplomat that Thailand was like a "golden bell" that had to be defended from the outside, as for example in Laos, and remarked that he "would not give a cent for what the Persians would think of us if we did not defend Laos."[28]

Each of Rusk's suggestions, each of his questions, pointed to the same concern. Could American troops secure an airfield? Could

Laos be held from the 17th parallel to the Mekong? He suggested putting American and Thai forces into Vientiane together, evacuating them by helicopter if they could not hold. "Even if they were defeated they would be defeated together and this would be better than sitting back and doing nothing." Rusk thought the United Nations could be brought in if a cease-fire was not agreed upon quickly. Throughout the discussion, Rusk was eager for limited military action to demonstrate the commitment to defend the victim—and hopeful of at least symbolic collective action to uphold the principle of collective security. The JCS shared his concern for holding as much of Southeast Asia as possible, but batted back each of his ideas for limited action, more fearful than Rusk of escalation. The stalemate in Washington held until the cease-fire was announced May 3.

The opening of the conference in Geneva was delayed for several days while Rusk and Gromyko argued about who would represent Laos. Rusk refused to accept the Soviet demand that representatives of the Pathet Lao be seated—an outrageous position given Pathet Lao superiority on the battlefield. The argument was not, of course, procedural. Rusk wanted only representatives of the pro-Western regime and of Souvanna Phouma's neutralists involved in the discussions. Had he been successful, the chances of a center-right government emerging in Laos would have been greatly enhanced. Given opposition in Congress and on the American Right to a coalition government including Communists, the administration may have considered opposition to Pathet Lao participation a necessary opening position. On May 14, Rusk rejected a Soviet-British compromise that would have let representatives of all three Laotian factions attend as individuals, not delegations. He was willing to let the Pathet Lao representatives attend as observers or consultants, but not as equals of the Lao government. The next day Rusk accepted the Anglo-Soviet arrangement. The President, who was eager to get on with the discussions of substance, was generally less patient with negotiating postures than Rusk—or Harriman, who thought too much had been yielded. [29]

Rusk remained in Geneva to offer the opening presentation for the United States. He refuted Chinese charges that the United States threatened the peace of Southeast Asia, arguing that the only threat there and elsewhere in the world came from those who preached peaceful coexistence while trying to impose their political system on others, *e.g.*, the Communists. But the heart of Rusk's statement was his call for a neutral Laos. Disagreements between the United States and the People's Republic of China would not be resolved at Geneva, but they might agree to spare the people of Laos from the consequences of differences between others over larger issues: "it is their country and not an appropriate target for ambitions with which they need not be involved."[30] At the very least in Laos, where pro-Western forces were faring poorly, the United States desired to separate local problems from the central confrontation with the Soviet Union. It became apparent that Khrushchev, too, was prepared to avoid complication in an area of peripheral interest to the Russians while he directed his energy toward Berlin and the strategic balance between the superpowers.

Rusk returned to Washington and left the negotiation to Harriman. Kennedy, Rusk, and Harriman agreed that they could accept a neutralist regime under Souvanna Phouma, provided its nonalignment would be accepted by the Communists. In the fourteen months of negotiation and cease-fire violation that followed, Rusk and Harriman were persuaded that the Russians were acting in good faith. But just as the United States had great difficulty bringing General Phoumi and the Lao Right into line, so the Russians seemed unable to control the Pathet Lao or the North Vietnamese who appeared to direct Pathet Lao operations. Rusk concluded that Moscow's influence with Hanoi had declined and came to see Peking as the deus ex machina of Communist aggression in Southeast Asia. A special CIA report late in June confirmed Rusk's estimate of the extent of Russian and Chinese involvement in Laos.[31]

Of all the subordinates to whom Rusk tried to delegate responsibility, Harriman proved the man most eager and, perhaps, most able to exercise it. Rusk met frequently with the task force on Laos set up in Washington to support Harriman. He and McNamara met frequently with Kennedy and Bundy to discuss Laos, but it was Harriman who conducted the negotiation almost entirely on his own, more often than not reporting directly to the President. When the agreements were finally signed, in July, 1962, Rusk was greatly pleased with Harriman's work. Laos was to be neutral, under the leadership of Souvanna Phouma. A cease-fire would be supervised by the International Control Commission established in 1954. All foreign troops were to be withdrawn and Laos was not to be used as a sanctuary for interference in the internal affairs of other countries—a provision designed to end North Vietnamese infiltration through Laos into South Vietnam. The North Vietnamese never withdrew all of their forces, nor did they cease using infiltration routes in Laos, but for about two years their level of involvement in Laos was deemed tolerable. In Kennedy's lifetime, Laos did not become a matter of deep concern again.

6

The three early crises of 1961—Cuba, the Congo, and Laos— were inherited and avoidable. They derived, at least in part, from American interference in the internal affairs of other peoples in the name of anti-Communism. The Eisenhower Administration had prepared plans and trained forces to overthrow Castro, was implicated in efforts to eliminate Lumumba, and was directly responsible for the creation of a Rightist, pro-Western regime in Laos. Of the three, the crisis in Cuba was most escapable. Kennedy had only to say no to the CIA. With all that might be said about plans gaining their own momentum, Kennedy had the power to cancel the operation, and the good sense afterward to accept with grace the responsibility for carrying it out that neither he nor his administration could shirk. In both the Congo and Laos, local conditions and blunders by the Eisenhower Administration left Kennedy and his advisers less leeway and they were fortunate to obtain tolerable results.

The Kennedy Administration was much like its predecessor in its determination to contain Communism and in its apprehension about Communist intentions. In Cuba the principal difference between the two administrations was the reduction of American military support for the exiles. In Laos, Kennedy settled for a neutralist regime out of necessity, though it would be fair to argue that men like Rusk, Bowles and Stevenson had long maintained that independent, neutralist regimes were all that the United States needed in the Third World. In the Congo, determined opposition to Tshombe's compradore regime in Katanga differentiated Kennedy's policy from that of Eisenhower—although the basic aim of containing the Left was unchanged. The difference in means, when not dictated by circumstances, as in Laos, reflected the greater confidence in democratic centrism that seemed to distinguish Democrats from Republicans in the common task of checking the expansion of Communism. But the three crises were discrete, as were the responses, and allowed for little generalization.

The three crises were more revealing of Rusk's modus operandi. In the Cuban situation, his anti-Communism was tempered by his commitment to other traditional American principles. Rusk's patriotism was based on his conviction of American liberal exceptionalism. He was leery of having his country involved in a bad cause and opposed using American military power against tiny Cuba. He was uncomfortable about interfering in the internal affairs of another people. And perhaps most of all, he cared deeply about the reputation of the United States, about the effect American actions might have on world public opinion. Obviously, he yielded on the most important point, acquiescing in the decision to launch the attack. He was rigid only in his insistence on steps to absolve the United States from complicity.

The crisis in the Congo demonstrated his continued faith in and hope for the United Nations, particularly in its use of an international armed force to keep the peace. At the end of this particular phase of the crisis, he was more skeptical about the efficacy of such forces than he had been in the 1940s, but the fervor of his earlier commitment carried him through 1961. The Congo crisis also revealed that Rusk, unlike the Atlanticists, was willing to antagonize NATO allies in order to obtain justice for and to seek friends among Third World countries.

Rusk's speech at the SEATO meeting in March, 1961, was particularly revealing and portentous. The Wilsonian commitment to aid weak countries gave an edge to his words. He hoped the UN would help, as Wilson had hoped the League would do what the United States could not do alone. He hoped SEATO might help. But if no one else would help Laos, this tiny victim of Communist aggression, then the Yanks were coming. Proudly, even defiantly, he insisted that the Truman Doctrine protected Asians as well as Europeans, that the United States would protect the free people of Laos. Here was Rusk the universalist linking himself in his own mind with Marshall as against the narrower vision of men like Acheson and Herter.

In the Laotian situation, Rusk's rhetoric may have been hyperbolic, as in his "Slavic Manchukuo" speech—and it was surely designed as a warning to the Communists as well as a stimulant to his more immediate audience in Bangkok. But unlike the "Slavic Manchukuo" speech, Rusk's theme in March, 1961, was not contrary to anything he was saying or writing privately. Indeed, the words convey the essence of his thought on America's role in world affairs. Eisenhower's responsibility for the danger to the people of Laos was easily brushed aside in face of what might be the last opportunity to save them from Communist imperialism.

What emerge clearly in these early tests are Rusk's commitment to the protection of the weak everywhere and his conviction that in the 1960s Communism presented the gravest danger to the aspirations of all people. He had concluded that the United States had a responsibility to counter Communist imperialism wherever possible, to preserve the opportunity of all free peoples to choose democracy. It was a bold vision for so quiet and modest a man. That so heavenly a vision might bring hell on earth was beyond his comprehension.

CHAPTER EIGHT

The Central Confrontation: Kennedy vs. Khrushchev

Wherever the Cold War might be found at a given moment, the principal participants were the Soviet Union and the United States. On January 6, 1961, Khrushchev provided the American President-elect and his advisers with a foreshadowing of what the future might bring. Addressing a Communist Party meeting in Moscow, Khrushchev reiterated his commitment to peaceful co-existence with the West, but stressed one exception: wars of national liberation. Such wars were deemed just wars, worthy of Soviet support. To the faithful, he also boasted of economic and technological progress and predicted victory for "socialism."

Kennedy did not interpret Khrushchev's speech as a convention-style rabble-rouser. He directed all of his advisers to read it and they dared not ignore the Russian stress on guerrilla warfare and subversion in the Third World. Llewellyn Thompson, American ambassador to Moscow, was troubled. In a cable sent on the eve of Kennedy's inauguration, he described Khrushchev's words as a "Declaration of Cold War"—"if taken literally." Two other Soviet experts for whom Kennedy had high regard, Kennan and Bohlen, agreed that Khrushchev should be called to account for the incompatibility of his persistent calls for peace and what Bohlen saw as the violent hostility of the January 6 speech. Kennedy and Rusk took the Soviet leader's words as an indication of renewed Russian commitment to world revolution. Beginning with his inaugural, Kennedy tried to warn the Russians of American determination. In the months that followed, Rusk rarely missed an opportunity to signal to the Russians the willingness of Americans to accept the new challenge.[1]

However much the Russians may have hoped to gain from stirring the pot in distant places, Rusk was convinced that Germany remained their highest priority. On January 28 he warned Kennedy that Khrushchev's truculence would mean renewed Soviet pressure on Berlin. He was outraged by a congratulatory cable from the East German Communist leader, Walter Ulbricht, to Kennedy. Advising Kennedy not to respond, Rusk described the cable as "an act of extreme impertinence." He described Ulbricht's German Democratic Republic as "an artificial regime created by Soviet fiat and imposed upon the seventeen million people of East Germany." It had never been legitimized by any democratic process and was merely an instrument of Soviet control.[2]

In his campaign speeches Kennedy had talked of negotiations with the Russians to resolve some of the questions that had led to recurring crises over Berlin. After his inaugural he instructed Thompson to notify Khrushchev that the new administration would need some time to prepare its position.[3] Rusk, however, seemed not at all eager to initiate discussions. Nor did he appear to believe that the affairs of Berlin or the larger question of German reunification were negotiable. But Khrushchev was not to be denied.

On February 17, just a few days after the West German foreign minister met with Rusk to express his government's fears about the resoluteness of the Kennedy Administration, the Russians informed Bonn that the time had come to end the anomalous condition of Berlin as an occupied city. West Berlin should become a "free city." The Russians were prepared to discuss West German interests in Berlin, but warned that if agreement on a peace treaty could not be reached, they would sign a separate pact with East Germany. In the weeks that followed, Khrushchev found a variety of ways to intensify the pressure. The Congo, Cuba, and Laos preoccupied Kennedy, Rusk, Bundy and other top advisers for several months and Rusk argued against a summit meeting between the American and Soviet leaders. In mid-May, however, Kennedy decided that the time had come to meet his adversary, to take the measure of the man, to determine the prospects for the future. They scheduled a meeting for early June, in Vienna.

Khrushchev's reasons for renewing the crisis on Berlin are by no means clear. Soviet fear of West German "revanchism" seemed genuine, as did Khrushchev's desire for Western recognition of East Germany and the Oder-Neisse boundary separating it from Poland. Acceptance of a divided Germany by the West was the single most important step toward stability in Central Europe and toward confirming Russian gains during and immediately after World War II. Removal of Western forces from Berlin would eliminate an embarrassment to the Soviet Union and a threat to the stability of Ulbricht's regime, from which a steady flow of refugees fled into West Berlin. Khrushchev also appears to have been seeking a Western retreat that would indicate to the world a shift in the balance of power toward the Soviet Union. In the campaign of 1960, Kennedy and his supporters had been sharply critical of Eisenhower for allowing a "missile gap" and they appeared to believe that strategic superiority had been lost to the Russians. If so, they would understand that Khrushchev was now claiming the rewards of superiority.

Other possibilities exist. Khrushchev doubtless wanted to test the new American leadership. There is evidence that his own leadership was being challenged and that he may have been forced toward confrontation with the United States when he would have preferred to work on the perennial problems of Soviet agriculture. But, as he phrased things in his inimitable fashion, "Berlin is the testicles of the West. Everytime I give them a yank they holler." It was clear that he was reaching all along, but the first yank did not come until he and Kennedy met in Vienna.[4]

Kennedy went to Vienna prepared to discuss Berlin, but really primed to demonstrate his skill and determination to resist what he saw as Soviet expansionism in Laos or through other wars of national liberation. Khrushchev agreed that Laos should be neutral, but not without lecturing Kennedy on the inevitability of victory for the Pathet Lao. He criticized Kennedy's desire to separate the Third World from the Soviet-American confrontation as an attempt to deny Moscow the fruits of impending victory. Berlin, however, was unquestionably Khrushchev's primary concern. He was most threatening in his remarks about Germany and he presented Kennedy with an aide-memoire setting a December, 1961, deadline for agreement on a peace treaty, after which the Russians would proceed unilaterally. If the West interfered, there would be war. Kennedy countered with a warning that the United States would fight to maintain access routes to Berlin, but without apparent effect.

After the Vienna meeting Rusk stopped off in Paris to brief the NATO ministers. He suggested that the seriousness of the Soviet threat might be determined by whether Khrushchev would risk prestige by publicizing his demands. On June 10 the Russians published the aide-memoire, leaving no apparent room for maneuver. Soviet demands were not negotiable.[5]

Kennedy's advisers had been preparing contingency plans since entering office and in June they applied themselves to the specifics of Khrushchev's position. Acheson played a central role in the earlier planning and in the debate within the administration on how to respond. He advised against negotiation on the ground that the Western position in Berlin and on Germany was not negotiable. The West German government feared negotiation and adamantly opposed recognition of the East German government, de facto or de jure. The power of NATO depended on the support of West Germany and it was important not to allow the Russians to drive a wedge between Bonn and Washington. Acheson advised mobilization of American forces and negotiation with NATO to demonstrate the West's readiness for war.

Kennedy was not pleased with the kind of response Acheson and West German chancellor Konrad Adenauer considered suitable. Despite the German political situation, which precluded advocacy of a divided Germany, Kennedy found a de facto two Germanies policy perfectly sensible. Although determined to yield nothing of substance, he was not persuaded that the kind of brinksmanship inherent in Acheson's position was necessary. Was it necessary to appear so intransigent? Wasn't there some kind of language that could be used that would keep both Adenauer and Khrushchev happy? If there were no negotiation, wasn't there grave risk of an explosion over Berlin?

There were others among Kennedy's advisers who urged negotiation. None of these men favored concessions to the Russians, but they tended to view Soviet motives differently than did Acheson.

Bohlen and Stevenson were reputedly among those who thought Khrushchev might be acting defensively to avoid the collapse of East Germany and the consequent danger to the Soviet position in Eastern Europe. They encouraged Kennedy to avoid a confrontation and to signal a willingness to reduce some of the irritants of the situation in Berlin without yielding basic Western rights.

Rusk, supported by McNamara and Henry Kissinger, an outside consultant, opposed Acheson's position as bellicose, provocative. He advocated negotiation, but was much closer to Acheson than to the views attributed to Bohlen and Stevenson. He did not think the Berlin question could be solved. He saw nothing that the West might yield. Rusk wanted to talk the question to death, to drag out old arguments, to sit with the Russians and be as repetitive in maintaining the American position as the Russians were in their demands. Talking might ease the tension and in the meantime the United States would strengthen its capacity to fight, if necessary, demonstrating its determination to resist. Rusk also spoke against American unilateralism. Despite Bundy's skepticism he persuaded Kennedy to agree to a meeting of American, British, German and French foreign ministers in New York at the opening of the General Assembly session. Characteristically, he urged UN involvement.[6]

Although Rusk's views were clear enough, his position and the deliberate speed with which the State Department labored over a reply to the Soviet aide-memoire frustrated Kennedy. A month passed without a negotiating position being developed by the Department and Kennedy could not understand the delay. Working with Bundy and Sorensen, he could prepare a statement in a matter of days, perhaps even hours. Why in hell was the bureaucracy so constipated? At times Kennedy's irritation focused on Rusk.

The Department's deliberateness doubtless reflected bureaucratic inertia, but the failure to deliver a speedy answer to the President had two more important reasons. First, Rusk was determined not to act unilaterally, but to devise a negotiating position that would have a reasonable chance of acceptance by France, Britain and Germany—a task of extraordinary complexity given British eagerness to negotiate, France's refusal to negotiate and Germany's intense apprehension. In addition, Rusk and his aides were aware that their Soviet counterparts would examine the

American reply microscopically in search of the slightest change in nuance over earlier American positions on Berlin, seeking the slightest crack in which to drive a wedge between the United States and its allies, seeking any sign of softness. Past statements and minutes of previous discussions had to be reviewed carefully, desk officers had to probe—and this all took time. Perhaps the process was too slow, but some analysts have subsequently concluded that Kennedy in this instance and in others put too high a premium on quickness to the detriment of wisdom.[7]

The second reason for Rusk's failure to provide Kennedy with a "good clear negotiating position" was that Rusk did not believe one existed. He wanted to negotiate as a means of "taking the fever" out of the situation, but believed it would be a mistake to lead the Russians to expect that the United States was prepared to give anything away. He had long experience with Soviet whittling tactics and preferred to begin with the Western position of 1959. Offer the Russians the reunification of Berlin and Germany on the basis of free elections. The Russians would reject this, of course, Rusk and Gromyko would argue endlessly, the United States would remain firm, the Russians would give up until next time—and nothing would happen. Rusk thought the President too eager to negotiate, too optimistic about accomplishing something. So he stalled.[8]

With a speech he delivered July 25, Kennedy heightened the tension enormously. He discussed Berlin in a global context, seeking to explain its importance to the American people, to explain why he was prepared to risk war. He explicitly stated his perception of America's vital interests in Berlin, accepting the possibility that the Russians would deem all unmentioned issues as points on which the United States would yield to pressure. The American military presence in West Berlin was not negotiable; nor was access for Americans to the city. The security of West Berlin would be guaranteed by the United States. Access between East and West Berlin, the importance of which had been argued among his advisers, was not included in his list. Finally, the President announced a partial mobilization of reserves and an increase in the draft. American conventional forces would be augmented and the Russians were warned against miscalculating the determination of the United States. Kennedy formulated the American position unilaterally, very likely contrary to Rusk's judgment. Macmillan clearly approved. De Gaulle and Adenauer were as clearly troubled. The next step would be Khrushchev's.

Public statements by Kennedy and Khrushchev subsequent to their meeting in Vienna allowed for little complacency in Europe or the United States. The Russians had created a crisis and the Americans showed no inclination to back away. In Berlin the flow of refugees from East to West became a torrent as thousands seized what they thought might be their last chance to escape Communist rule. In July alone, 30,000 East Germans fled to the Western sector of Berlin. The Ulbricht regime appeared to be in danger of imminent collapse. Rumor of intensive civil defense preparations came out of Moscow and Kennedy asked Congress for funds for fall-out shelters. All over the United States fall-out shelters were designated, built and stocked. If it was nuclear war the Russians wanted, America would be ready.

On July 27, Khrushchev talked with McCloy and left him with no doubt of his determination to avoid war. But the danger may have been greater than Khrushchev or any Americans realized at the time. Kennedy was not the only bloc leader with unruly allies—or the only superpower leader with powerful internal opposition to his policies. From Peking came constant pressure for a more aggressive policy toward the West and Ulbricht was frantic in pursuit of ends which were not necessarily congruent with those of the Soviet Union. Within the Kremlin, opponents of peaceful coexistence and of Khrushchev's control of the Soviet government may have driven him farther toward the precipice than he had intended to go. Ulbricht pressed ceaselessly for permission to cut off the flow of refugees out of East Germany. As the rate increased sharply in August, permission was granted.

On August 12, 4,000 East Germans crossed over into West Berlin. On August 13, the East German police began to erect barriers cutting off West Berlin from the East. It was a dangerous step that might provoke Western action, but the danger to the East German regime was too great for further delay. Moreover, there were signs that the United States might not respond. Kennedy had said nothing about movement between East and West Berlin. The *New York Times* had reported that Rusk was worried about the explosive situation in East Germany. The barriers, just barbed wire at first, infringed upon none of those interests Kennedy had deemed vital. Unchallenged, the barriers would ease the pressure on East Germany and might defuse the entire crisis.[9]

The Soviet gamble worked. Rusk protested, but the United States did not launch its forces against the barricades. In despair, Germans watched the barricades turn into the Wall while all that came out of Washington were words and, some claimed, an audible sigh of relief. The immediacy of the crisis retreated as the United States shrank from the risk and onus of firing the first shot. To smash the barriers required the United States to take the offensive in a situation in which the stakes were very high for the Soviet Union. As Rusk explained to a critic a month later, he had no doubt that if an attempt was made to knock down the Wall, the Russians would come out shooting.[10]

Khrushchev had achieved his minimum goal. The drain on East Germany had halted. To Kennedy and those of his advisers who looked to an eventual two Germanies, that was a small price to pay if further danger could be averted. Rusk was more sympathetic to West German aspirations and perhaps more profoundly moved by a sense of what the barriers might mean to Germans who had hoped to escape from Ulbricht's Stalinism. When the Wall went up, Bundy and Kennedy thought the time had come to go ahead with negotiations. Rusk opposed, ostensibly on the grounds that negotiations should be conducted at the four-power ministerial level, including the British and the French. It is also possible that he thought that in building the Wall the Russians had done all they dared do, and that it was inadvisable to negotiate while the mortar was still wet on so morally repugnant an act. He consistently resisted negotiating under threat or as an apparent reward for wrongdoing. As always, Kennedy, however, was impatient. Under instructions from his President, Rusk eventually persuaded the British, French and Germans to allow him to meet with the Russians—not to negotiate but to determine whether a basis for negotiations existed.[11]

In the latter part of August the Russians stepped up their pressures on West Berlin, perhaps because the mild American response to the Wall strengthened that faction in the Kremlin in favor of a more aggressive policy. More threatening was the sudden

Soviet announcement on August 30, that the Russians would resume nuclear testing. But it was also in late August that Kennedy
received new intelligence estimates that persuaded him that Soviet
claims to strategic superiority were false, that the United States
retained the upper hand. In addition, General Lucius D. Clay,
symbol of an earlier stand in defense of Berlin, took charge there
and vigorously, even provocatively, repelled further East German
and Soviet attempts to encroach on Western rights.

Early in September, in a maneuver interpreted as an indication
that Khrushchev was trying to circumvent his own war party, the
Russian leader sent word to Kennedy of his desire to open up a
secret "back-channel" correspondence with the American
President. It was obvious that his stated reason, to by-pass Rusk,
tool of the Rockefellers, was not genuine, for he quickly agreed to
Kennedy's stipulation that Rusk be shown all letters. The ensuing
correspondence eased some of the tensions and Khrushchev attempted further to reassure the Americans in conversation with
McCloy and in instructions to the Russian delegates to the disarmament talks. On September 20, Rusk appeared before the Senate
Foreign Relations Committee to advise that he would begin discussions with Gromyko on the following day.[12]

Rusk was dubious about reaching any agreement with the Russians through the talks. He thought it was clear that Khrushchev had
not modified his demands and that the list of three vital Allied
interests formulated by Rusk and his Berlin Task Force would be
unacceptable to the Soviet leader. NATO was unanimous in insisting on continuation of a Western presence in West Berlin, on
physical access to the city, and on its viability. He left no doubt
among the Senators present that there was little leeway for negotiations: "Our basic position is that these fellows ought to leave us
alone and leave our rights alone." Fulbright, recognizing the administration's stress on access to the city, asked if a Khrushchev
guarantee of free access would circumvent the problem of East
German control of access routes. Rusk conceded such a guarantee
would be important, but went on to express doubt of the value of a
Russian promise. He did perk up, however, when Fulbright offered
suggestions for UN-supervised access to West Berlin.[13]

Rusk and Gromyko met three times in late September. Gromyko

indicated Soviet awareness of the danger inherent in the confrontation and informed Rusk that his government was prepared to delay
its deadline on an agreement if the Americans were serious about
negotiating. A little more of the pressure was relieved. Rusk focused
his position on access to West Berlin, calling for four-power guarantees of Western access. To assure East German compliance without
granting recognition to Ulbricht's government, Rusk proposed that
the German Democratic Republic adhere to the four-power agreement in a separate agreement with the Soviet Union. He suggested
that specific arrangements for civilian access from West Germany be
determined by officials of East and West Germany and guaranteed
by the Americans, British, French, and Russians. As an incentive,
Rusk offered the possibility of arms limitation in Central Europe, a
subject dear to Russian hearts. The talks were continued in October. [14]

Khrushchev unquestionably found enough in Rusk's proposals to
justify to his comrades the withdrawal of his deadline for a German
peace treaty. The French and Germans, however, were not at all
pleased. De Gaulle utterly opposed negotiation as implying a loss of
nerve. Adenauer thought he recognized a weakening American
resolve and was easily persuaded that Rusk and Kennedy were
insensitive to West German interests. Kissinger was apparently one
of those who spread rumors that Rusk was weak and would compromise to the point of producing something akin to the Munich
settlement. Arms limitation in Central Europe was quickly vetoed
by Paris and Bonn. When Khrushchev, seeking a way out of the
crisis, expressed satisfaction with the seriousness of the initial
American position, not only Bonn and Paris but Americans suspicious of Rusk's tenacity feared appeasement. After all, Adolf A.
Berle noted in his diary, Rusk had been afraid to take chances on the
Bay of Pigs. [15]

Kennedy, however, was highly pleased by Rusk's performance. [16]
He had, of course, approved the negotiating position and was
satisfied that Rusk had conveyed the administration's convictions
and resolve. He was coming to appreciate Rusk's skill as a negotiator
and the reasons for Rusk's caution in developing the American
position. If agreement could be reached on American terms, the
administration would win an impressive victory. If, as seemed

assured, the crisis was over without agreement, the United States was quite content with the status quo.

Khrushchev's statement withdrawing the deadline for a peace treaty came on October 17, the opening day of the Twenty-second Communist Party Congress. On October 21, Roswell Gilpatric, Deputy Secretary of Defense, delivered an address warning the Soviet Union that the United States could absorb everything with which the Russians could strike and be able to devastate its enemies in retaliation. Gilpatric was unusually specific in enumerating American strategic weapons. On the next day Rusk indicated that he had cleared Gilpatric's speech and he reasserted its substance. On this occasion, Khrushchev, sometimes enraged by what he perceived as American threats, did not respond in kind. On October 26, however, there was an ominous confrontation between American and Soviet tanks across a checkpoint between East and West Berlin. General Clay had ordered the American tanks into position to prevent further "salami tactics" by East German police. Ulbricht called for help and the local Soviet military commander sent his armor rumbling forward. But suddenly, on the 27th, the Soviet tanks withdrew.

Gilpatric and Rusk were presumably attempting to advise the Russians—*and* the French and Germans—that the American willingness to negotiate did not derive from fear, that the panic about the "missile gap" had ended. Khrushchev continued to stress the seriousness of the American negotiating position, and the tank confrontation, as dangerous as it was, appears to have been the work of local commanders, Russians as well as American. One historian has argued persuasively that American resistance and assertiveness helped Khrushchev against the more violently anti-Western opposition at the party Congress; that the movement of Soviet tanks to the checkpoint had been arranged by Khrushchev's opponents at the Congress in collusion with Ulbricht—and that their removal signaled a partial victory for Khrushchev and his interest in peaceful accommodation with the West. [17]

Friction in and about Berlin continued, but the aura of crisis was fast disappearing. In January, 1962, Ambassador Thompson began a series of talks with Gromyko that continued into March. He continued to press for Soviet guarantees of Western access to West Berlin, indicating a willingness to accept an international control authority in which East Germany might participate—without recognition by the United States. Gromyko showed no interest and in February the Russians began to harass Western military and civilian flights into Berlin—yet the Russians continued to talk even as they tried to increase the pressure and the West resisted.

In late February, Rusk announced he would head the American delegation to the Eighteen Nation Disarmament Conference at Geneva. Two weeks later the Russians announced that Gromyko would be there. Rusk did not wish to negotiate with Gromyko about Berlin. As always he believed it was a mistake to negotiate under the gun. Soviet harassment of the air corridors to West Berlin should cease first. Once again Kennedy was eager to proceed and Rusk obeyed orders. He and Gromyko met almost daily for two weeks, March 11-27. Although no agreement was reached, Rusk was pleased with the negotiations. Although he had conceded nothing, Gromyko remained agreeable. The Soviet foreign minister repeated the Kremlin's formulae ad nauseam, pressing for Western concessions. When it was time for Rusk to return to Washington, Gromyko expressed the desire that negotiations continue in Washington between Rusk and the new Soviet ambassador, Anatoly Dobrynin.[18]

Shortly after his return to the United States, Rusk held a top-secret briefing for the Foreign Relations Committee. He explained that he and Gromyko had gotten nowhere on the substance of the Berlin question, but he was obviously content with the results of the talks. The Russians had shown no inclination to heat matters up and create a new crisis. They were also eager not to record a diplomatic impasse. Rusk was encouraged by their willingness to talk. He had resisted pressure to come up with new Western positions, without anything new from the Russians. "But we kept at it. I think perhaps our job is to stay with it." He was obviously pleased with himself for being as repetitive as Gromyko, perhaps wearing Gromyko down this time.[19]

Fulbright asked Rusk why the Russians seemed reluctant to press for a showdown and wondered if problems with China might be relevant. Rusk thought the prospects of a Sino-Soviet split, if they seemed serious to Moscow, might indeed induce caution. There was also the possibility that the quarrel might induce the Russians to be more aggressive, to prove the superiority of their approach to the Chinese.[20]

Rusk had another theory that precluded optimism about the ultimate outcome of the Berlin question. He suggested that the Russians might have decided on a crash program to redress the strategic imbalance and might want to delay a showdown until this program was completed. He noted intelligence reports that the Russians were undertaking a massive effort in missiles. What would they do if they achieved parity? Or superiority?[21]

If Rusk or Kennedy had any expectation of Soviet concessions leading to an agreement during the talks with Dobrynin—and Rusk did not—they were doomed to disappointment. From mid-April to the end of May, Rusk and the Soviet ambassador discussed their respective positions, without progress. On the sidelines Adenauer had already done what he could to preclude success, including a public prediction of failure. Once the Russians determined that the United States would not be persuaded under any circumstances to remove its forces from West Berlin, they appeared to have lost interest and the whole question of Berlin seemed to fade away.

In fact the Berlin question, caught up as it was in the Sino-Soviet debate about tactics appropriate to hasten the world-wide victory of socialism and the related policy debate within the Soviet leadership, could not disappear. It could not be resolved before the Soviet leadership could agree as to method. In retrospect it seems clear that Rusk's hypothesis about the Russians delaying until completion of their missile program was very close to the mark. Khrushchev had apparently been persuaded to make one more try to pull at the West's testicles, but under more propitious circumstances—with the United States in the shadow of Soviet missiles in Cuba.

Reflecting on the situation in July, Rusk told Cyrus Sulzberger of the *New York Times* that he thought Khrushchev greatly worried by the unpopularity, the internal weakness of the Ulbricht regime in Germany. The Russians feared and hated the Germans, and were intensely apprehensive about the possibility of nuclear weapons in German hands. He argued, however, that Russian pressure on Berlin was counterproductive. Despite the fact that he and Kennedy had been very rough with Bonn in the spring, Rusk gave no indication of a willingness to modify the status quo in Germany in a direction that might ease Soviet fears. He was not unaware that a rapprochement between the two Germanies, acceptance of the long-term division of Germany, was the most promising answer. But he knew that Adenauer was unalterably opposed and could not be forced in that direction by the United States. American pressure might shatter NATO. Certainly de Gaulle would be outraged and perhaps other allies would be deeply troubled by American willingness to bludgeon a friend on an interest so central to that friend's concerns. No, the Germans would have to move in that direction voluntarily and that would probably have to wait until the despicable Stalinist, Ulbricht, had been replaced by a less reprehensible figure—and until Adenauer had passed from the scene. Rusk's task was to contain the crisis and to move back from confrontation until a new and, with luck, a more enlightened German leadership appeared on both sides of the iron curtain. Miracles were not his forte.[22]

There was one weakness to his approach, of which he was well aware—and he knew it might prove fatal. The Russians might not wait and the whole damn world might get blown up. In October, as he viewed the United States and the Soviet Union "eyeball to eyeball," on the brink of a nuclear holocaust, he knew it was all out of his hands.

2

Andrei Gromyko, Foreign Minister of the Soviet Union, had requested and received an appointment to see President Kennedy on October 18. Martin Hillenbrand, director of the Berlin Task Force, drafted a memorandum, which Rusk signed, and some "talking points on Berlin" for the President's use. Hillenbrand did not expect Gromyko to say anything new about the Berlin question, although he thought it remotely possible that the Russians would propose a compromise of little substantive value that would assure a public relations triumph for a heads of state meeting. Other contributors to the memorandum and "talking points" mentioned Laos, disarmament, and problems relating to nuclear weapons.[23]

The "talking points on Berlin" succinctly summarized seventeen months of confrontation and negotiation:

Both sides have seemed to agree that these many talks have been useful, and that a certain amount of progress has been made in clarifying respective positions. No one could realistically claim, however, that much progress has been made toward an understanding on Berlin which would remove this problem as a point of possible confrontation in which a grave danger of war inheres.

Hillenbrand advised continuing the conversations through the ambassadors in Moscow and Washington. He and the expert on Soviet affairs advising him thought it important to warn Khrushchev that it was a "dangerous illusion" to suppose, as he had indicated on several recent occasions, that the West would not fight over Berlin. Hillenbrand was also eager to have the Russians led away from the assumption that the Berlin problem was "entirely" a matter of Adenauer preventing his allies from taking a more reasonable position. The leaders of the West were united on the issue.

What Hillenbrand did not mention—because he did not know—was that the United States and the Soviet Union were verging on nuclear war over Cuba. Three days before he prepared his memorandum for Kennedy, an American U-2 flight had returned with unmistakable evidence that the Russians were building missile sites in Cuba. For Rusk, who would meet Gromyko for dinner on the 17th, and for Kennedy, Berlin had slipped into the background.

The Kennedy Administration had not been inactive toward Cuba since recovering from the stupidity of the Bay of Pigs operation. Rusk had led a moderately successful diplomatic effort to isolate the Castro regime within the hemisphere. He had been persistent but much less successful in winning support from the NATO allies for American economic warfare against Cuba. The United States did not contemplate further attempts to use force to overthrow Castro, either directly or indirectly, through Cuban exiles. Nonetheless the American government was less vigorous than it might have been in suppressing piratical acts by exiles against Cuban vessels and territory. Kennedy and Rusk had both stated publicly that a Communist regime in Cuba was intolerable. Worst of all, the Kennedy Administration was experimenting with a variety of covert operations some of which were designed to humiliate Castro—and others to murder him.[24] Castro's intelligence services were apparently aware of some of these plots. It is clear that the Cuban government had reason for anxiety, reason to lean more heavily on the Soviet Union, reason enough to allow the Soviet Union to build missile sites directed against the United States.

Khrushchev's purpose in placing the missiles in Cuba is not clear. Cuban fears and an obligation to allay them were doubtless an element in his thought. The events of the previous year had demonstrated the difficulty of improving the Soviet position in the world, particularly in Europe, while the Americans were aware of their strategic superiority. The placement of intermediate-range missiles in Cuba was very likely seen as a short cut toward parity with the United States in strategic weapons. Once the missiles were operational, a new crisis on Berlin might be initiated—with very different results. When Kennedy and Gromyko talked on October 18, one of Gromyko's remarks seemed to hint at the possibility of trading Cuba for Berlin.[25] There seems little doubt that Khrushchev's priorities placed Berlin well ahead of Cuba or any other areas on the periphery of Soviet power. Finally, remarks by Kennedy that implied there were circumstances under which he might feel obliged to launch a preemptive strike against the Soviet Union, may have increased the internal pressures driving Khrushchev toward a more aggressive policy. It is clear, however, that while assuring Kennedy that offensive weapons would not be placed in Cuba, that nothing would be done to embarrass the administration during the Congressional election campaign, the Soviet Union rapidly proceeded to build missile facilities that appeared to some to pose a threat to the security of the United States.

On August 22, John McCone, Director of the Central Intelligence Agency, advised Kennedy, Rusk, and McNamara that he suspected the Russians of placing offensive missiles in Cuba. Rusk and McNamara, studying the evidence available to McCone, disagreed. They conceded that the Russians were aiding the Cubans with a defensive build-up, but were not persuaded that anything more threatening was occurring. Neither the Secretary of State nor the

Secretary of Defense expected the Russians to take the risk of installing offensive weapons in Cuba. The administration had left no doubt that such action would be intolerable. On September 19, the U.S. Intelligence Board concluded that the Russians would not put nuclear missiles in Cuba.

For Rusk the pattern of the Truman era debate over policy toward China seemed to be recurring. The Republican opposition this time had chosen the administration's Cuban policy as its target, insisting irresponsibly that something be done to get rid of the menace of Communism 90 miles off America's coast. Rusk and his colleagues would have liked nothing better, but the risks were too great, the price too high. Castro was simply not a great enough threat to challenge the Soviet commitment to him or to reap the anger of most of the rest of the world by invading Cuba. As the election approached, Republican pressures intensified and increasingly the administration defended itself by insisting that Cuba was not an offensive threat. In a televised interview with John Scali of ABC, taped on September 29, Rusk insisted that the military situation in Cuba revealed a "configuration of defensive capability."[26] As Republicans like Senator Kenneth Keating rumbled about Soviet missiles in Cuba, the administration, not wanting to find offensive weapons there, pressed into denying their existence, rejected the mounting evidence. As with Korea in 1950, an administration that was mistrustful of the Russians was pushed by more extreme domestic opponents into underestimating Khrushchev's willingness to gamble. The result of the miscalculation in 1962 was infinitely more frightening, but ultimately less costly.

On October 14, it was Bundy's turn to assure an American television audience that there was no evidence the Russians were preparing an offensive capability in Cuba. He saw no "present" likelihood that they would try to do so. On the same day a U-2 flight over western Cuba returned with unmistakable evidence of a ballistic missile complex under construction at San Cristobal. The films were processed on the 15th and by midnight Rusk, McNamara, Bundy—all the top policy makers except the President—were aware that the United States and more especially the Kennedy Administration faced catastrophe.

Briefed as he got out of bed the next morning, Kennedy called a meeting of an ad hoc group that came to be called the Executive Committee of the National Security Council. What were the Russians trying to do? What did it mean? How should the United States respond? The United States had contingency plans for such an occasion, plans that called for an invasion or an air strike. Preparations for both commenced but Rusk and Paul Nitze argued successfully that an immediate attack was too risky, that the American response would have to be reconsidered. Nitze, however, thought an air strike against the missile sites was the appropriate response and he was supported by Maxwell Taylor, newly appointed Chairman of the Joint Chiefs, and Douglas Dillon, Secretary of the Treasury. McNamara, Ball and Gilpatric led the opposition to an air strike. McNamara contended that Soviet missiles in Cuba meant little more than Soviet missiles in Russia. No matter where the Russians might launch their attack, the United States would retaliate and destroy the Soviet Union. When others argued that missiles in Cuba would reduce and might eliminate the American strategic advantage, McNamara was unperturbed. He contended that parity was inevitable and there might be an advantage to American security if the Russians achieved it sooner rather than later. Such blasphemy was heard, but little tolerated.

Rusk was convinced that the missiles had to be removed, but deliberately refrained from advocating a course of action. In the first meeting of the "ExCom" and in a number of those that followed, some of his colleagues were puzzled, even critical of his reserve, of his apparent unwillingness to commit himself. He did not lead the discussions, although McNamara, as always, deferred to him. Indeed, he did not attend all of the sessions, to the disgust of Acheson, himself present because Rusk sought his advice. In this crisis Rusk's favored mode of operation was evident. His task was not to be an advocate, but rather to probe all possibilities, listen to all arguments without becoming identified with any. When every point on the compass had been touched, he would be ready to advise the President. He worked throughout the crisis with task forces concentrating on particular aspects of the problem, especially with Llewellyn Thompson's group trying to estimate Khrushchev's likely responses. In the early stages of the crisis, while the administration was trying to work behind a facade of business-as-usual, he kept up with routine affairs. And he saw the President frequently. Although some of his colleagues and subordinates and later analysts have been critical of his role, no one has recorded any indication that the President was dissatisfied with Rusk's performance.[27]

After two days of discussion, even McNamara was persuaded that the President had to respond strongly. For domestic political reasons as well as for his image abroad, he had to demonstrate that the United States could not be deceived and challenged with impunity. The choices quickly reduced to an air strike against the missile sites or a blockade, with an air strike or invasion to be readied if the Russians did not respond appropriately to the blockade. Acheson was the most forceful advocate of an air strike, arguing that the risk of allowing the Russians to ready the missiles was greater than the risk of Russian retaliation if the United States attacked the sites. He was supported by Dillon, Nitze, McCone and the Joint Chiefs. When consulted by the President several days later, Senator Fulbright urged military action rather than a blockade. But McNamara, Robert Kennedy, and Sorensen resisted and fell back on the blockade.

On October 18, the day Kennedy was to meet with Gromyko, Rusk took the lead in a morning meeting. He spoke against a surprise attack on the missile sites, raising two objections. Khrushchev was reputed to be impulsive. How would he respond to an attack that would almost certainly kill the Russians at the sites? Wasn't the risk of nuclear war too great? He also warned that Latin American opinion in particular and world opinion in general would be hostile to the United States if it launched an attack without warning, without some effort to have the missiles removed by peaceful means. To some of the participants in the meeting, it seemed clear that Rusk had come down on the side of the advocates of a blockade.[28]

In the afternoon he appeared to reverse himself. Now he argued—or appeared to argue—that if the Russians had not stopped construction on the sites by October 23, the United States should notify its allies of its intent to use force. On the 24th, an air attack should be launched with a simultaneous public statement of what the United States was doing and why—and a warning to Khrushchev that counteraction would mean war.[29]

What had persuaded Rusk to change sides so abruptly? In fact, as was very likely clear to those who knew his approach, Rusk was not advocating either position. He had refined and was now posing both arguments to determine if there were any other considerations. It was approaching time for a decision—and action. In the evening, after meeting with Gromyko, the President would attend the "ExCom" session. Assuming Gromyko provided no surprises, the existing choices were clear.

Kennedy did not pick up Gromyko's hint of a possible accommodation of differences over Berlin and Cuba, but quickly regretted his decision to give no indication of undue concern. Bundy had thought it might be useful to confront Gromyko with the evidence and demand withdrawal, but Rusk and Thompson were opposed and reassured the President after Gromyko left. They argued that there was no point in saying anything to the Russians until Kennedy had decided what action he would take. To do otherwise was to yield the tactical advantage to the Russians.[30]

In the evening Kennedy's advisers reached a tentative agreement on the blockade, at least in part because the President was not persuaded that the air strike would suffice. He may indeed have feared that the military was attempting once again to draw him into an invasion of Cuba. Thompson warned against the possibility of Khrushchev's responding irrationally if Russians were killed. As the consensus on a blockade was approached, Rusk kept raising questions, still trying to be sure that all possibilities had been considered. His questions were answered to his and Kennedy's satisfaction. They would begin with a blockade. If the Russians did not stop construction of the sites and withdraw the missiles, an air attack would follow.[31]

On the 19th, the Joint Chiefs stressed their reservations about a blockade and Kennedy wavered. On the 20th, Rusk came forward to keep the consensus from breaking up. He read aloud a one-page memorandum he had written by hand, recommending the blockade. He included a list of the arguments for a blockade, stressing the fact that it, unlike the air strike, was reversible. The debate was over that Saturday morning. American forces would be moved into position and on Monday the Russians and the rest of the world would be informed of Kennedy's decision.[32]

One hour before Kennedy addressed a nationwide television
audience, Rusk met with Dobrynin to inform him of American
intentions. At 7:00 PM, Eastern Standard Time, the President told
the American people of the discovery of the missile sites, the
meaning of the sites to the United States, and of the action the
United States was taking. To Americans, to informed people
everywhere, there came an awareness that they hovered on the
edge of extinction. No one was more aware of the danger of nuclear
incineration than Rusk, as he spoke somberly to the ambassadors of
the neutral and nonaligned countries. He did not try to persuade
them of the righteousness of America's cause, merely telling them
personally of what had been found and what would have to be done
by the Soviet Union if war was to be avoided. With a sense that they
might never see each other again, each ambassador shook Rusk's
hand, more often than not murmuring a word or two of hope or
support.[33] Now the initiative had passed to Khrushchev. His choice
was war or surrender and the answer could come as swiftly as an
intercontinental ballistic missile.

The hours passed and Tuesday morning the sun rose as always. A
weary Rusk congratulated his undersecretary on the fact of survival.
That morning the Organization of American States met and to the
delighted surprise of Kennedy and his advisers voted 19-0 in favor of
the proposed American resolution calling for a "quarantine" on
offensive weapons to Cuba until the missiles were removed. Fourteen votes were needed and the administration had been apprehensive, but Rusk and Edwin M. Martin, his Assistant Secretary for
Latin American Affairs, found the OAS diplomats responsive. Martin's effort was brilliant, but he attributed his success to Latin
American attitudes toward Kennedy and to Rusk's great patience in
meeting after meeting with Latin American ambassadors and
foreign ministers over the years. On the same day Acheson flew to
Europe to brief NATO leaders, who quickly pledged their support.[34]

The initial Soviet response was verbal: a condemnation of American piracy and a denial of the offensive nature of the weapons they
were supplying Cuba. Construction on the missile sites continued
frantically and twenty-five Soviet ships continued to move toward
Cuba. On Wednesday, October 24, the Russians rejected the

American "quarantine" and that morning Soviet submarines joined the cargo ships steaming toward confrontation with blockading vessels of the United States Navy. Resisting civilian control, an eager Navy hierarchy moved its vessels outward, toward what was theoretically a more effective blockade but in fact left less time for Khrushchev to reconsider. On Cuba, Soviet ground forces, armed with tactical nuclear weapons, readied themselves for battle. World War III, the "last" world war, was approaching rapidly.

That evening, however, the Soviet vessels stopped on the high seas. By Thursday, October 25, it was clear that the ships believed to be carrying offensive weapons had turned back. A confrontation at sea was to be avoided. Americans watching as Walter Cronkite plotted the ship movements on the evening news sighed with relief. Kennedy and his advisers shared the relief, but they were also aware that the Russians were working frenetically to get their missiles in Cuba operational. As Nitze noted, the difference between war before the missiles could be used and war afterward would be millions of American lives. Rusk and the others agreed that the United States would have to attack before they were ready. The Russians were so informed. Intelligence estimates indicated that some of the sites might be completed by Sunday, October 28, conceivably by Saturday.[35]

Early Friday afternoon Aleksander Fomin, the top Soviet intelligence officer in the United States, suddenly contacted John Scali, ABC's State Department correspondent, to ask if his friends in the Department would consider offering a public pledge not to invade Cuba if the Russians dismantled the missile sites, removed the missiles, promised never to reintroduce them, and allowed UN inspection to verify the removal. Fomin left no doubt that his approach was urgent. Scali went immediately to Roger Hilsman, State's Director of Intelligence and Research, who passed the information to Rusk, Kennedy and others. Rusk remembered the unofficial exchange of views that had led to the cease-fire in Korea in 1951 and quickly recognized the potential in the Fomin-Scali exchange.[36]

Rusk called Scali to his office and handed him a piece of paper on which he had written:

I have reason to believe that the USG sees real possibilities and supposes that the representatives of the two governments in New York could work this matter out with U Thant and with each other. My impression is, however, that time is very urgent.

He asked Scali to give the message to Fomin and to tell him that it came from the "highest levels in the government of the United States." Scali was to say that time was very short, no more than two days.[37]

While Scali conveyed Rusk's message to Fomin, a long cable arrived from Khrushchev to Kennedy. The Soviet leader left no doubt that he understood the danger of the situation, that he desired to avoid conflict, and that he was prepared to negotiate. He did not, however, indicate his terms. Nonetheless, when Rusk put together Khrushchev's cable and the settlement outlined by Fomin, he concluded that the crisis was over, that the Russians were prepared to back off. Thompson reinforced this estimate of the situation. Rusk and Thompson apparently suspected that Khrushchev had been struggling with other Soviet leaders more eager to call the American "bluff" and had chosen a direct line to Kennedy and the Fomin approach as a way of circumventing obstructions. When he briefed reporters over the next few days Rusk urged them not to speak of a Soviet surrender lest they give sustenance to what might be a more aggressive faction in the Kremlin.[38]

Acheson did not share Rusk's optimism. He suspected the Russians of stalling until some of the missiles were operational. This fear was never far from the minds of Kennedy's other advisers. The President concluded that he would have to demand cessation of construction before negotiations might begin.

Saturday morning a new message from Khrushchev complicated matters. The Soviet leader now specified his terms for removal of the missiles in Cuba: removal of the American missiles threatening the Soviet Union from Turkey. Kennedy was outraged to learn the missiles he had ordered removed as an unnecessary provocation were still in place, but with the exception of McCloy and Stevenson, his advisers insisted there be no trade. Rusk and Ball argued that although the missiles were obsolete and would be removed shortly, a trade might have a damaging effect on American allies. They might fear that whenever the United States was threatened it would be willing to sacrifice the protection it offered its allies—just as de Gaulle claimed. Rusk suggested that the Turks be advised to reject Khrushchev's demand as irrelevant to a crisis over Cuba. Finally, Rusk again sent Scali to Fomin. Scali was directed to try to find out what the Russians were up to, to warn Fomin that the American leadership suspected a doublecross, that a trade for the missiles in Turkey was out of the question.[39]

Later in the day, Thompson and Robert Kennedy came up with the famed "Trollope ploy," the idea of responding to Khrushchev as if only the terms suggested by Fomin had been received—ignoring the reference to the missiles in Turkey.[40] At the same time the President, his brother, Rusk, and others decided that they would inform Dobrynin that although the trade proposed was unacceptable, the Russians could be assured that the American missiles were coming out. Their warheads were removed in the midst of the crisis. At Thompson's suggestion, the President sent his brother to speak to Dobrynin so that there could be no doubt that the message conveyed his personal commitment. Sunday morning it was all over. Khrushchev announced he had ordered the arms Americans described as offensive to be dismantled and returned to the Soviet Union.

There was no shortage of details to be worked out in the days, weeks, and months that followed. Castro never permitted UN supervision or verification and there were delays getting out the bombers and Soviet troops. But the gravest crisis of the Cold War had ended with a victory for mankind.

3

Rusk's performance during the Cuban missile crisis was far superior to the way in which he had functioned during the Bay of Pigs proceedings. In October, 1962, he worked extremely well with Kennedy. He reached out in all directions to collect ideas and information. He listened at some of the "ExCom" meetings, checked in with task forces examining particulars of the problem, and contacted a number of outsiders, oblivious to the crisis but possessed of expertise on some relevant matter—like the strategic importance of the Jupiters in Turkey. As the discussions developed at "ExCom," he scouted the alignment of forces within the administration, preparing to protect the President as he had not done in early 1961. He may have been less solicitous of the President's personal interests than Bundy, Sorensen, and Robert Kennedy, but because he was not part of the palace guard, he could play the role of the President's stalking horse most effectively. The others might be assumed to speak for the President. When Rusk spoke presidential deniability was more credible.

As the drama unfolded, there had been a consensus in favor of a strong response. Only McNamara demurred, but he was persuaded by Nitze, Rusk and perhaps by the combined weight of the other judgments. When discussion about action boiled down to two choices, blockade or air strike, and the debate became repetitive, Rusk interceded, summing up the arguments for each. When it became clear that Kennedy preferred the blockade and the Pentagon began to prepare a record of opposition, Rusk came forward again to force agreement—a role which he and not the President's men had to play. A year and a half earlier, Rusk had been ineffectual in preventing the Bay of Pigs operation, but in October, 1962, his was a virtuoso performance.

The Kennedy Administration's management of the missile crisis was impressive, successful, and generally viewed as its finest hour in foreign affairs. It should be noted, however, that the crisis may have been avoidable. First, there can no longer be any doubt that in addition to provocative statements about the need to eliminate the Castro regime, the administration was acting provocatively against Castro in particular and Cuba in general. Second, the build-up of American conventional forces, supplementing American strategic superiority, stimulated the arms race. In this context, Kennedy's apparent willingness to consider a preemptive strike against the Soviet Union may have generated unbearable pressure on Khrushchev for a major foreign policy success with which to contain Peking and the opposition at home.

The Kennedy Administration may also have risked nuclear war unnecessarily. A later analysis prepared within the administration suggested that Kennedy's advisers had exaggerated the risks of Khrushchev's starting a nuclear war.[41] It is not unreasonable, however, to consider the possibility that McNamara was right: that parity was inevitable and that the gap was merely being closed sooner rather than later; that Soviet missiles in Cuba were strategically tolerable. By making considerably less of the discovery of the missiles, by publicly accepting Soviet claims that they were defensive, and indicating no fear, the rest of the world might have been impressed by American confidence, rather than being appalled by American cowardice. The only clear and imminent danger in the missile crisis was to the political future of the Kennedy Administration.

However worthy these arguments may be, they are, nonetheless, hypothetical. For whatever reason, Khrushchev decided to place missiles in Cuba while attempting to assure Kennedy that he would do nothing of the sort. The evident deceit leaves little doubt that Khrushchev hoped to score a diplomatic and military coup against the United States. Kennedy and his advisers were persuaded that a strong response was necessary. Their plans were conceived carefully and executed with an appropriate balance of courage and caution.

In the immediate aftermath of the crisis, Rusk stressed the limits of the lesson learned. Fearful that Khrushchev's retreat in Cuba might be interpreted as evidence that the Russians would back down whenever the Americans expressed willingness to risk war, he insisted the Cuban model might not work elsewhere. He did not reveal the assurances about the Jupiters that Robert Kennedy had given Dobrynin—or that the missiles had been disarmed. Instead he noted that for the United States, an island 90 miles from its shores was the ideal place for a showdown. Elsewhere, as for example Berlin, the advantages of naval superiority and short supply lines would be lost—and the outcome might be very different.[42]

Gradually Rusk and countless others came to see the missile crisis as a watershed in Soviet-American relations. Thereafter the actions of both sides were dictated by greater prudence and a desire for detente. In the last year of Kennedy's life, much of the tension drained out of the confrontation. A Moscow-Washington "hot-line," permitting direct and immediate communication between the two leaders, was established and an agreement reached for a partial test-ban treaty, ending atmospheric testing by the two superpowers and easing, ever so slightly, the pressure of the arms race.

Neither in the Kennedy Administration nor in Khrushchev's Kremlin could a consensus be obtained for more steps toward detente. Further improvement of relations would depend upon the performance of each country in the last months of 1963 and on through the election campaign of 1964. Unanticipated in 1963, as matters drifted, was the fact that both Kennedy and Khrushchev would be gone from the scene by then—one murdered and the other brusquely pushed aside.

Soviet-American relations in the year following the missile crisis were uneven, a parody of Lenin's "two steps forward, one step back." Kennedy seemed exuberantly confident after the missile crisis. As the grimness of October faded, so did the gloomy prophecies that had characterized administration views of the world in 1961. The administration was prepared to believe Khrushchev's insistence that he wanted to concentrate on Russia's agricultural problems, and in October, 1963, arranged to sell him wheat. Khrushchev subsequently announced a reduction in Soviet military spending, but harassments in and around Berlin recurred sporadically. And from a Russian viewpoint, Kennedy spoke out of both sides of his mouth. In June, 1963, he gave a moving speech at American University, reaching toward an end to the Cold War. But the previous December, speaking to Cuban exiles, he promised that there would be no coexistence with the Castro regime. The speech he planned to give in Dallas, in November, 1963, designed no doubt to woo right-wing Democrats, resumed his Cold Warrior stance. The direction in which Kennedy was headed at his death was by no means clear—and would not be until—and if—he was reelected.

Rusk, too, seemed inconsistent in the year that followed the missile crisis. He was never as optimistic about ending the Cold War as Kennedy seemed to be in the American University speech, but he was second to none in the quest for points of accommodation. Kennedy and Harriman played the central roles in deciding the American approach and negotiating the test-ban treaty with the Russians. According to Llewellyn Thompson, however, a key turning point in the discussions came when Rusk took Dobrynin for a ride up the Potomac on the presidential yacht. Reinforcing Dobrynin's personal interest in a treaty, Rusk succeeded in getting the Russians to reverse their position. Similarly it was Rusk who carried the burden of selling the treaty to a wary Senate. In closed hearings he stressed Khrushchev's difficulties with the Chinese to persuade conservative Senators that Khrushchev had an interest in ending atmospheric tests and improving relations with the United States. Rusk trusted Dobrynin in a way he had never trusted his predecessor, Mikhail Menshikov. He came to accept the sincerity of expressed Soviet desires for peace with the United States. But he never surrendered the conviction that the Soviet Union was forever committed to world revolution. [43]

Rusk's public statements in 1963 warned against euphoria. He insisted that the Soviet-American relationship could not be characterized as "detente." Much like Acheson and Dulles before him, he seemed troubled by the danger of complacency in the United States and in NATO. He was afraid that Americans and West Europeans would relax, become unwilling to make the sacrifices necessary to deter Communist aggression—and invite it once more, as they had by demobilizing after World War II. In a speech in Germany in October, 1963, he warned that Soviet leaders had not abandoned their goal of world domination. They would pursue that goal by every "safe" means. The "hot-line" and limited test ban treaty were useful but small steps toward peace. "Genuine detente" would come with progress on Berlin, German reunification, Vietnam, Laos, and Cuba. The Russians still blocked progress on disarmament by rejecting procedures for inspection and verification. Foreign affairs analysts might talk of the Cold War in the past tense, but it remained very much a part of Rusk's present. Nonetheless, elements of common interest existed and were to be sought. To a group of American businessmen, Rusk spoke of the need to "discover whether bridges might not be thrown across, along which some elements of peace can be gradually built." [44]

Trust the Russians, but not too far. Keep up your guard, but keep probing for opportunities to develop mutual interests, to build on them. Intrigued, he watched the Sino-Soviet rift widen and wondered what hope it might offer America and its friends.

CHAPTER NINE

The Perils of Asian Communism

After the election of 1960, Chiang Kai-shek's friends in the United States became apprehensive. Bowles, Stevenson, and Rusk—the three men who were *persona grata* to the *New Republic*—were allegedly interested in changing American policy toward China. Working through the Committee of One Million, the principal remaining front organization for the China Lobby, Chiang's supporters reprinted Rusk's "Slavic Manchukuo" speech. In an introduction they blessed him as one of the few public figures to recognize the threat of Communist China in 1951 and to have the courage to speak up in warning. Proceeding from that questionable analysis of the past, the Committee of One Million pronounced Rusk's 1951 statement to be of continued validity in 1961.[1]

Rusk was not seeking to return to 1951, but did seem to feel a deep hostility toward the Chinese Communists, stemming from the Korean War. Chinese intervention in that war had cost thousands of American lives for which loss he had to share responsibility. Chinese diatribes against the United States had questioned the purpose for which those Americans had died. And Rusk seemed anguished by a sense that the Chinese Communists had betrayed men with whom he had worked so closely—Jessup, Davies, and others who had withheld support from Chiang, only to be consumed by McCarthyism when Chinese intervention seemed to belie their assumptions.

But Rusk also understood that the People's Republic of China was likely to be around for a very long time and that it had to be involved in a variety of world affairs, in the United Nations and in arms control. Indeed, Rusk shared the view that had become widespread in the foreign policy establishment—and even in the executive branch of the government—during the 1950s: the Communists were in control of China and the United States should pursue a "two Chinas" policy. Opposition to recognition of the People's Republic and to its being seated in the UN, fanned furiously by the China Lobby, was strongest in Congress. Even John Foster Dulles, however, thought Congress might be ripe for change as early as 1956, and asked Rusk to work with Walter George, the Democrat from Georgia who chaired the Foreign Relations Committee. Rusk's task was to persuade George to accept a "two Chinas" policy and then to work with him to attain majority support or to at least neutralize the opposition. George chose to resign that year, in the face of a primary challenge from Herman Talmadge, and Dulles' plan was killed. According to the Chinese Communists, Eisenhower in September, 1959, convinced Khrushchev of the wisdom of a "two Chinas" policy and the Soviet leader tried to sell it to them.[2]

Conceding the mainland to the Communists, Rusk had shared in plans during the Truman era to preserve a separate China on Formosa or Taiwan, as it came to be called increasingly in the 1960s. Without any affection for Chiang, Acheson, Rusk and others hoped to save the island for the non-Communist world. The Joint Chiefs were forever interested in using Taiwan for harassing the People's Republic, but Acheson and Rusk seemed to retain the hope that decent government might emerge there. So covertly at first, the United States had encouraged the separation of Taiwan from the mainland and, in the absence of any likelihood of one big friendly Chinese government, pursued a de facto "two Chinas" policy which it was increasingly willing to proclaim. Unfortunately, a "two Chinas" policy suited neither Peking nor Taipei—nor the Congress, notoriously receptive to the blandishments of the latter.

When Kennedy appointed Rusk as Secretary of State, Rusk was prepared to recommend a less hostile posture toward the People's Republic. It was time to begin tying the Chinese with those "little threads" that would eventually draw them into the community of nations. But unlike a number of his colleagues, Bowles for example, he did not champion rapprochement. He was not prepared to lead a crusade. Kennedy quickly left Rusk without any doubt that he considered overtures to the People's Republic to be too risky. Eisenhower had threatened to come out of retirement to oppose any effort to seat Peking in the UN and opposition to recognition was intense on the Hill. Publicly and in private, Mao and his representatives had been belligerent and uncompromising. To Kennedy there seemed no point in stirring up the animals—or "primitives" as Acheson had labeled the McCarthyites—in circumstances that held so little promise. Pointedly, Kennedy told Rusk that he did not want to reopen the question of policy toward China and did not want to read about rumors that the Department of State was contemplating changes. Rusk did not presume to question his President's assessment of the domestic political context.[3]

In his confirmation hearings Rusk ruled out the possibility of recognizing the People's Republic, but only because the Peking government demanded abandonment of Taiwan as a prerequisite. Implicit in Rusk's response was the possibility of recognition should Mao and colleagues ever accept the concept of "two Chinas". In a later briefing, he offered parallel comments on a UN seat for China. Substitution of the "Peiping" regime for Taipei was unacceptable. Rusk left the Senators with his conviction that the Chinese needed to be participants in major international conferences, especially those relating to arms limitation. The Kennedy Administration planned no changes, but Rusk was not above an educational program to prepare Congress for the future.[4]

When Stevenson and Harlan Cleveland, Assistant Secretary of State for International Organization, expressed the desire to undertake a campaign for two Chinas at the United Nations, Rusk approved. He knew, of course, that the President did not. Sent to see Kennedy, Stevenson and Cleveland found the President willing, provided Congress and the Taipei government approved. Obviously neither would consider the change and Stevenson and Cleveland became intensely aware of the magnitude of the lobbying they would have to do. Similarly, Bowles found Rusk and Kennedy receptive to his proposal to work with the People's Republic on its food problems, an obviously humanitarian project unlikely to provoke domestic outrage. If the Chinese responded favorably, food aid would be a relatively hazardless way to ease Sino-American tensions. If the Chinese rejected the overture, Bowles and his followers would ease their pressure on Kennedy for more important policy changes—which is what happened. In both cases the technique Kennedy and Rusk used to manage their subordinates allowed the latter freedom to break their lances without compromising the President or the secretary.[5]

There seems little doubt that Rusk was genuinely in favor of ending the rigidity of the American posture. In May, 1961, he offered Kennedy a shrewdly conceived plan for winning Chiang's support for seating both Peking and Taipei in the United Nations. Kennedy was scheduled to meet with Henry Luce, Chiang's most powerful American supporter, and Ch'en Cheng, Chiang's Vice President. Rusk suggested that Kennedy advise his visitors of the need for a new strategy to protect the Republic of China's seat in the UN. He feared that the next vote, if posed as a simple choice between Taipei and Peking, would result in the expulsion of Taipei. Rusk contended that he could probably get majority support for keeping Taipei in the UN with some version of the two Chinas concept. If Chiang accepted, Rusk thought it unlikely that Mao would accept—and both Taipei and Washington would be spared the onus of excluding Peking. Rusk asked Kennedy to warn the Chinese and Luce that the United States could not stress the aim of keeping the People's Republic out because this strategy would lose votes. Most of all, Washington needed restraint from American leaders of opinion, from Chiang's friends.[6]

What was posed as a clever idea for saving Taipei's place in the UN was in fact an attempt to muzzle the China Lobby so that Rusk, Stevenson and Cleveland could work toward a two China solution in the UN. If Taipei, fearful of losing all, would agree, Congressional opposition would fade, and Kennedy's two conditions would be met. If in the end, Peking rejected the compromise, there would still be gain for the Kennedy Administration with American liberals and world public opinion: we tried.

It seems unlikely that either Chiang or Luce would have taken the bait. Both opposed a two Chinas policy to their last days. But in 1961 the culprit was neither Chiang nor Luce but Kennedy. In August, before the General Assembly convened, Kennedy decided—without consulting Rusk—to offer Chiang a secret promise to veto representation for the People's Republic if the United Nations voted to seat the Peking government. Bundy, who was present when Kennedy came up with the idea, tried unsuccessfully to dissuade him. Kennedy believed that domestic pressures would require him to use the veto and he might as well promise in advance and bank some capital with Chiang. Perhaps it would be easier to deny Taipei's demands for approval of offensive operations against the mainland.[7]

Had Rusk been consulted, he would doubtless have explained to the President a little of the complexity of attempting to use the veto—a problem he often discussed with Chiang's representatives. Very likely he would have annoyed the President. Like most men who attain power, Kennedy was not receptive to arguments that prevented him from acting. Moreover, Kennedy's attitude toward the People's Republic appears to have been much less flexible than some of his admirers believed. He had been an early purveyor of the China Lobby line, attacking John K. Fairbank and Owen Lattimore for betraying China to the Communists years before Joe McCarthy had ever heard of the two men. His brother Robert had not been sympathetic to Rusk's efforts to rehabilitate victims of McCarthy and the China Lobby. The fact of his unwillingness to move toward an extraordinarily modest two Chinas policy appears to be more important than the explanations for his stand offered by later apologists. Early in March, 1961, Kennedy astonished Washington observers by joining the prime minister of New Zealand in an attack on the "hostile and aggressive attitude of the Chinese Communist regime and the particular menace it poses to the peace of Asia, Africa and Latin America." It was clear to almost everyone that the Soviet Union was underwriting Communist activities in Laos, the Congo and Cuba: why attack Peking and ignore Moscow? A *New York Times* reporter speculated that Kennedy was beginning a campaign to keep the Chinese Communists out of the UN. His secret promise to Chiang leaves no doubt that this was one of his intentions. Kennedy was not an ideologue and by 1961 most of the rightist tendencies he had evidenced earlier in his career had disappeared. Toward the People's Republic, however, he seems to have retained an enduring hostility.[8]

Khrushchev and Mao were at least as important as any subliminal anger on the part of Kennedy or Rusk in shaping American apprehension about the People's Republic. In the three years of the Kennedy Administration, the American public's fear of the Soviet Union declined, but expectations that the Chinese would start World War III rose sharply. In April, 1964, a Gallup poll showed that by a margin of approximately two to one, Americans saw China as a greater threat to world peace than the Soviet Union.[9] Among college-educated respondents, the ratio was almost four to one. In part, the public was reflecting administration statements, but the question remains: why did Kennedy, his advisers, and the American people perceive so grave a danger from China? The answer appears to derive from the Sino-Soviet split, from what Khrushchev and Mao were saying to each other and to the United States.

During a top-secret briefing of the Senate Foreign Relations Committee in February, 1961, Rusk was asked about reports of friction between the Chinese and their Russian mentors. He replied that he thought the tensions were genuine, that there was a debate underway in the Communist bloc, and that the Chinese were leading the most aggressive wing. In a different context, he spoke (prematurely) of having entered a new period of civility in Russo-American relations, but of finding the Chinese as bellicose as ever. He noted that they had attacked the Kennedy Administration as vigorously as they had its predecessor. He might have noted that Peking had reacted hostilely to his appointment as secretary, charging him with a major role in "US aggression" in Korea and in plotting the "forcible occupation" of Formosa. Later in the year, he and Fulbright found the Chinese bogey useful in their efforts to fend off cuts in the administration's foreign aid bill. Fulbright argued against changes in Kennedy's request "in these very serious times when the Chinese Communists were showing very aggressive tendencies."[10]

But for the rest of 1961 and most of 1962, as evidence of Chinese aggressiveness proved scarce and the Russians seemed to stir trouble everywhere, not least in Berlin and Cuba, Rusk minimized the Sino-Soviet split. Yes, there were tensions, but he saw no opening for American policy. In a speech given in May, 1962, Rusk demonstrated his determination not to repeat the mistake he, Acheson, and Jessup had made in 1949–1950. He reported apparent "differences of view" among Communists on the "pace and tactics" of their effort to communize the world, as well as on ideological and internal political questions. But it made no functional difference: "both of the major branches of the Communist movement are determined to bury us, and each seems intent on demonstrating that its method of interring us is the more efficacious." The point he underlined in his speech was that Khrushchev talked of peaceful coexistence while approving wars of national liberation—an effort "to impose Communism by force while escaping the penalties for massive aggression." Yes, Khrushchev was more afraid of world war than Mao professed to be, but he was no less intent to force Communism on unwilling peoples.[11]

Within the Kennedy Administration, men like Bowles and John Kenneth Galbraith, the highly articulate ambassador to India, supported by James C. Thomson of the White House staff and some of the younger State Department specialists on Chinese affairs, pressed a different image of China. They could not erase Mao's words, the threats that emanated from Peking, but they argued that this rhetoric was extraordinarily belligerent because China lacked the means to act. They stressed the prudence and defensiveness of Chinese behavior. As Khrushchev precipitated one crisis after another, the view of a China moderate in action began to gain. In early 1962, when Chiang determined to launch a major operation against the mainland, those who thought Peking could be led toward a constructive role in world affairs had no trouble persuading Rusk to take the lead in squelching American proponents of Chiang's dream. Rusk insisted that the Communist military build-up opposite Taiwan was defensive. At year's end a commentator unsympathetic to the People's Republic expressed wonder at that nation's "remarkable quiescence" in early 1962.[12]

Two events in October, 1962, seem to have destroyed the effort to moderate the American view of Mao's China. The first, curiously, was the Cuban missile crisis. Initially, the focus of Kennedy and his advisers was on Khrushchev's adventurism, impulsiveness, and deceitfulness. When the crisis was over, the Soviet leader's determination to avoid war, the genuineness of his hope for peaceful coexistence, were accepted by the Kennedy Administration. Survivors of that incredible week in October came away with the conclusion that Khrushchev had been driven by the pressures of the

Chinese in collusion with his enemies in the Kremlin. The source for this view appears to have been the Soviet ambassador, Dobrynin, in whom Rusk and Llewellyn Thompson seem to have had unusual faith.[13] For the first time Rusk believed he was getting some insights into the decision-making process in Moscow—and the Chinese image in his mind was much the worse for it. Chinese abuse of Khrushchev for his retreat in the missile crisis was not likely to have undermined this new conception of the meaning of the Sino-Soviet split.

The second event, the Chinese attack on India, occurred in the midst of the missile crisis. Whatever Rusk's view at that moment of the significance of Sino-Soviet tensions, neither he nor any of Kennedy's other advisers indicated any suspicion that the Chinese action was part of a coordinated movement by international Communism. They were aware of Moscow's successful efforts to woo India and of the Soviet refusal to support Chinese territorial claims on the Sino-Indian border. The march of Chinese troops underscored Peking's determination to be independent of Moscow. Most important, it impaired those in the administration who were arguing that the People's Republic was not aggressive and expansionist. They might note, as some including Rusk did, that the territory in question had been claimed by Chiang earlier. They might argue, as scholars would later, that the Indians had provoked the attack. But it was to no avail. Chinese willingness to use force and the ease with which they routed the Indians seemed to demonstrate aggressiveness. Perhaps most important, in attacking India they attacked a nation which had captured the sympathies of American liberals— that segment of American society receptive to the image of a prudent China. In particular, they stilled the voices of two of the most voluble advocates of a new policy toward China, Bowles and Galbraith, both of whom had deep attachment to India.

By early 1963, as the Kennedy Administration made halting progress toward detente with the Soviet Union, Washington's verbal attack on Peking mounted. Internally, Rusk had concluded that continued difficulties in Laos reflected a loss of Soviet influence in the region. He was persuaded that the Russians were making an effort to implement the Geneva agreement of 1962, but that Chinese influence in Hanoi had eroded Soviet leverage. Similarly, unrest in

Africa was now increasingly attributed to a Chinese offensive there. Even when the Russians behaved unpleasantly, there seemed a tendency in Washington to believe that Khrushchev was being goaded into appearing tough by the Chinese.

Twice in the spring of 1963, Rusk used the Sino-Indian war as his text in sharp attacks on the People's Republic. In April he told a SEATO meeting that China's "blatant aggression" was of tremendous historic significance: "it revealed for the whole world Communist China's readiness to turn even on those who have tried to be a friend and to resort to overt aggression whenever its expansionist aims are thereby served." In June he explained to the Senate Foreign Relations Committee that "the Chinese aggression of 1962 . . . demonstrated for all to see—and for the Indians to see—the true nature of the conflict between two radically different political and social systems and the difference between the Communist and the free world's concept of peace." As tensions with the Soviet Union eased, Rusk focused on the Chinese in his verbal war against Communism. [14]

Concern about the threat posed by the Chinese Communists seems to have been genuine. While the United States negotiated with the Russians for a test-ban treaty, Kennedy brooded about the imminent danger of the Chinese creating their own small nuclear force. He worried constantly about Chinese intentions and, on July 31, 1963, he called a National Security Council meeting for the purpose of discussing possible Chinese aggression. For that meeting, the CIA produced a special estimate which discounted the likelihood of a direct Chinese military offensive into India, Southeast Asia or anyplace else. Intelligence analysts argued that the Chinese were not likely to act recklessly, that despite their rhetoric they had followed a cautious policy, and had shown respect for American power. However much Kennedy and his advisers may have been comforted, they were most attentive to and chilled by estimates that Peking was likely to increase its subversive efforts, its support for revolutionary movements in Southeast Asia. If this was to be the challenge, they were prepared to meet it. [15]

In his last news conference, Kennedy indicated that the United States was not wedded to a policy of hostility toward the People's Republic, but had no plans to resume trade with Mao's China. [16] He provided a hint of flexibility for the liberals and an assurance of inaction for the conservatives. After his death, men who worked with him suggested that he planned to change policy toward China after he was re-elected. They explained that he had been deterred from moving toward an accommodation with the People's Republic not only by domestic political opposition, but by Rusk's rigid hostility toward China. This may be true, but it is highly unlikely. First, it is difficult to separate those threads of policy that derive from Rusk from those deriving from Kennedy. Second, it is unlikely, given Rusk's conception of his constitutional role, that he would have blocked any initiative Kennedy wanted. Finally, where the record does indicate differences between the two men, it suggests that Kennedy had greater sympathy for Chiang than did Rusk and that initiatives for a more realistic policy came from Rusk and were blocked by Kennedy, rather than vice versa.

Roger Hilsman's Commonwealth Club speech, delivered several weeks after Kennedy's death, can be viewed differently if Kennedy rather than Rusk is considered the obstacle to change. Although hardly a revolutionary departure, the speech created a sensation at the time. It was the first official statement of American willingness to concede that the People's Republic was likely to endure and of the desire for the United States to reach an accommodation with Peking on a two Chinas basis. Thomson of the White House staff later reported that he and like-minded colleagues in the White House and State Department had slipped Hilsman's speech by Rusk and the unwitting new President, Lyndon Johnson.[17] The implication was that Rusk was an obstacle to a policy with which Kennedy was in sympathy.

There seems no reason to doubt that Kennedy did lead Thomson and others to believe that he favored a change, but the fact is that while Kennedy lived, no such statement—even one as tepid as Hilsman's—was possible. Only a few weeks after his death, a fresh position was announced—and with approval of Rusk. Hilsman has left no doubt that Rusk approved the substance of his speech in advance, that it was not slipped by the secretary.[18] Moreover the implications of the speech had been endorsed by Rusk since the 1950s. It is possible, indeed probable, that Kennedy and not Rusk was responsible for the inflexibility of American policy toward China.

The differences between Kennedy and Rusk on policy toward China seem trivial in comparison with an assessment of the Cold War on which they and Kennedy's other national security advisers agreed in 1963. In the missile crisis, as in the Berlin crisis of the year before, they had tamed the Soviet Union. Khrushchev would not trifle with the United States again; the revolutionary thrust of the Soviet Union had been blunted. To be sure the Russians could not be trusted and, unchecked, would try to expand their influence. The United States would have to remain strong and ready. But the possibility of Soviet-American detente, of peaceful competition seemed great. There remained one major task before anyone could speak of the end of the Cold War. The Chinese Communists would have to be taught the same lesson. Their revolutionary fervor would have to be brought under control. It seemed clear the Chinese would not attempt, could not attempt, any frontal assault against Western positions. They would test the United States through indirect aggression—by supporting the "war of national liberation in Vietnam." It was in Vietnam that the contest would be fought, in Vietnam that the Chinese Communists would be taught the same lesson the Russians had learned, in Vietnam that the last battle of the Cold War would be fought and won.

2

Rusk and his colleagues in the Truman Administration had spoken of the importance of Southeast Asia to the security of the non-Communist world. Often the State Department seemed willing to offer such statements as substitutes for the more aggressive military posture sought by the Pentagon. Financial assistance to the French in Indochina was forthcoming because Congress had appropriated funds for use in the "general area of China" and Acheson preferred not to waste the money on Chiang Kai-shek. He announced aid to France one day after the French pleased him with the Schuman Plan, their acceptance of his call for integration of Germany into

NATO. After the outbreak of war in Korea focused attention on Communism in Asia, a development highly embarrassing to the Truman Administration, financial support for the French contribution to containment in Southeast Asia increased.

The French continued to fare poorly, despite large-scale American aid. Inevitably, the United States government contemplated direct military intervention. A CIA report in December, 1953, warned that even if the United States defeated the Viet Minh on the battlefield, guerrilla action could continue indefinitely and would preclude non-Communist control of Indochina.[19] Early in April, 1954, as France faced defeat, Admiral Arthur W. Radford, chairman of the Joint Chiefs, urged the use of American air and naval power to turn the tide. Although Vice President Nixon and Secretary Dulles shared Radford's estimate of the importance of Indochina, the Congressional and allied support demanded by Eisenhower was not forthcoming. Radford's plan was not implemented and the French ultimately surrendered at Dienbienphu.

Elsewhere in the military establishment, the crisis in Indochina evoked the "lessons" of the Korean War. The Pentagon did not want to be involved in a limited war: "whether or not the action can be limited to Indochina once U.S. forces and prestige have been committed, disengagement will not be possible short of victory." For the United States, "Indochina is devoid of decisive military objectives." The Joint Chiefs objected to that they called a "static" defense. They wanted to carry the war to the aggressor, "in this instance Communist China." Still bitter over the restrictions imposed on action during the war in Korea, the leadership of the American military, especially the navy and air force, determined not to be hamstrung again. They were eager for another shot at the Chinese, for a chance to repay the punishment suffered in Korea. China was viewed by the military as the enemy in Southeast Asia. The Vietnamese were pawns, of little independence or importance.[20]

Eisenhower had no difficulty restraining the Joint Chiefs. His military judgment was not easily impugned by Admiral Radford or rightist Congressmen or columnists. Events in Indochina moved rapidly and in July, 1954, the Geneva Agreements allowed France to depart with a modicum of dignity. The armistice called for the two sides to regroup on either side of the seventeenth parallel, with provision for an election in 1956 to provide Vietnam with a single government. Although close to a military victory over France, Ho Chi Minh accepted this political compromise because the Viet Minh were expected to win the election easily and unification of Vietnam under Communist control could be attained without further loss of life. The United States was not a signatory to the Geneva Agreements and did not endorse them, but a series of American statements allowed for assumption that the agreements would be respected by the United States.

Eisenhower had other ideas. Military intervention in support of the French had been out of the question. Use of American forces to fight in Southeast Asia had no appeal. But if a Vietnamese nationalist regime, free of the stigma of French imperialism, chose to resist Communism in southern Vietnam, the United States would be sympathetic. Sympathy might be spelled out with economic aid, technical assistance, and military advisers. Careful inspection of candidates in Saigon led to selection of Ngo Dinh Diem, premier of the southern regime, as the instrument for American policy. An ardent nationalist who had won even Ho Chi Minh's respect, Diem had traveled widely in the United States, accumulated powerful friends, and was deemed the man most likely to succeed in establishing an anti-Communist state below the seventeenth parallel. Rivals were warned off, the French were eased out, and in January, 1955, American aid, including military assistance, began to flow directly to Diem's regime—contrary to the intent of the Geneva Agreements.

The election scheduled for 1956 was never held. The Eisenhower Administration was aware of the popularity of Ho's Viet Minh and Diem required no instruction. The freedom of the Vietnamese people to elect a Communist government was not a freedom for which the United States was prepared to expend any capital. Hanoi's efforts to arrange the election were rebuffed and Ho was able to elicit only slight verbal support from the Soviet Union or the People's Republic. In the late 1950s two separate republics existed on either side of the parallel. With American support, Diem determined to create an independent state in the south. Ho Chi Minh concentrated on carrying out the revolution in the north.

In Washington, a National Intelligence Estimate of July, 1956, noted little traffic coming south from Hanoi. A few cadres, some supplies, trickled in, but nothing worthy of alarm. The Russians seemed remarkably disinterested in Vietnam. The Chinese were more involved, but there was probably a mistrust of the Chinese that transcended Marxist comradery. Diem's Vietnam seemed quiet. He had suppressed the Viet Minh and brought the armed sects around Saigon under control. But 8-10,000 armed Communists were believed present in the south, capable of harassing Diem's troops and of widespread intimidation. They could easily reassert their influence in the rural areas. And the intelligence community worried about Diem's direction, about "the trend toward authoritarian rule through the political parties led by Diem's relatives and small circle of trusted associates."[21]

In fact, by the end of 1956, Diem's regime had become repressive, at least as indifferent to human rights as the Communist regime to the north. Opposition to Diem, most of it non-Communist, was suppressed by an active secret police, trained in part by American advisers. Hanoi declined to intervene, but Diem's tactics greatly facilitated recruitment by southern Communist cadres. Hatred of the Saigon government drove opponents into the arms of the group best organized to resist that regime. In 1958 and 1959, guerrilla activity increased sharply and in December, 1960, with the blessing of the Hanoi government, the National Liberation Front (NLF) was organized to overthrow the Diem regime.

As Diem's rule became increasingly unpopular among the people of Vietnam, there was occasional criticism by Americans who hoped to see a democratic alternative to Communism develop there. But the National Security Council in 1956 and 1958 restated the proposition that "the national security of the United States would be endangered by Communist domination of mainland Southeast Asia"; that "the loss to Communist control of any single free country would encourage tendencies toward accommodation by the rest;" that "the loss of the entire area would have a serious adverse impact on the U.S. position elsewhere in the Far East, have severe economic consequences for many nations of the free world . . . and could result in severe economic and political pressures on Japan and India for accommodation to the Communist bloc." With so many dominoes ready to fall, the anti-Communism of the Diem regime appeared more important than its record on civil liberties. In 1956, resistance to "Chinese Communist aggression" seemed central to policy in Southeast Asia. By 1958 there was thought of weakening the Communists in the North as well as South and bringing the peaceful reunification of Vietnam under "anti-Communist leadership."[22]

The alarm had sounded in August, 1960, about two months before Kennedy was elected President. A special intelligence estimate noted that the American ambassador in Saigon had been warning about deterioration of conditions there, about the ripeness of Vietnam for Communist-led guerrilla operations. The analysts concluded that trends were "adverse to the stability and effectiveness" of Diem's government. Criticism of Diem's leadership was increasing even in Saigon, within the government. Diem's regime was considered in danger of collapse if there were no changes. Moreover, "indications of increasing dissatisfaction with the Diem government have probably encouraged the Hanoi regime, supported and guided by the Chinese Communists, to take stronger action at this time."[23]

The Kennedy Administration thus inherited a civil war in Vietnam in which the American-supported regime was declining in popularity and power. The Communist opposition had reconstituted itself under the aegis of the National Liberation Front with every likelihood of increased support from the north. Kennedy was aware of what was happening. His interest in Vietnam had been whetted by a report from Edward Lansdale, the legendary hero of Ramon Magsaysay's victory over the Huks—the Filipino equivalent of the Viet Cong. On January 28, 1961, the President designated four crisis areas for immediate and concentrated attention: the Congo, Cuba, Laos, and Vietnam.[24] Of the four, Vietnam engaged Rusk least in 1961. Indeed, as Rusk tried to manage crises all over the world, McNamara quickly came to dominate the issue in which the Pentagon seemed most interested. Southeast Asia was the choice arena for a major application of American military power.

Kennedy and his advisers had to deal with Laos first, but soon they all agreed that Vietnam was more important. Vietnam was pivotal in the region. As Laos went, so went Laos. Efforts toward a settlement in Laos were aimed in large part, therefore, at improving the situation in Vietnam by having Ho's forces withdraw from Laos and by eliminating their supply lines and sanctuaries. Still another reason for focusing on Vietnam was the alleged willingness of the Vietnamese to fight. Unlike the placid Lao, the Vietnamese fighting man had won the respect of American military observers.

The assumptions of Rusk and Kennedy were not different from those of the Eisenhower Administration. Both men were on record in opposition to European imperialism. Rusk, like his friend Jessup, thought the European role in Southeast Asia was not only wrong but doomed because of the post-World War II weakness of Europe. An American role in Vietnam would be different. The United States wanted nothing for itself. Americans came not as colonial masters but as friends and supporters of Vietnamese national aspirations. Unlike Europe, the United States had the power, military and economic, to do the job. Douglas Dillon, who held important posts in both the Eisenhower and Kennedy Administrations, thought Southeast Asia peripheral to American interests.[25] Its "loss" was tolerable. His views were not uncommon among the Europe-oriented members of the foreign policy establishment, but were not shared by Rusk or other liberals in the new administration. Bowles, Stevenson and Williams, as well as Rusk, determined to broaden American perspectives, to win attention for Africa and Asia. For them the problems of Southeast Asia were not peripheral.

In a news conference early in May, 1961, Rusk spoke of increased Communist activity in southern Vietnam and indicated the Kennedy Administration's determination to prevent "liberation" of the area under Saigon's control. He announced that Kennedy had authorized an increase in military assistance to strengthen Diem's troops. The next day, the President's advisers discussed the possibility of introducing American combat forces into Vietnam. Rusk wanted American troops kept out. He did approve of increasing military advisers in Vietnam. Up to 100 additional men might be sent, a few at a time, and spread around to avoid attention. Rusk was not seeking a symbolic gesture to warn Hanoi, Peking or Moscow, but a small effort to improve the performance of Saigon's forces. He was clearly uncomfortable taking any action that might be construed as violating the Geneva Agreements. He did not wish to have the augmentation of military advisers discussed with the British or with members of the International Control Commission which watched for violations.[26]

Later in the month Rusk argued publicly that the problems in Vietnam could not be solved solely in military terms. The ability to withstand subversive efforts depended upon the quality of a society, on the well-being of its people. A trifle obliquely, he was hinting that political reform was necessary in Saigon. Questioned by reporters, he promised a strong effort to "reinforce" the situation in Vietnam, but refused to commit himself on possible intervention by American troops. Pointedly, he refused to concede that Southeast Asia was on the periphery of American concerns. There was much that could and should be done there.[27]

After meeting Khrushchev in Vienna, Kennedy was looking for an issue or area in which he could demonstrate the credibility of American power. As conditions in Vietnam continued to deteriorate, that tiny country looked more and more like the place to act. Hampered by the Geneva Agreements of 1954 which precluded the build-up of foreign troops, Kennedy simply decided that Hanoi's violations of the agreements were sufficient to justify an American decision to ignore the limits. An August, 1961, intelligence estimate reported that "a major Hanoi-directed Communist offensive against the Diem government" was underway and predicted an increase in the pace and scope of Hanoi's "paramilitary activity" in the months ahead. The outlook was for a long and difficult struggle, but the Communist threat could be brought under control with "continued high levels of US aid" and a strenuous effort by the Saigon government.[28] Kennedy, Rusk, Bundy, and McNamara agreed that the United States could not stand by and allow southern Vietnam to be overrun. The situation was retrievable.

A September report by the Department of State's own intelligence analysts was more ambiguous. Hilsman's staff concluded that the substantial increase in American aid had given Diem a reprieve, but it was not clear that he had been able to end the erosion of his support. The counterinsurgency program, so dear to Hilsman and Kennedy, was taking hold, but there was no improvement in security. In October, the Joint Chiefs returned to the offensive, arguing that "outside"—presumably American—intervention was

necessary because their advice for military action short of intervention had been ignored. General Lyman L. Lemnitzer, Chairman of
the Joint Chiefs, insisted that "we cannot afford to be preoccupied
with Berlin to the extent that we close our eyes to the situation in
Southeast Asia, which is not critical from a military viewpoint." A
special intelligence estimate of the same date as Lemnitzer's letter
confirmed part of his analysis, noting a rapid increase in the size and
scope of Communist operations in the south. Although it was clear
that supplies were being infiltrated from the north, the Viet Cong
effort was still viewed as "largely a self-supporting operation" composed of local recruits led by cadres who were southerners. Kennedy held back, sending General Taylor and Bundy's deputy, Walt
Rostow, to study the situation in Vietnam.[29]

Much has been written of the Taylor-Rostow mission, implying
that Rusk's failure to insist on a high-ranking representative from
the State Department was a conscious decision on his part to turn
Vietnam over to the Department of Defense. Neither Taylor nor
Rostow, however, was working for Defense. They both served on
the White House staff and traveled as the President's men. Both
shared Kennedy's devotion to counterinsurgency and were expected to return with recommendations that would support the
President's desire to step up the counterinsurgency program rather
than the desire of the Chiefs to introduce American combat forces.
All Kennedy's information pointed to the need to improve forces
defending the Saigon regime and he sought confirmation of his
approach from someone whose military authority was not easily
challenged. No one could have served the President's ends better
than Taylor. No political adviser was more likely to support Taylor's
views than was Rostow—whose liberal credentials were still intact.
There was no apparent need for a State Department role other than
that the ambassador could play. There was no role for Schlesinger or
Bowles whose views on military strategy were respected by no
one—and Kennedy was not looking for political advice.

Unfortunately for Kennedy and ultimately for the people of
Vietnam and the United States, General Taylor recommended the
introduction of American combat forces. He suggested that 8,000
men be sent to Vietnam under the guise of working on flood relief
and warned that the struggle against the Communist guerrillas

might be lost without such direct American intervention. Kennedy hesitated and his reluctance to endorse Taylor's report was reinforced by a cable from Rusk who was in Japan.

Rusk had no reservations about the importance of Southeast Asia and the importance of preventing further Communist expansion there. He did fear that the President might act precipitantly. Too often in the past year Kennedy had grown impatient with discussion, moved rapidly and unwisely. Rusk wanted Kennedy to understand the danger of direct American intervention, to understand what he was undertaking. Pressing the State Department's belief in the need for political reform in Saigon, Rusk asked how a "handful" of American troops could have decisive influence if Diem was unwilling to take steps necessary "to consolidate non-Communist elements into serious national effort." If the Saigon government would not transform itself into something worthy of support, Rusk was "reluctant to see U.S. make major additional commitment American prestige to a losing horse." The introduction of 8,000 combat troops, under whatever guise, would violate the Geneva Agreements and constitute a major step toward Americanization of the war. Once American power and prestige were committed, there could be no retreat. Was the President prepared to make such a commitment to Diem?[30]

Kennedy's answer was "not yet." The Taylor-Rostow report unquestionably intensified the pressure on the President to send troops to Vietnam. Early in November, McNamara supported the call for troops. A few days later, however, McNamara and Rusk signed a joint memorandum that read like a model of bureaucratic compromise. They agreed that the United States had to commit itself to prevent the fall of southern Vietnam to the Communists, reasoning that the fall of the Saigon regime would result in the rest of Southeast Asia accommodating itself to the Communists, the destruction of SEATO, and undermining of the credibility of American commitments elsewhere. The two secretaries advised the President that he be prepared to introduce American combat forces, perhaps even to strike at the source of aggression in North Vietnam, but they recommended deferring deployment of combat units. With support from both State and Defense, Kennedy was free to delay his decision.[31]

The joint memorandum was a characteristic Ruskian compromise. The common denominator among Kennedy's advisers, the importance of containing Communism in Southeast Asia, formed the preamble. The validity of the argument for combat troops was conceded, but for a variety of reasons centering on Rusk's belief that Saigon's performance was critical, the dispatch of troops should be delayed and less drastic steps tried first. American forces might be divided into two categories, modest-sized "support" units and larger combat units. Small support units should be sent immediately. Introduction of larger combat units was, however, very "complicated." It might lead to escalation by the Communist bloc. Even if the Communists did not match the American escalation, Rusk and McNamara noted another dilemma: if there were a strong effort by the South Vietnamese, American combat forces might not be needed; "if there is not such an effort, United States forces could not accomplish their mission in the midst of an apathetic or hostile population." Rusk and McNamara viewed the introduction of American forces as a means of improving morale in the South and, implicitly, of warning off the Communists.

Rusk also began a series of public statements designed to justify increased American assistance to the Saigon government. Although aware that Diem's tribulations were to some extent self-inflicted and conscious of intelligence reports indicating that the southern Communists, the Viet Cong, were largely self-supporting, he chose to focus on Hanoi's violations of the Geneva Agreements. He was unquestionably correct in contending that violations existed, that supplies and cadres were being infiltrated from the north. He knew, however, that although the Viet Cong had Hanoi's support, Hanoi's role was not responsible for the growing crisis in the south. If a villain had not existed, it would have been necessary to invent one to permit the kind of action the United States contemplated. Pressed by a reporter at a news conference in December, Rusk argued that it was not a violation of the Geneva Agreements "to take steps to protect oneself against the other party's breach, even though in the absence of such a breach those steps might not be considered normal." The logic was tortured, but the position of the United States government was clear.[32]

The decisions following the Taylor-Rostow mission were the most important steps taken by the Kennedy Administration. The key decision was to send American troops, "support" units to strengthen Diem's effort against the Communist-dominated insurgency. These support forces quickly engaged in combat operations, accompanying Vietnamese pilots on combat missions, flying the helicopters that carried Saigon's troops into battle, and shooting back as necessary for "self-defense." Kennedy and his advisers had taken the first important step toward Americanization of the war.

Rusk's part in the process of reaching this decision seems to have paralleled his role at the time of the decision to go ahead with the Bay of Pigs operation. More comfortable with Kennedy by November, he was less hesitant about expressing reservations. Once again he was much concerned with America's image. Once again, when an appropriate cover could be found for improper actions, he acquiesced. Rusk wanted to see the Saigon government reform, wanted to see the Vietnamese mobilize their own society and win their own battle against the Communist insurgency. He did not want to see the war Americanized. He did not want to have the United States committed to a moribund regime. But it was important to stop the Communists and if the best military analysts thought American military intervention was necessary and might succeed, Rusk would go along. He argued the State Department's case for reform in Saigon and qualified the style of intervention, support rather than combat troops, a distinction that had hardly more than cosmetic value at the outset—and soon lost even that.

Among Kennedy's advisers, Rusk was the most skeptical of any good coming from a commitment to Diem, but he yielded to none in his conviction that American interests required a non-Communist regime in southern Vietnam. If Kennedy could have been deterred from underwriting the Diem regime—and he almost certainly could not have been—Rusk's reservations might have offered an acceptable escape. But Rusk would not have chosen to avoid further effort to stave off a Communist victory in southern Vietnam, so long as there was any hope of success, of preserving the area for the extension of democracy. Tactically, he easily differentiated himself from the Joint Chiefs and conservative Cold Warriors. In Vietnam as always he attempted to minimize the use of American power. Ideologically he was more concerned than most of Kennedy's advisers about the quality of the Saigon government and more convinced of the importance of decent government in the struggle against Communism. Nonetheless, operationally, the Communists had to be stopped and when the modest steps he urged failed, he could not abandon the cause. In the end he was but a few paces behind the Joint Chiefs, a distance that hardly entitled him to be spared the criticism the war soon engendered.

Once the decision was made to introduce American forces, Rusk deferred to McNamara's judgment on matters of military strategy. He did not cease in his efforts to leave the war a Vietnamese war, but he considered logistical questions and determination of the troops necessary for particular missions to be matters for the Pentagon. He sat in on various task forces working on Vietnam, but did not involve himself deeply in their operations. In Harriman and Hilsman, successively his Assistant Secretaries for the Far East from October, 1961, to December, 1963, he had men who enjoyed his willingness to delegate authority and had direct access to the White House. For much of 1962 and 1963, when most decisions on Vietnam merely modified existing policy, Rusk voluntarily stayed on the sidelines, restricting himself to efforts to win public support and to diplomatic efforts to ease mounting international apprehension over America's course in Southeast Asia.

In February, 1962, Rusk returned to Davidson College, his alma mater, to deliver a speech on Vietnam. It was a rousing address, appealing to American ideals, to traditional commitments to self-determination and opposition to aggression. He condemned the North for systematic violations of the Geneva Agreements designed to destroy "a new and promising country in the south of that divided country." He insisted that the stakes were great: the independence of all of Southeast Asia. "And beyond this region," he warned, "the international community confronts a question that affects the lives of men and women—and of nations—on every continent: Shall this form of external aggression be allowed to succeed?" As part of what would soon become a familiar litany, he pointed to Korea as a country in which the "international community proved that overt aggression was unprofitable." In Vietnam, "we" would have to prove that "semi-covert aggression across international boundaries cannot succeed."[33]

There is no reason to question Rusk's commitment to the idea of collective security. The problem of coping with "indirect" or "semi-covert" aggression had troubled him since the late 1940s, when the Truman Administration was trying to help the Greek government. His variation on the "domino theory", however unattractive, had some substance and was based on repeated assessments by the intelligence community. But it is clear that Rusk was *not* being candid with his audience in his discussion of violations of the Geneva Agreements or his reference to violations of "international boundaries."

Rusk was well aware of a long history of violations of the Geneva Agreements by the Saigon government with the connivance of the United States. He was aware of American violations and the dissatisfaction with American actions expressed by the International Control Commission. He was well aware that the so-called "international boundary," across which men and supplies were unquestionably moving from the North, existed only because Diem, supported by the United States, had refused to hold the elections scheduled in 1956. And those elections had not been held because Diem and his American patrons knew the Communists would win the elections and unite the country under Ho Chi Minh. The Republic of Vietnam's existence depended on a violation of the Geneva Agreements. Rusk might justify that violation by an appeal to "higher law", preserving the area for the subsequent extension of democracy, but at Davidson he was arguing a brief, not informing the American people.

In his determination to couch his argument in an appeal to American ideals Rusk included one puzzling statement. With all his concern for Southeast Asia, he presented American policy as altruistic: "The United States has no national requirements in that area." Was Southeast Asia vital to the security of the United States—or was American action there just another example of the selfless use of power for world peace and the well-being of less fortunate peoples? Perhaps it might be argued, as Rusk and others did in the years that followed, that both the ideals and interests of the American people were being served by American policy toward Vietnam. That is not, however, what Rusk argued at Davidson. Ultimately he may have come to believe that, but the words at Davidson reflect what Rusk wanted America's war in Vietnam to be: a selfless crusade on behalf of a people whose yearning for freedom the Communists threatened to frustrate. Long after most of the rest of the world was sickened by the agony Americans were inflicting on the Vietnamese, Rusk clung to that vision. He had to.

The war went on in Vietnam. More and more American "advisers" and "support" forces entered Vietnam and found themselves involved in combat. Estimates of the war's progress varied. In December, 1962, the State Department's Intelligence and Research Bureau concluded that at best, the rate of deterioration had declined. Counterinsurgency activities by Saigon's forces were improving, but the Viet Cong had also improved their capabilities. It was going to be a long war. [34]

In the early months of 1963, Rusk, supported by intelligence estimates, became markedly more optimistic about the course of the war. On a trip to Los Angeles in February he was asked by a reporter if the United States had a "no win" policy in Vietnam. He denied the charge vigorously. The Kennedy Administration was providing the support necessary for the South Vietnamese to win their own war "and they are beginning to win it." Rusk detected "a turning of the corner." Early in April he told the House Committee on Foreign Affairs that the guerrilla operations Hanoi was directing against the South had been "curbed." Generally he thought it might be said that "the threat to Southeast Asia has been brought under control." A few days later he told the Council of SEATO foreign ministers that although the struggle in Vietnam had intensified, there was a basis for encouragement. He thought the Diem regime had found the correct strategy for eliminating Communist terrorism. The struggle might be "protracted and bitter" but he conceded "no doubt of ultimate victory." [35]

A CIA estimate of mid-April was less optimistic. The analysts believed that Communist progress had been blunted. The Viet Cong had been hurt by American "involvement"—a marvelously ambiguous term—but had not been hurt mortally. Assuming no increase in external support by the North Vietnamese, the Viet Cong could be contained, but no one could be sure. The situation remained "fragile" and there was doubt that the Saigon government would carry out the reforms necessary to convert military success into "lasting political stability."[36]

The possibility of increased support from Hanoi worried Rusk and his colleagues. Rusk thought the Russians eager to stabilize Southeast Asia and sincere in their efforts to end the fighting in the region. But as early as March, 1962, in a top-secret briefing of the Senate Foreign Relations Committee he evidenced fear that the Russians were losing influence with Ho's government, that the pro-Chinese wing of the Vietnamese Communist Party had gained ascendancy in Hanoi. The Chinese could be expected to urge the North Vietnamese to greater efforts to destroy the Diem regime. In March, 1963, Rusk began a public campaign against Chinese imperialism in Southeast Asia, a paraphrase of his Truman era attacks on Russian imperialism in China. "The peoples in Southeast Asia," he insisted, "do not wish to be absorbed either by Communism or by the Chinese. And this means that they are particularly concerned about being absorbed by Chinese communism." As the Chinese role in Hanoi seemed to increase, Rusk inclined to blame their bellicosity for renewed aggressiveness by the North Vietnamese. At no time does he appear to have appreciated the determination of the North Vietnamese to unite their country, quite independently of the advice they might receive from fraternal parties. Nor does he seem to have recognized the likelihood that Soviet or Chinese influence in Hanoi might rise or fall in direct proportion to the willingness of the two allies to support North Vietnam's conception of its interests.[37]

Criticism of the American "involvement" in Vietnam increased at home and abroad and Rusk usually bore the brunt of defense. In late April he addressed the Economic Club of New York and told his audience that Vietnam was "a sector of vital importance to the future health and security of the free world." He denied indignantly that the war was a civil war, insisting it was "an aggression organized, directed, and partly supplied from North Viet-Nam." Clearly the fiction that the seventeenth parallel was an international boundary had taken root in Rusk's mind, an easy analogue with the thirty-eighth parallel in Korea and the line that divided East and West Germany. He explained the danger the "loss" of South Vietnam would constitute for Southeast Asia, but there were, he insisted, "larger reasons" why the defense of South Vietnam was vital. Again, Rusk was carried away on the wings of a rhetoric that seemed to spring from an idea central to his being. Americans could not be indifferent to the fate of fourteen million people who had fought against Communism. Since 1947, it had been the attitude of the United States to assist peoples who resist Communist aggression. And on and on. We were not alone in Vietnam—100 other nations were helping. Ours was not a combat role. The strategic hamlets were working. Finally, with all of his steel bared, he declared: "I cannot understand anyone who would quit, withhold our resources, abandon a brave people to those who are out to bury us and every other free and independent nation . . . this is a battle to the end between freedom and coercion." To the astonishment of men who had worked with him on UN affairs in the 1940s, Dean Rusk had become an ideologue.[38]

Unfortunately for Rusk, for the American people, and especially for the people of Vietnam, the "fragile" situation in South Vietnam shattered in June, 1963. In the end not even hundreds of thousands of American fighting men could put South Vietnam back together again. Diem's regime had become more rather than less repressive in the years since Kennedy's inauguration. Many observers, Vietnamese and American, pointed to Diem's brother, Ngo Dinh Nhu, as the culprit. Nhu and his wife, the latter known to American correspondents as the "Dragon Lady," were considered the powers behind the throne, isolating Diem from the people, leading him to believe all dissent was Communist-inspired, and seizing for themselves the instruments of coercion. In May the regime came into conflict with Buddhists in the city of Hué, who launched a protest demonstration. Government forces opened fire, killing several demonstrators. The protest spread through the coastal cities and the Americans in Vietnam began to worry about its effect on the war. They urged Diem to be conciliatory. The Nhus urged him to crush the Buddhists. On June 11 a Buddhist priest sat cross-legged in a major Saigon intersection, doused himself with gasoline, and set himself afire—a scene which horrified Americans and people all over the world, who watched it shortly after on television. A *modus vivendi* was worked out under American pressure, but it broke down during the summer. By August the protest movement was out of control and Diem seemed immobilized by the countervailing pressures from the American embassy and from his brother. On August 21, Nhu struck. The Diems' private security army raided the Buddhists' pagodas shortly after midnight. With billy clubs and truncheons the Buddhist movement was suppressed.

In Washington, Rusk and Kennedy were repelled and terribly embarrassed by the brutal action of Nhu's men. For cosmetic reasons alone, they did not wish to be associated with a tin-pot dictatorship that survived by Gestapo methods. No sleight of hand could provide the Diem regime with an image of men striving to preserve the freedom of their people. At the very least, the Nhus had to go. And the man capable of conveying Washington's demands unequivocally, Henry Cabot Lodge, was on his way to Saigon.

During the summer, Kennedy had decided to replace the American ambassador in Saigon who had become closely associated with the policy of support for Diem. The President wanted to send Edmund Gullion, a career diplomat whom he had met in Indochina in the 1950s and for whom he had a high regard. Rusk persuaded him to send Lodge—just as he had persuaded Acheson to bring Dulles into Far Eastern Affairs in 1950.[39] Lodge was to the Republican Party of 1963 what Dulles had been in 1950: the personification of its liberal internationalist wing. In both instances Rusk sought to coopt part of the Republican Party, to outmaneuver neanderthals like Knowland in 1950 and Goldwater in 1963.

On August 24, Ambassador Lodge received a cable from Washington that contained a thinly veiled instruction to precipitate a coup against the Diem regime. Lodge was to inform interested Vietnamese military leaders that the United States could not long support a government which included Nhu or suppressed the Buddhists. If Diem would not rid himself of Nhu, the possibility of alternative leadership of the Saigon regime should be investigated. Should the central government collapse, the generals were to be assured of a continued flow of military supplies.[40]

The cable was drafted by Ball, Michael Forrestal, Harriman and Hilsman, at the instruction of the President and in consultation with the Secretary of State. Rusk was determined not to tolerate the desecration of the pagodas. He argued that to acquiesce in the increasing repressiveness and brutality of the Diem regime would lead to disaster. The American people would not support so reprehensible a regime, nor would the people of Vietnam. "The decision would then be whether to get out and let the country go or move United States combat forces into Vietnam and take over." Diem and Nhu could not prosecute the war and their continuation in office would have adverse international repercussions. Rusk was ready for a change of government in Saigon although he was not as willing for the United States to take responsibility as were the men who drafted the cable. Despite his scruples, the administration decided to invite a coup against a rotten dictatorship that did not offer its people a decent alternative to Communist domination. Heaven, now located on Pennsylvania Avenue, had withdrawn its Mandate from the Diem dynasty.[41]

Rusk had not changed his mind about continuing the effort to contain Communism in Southeast Asia. He did not want to surrender South Vietnam and did not want American troops to have to fight the war for the Vietnamese. Removal of Nhu and transformation of the Saigon regime into something more approximately liberal democratic was his alternative to an American war or surrender. He did not realize that it was too late.

McNamara, Taylor and CIA Director McCone later expressed reservations about a coup and Lodge's instructions were modified, but it was the initial timidity of the Vietnamese generals that precluded action in August or September. For McNamara and Taylor the absence of a coup was a relief and they determined to get on with the job. The National Security Council met on August 31, with Vice President Johnson chairman in the President's absence. Paul Kattenburg, a foreign service officer heading the Interdepartmental Working Group on Vietnam, offered an analysis of the situation in the south very close to that Rusk had argued when demanding Diem's removal. But Kattenburg went a step further. In the absence of a coup and given the certainty that Diem and Nhu would not reform, he recommended that the United States withdraw from Vietnam. He thought it likely that Diem would call for American withdrawal within six months in any event.[42]

Kattenburg's analysis was rejected by Taylor, McNamara, and Ambassador Frederick E. Nolting, Lodge's predecessor in Saigon.

None accepted his pessimistic estimate and all were eager to restore communication with Diem and revitalize the war effort. Rusk was ambivalent. He still wanted Nhu out, but in the absence of a coup he saw no choice but to muddle on. To withdraw and leave the field to the Communists was unacceptable. Somehow he hoped to avoid Americanization of the war. He concluded the meeting by stating that the United States would proceed on the assumption that "we will not pull out of Vietnam until the war is won, and that we will not run a coup."[43]

And so the United States muddled on. September was relatively uneventful. Kennedy publicly expressed dissatisfaction with Diem's course to Walter Cronkite. Lodge left Diem, Nhu and a host of Vietnamese politicians and generals with no doubt of American displeasure with Nhu's attacks on the Buddhists. Comparable signals were sent throughout September and October. At last, on November 1, the generals struck. Unhappily, in the course of carrying out the coup, they murdered Diem and Nhu. The murders were regretted—Diem's if not Nhu's—but the coup brought a great sense of relief to Washington. The cause of freedom had been purged of the stigma of repression. The people of Vietnam could be mobilized to use American assistance to defend themselves against Communist oppressors. On with the war. On to victory.

Lodge reported that morale in the Vietnamese armed forces had improved greatly after the coup. He was convinced that the war would be shortened. But there were some danger signs. In October the State Department's Intelligence and Research Bureau offered an analysis of the military situation that implicitly questioned Pentagon estimates. Rusk's men suggested that there had been an unfavorable shift in the balance since July, 1963, and that all of the gains of the first six months of the year had been erased. The Joint Chiefs were furious with the implication that their estimates were inaccurate and Rusk chose to apologize to McNamara—not for the estimate, but for the indiscretion of having circulated a military appraisal to other departments without seeking the views of the Department of Defense. In the weeks that followed the coup, to the horror of Kennedy and all of his advisers, it was discovered that Diem's regime had regularly and substantially falsified reports on the military situation and the progress of the strategic hamlet program. The sophisticated analyses of the Pentagon had been based on false statistics. The military situation in Vietnam was in fact far worse than anyone had imagined.[44]

The fault for the disastrous state of the war against the Viet Cong was Diem's, but it was too late to withdraw and allow him to take the blame. Had Kennedy and his advisers realized how desperate the situation was in August, perhaps they would have been more receptive to Kattenburg's advice. But not likely. Rusk could not easily have brought himself to advise abandoning 14½ million freedom-loving Vietnamese to the Communists. McNamara and Taylor would not have been ready to concede that the situation was beyond the point where American power could retrieve it. Kennedy and those who protected him politically were not likely to risk the "loss" of Vietnam before he was elected for a second term. There were still lessons to teach the Chinese, and anti-Communists at home to be appeased.

Complicity in the coup against Diem greatly increased American responsibility for the future of South Vietnam. Long before the limits of that responsibility could be defined, John F. Kennedy met an assassin's bullet. Had he lived, those who loved him are persuaded he would have ended the war. Perhaps, but not likely. There were approximately 600 American advisers in Vietnam when Kennedy was inaugurated. When he died, there were over 16,000 American soldiers there—and they were not merely advising. Kennedy had maintained close control over policy toward Vietnam from the very beginning of his administration. He was de facto head of the Vietnam Task Force, master of all the detail. Lansdale's ideas intrigued him. He was exhilarated by the counterinsurgency programs. The desire to appear active and powerful, the need to win, all of the *machismo*, were tied up in Vietnam. Doubtless he did tell those who wanted to hear it that he was looking for a way out of Vietnam. He told others that withdrawal was impossible; that it would have ramifications in India, perhaps all the way to the Middle East.

Kennedy died, Rusk and most of his other advisers stayed on to guide another President. The war in Vietnam went on.

CHAPTER TEN

Friends, Neighbors and Their Quarrels

In the 1950s, as Western Europe recovered from the ravages of World War II, gratitude toward the United States as liberator, provider, and protector faded. On the whole the new European attitudes toward the United States were welcome signs of a declining dependence. Unfortunately, independence on the part of its European allies was welcomed little more by the American government than it usually is by the parents of teen-agers. Washington was not prepared to accept its friends as full partners in the alliance. A pattern of unilateral action in NATO's best interests had characterized the foreign policy of John Foster Dulles. Moreover, the United States had not hesitated to ignore interests its friends considered vital. In Britain and in France there was a legacy of resentment over the American role in the Suez crisis of 1956 when the United States joined the Soviet Union to condemn the Anglo-French-Israeli attack on Egypt. In France there was also some bitterness over the failure of the United States to come to the rescue in Indochina in 1954.

As the Soviet Union developed the capacity to launch a nuclear attack against the United States, some Europeans came to doubt the American commitment to defend them. If the Russians invaded Western Europe or struck Paris with an atomic bomb, would the United States strike Moscow, knowing full well the Soviet Union could retaliate against Washington? The European allies Kennedy and Rusk confronted were less grateful, more independent, more

193

suspicious, more truculent than they had been when Rusk served President Truman, in the heyday of the Marshall Plan.

Kennedy's campaign and the views of men like Rusk, Bowles and Stevenson worried the NATO allies. There was apprehension about their seemingly inordinate concern for Africa and Asia, fear that American interest in Europe would decline. In that Rusk and Bowles were less Euro-centered than Acheson, Dulles and Herter, uneasiness in European capitals was not irrational. But the ambivalence of European leaders was clear. They wished to demonstrate their independence, to show they no longer needed the United States. But they were also afraid that the United States would neglect them.

The Berlin crisis posed the principal test of the alliance during the Kennedy years and, despite intense irritation with de Gaulle among American and British leaders and tension between Bonn and Washington, there were no enduring rifts. The NATO allies were steadfast during the crisis over the Cuban missiles. Two less sharply focused issues proved more troublesome and were not resolved to Washington's satisfaction while Kennedy lived. One was the matter of strategic posture and control of nuclear weapons within the alliance. The other involved the vision of a united Europe and steps toward further European integration, specifically admission of Britain to the Common Market. From the vantage point of Washington, de Gaulle appeared to be the obstacle to a happy ending, but the "theologians" of European unity, led by Ball, proposed solutions that created more problems than they solved.

The Europeanists in the Department of State thought Rusk less interested in Europe than he was in Asia—or even Africa. They were wrong, but there was some substance to their view. Rusk had to focus on the crises of the hour. Most of these came in the underdeveloped world, as the United States and the Soviet Union sought new arenas in which to test their power. Rusk was bored by economic issues, worked with them only if he had to, and was delighted to allow Ball to relieve him of such worries. He delegated economic problems to Ball and, as these involved the next steps toward European integration, left the politics of integration to him as well. Rusk appeared annually at the NATO meetings, paid homage to Adenauer and de Gaulle, maintained a warm friendship with Paul-Henri Spaak, but it was Ball, Jean Monnet's disciple, who dominated the day-to-day relations with continental Europe. It was Ball who became the force behind the effort to drive Britain into the Common Market and to solve the nuclear weapons control issue with the Multilateral Force (MLF).[1]

The basic change in American strategic arms doctrine during the Kennedy years was the shift from reliance on nuclear weapons, "massive retaliation," as a means of deterring Communist attacks, to a strategy labelled "flexible response." The Eisenhower Administration's choice of a threat of general nuclear war to deter its adversaries was deemed inadequate by a host of prominent experts in the late 1950s. Generals Ridgway, James Gavin and Taylor, and civilian strategists like Kissinger, Robert E. Osgood, and Albert J. Wohlstetter varied in their assessments of the usefulness of nuclear weapons but agreed on the need for building limited-war capabilities. The United States had to be able to respond at a level below that of total war.[2]

Guided by Nitze, leading Democrats, including both Acheson and Bowles, had been early critics of massive retaliation, of the Eisenhower quest for "more bang for the buck." In the campaign of 1960, Kennedy placed himself unequivocally in the fore of proponents of a flexible response, arguing in a review of Liddell Hart's *Deterrence and Defense* that Soviet acquisition of nuclear weapons systems assured mutual devastation in a nuclear war. The "free world" could not be protected by a threat of massive retaliation. He insisted that "responsible leaders in the West will not and should not deal with limited aggression by unlimited weapons." All kinds of potential Communist aggression had to be deterred. As soon as the Kennedy Administration assembled, Rusk urged a new, more flexible strategy, as essential to American diplomacy. McNamara required little persuading. All that was needed was money.[3]

Nitze's goal was American superiority in all aspects of military capability. If the Communists could be beaten on land, at sea, and in the air, anywhere in the non-Communist world, an attack was not likely. Rusk and McNamara were more sympathetic to the arguments of supporters of arms control. To avoid a perpetual arms race, nuclear parity would have to be accepted. But all agreed that a rapid build-up of and stress on conventional forces was necessary. To this end, Kennedy immediately committed himself. It would be costly, but his economic advisers assured him that once they revitalized the economy, the expense could quite readily be borne. Kennedy instructed McNamara to determine his requirements without regard to budgetary constraints. There would be no price tag on American security. Inter-service rivalries were muted by providing enlarged budgets for all. Kennedy's military expenditures quickly exceeded peacetime records. American forces would be ready for action in any place, at any level of violence. [4]

The new American strategy might have provided comfort to peoples in far-off places, "on the periphery," as the Europeanists might have said, but the NATO allies did not like it. Least of all did the Germans like it. If the Red Army moved West, the Germans had little use for the idea of attempting to stop it by conventional means, no interest in becoming a battleground while Americans thousands of miles away coolly decided when the situation was sufficiently desperate to unleash missiles against the Soviet Union. And when Adenauer met with de Gaulle, the French President warned against relying on the Americans. In the face of Soviet nuclear weapons, de Gaulle was contemptuous of the American commitment. He saw the stress on limited, conventional responses as evidence of American hesitance to share the risks. A limited war would be limited to Europe and the Americans and Russians could destroy each other's proxies without damage to themselves. For France the answer would be an independent national nuclear deterrent. De Gaulle did not urge Adenauer to seek his own nuclear capability, but the apprehensions he fanned led to German dissatisfaction with American unilateral control of the alliance's strategic weapons.

De Gaulle's arrogance and blatant anti-Americanism led some American leaders, especially Ball, and to a lesser extent Rusk, to focus on the French leader as the cause rather than a symptom of European discontent. Perhaps too eager to fight Monnet's battles, Ball called for a frontal attack on de Gaulle, but was held in check by Kennedy. Rusk kept his anger under control, but there were more than enough witnesses to the ability of de Gaulle to penetrate his blandness. [5] De Gaulle was questioning the credibility of America's commitment, an intolerable affront to a central article of Rusk's faith in his own country. There were indications that Rusk's stress on honoring the vaguest of American commitments, to the Saigon regime, may have been a response to de Gaulle's goading. Not only would the United States honor the most sacred of its commitments, those of the Atlantic alliance, it would honor promises whose very existence was controversial. In Vietnam, Rusk would demonstrate to doubters the seriousness with which his country took its commitments.

Rusk tried to reassure NATO friends of America's steadfastness at a Council meeting at Oslo in May, 1961. Those present professed to be favorably impressed by what he had to say, especially by his grasp of their problems. But he had nothing but words to offer—and words could not stem the mounting dissatisfaction with America's monopolistic control of the alliance's strategic weaponry. Nor could Rusk's stress on the need for Europe to understand that there were no longer any peripheral areas in the struggle with the Communists have eased apprehension about American priorities.[6]

The closest Rusk came to the core of the problem was an offer to assign five Polaris submarines to the NATO military command. The submarines would remain, however, under American control. Their nuclear missiles could not be fired without the permission of the President of the United States. Europe wanted more and there was sentiment in the United States for meeting the demand. General Lauris Norstad, an American officer serving as NATO commander, called for making NATO a nuclear power and the *New York Times* endorsed Norstad's idea on the eve of the Oslo conference. Something had to be done and after months of discord an idea that Robert Bowie had developed in the last year of the Eisenhower Administration was resurrected. Europe might be offered partnership in a multilateral force that would have nuclear weapons at its disposal.[7]

For over a year McNamara and his aides strove mightily to rationalize American military strategy and maximize its cost-efficiency. One policy on which he and Kennedy quickly agreed was to bring nuclear weapons under tighter control. In May, 1962, he told the NATO ministers of his determination to have all NATO's nuclear weapons controlled from one source, obviously Washington. The United States would provide a nuclear umbrella and the allies could provide conventional forces. In June, he delivered a speech belittling small nuclear forces, such as the British possessed and the French were developing. Such forces he deemed worthless as deterrents, "dangerous, expensive, and prone to obsolescence." There seems little doubt that McNamara was right. Yet his words, accurately reflecting American policy, demeaned the effort of his allies and increased resentment at Washington's domination of the alliance's nuclear strategy. First Kennedy put "locks" on American nuclear weapons in Europe and now he was advising his allies to dispense with independent national nuclear capabilities.[8]

The core of the problem seems to have been fear that the West Germans would follow the British and the French in developing nuclear weapons. The prospect of Germans armed with nuclear bombs created discomfort in the United States and Britain. It apparently terrified the Kremlin. If the Germans were allowed to develop a nuclear capability, all hopes of agreement to limit arms would be lost. There was the danger that the Russians would be so provoked as to strike before the "revanchists" in Germany were ready to turn on them. Few prospects were more threatening to the peace and stability of Europe than a nuclear-armed Germany. And yet the United States, largely dependent on German troops for NATO's conventional forces, could not long deny the Germans what other allies claimed as a sovereign right. Again, the multilateral force offered a possibility for finessing German pressures. Indeed, that was how the idea originated in 1960. If a NATO nuclear force could be created, in which the Germans shared an illusion of control over nuclear weapons, under conditions of equality with the British and the French, perhaps they would be satisfied.

A week after McNamara's speech, Rusk went to Bonn to discuss a variety of problems with Adenauer and other German leaders. He found them more flexible on a Berlin settlement than he had anticipated and thought he had assurance of support for Britain's admission to the Common Market. Nonetheless, he came away skeptical of Adenauer's ability or willingness to resist de Gaulle's blandishments. In a cable to Kennedy and Ball, Rusk warned that there could be no doubt that multilateral arrangements would be necessary to head off German pressure for nuclear weapons. Ball was ready with a plan, developed by Henry Owen of the Policy

Planning Staff, that would offer something to the Germans, something to other Europeans unwilling to rely on American nuclear
protection, and advance Ball's dream of an integrated Europe. On
July 4, Kennedy declared that as soon as the Europeans achieved
the necessary political integration, as soon as there was a united
Europe, the United States would remove the obstacles to control
over nuclear weapons. He offered no blueprint, made no demands.
The Europeans could do with the idea as they liked. In Ball's mind,
there was very likely the expectation that Monnet or his equal
would take over, as in 1948. But except for Ball, Owen, and a few
other middle-echelon officials in Washington, interest was not
deep.[9]

The first major victim of the McNamara-Ball war on independent
national deterrents was the Air Force project for Skybolt, an air-to-
ground missile intended to extend the life of manned bombers.
McNamara saw no point in spending money on such a project when
it was apparent that intercontinental missiles were the weapons of
the future. Skybolt would be obsolete by the time it was ready.
Britain, however, had been promised the opportunity to purchase
Skybolt missiles and, unable to afford intercontinental missiles, was
dependent on Skybolt for its future as a nuclear power. McNamara
was unsympathetic to the British desire for an independent nuclear
force. Ball and the other European integrationists in Washington
saw Skybolt as an obstacle to their plans, an example of the
Anglo-American "special relationship" of which de Gaulle constantly complained. Their aim, in any event, was to push Britain
toward the Continent, not to encourage British independence. If
the project were cancelled, deGaulle might be more receptive to
admitting Britain to the Common Market.[10]

The question of whether to continue with Skybolt was precisely
the kind of issue on which Rusk deferred to McNamara. But he was
aware of the political problem. Accepting McNamara's argument,
Rusk nonetheless warned Kennedy that cancellation of the project
would create serious trouble for the British government, both in
terms of defense planning and domestic politics. McNamara promised to discuss these matters with his British counterpart, to give
him time to prepare Macmillan's cabinet and the public. Neither

Kennedy nor Rusk was as comfortable as Ball in surrendering the close relation with Britain and they were anxious to avoid either gratuitous affront or to cause trouble for Macmillan.[11]

Something happened. McNamara may have failed to indicate to Peter Thorneycroft, the British Defense Minister, that the issue had been decided: there would be no Skybolt. Conceivably Thorneycroft or Macmillan handled the information they had badly or, less likely, they allowed a crisis to develop as a means of forcing Kennedy to provide an alternative weapon. Perhaps all concerned had been preoccupied with the Cuban missile crisis. Whatever the circumstances, Kennedy went to Nassau to meet Macmillan in December, 1962, without any expectation of the Skybolt issue precipitating major difficulty. Leaving technical military matters to McNamara and the pushing of the British toward the Continent to Ball, Rusk stayed in Washington for a ceremonial engagement with the diplomatic corps.[12]

Kennedy's intention at Nassau was simultaneously to kill Great Britain's independent deterrent and call once more for a multilateral NATO force. He quickly realized that Macmillan had not prepared the British public for the loss of a credible national nuclear force and faced serious political trouble if he returned to London empty-handed. Kennedy was sympathetic and pressed McNamara and Ball for a means to help Macmillan. They recommended that he offer to supply the British with Polaris missiles without nuclear warheads. Ball urged that the same offer be made to de Gaulle, to avoid any appearance of favoritism. If the British and French provided warheads and built submarines to launch the missiles, Kennedy stipulated that the missile-bearing vessels be assigned to NATO forces, although the British held out for the right to use the missiles independently when "supreme national interests" were at stake. Macmillan took what he could get and survived the onslaught of critics who ridiculed his claim to have preserved Britain's independent deterrent. De Gaulle rejected the American offer and evidenced no interest in Kennedy's conception for a NATO nuclear force. He remained determined to have his own.[13]

Of the major figures in the Kennedy Administration, Rusk was probably the man least troubled by the Nassau fiasco. He simply did not share the determination of McNamara or Ball to eliminate Britain's nuclear deterrent or end the special relationship. He had warned Kennedy of the consequences of cancelling Skybolt and left McNamara and Ball to tidy up their dirty work. Had the British come away empty-handed, Rusk would have had regrets, but he had accepted decisions with which he had less sympathy and he could accept this one. The two steps forward, one step backward of the Nassau agreement left the Anglo-American relationship a little closer to where Rusk thought it should be.

Ball and Owen were determined to proceed with a multilateral force. They persuaded the President to send Livingston Merchant, a retired diplomat, to Europe and pressed for an internationally manned—mixed crew—fleet of missile-bearing surface ships. Kennedy was skeptical. If the Europeans wanted MLF, he was prepared to be supportive. He was not willing to impose it on them. Rusk shared Kennedy's skepticism, and Bundy's initial enthusiasm faded. McNamara was sympathetic, but not committed. Some of his advisers, like Nitze, thought the idea absurd. Unless the United States was willing to relinquish its veto over the use of the multilateral force, the Europeans would not be satisfied. If the United States was prepared to surrender its veto—and Rusk was "absolutely opposed"—both the Soviet Union and the American Congress would be outraged. In June, 1963, on a trip to Europe, Kennedy recognized European reluctance and agreed with Adenauer that MLF would be put aside for further study. Ball and Owen did not surrender their idea, but nothing more came of it during Kennedy's lifetime. Similarly, although a hesitant Britain responded to American prodding and applied for admission to the Common Market, de Gaulle resisted the pleas of Washington and his other allies and vetoed Britain's admission. No progress was made toward Ball's vision of a united Europe—and neither Rusk nor Kennedy seemed deeply concerned.[14]

Kennedy and Rusk had come to office determined to improve relations with their NATO allies, but failed. In particular, relations with France deteriorated rapidly. Kennedy, like Eisenhower, rejected de Gaulle's proposal for a London-Paris-Washington *directoire* over Western affairs.[15] Thwarted, de Gaulle gradually withdrew support from NATO and insisted on underlining the independence of France, to the detriment of American conceptions of European unity. The other allies differed primarily in their willingness to pay lip service to American views. They were no more willing to respond to requests to increase conventional forces, or aid less developed countries, or contribute to NATO's budget. When Rusk gave an inspirational speech extending the frontiers of NATO's concern, denying that any area could be called "peripheral," his colleagues applauded, but they were not willing to have their countries play more active roles in Africa or Asia. Washington's balance of payments problems aroused little sympathy in Europe; nor did American insistence on restrictions on trade with the Soviet Union. No longer fearful of a Soviet invasion or internal Communist coup, no longer abjectly dependent on American aid, the nations of Europe defined their own interests and did much as they pleased. Why should Europeans demonstrate more concern for American interests in Vietnam than the United States was willing to demonstrate for Belgian, British or French interests in the Congo, Dutch interests in West New Guinea, or Portuguese interests in Angola? Why shouldn't the richest nation of the world bear the overwhelming financial burden of alliance defense? Why should the United States alone have an independent nuclear deterrent?

Rusk put the best light he could on differences among the allies. Asked constantly about the meaning of de Gaulle's actions, he insisted that de Gaulle remained committed to the alliance. Disagreements were merely over organizational problems. DeGaulle could be relied upon against any threat from the Soviet bloc to the NATO area. By implication, it was clear Rusk was not depending on France in Asia. Little was said about the reservations expressed less dramatically by other friends. Rusk, Kennedy and most everyone else concerned with foreign policy doubtless wished the Europeans would be more cooperative, more receptive to American ideas, but they understood that the age of American hegemony had passed. Leadership in the alliance would require more subtle techniques and considerable patience. At least publicly, the administration was patient, if not always subtle.

2

Rusk was marginally involved in other issues during the Kennedy years. Some of these involvements are useful to illustrate his commitments and priorities and some indicate points on which he differed from Kennedy and others in the administration. Perhaps most interesting are those occasions when he was forced to choose among the principles he held dear, as between anticolonialism and the peaceful settlement of disputes; between adherence to the UN Charter and containing Communism.

Rusk shared Kennedy's ideas for a new policy toward Latin America, but rarely handled affairs in the Americas outside of Cuba. His commitment to liberal democracy was readily apparent in his desire for policies that would prevent more Castros *and* more military dictators. He shared the prevailing view among liberals that military dictatorships were breeding grounds for Communism. Although his commitment to social and economic reform for Latin America was apparent while he was President of the Rockefeller Foundation, neither he nor the Department of State had much to do with the initiation of the Alliance for Progress. Adolf Berle's task force and a plethora of White House advisers dominated policy until at least June, 1961. Rusk had little taste for competing with Berle, Schlesinger, or Goodwin. There were other areas that seemed more important and he all but abdicated the field.

After Trujillo's assassination in 1961, Rusk and the Department of State had thoughts of creating a model democracy in the Dominican Republic. When the late and unlamented dictator's son Ramfis and his uncles were reported to be planning a military coup, the Department recommended that the United States take steps to get the remaining Trujillos to leave the island. Rusk's subordinates feared a coup would polarize the country and drive the non-Communist opposition into an alliance with Castroites. If Ramfis succeeded, his regime would be one that the United States would be uncomfortable supporting and there would be complications with Venezuela and the OAS. "Castro-Communism" had to be prevented and as democratic a government as possible had to be established. It was clear in the memorandum Rusk signed for Kennedy that the goal of a democratic Dominican Republic was flexible; but there was no leeway in the determination to have a friendly, stable, and non-Communist regime. Acquiescence in the brutal Duvalier regime in Haiti underscored the point. If it were overthrown, a Castro-style government might follow. Some things were worse than corrupt dictators.[16]

Rusk and Kennedy succeeded in finding other fields in which

Ramfis might play, but they were less successful in Peru in 1962. The administration was angered by a military coup in July and decided to use Peru as an example for other would-be military dictators. The United States suspended diplomatic relations and cut off an aid program. American officials publicly condemned the coup. Soon it was clear that the junta had considerable public support and when it uttered the obligatory catechism about returning to constitutional processes, aid and diplomatic relations were resumed. There appears to have been little doubt in Washington about the validity of the conception of using one country, like Peru, as an example to deter ambitious generals elsewhere in the hemisphere.[17]

If the money Kennedy and Rusk wheedled out of Congress for the Alliance for Progress is evidence of their conviction that economic and social progress was the best way to impede Communism in Latin America, the Kennedy years abound with evidence that containing Communism was their highest priority there. Aid to Haiti was suspended as an indication of disapproval of Duvalier—until Haiti's vote was needed to pass an OAS resolution declaring that Cuba had excluded itself from the OAS by embracing Marxist-Leninism. Rusk personally decided that there was too great a risk of British Guiana following Castro's example if Cheddi Jagan were allowed to lead that country when it was granted independence. At Rusk's insistence the British government manipulated the elections to facilitate the victory of a coalition led by Forbes Burnham, Jagan's opponent, of whom the British were themselves most apprehensive. In 1963, coups in Argentina, Guatemala, and the Dominican Republic brought right-wing military regimes to power. However uncomfortably—and the overthrow of the democratically elected regime of Juan Bosch in the Dominican Republic was especially troubling—Kennedy and Rusk quickly made their peace with the new anti-Communist leaderships.[18]

When Kennedy died, the administration might boast that it had permitted no new Castros in the Americas. But it had failed to prevent the emergence of new Batistas—or the continuance of old Duvaliers. Communism had not spread in the Americas, but neither had democracy. The optimism the *Alianza* had brought in 1961 was gone. Enthusiasm for the program had faded in both Latin America and the United States. There had been little progress—and there was little hope.

The Rusk-Kennedy commitment to liberal democracy—and its limits—was similarly illustrated in Korea where in May, 1961, the Army deposed the democratically-elected civilian regime of Premier John Chang. The American government opposed the coup and its representatives in Seoul, military as well as civil, unhesitatingly expressed public support for Chang. To no avail. The junta leader, General Pak Chong-hui, undoubtedly wanted and was likely to be dependent on American support, but first of all he wanted power. Weeks passed and Pak resisted all the pressure Washington dared bring to bear. By the end of August, the American ambassador in Seoul was ready to give up. It was too risky to remain at odds with Pak. The North Koreans might calculate that they could attack without fear of American intervention. The repercussions of an apparent invitation to an invasion by the North, both domestically and internationally, were too serious to gamble any longer. Rusk agreed with the ambassador's recommendation that Pak be invited to the United States. A visit would have a "stabilizing" effect on the Korean internal situation and enhance Pak's international prestige. It would serve as a warning to the Communists that the United States had not wavered in its determination to defend Korea. And while Pak was in town, Rusk wrote, "we would also have the opportunity to stress the dangers of prolonged military rule and the need for the restoration of representative civilian government."[19]

Ostensibly stuck with Pak, Rusk wished to strengthen him as a means of keeping the Communists at bay. Containment was, after all, the purpose of American involvement in Korea. Nonetheless, it was important to explain the need for democratically-elected civilian regimes to the general. Pak was slow to learn and left no doubt that he had no intention of restoring the civil government. Rusk remained dissatisfied, and succeeded in maintaining mild pressure. Finally, in 1963, Pak came up with a clever solution. He scheduled elections, designated himself a civilian, restricted the freedom of his opponents to campaign, and managed to eke out a plurality. Now the Americans could be happy, perhaps even quiet. Korea had elected a civilian president. The Kennedy Administration and its successors learned to live with it, as it became increasingly corrupt and repressive in the years that followed, ending only with the murder of Pak in 1979.[20]

Elsewhere in Asia, relations with the nations of the subcontinent indicated some distinctions between the attitudes and assumptions of Rusk and those of Kennedy and Bowles. India, and particularly Nehru, engaged Kennedy intellectually. He was eager to meet and talk with Nehru as a great historical figure. Kennedy was also tempted by the vision of Bowles, Galbraith and other liberals of supporting India as a successful model of democratic development. If democratic India could modernize more rapidly than totalitarian China, Communism might be less attractive to developing countries. Although India was a leader among the nonaligned nations, Kennedy and Bowles in particular seemed to assume that India's successes were victories for American interests. After the Sino-Indian border war in 1962, Bowles was eager to become India's arms supplier, confident of drawing the Indians into America's orbit. Kennedy and the White House staff were also hopeful of persuading the Indians to come to terms with Pakistan over Kashmir, to end the confrontation between two American friends.[21]

Rusk always favored economic assistance for India, but had little expectation of banking any goodwill in return for American largesse. Although the Pakistanis were allies of the United States, Rusk thought that in a general war with the Communist bloc, India would prove a better friend. He had few illusions about Pakistani friendship, understanding that it was based primarily on the hope of getting arms to use against India. Short of a general war, however, he did not expect to be able to win India over to the West. In 1963 he pressed for a commitment to defend India against air attack, but opposed Bowles' proposals for arms sales to New Delhi. The Kashmir issue had been a focus of his attention since 1948 and he understood better than most how long the odds were of facilitating a settlement. But what distinguished Rusk most from his colleagues was his anger over Indian self-righteousness and Indian criticism of the United States. In particular, Rusk quite reasonably held the Indian government responsible for the behavior of Krishna Menon, its ambassador to the United Nations, justly famed for his vitriolic attacks on the United States and, of course, Pakistan. Here again was that deep strain of patriotism that brought outrage close to the surface when the United States was maligned. Menon, like de Gaulle and Chinese Communist propagandists, offended Rusk. Always, his anger was controlled, but he never forgave.[22]

Rusk, in the 1960s, was profoundly troubled by the alacrity with which Third World countries were willing to act in violation of the UN Charter to serve their ends. Nehru and Menon preached virtue to the United States, but did not hesitate to send troops to take over the Portuguese enclave of Goa when they determined that Goa was part of India. Rusk was markedly sympathetic to the Portuguese in this instance. In his mind, the question was not one of colonialism. It was Rusk, after all, who had tipped the scales against the Europeanists in favor of the African Bureau's attack on Portuguese imperialism in Africa. The issue over Goa was adherence to the UN Charter which prohibited use of force in such a situation. Convinced of his righteousness, Nehru chose to ignore the legal and peaceful methods provided by the Charter and grabbed what he wanted. Moreover, the UN itself, where control of the Assembly was passing into the hands of Third World nations, ignored the Indian violations of the Charter.[23]

A dispute between the Netherlands and Indonesia over West New Guinea posed comparable problems. The Dutch retained control of the territory after Indonesia won its independence, but Sukarno, President of Indonesia, claimed West New Guinea—West Irian—as part of his country. Kennedy's advisers agreed that Sukarno's claim was questionable, but warned the President that Indonesia would use force if necessary to obtain control over the territory. Indonesia had the largest and best-equipped armed forces in the region and was deemed more than a match for the Dutch, should push come to shove. The United States wanted a peaceful settlement and it did not want to offend its Dutch allies or risk alienating a very left-leaning Sukarno. What to do?

There were two American goals: 1) keeping Indonesia out of the Communist camp; 2) handling the claims to West New Guinea in a legal and peaceful manner. There was no disagreement on the first goal within the administration. On the second, however, tension developed between the White House staff and Rusk. There was a tendency on the part of the staff to be impatient with Rusk, especially when he seemed mired in principle. Few of Bundy's young men were aware of the central role Rusk had played in the Truman era in assisting Jessup at the birth of the Indonesian Republic. He was suspected of being too sympathetic to a NATO ally. The issue seemed clear-cut. Sukarno wanted West Irian. He had the power to take it. The Dutch could not stop him and the United States, determined not to provoke him, would not interfere. The United States should simply state the case to the Dutch directly and tell them to get out of the way.[24]

Rusk resisted this approach. Indonesian control of the Papuans in the territory was hardly likely to be more benign than that of the Dutch. Sukarno had become an obnoxious bully and appeasement would make him worse. Rusk wanted to exert every effort to bring the problem before the United Nations and have it resolved in a manner consistent with the Charter. In April, 1961, after mustering support from Senator Fulbright, he recommended that Kennedy seek a UN trusteeship for West New Guinea. In talks with the Dutch ambassador to the United States, he encouraged him to internationalize the issue by taking it to the United Nations. The Netherlands had become a weak country, threatened by an aggressor, and the UN existed to handle such problems. Rusk asked Kennedy not to press the Dutch to meet directly with Indonesia.[25]

By October, 1961, the White House staff was urging Kennedy to twist Rusk's arm. A device to ease Dutch pain was acceptable, but what mattered was to get the Dutch to turn the territory over to Indonesia quickly, before Sukarno decided to use force. Robert H. Johnson, who served as Bundy's expert on the subject, advocated American pressure on the Dutch. He claimed support from the Far East Bureau at State, but acknowledged the opposition of the West Europe and International Organization sections. He considered the Dutch call for self-determination for the Papuans to be a sham. Rusk and Cleveland at International Organization did not.[26]

In the first half of 1962, American pressures were directed primarily toward getting the Dutch to accept terms that would disguise their surrender. Rusk accepted Kennedy's decision, as always, but was not willing to let Sukarno get off lightly. Sukarno was another tin-pot dictator who needed a lecture against aggression. On the eve of a settlement, Bundy had to ask Kennedy to call Rusk off. Rusk was showing a "considerable eagerness to be tough with Sukarno." Bundy conceded the need to be tough might exist, but did not want to reveal this mood to the Dutch. He did not want to risk stiffening their resistance and precluding a peaceful settlement. In August, under the guidance of Harriman and Ellsworth Bunker, an arrangement was signed at the UN for administration of the territory to pass from the Netherlands to the UN in six weeks and on to Indonesia four and a half months later. Sukarno would not wait and the Dutch were merely spared the humiliation of turning the land directly over to Indonesia. After six years of Indonesian rule the Papuans were promised a plebiscite to determine their future, but there could be little hope Sukarno would honor the promise.[27]

Clearly, Rusk had a greater commitment to the principles of the UN Charter than did many of his colleagues in the Kennedy Administration. He had less patience with Third World leaders quick to condemn Western imperialism but indifferent to those aspects of the Charter that prohibited aggression. He was less sure that appeasement would result in nations like India or Indonesia acting more responsively to American interests. The cool pragmatism of Kennedy, the White House staff, and men like Harriman left Rusk feeling queasy.

One other case, in Africa, highlighted another Rusk concern, another difference between him and some of his colleagues. Kennedy had come to office determined to woo Nkrumah, the radical nationalist leader of Ghana. Nkrumah, like Nehru, was a spokesman of the nonaligned nations. In June, 1961, Kennedy wrote Nkrumah a warm letter, promising to help Ghana with the construction of the Volta Dam. By September, Kennedy was having second thoughts, as Ghana prepared to send four hundred cadets to the Soviet Union for training. Nkrumah seemed to be paralleling Soviet bloc policies in the UN and in his public addresses. In December, Kennedy called a meeting of the National Security Council to consider canceling the offer to build the Volta Dam. The President questioned helping Ghana, given the leftward turn it had taken internationally and the increasingly dictatorial manner of Nkrumah's rule at home. Kennedy thought he would get no support for the project

from Congress. The President's brother Robert advocated withdrawing the offer and was supported by Secretary of the Treasury
Dillon. They argued that Nkrumah was no friend of the United
States. It was Rusk who vigorously opposed cancellation of the
project.[28]

Nkrumah was precisely the kind of Third World leader who
tended to outrage Rusk. He seemed to have a double standard when
he criticized Western actions and approved those of the Communist
bloc. He was creating a personal dictatorship at home. But, Rusk
argued, the United States had made a *commitment*. The President
had personally committed himself and a refusal to go forward with
the plan would be misunderstood all over Africa. Rusk advocated
enlisting British assistance to turn Nkrumah toward a more reasonable course and Ball reminded Kennedy that his letter in June had
been made "warmer" at Kennedy's insistence. Grudgingly, Kennedy continued the project. Rusk's concern for his nation's word was
transcendent. Commitments had to be honored.

3

In one area of the world, the Middle East, the Kennedy Administration faced no grave crises. Kennedy alone of the first five postwar
presidents was spared the trauma of an Arab-Israeli war. No one
threatened to turn off the oil spigot and neither the Russians nor the
Chinese Communists appeared to extend their influence in the
region. The Arabs quarreled among themselves. Coups occurred in
Syria and Iraq, and Saudi Arabia and Egypt became involved in a
civil war in Yemen. The Yemeni struggle worried Washington
where there was fear it might spread, upsetting the balance among
radical and conservative Arab states and affecting Saudi oil fields.
These problems were mild compared to Rusk's experiences in the
1940s. Neither he nor the President made more than sporadic forays
into Middle Eastern affairs.

Ever since the Suez crisis of 1956, Gamal Abdul Nasser of Egypt
had towered over the Arab world. Kennedy thought it urgent to
pacify Nasser, perhaps less to win him over than to minimize the
hostility that followed from American support of Israel and Saudi
Arabia. It seemed sensible to improve relations with Egypt, and

Kennedy was willing to expend not only his charm but also the domestic political capital necessary to get Congressional approval of aid for Egypt. Rusk was doubtful. Nasser was another of those Third World leaders who fed his people with tirades against the United States and opposed American policies all over the world. In the early months of 1961, Nasser was channeling aid to antigovernment factions in the Congo, serving as a likely Trojan horse for the extension of Communist interests. But the President wanted to try to reach Nasser and Phillips Talbot, Assistant Secretary of State for Near East and South Asian Affairs, concurred. Once it was agreed that aid would be limited to food, Rusk acquiesced. As he antici- pated, the hope of Kennedy and Talbot that Nasser would be more amenable proved unrealistic.[29]

UN forces kept the border between Egypt and Israel quiet and assured Israeli passage of the Straits of Tiran. There was little stirring along that front. Nasser's major adventure in the Kennedy years came in Yemen where republican forces sympathetic to Nasser rebelled against the Imam. Nasser intervened, sending as many as 70,000 Egyptian soldiers as well as planes and administra- tive advisers. The royalists proved surprisingly resolute, received aid from Saudi Arabia and Jordan and, Rusk suspected, surreptitious aid from Britain.[30]

The United States had no interests in Yemen, but feared an expansion of the war to Saudi Arabia. The aim of American policy was to contain the struggle to Yemen. The outcome was not important. When the Soviet Union recognized the republican re- gime immediately, Washington chose to follow suit, after a decent interval. The Kennedy Administration was persuaded that the rebellion was a legitimate Yemeni affair, aimed at modernization of a tribal society. Most of all, Kennedy and his advisers did not want the United States identified with the forces of reaction.

In the months that followed, the United States acted with restraint, trying to get the Saudis and Egyptians to go home and leave the Yemenis to work out their destiny. Finally in April, 1963, Rusk's friend Ralph Bunche, acting for the UN, and assisted by the ubiquitous Ellsworth Bunker, succeeded in arranging an agreement for withdrawal. Unfortunately the agreement was not carried out, and years passed before Nasser could extricate himself. A squadron of American jets posted temporarily to Saudi Arabia may have helped to assure the Saudis and to serve as an expression of American earnest for Nasser. Though the struggle continued, American ends had been served.

As most of the other nations of the region struggled with their internal problems, some more peaceably than others, Rusk's only other concern of note was the Central Treaty Organization, CENTO. He had a low regard for the organization, but attended its annual meetings faithfully. Once there he stroked other ministers as necessary, said the obligatory words of praise for nations involved, pledged American moral support—and rejected requests for arms or the development of CENTO forces comparable to those maintained by NATO.[31]

Before the decade of the 1960s ended, Rusk would have opportunity to cope with crises in the Middle East. But these would come after the death of John F. Kennedy.

CHAPTER ELEVEN

From Camelot to the Pedernales

After the first six months of 1961, the working relationship between Kennedy and Rusk improved immensely. McGeorge Bundy and Luke Battle labored mightily to bring order to both ends of their channel. The President's confidence in Rusk rose during the summer and fall, and evidence of Kennedy's increased trust and reliance reassured the secretary and gave him greater stature in the administration. In the last years of Kennedy's life the two men worked well together. To the end, however, their contacts remained formal. Rusk never played touch football on the White House lawn, nor did anyone ever push him into Ethel Kennedy's pool. His relations with the President's brother Robert were decidedly cool and may have posed an obstacle to more extensive social ties between the Rusks and Kennedys. It seems unlikely, however, that Rusk and his wife would ever have been comfortable with the jet-setters whom the Kennedys cultivated; nor could they have afforded to maintain the pace.

Throughout the Kennedy years, Rusk was one of the central figures in American foreign policy. Kennedy, however, dominated that process and often served as his own chief of task force on issues that attracted his attention. He was able to do this in part because of the skill of Bundy—whom Rusk would dearly have liked as his undersecretary. Bundy's influence on what the President read, on the President's direction, was great, but he was scrupulously careful to avoid any usurpation of the secretary's duties. Similarly, McNamara, sure of his own influence, always deferred to Rusk. The pattern that emerged appeared to be one in which Rusk was again, as in the

Truman era, part of a triumvirate, shaping policy. But any similarity between the two situations was highly superficial. Jessup and Rusk had been Acheson's subordinates, not his bureaucratic rivals. In the Kennedy years, Rusk had to compete with men who were directly responsible to the President, not the Secretary of State. Unlike Acheson's rival, Secretary of Defense Johnson, whose competence was widely questioned, Bundy and McNamara were men of powerful intellect and forceful personality. Rusk's status was never more than that of first among equals—and few would grant him that. Finally, in Kennedy, Rusk served a President far more confident in foreign affairs than Acheson's "captain with the mighty heart."

In 1964 Schlesinger reported that Kennedy had intended to replace Rusk in his second administration.[1] No one will ever know what Kennedy would have done in this situation any more than any other. It seems likely that Kennedy did raise the possibility of appointing a new Secretary of State if he were reelected. Men of high repute both confirm and deny the likelihood, suggesting that Kennedy was of two minds and seeking the judgment of others. It is at least conceivable that the President was whetting the ambition of some subordinates and outsiders either for his own amusement or to strengthen their efforts on his behalf in the 1964 campaign. Rarely noted, however, is the fact that Rusk had informed the President of his desire to resign after the election.[2] Rusk was tired. He had not been as exhilarated by power as McNamara or Harriman or Ball. Lacking outside means, he was financially pressed. A man will suffer much when he can be convinced that he alone can do a job that needs doing. Kennedy had not attempted to so persuade Rusk.

2

The implications for American policy and actions of the Kennedy-Rusk relationship do not seem important. Differences, when discernible, were not great. They were both intensely anti-Communist and dedicated to preventing the expansion of Communism, whether Soviet, Chinese or indigenous to Africa, Asia, or anywhere else. Both were persuaded that Khrushchev and Mao were committed to world revolution and could be restrained only by evidence of American willingness to use force. Rusk was more hesitant about unilateral military action, more concerned about collective security, allies and the United Nations. When collective action was not possible, however, Rusk conceded the need to act alone, settling for symbols of allied support. Had Rusk been more assertive, as advocated by some of his critics, the attack on Cuba in 1961 might have been prevented. In no other instance does it appear that a warmer Kennedy-Rusk relationship or a more aggressive Secretary of State would have changed the substance of American policy.

In style the two men were easily contrasted, but seem in retrospect to have complemented rather than obstructed each other. Kennedy was more optimistic, more pragmatic. He was young, inexperienced, impetuous, impelled, like so many young lions, by an excess of *machismo*. The older man had worked with many of the problems before and was less convinced an appropriate American action could be found to solve them all. He never valued action for its own sake. Often fearing the worst in time of crisis, Rusk preferred to talk the problems to death. He was more principled than his President, but not inflexible. The President, the White House staff, and McNamara drove Rusk at a faster pace than he would have chosen for himself and into arenas he might have preferred to avoid. Rusk in turn checked their leaps with his deliberateness, forcing them to see all sides, to understand the history of a problem.[3] The resulting tension was salutary, though obviously no guarantee of wise policy.

Together, Kennedy, Rusk, Bundy and McNamara accomplished little in those "thousand days," but they met Rusk's primary goal. A few more years had passed without nuclear war. More positively, the Kennedy Administration in 1963 succeeded in cooperating with Khrushchev and friends to ease Soviet-American tensions, to drive that big mushroom cloud farther over the horizon. The limited test ban treaty of 1963 may not be the most memorable of achievements but it is impossible to overstate the progress it represented over the missile crisis of October, 1962. At the time of Kennedy's death, however, there were few indications that further progress was possible, either in arms control or in further reduction in tension between the two superpowers.

Kennedy and his principal advisers were well aware of the Sino-Soviet split, but derived scant satisfaction from it. The possibility of subtracting Chinese power from Soviet power seemed meager compensation for the increased risk of war posed by Chinese bellicosity. Neither Kennedy nor Rusk evidenced any sympathy for the argument that Mao's actions belied his bluster. Rusk was prepared to go a little farther than Kennedy toward bringing the Chinese into the world community. He was no less convinced, however, than his President or Bundy or McNamara that the Chinese challenge would have to be met. Regrettably, the only line they could draw was in Vietnam, where Chinese involvement was marginal. The critical assumption, central for the American leaders, was the one Rusk had made during the Korean War, that all Communists were hostile. It did not matter whether they were united, independent or satellite. Each Communist country would in its way work against the interest of the United States. Yugoslavia was the exception that proved the rule—and not everybody was happy about Yugoslav policy. Intelligent men all, they realized China or Vietnam might prove an exception too, but they were highly doubtful and had neither heard nor seen anything to relieve their doubts. In Africa, for example, the Russians were quiescent, but now the Chinese were stirring trouble. Perhaps Kennedy or Rusk longed occasionally for less complicated days when the Russians seemed to control the Chinese.

The war in Vietnam was going poorly—worse indeed than Kennedy and his advisers realized. None of them doubted that the southern half of Vietnam had to be kept out of Communist control. All of them hoped the Saigon regime would do what was necessary without Americans in a combat role. Rusk alone expressed reservations about sending American troops to Vietnam. Once it seemed clear the Saigon regime could not survive without U.S. military forces, Rusk acquiesced, merely raising questions about the Americanization of the war. In later years, when the war was clearly lost, he thought he had been mistaken in trying to limit the size of American forces in Vietnam. Perhaps a massive intervention early would have demonstrated American determination and deterred the other side. Kennedy, Rusk, Bundy, and McNamara all underestimated the determination of the Vietnamese Communists and the cost of subduing them. They overestimated the cohesiveness of Vietnamese society in the south and the willingness of the American people to pay the price. Little of this was clear when Oswald's bullet found its mark.

NATO disintegrated in the Kennedy years, but it is hard to imagine anything that could have been done to retard the process. Few Europeans were willing to pay more for defense against a threat that seemed to be receding. Few enjoyed dependence on barbaric Americans. If anyone could have redirected Charles de Gaulle, it was probably Joan of Arc—and she did not make herself available. Not even George Ball was an adequate substitute. Kennedy and Bundy were more patient, probably more sympathetic with deGaulle than McNamara or Rusk. Perhaps left to his own devices Rusk, easily the most indignant of the group, would have provoked the French leader into being still more disruptive—but not likely.

In other areas of foreign affairs, there was little to instill optimism in men with perspectives like that of Rusk. The Alliance for Progress faltered. The administration's foreign aid program, for which Rusk lobbied relentlessly, was losing supporters even among liberal internationalists like Fulbright. In the United Nations a new majority had come into being, composed of emergent states not amenable to American leadership or sympathetic to American values. Anticolonialism took precedence over American concerns for peace, justice, and the containment of Communism.

Kennedy's legacy to Lyndon Johnson was a world increasingly less responsive to American power and leadership and an American people who were losing interest in an unruly world. Yet that world seemed less dangerous, as the United States and the Soviet Union groped toward detente. In November, 1963, the Kennedy Administration was adrift in foreign affairs. It planned no new initiatives and the President was already pointing for the election of 1964. But as Rusk might have said, there had been three years without nuclear war, without any new expansion of Communism, without an Arab-Israeli war, with but a handful of American war casualties. The UN, whatever its shortcomings, had survived Khrushchev's attacks. It wasn't a rose garden, but as the next few years would show, it could get a hell of a lot worse.

3

Rusk informed the new President of his desire to resign at the end of 1964. By then Johnson would have a firm grasp of all the issues and an appreciation of the capabilities of his inherited advisers. Once President in his own right, he would want his own men. Rusk does not seem to have been fishing for an expression of confidence, but if he had been, Johnson's response would have delighted him. With all of his overwhelming charm, the President assured Rusk of his respect and affection—and begged him to stay on. He needed Rusk—and no one bred for service could resist the call of a President who needed him.[4]

There was much to bind the two men. Most obviously, they had both felt peripheral to Kennedy's inner circle. Kennedy respected them, but had never been close to either. His brother Robert and many members of the White House entourage had been contemptuous of the Vice President and Secretary of State. Much of the mockery was public knowledge and two proud men had been wounded. Rusk had consistently, often personally, briefed the Vice President and done what he could to enable Johnson to participate. Each admired the other's restraint. Although Rusk had won the respect of the establishment that Johnson coveted in vain and Johnson had attained wealth beyond Rusk's dreams, they shared memories of being poor boys in the South. They had won their spurs, without family fortunes to aid them. Jocularly, they vied with each other's claims to having known greater poverty. Whose family had less land, less money, a more primitive house? Both were Southerners who had moved far in advance of thinking in their region on civil rights, determined to right the wrongs of centuries, to live up to American ideals. Both were great patriots, proud of the country that had allowed them to rise and determined to provide equal opportunity for all. Finally, Johnson, after long years in the House and the Senate, wanted a man who would be effective on the Hill. In 1963 and 1964, even Rusk's severest critics deemed him an unqualified success with Congress. Johnson and Rusk shared adversity as boys, a degree of humiliation in Kennedy's Washington, and a vision of a mission for Americans, at home and abroad. It proved to be a solid foundation for a warm and enduring relationship.

Johnson's approach to his Secretary of State and the changes he instituted in the process of reaching decisions on foreign policy reinforced Rusk's loyalty to the new President. On a personal level Johnson praised Rusk constantly. The White House Central Files contain countless letters from the President complimenting Rusk on a speech, on the way he responded to a question at a press conference or at a meeting, telling the secretary how extraordinary he was, how much he was appreciated.[5] Perhaps much of it was mere flattery, but is there a man or woman who would not treasure such letters after three years of being mocked?

Johnson's procedural changes were at least as gratifying. The Department of State was granted infinitely more independence than during the Kennedy years. Much less had to be cleared with Bundy and his staff. Ben Read, who had replaced Luke Battle as Executive Secretary, noted that Johnson immediately "made it quite evident that he had great faith and trust in Secretary Rusk and that he expected the Department to carry more of the load than it had been." Johnson always operated through Rusk. In the Kennedy years, desk officers and assistant secretaries frequently received calls or instructions from the President. Johnson never gave instruction to Rusk's subordinates without Rusk's knowledge. Any assistant secretary who approached the White House without the secretary's clearance was likely to be embarrassed. Johnson consistently demanded to know Rusk's views and was quick to advise Rusk if he thought a subordinate was finessing the secretary. Back-channels abroad that by-passed Rusk were abandoned. In contrast Johnson occasionally told Rusk that he wanted him to handle problems without anyone else knowing—although the Executive Secretary had to be involved if cables were necessary. Clearly the President was determined to strengthen Rusk's position. In return, declared an unsympathetic critic, "All he asked of Rusk, Rusk has given him, which is dog-like fidelity."[6]

Although Rusk's star had risen, he remained but one of several advisers to the President on international security. Bundy and staff continued to work in the White House. Bundy's relations with

Johnson were never as easy as with Kennedy and he was probably less influential. Certainly his staff declined in importance. Nonetheless, Bundy was too able to be left aside. After considerable initial difficulty in gaining access to the President, he reasserted himself and won Johnson's confidence. McNamara's skills had always been admired by Johnson and he lost none of the influence he wielded during the Kennedy years. McNamara's constant deference to Rusk as the President's principal adviser on foreign affairs was appreciated by Johnson and facilitated working relations among the men. From 1964 until Bundy resigned in 1966 and McNamara lost Johnson's confidence in 1967, Bundy, McNamara and Rusk were more nearly equals than in the Kennedy years. And with a President less sure of himself on foreign policy, when they agreed their combined influence may have been greater than before.

There was one new element in the administration of Johnson. To an extent unknown in the Kennedy Administration, Johnson relied on friends without official responsibilities for advice on foreign policy. He enjoyed the company and respected the judgment of Abe Fortas and Clark Clifford. Although the activities of these men were never humiliating to Bundy, McNamara, or Rusk, all three and their top subordinates were often puzzled by the Fortas and Clifford roles. It was always irritating to be overruled on the basis of advice given by someone less well informed. It was often infuriating when that contrary advice was given by someone who would bear no responsibility for it consequences.

In 1964 and 1965 a more forceful Rusk seemed to emerge. He did not lack for critics who, like Joseph Kraft, would be satisfied with nothing less than another incarnation of Acheson, but some commentators were pleased by the apparent change. There were reports that he had become more open, more disputatious at meetings. His stature rose to the point where many of those critical of him during the Kennedy years were gratified by Johnson's decision to retain him after the election of 1964. Perhaps with that Texan in the White House the establishment was merely relieved to have one of its own in Foggy Bottom. There was always the danger of someone like Big John Connally.[7]

Finally, there was Johnson himself—whose presence obviously constituted the most radical change in the policy process. Unlike

Kennedy—or the great Chinese emperors—he did not reach into the bureaucracy, either to stir or to observe. He did not involve himself deeply in the process. He preferred to work with his Cabinet officers—with the chiefs, not the indians. Unlike Kennedy, he did not relish and was not stimulated by debate and conflict among his advisers. He did not want them pleading three different courses. If at all possible, policy differences were to be worked out before Rusk, Bundy and McNamara met with him. He preferred large ratifying sessions, where dissent was not easily expressed, to meetings at which decisions would have to be hammered out. But he was also obsessed with the problem of "leaks" and seemed most comfortable at his Tuesday luncheon meetings, restricted to top national security advisers and a trusted aide or two. Once a decision was reached, Johnson did not like to have new questions raised. He abhorred vacillation and equated it with weakness. Men, presumably unlike women, made their decisions, carried them out, and lived with the consequences. Although Rusk, Bundy, and McNamara never ceased to encourage new ideas and dissent among their subordinates, Johnson's approach intimidated some of his advisers and inhibited the intellectual ferment that had characterized Kennedy's administration.[8]

Johnson's general ideas about policy and America's role in world affairs also differed in some respects from Kennedy's. Like Rusk, he was more sensitive about American prestige in the world. The United States always won. It must never be a loser. He was affronted by the rhetorical assaults on the United States by nations receiving American aid. More so than Rusk, he was willing to cut aid when benefits to the United States were not evident. The mystique of the Third World that stirred Kennedy, as well as Bowles and Williams and Rusk, never captured him. He had a Texan's interest in Mexico, but otherwise his attention focused more easily on where the power was rather than where it might be some time in the future. He was less ideological than Kennedy, less committed to liberal democratic regimes than to friends, less hostile to Communists because of their beliefs than because they were unfriendly to the United States. He was like Kennedy and so many Americans in his conviction that the United States had the power and wisdom to solve most of the world's problems, if the American people were willing to pay the price. Rusk, of course, was never as optimistic, but Johnson could not be reined in. He had less sense of the limits of American power than did Rusk or Kennedy. Perhaps he was most similar to Kennedy in his love of action. Motion was always better than inaction: do *something*. In the early years, his optimism was infectious and, conceivably, captured Rusk as well.

One characteristic that long-time observers of Johnson invariably called attention to was his instinct for finding the middle ground on an issue. Often he seemed unconcerned with the merits of a case, seeking instead the limits of each side, placing himself in the center. He was the seeker of consensus, of the Aristotelian mean. He was the moderate. This technique and the skill with which he executed it explained much of his success when he had been Senate Majority Leader. It had much to do with his popularity in 1964. Kennedy and most good American politicians had always appreciated the need for finding the center—an essential skill in a majoritarian political system. Johnson, however, seemed to continue the same mental process in situations where votes were not at issue and ideas had consequences: at meetings of his national security advisers. There he sought not the most popular course, but the most moderate, a compromise between those who advocated vigorous action and those who advocated doing nothing. In Vietnam, he invariably compromised between advisers who urged sharp escalation of American military activity and those who wanted to muddle on by escalating a little. It was a pattern most congenial to Rusk and, by some accounts, to the liberal mentality generally.

From November, 1963, to January, 1969, Rusk served as Lyndon Johnson's Secretary of State. Bundy left in 1966, replaced eventually by Walt Rostow, an able man but widely considered of lesser caliber. McNamara left early in 1968, having lost Johnson's confidence months before. Clifford, who replaced him, disappointed the President. In the end the faithful Rusk was left as the principal apologist for a disastrous policy in which he had initially had less confidence than those who departed.

CHAPTER TWELVE

In Goldwater's Shadow

Johnson's first year as President of the United States was dedicated to domestic affairs. At home his vision was of the Great Society, with more for everyone, especially the underprivileged and particularly the long-suffering blacks. But there was another domestic matter of hardly less importance. In November, 1964, the American people would elect their President and no effort could be spared to assure their choice of Lyndon Johnson. Not only his enormous ego, but his program for the American people required containing the Republicans, especially if they were led by Barry Goldwater. If at all possible, foreign affairs could wait until he was President in his own right. And, as he campaigned against Goldwater, he found it easy to see himself as the man of peace, the moderate, sensible statesman. He wanted a foreign policy to match. Johnson had no foreign policy initiatives as vital to him as his Great Society program. To the extent that foreign policy decisions could not be deferred until after the election, they would be made in the context of the campaign, as part of the effort to keep Goldwater out of the White House.

A survivor of the Palestinian brouhaha during the campaign of 1948, Rusk had no difficulty understanding Johnson's needs. To the surprise of some observers, the Secretary of State was active in the campaign—a marked departure from the Marshall model. He had, of course, always been sensitive to his President's political needs, but the Goldwater challenge was acutely provoking. The Goldwater wing of the Republican Party was raising fundamental questions about the bipartisan policy he and Marshall, Lovett and Acheson, Vandenberg and Dulles had worked so hard to create. He heard

223

overtones of McCarthyism and feared the ignorance and irrationality of "the primitives." These were men who questioned the value of the United Nations. Some, indeed, advocated withdrawal. They were nationalists who did not understand the interdependence of the modern world. They lacked compassion for the underdeveloped world. More often than not, their sympathies were with the imperialists rather than the oppressed. They were opposed to liberal democracy at home and abroad. They were rash men, who bruited about the use of nuclear weapons. If elected, Goldwater would demolish the edifice of liberal internationalism, wrought at such great cost—and there might be war, atomic war, and the end of us all. Unhesitatingly, Rusk responded to the charges and claims of Lyndon Johnson's opponents. They were dangerous men.

In one important respect, however, the distance between Rusk and the Goldwaterites was astonishingly narrow. Rusk remained convinced that the Communists, whether of Russian or Chinese persuasion, were bent on world domination. Tactically, the Russians had changed, but their goals had not. A speech he delivered to the OAS foreign ministers in July, 1964, might have come from Goldwater himself. "By its very nature international communism is aggressive and expansive. We see it at work in all parts of the world."[1] In the Johnson years, more strikingly than before, Rusk's conception of Soviet and Chinese policy as revolutionary rather than statist became apparent. At least in part, he seems to have been responding to a growing sense in Europe and even in Washington that the Cold War was over. Like Acheson and Dulles, he feared that Soviet "peace offensives" might be as dangerous as acts of aggression. If the peoples of Europe and the United States thought the Cold War was over, that there was detente, they would be unwilling to make the sacrifices necessary to contain Communism.

By the mid-1960s, Kennan and countless other commentators on world affairs were speaking of polycentrism, of the breakup of the bipolar world. Rusk himself acknowledged that nationalism remained alive behind the Iron Curtain.[2] But the policy implications were troubling. Both the British and the French refused to sacrifice profits to maintain economic warfare against the Soviet Union and its satellites. Rusk was particularly sensitive about their willingness to sell to Cuba. He was also unhappy about the refusal of his

European allies to support American policy in Southeast Asia. De Gaulle ignored American pleas and chose to recognize the People's Republic of China, threatening to undermine the barriers the United States had built in a hapless effort to isolate the Peking regime. The Europeans were unwilling to contribute more to their own defense or give the United States aid with its balance of payments problems. At home, influential men like Fulbright were talking as if the Cold War was over and questioning the foreign aid program. How much longer would Americans be willing to sacrifice? Convinced that rapid demobilization after World War II had tempted Stalin, Rusk feared that democracy would lose its will to resist the Communists if it appeared that the Cold War had ended.

To some extent, Rusk's strictures on the continued danger from communism were designed to hold the Western alliance together and to gain support at home for the foreign aid program. He was convinced that changes in Russian tactics derived from the demonstrated willingness and ability of the United States and its allies to respond to pressures with "counterforce." Whatever the sources of Soviet behavior, an apparent inability or unwillingness to respond would invite trouble from the Russians and Chinese. The capabilities of the free world had to be maintained, its willingness to meet force with force unquestioned. If Rusk seemed on occasion to exaggerate the danger as a means of inspiring his team, there were countless occasions when it was clear that he did not doubt the existence of a threat. Increasingly, in the mid-1960s, he worried about China. In 1964 he had evidence of efforts by the Chinese to expand their influence in Africa. He knew that in Indonesia, local Communists, abetted by Peking, verged on seizing control of their country. In Southeast Asia, Chinese influence appeared paramount as Mao urged his comrade Ho Chi Minh to drive the American imperialists from Vietnam. The Cold War was not over for Rusk. At very least the Chinese would have to be taught a few lessons about civility in world affairs. Then, slowly, they, like the Russians, might be brought into a world community governed by the United Nations Charter.

In one all-important respect, Rusk was very different from the Goldwaterites. He believed in ties to the Communist world. Prog-

ress in relations would be slow, glacially slow, but he had enormous
faith in the ultimate ability of contacts among nations to bring about
the world order to which he was dedicated. Surely the people of
Russia and China were like people everywhere, sharing common
aspirations, a desire for peace and material progress. He searched
incessantly for small areas of agreement, for ways to build bridges to
his adversaries. Agreements that reduced the danger of war—arms
control, for example—served the interests of both sides. He worked
assiduously to sell these to Congress, even when he was a trifle
skeptical. He enjoyed the relationship he had developed with
Dobrynin and even Gromyko did not induce despair. If only such a
relationship existed with the Chinese! In Kennedy's lifetime there
had been no progress. The Warsaw ambassadorial talks were valuable only as a means of keeping the lines open. Then, only weeks
after Johnson became President, Rusk approved Hilsman's "two
Chinas" speech, an ostensibly bold initiative in December, 1963. If
the Chinese would take the bait, perhaps they could be drawn in,
and tied in with those little threads. Anti-Communist and Cold
Warrior he remained, but unlike General Curtis Le May and other
Goldwaterites, he was not looking to bomb anyone back to the stone
age. He remained patient, as perhaps only a Southerner could, and
kept trying.

2

Traditional Cold War concerns continued to loom large in the
Johnson Administration's view of Latin America. Castro remained in
the saddle in Cuba and there was evidence that he was trying to
"export revolution" to other countries in the region. In Brazil the
policies of President Joao Goulart were deemed leftist, Communists
were thought to be in key places in his government, and apprehension mounted in Washington. In Chile, Salvador Allende, a Marxist,
presented a threat to the election prospects of Eduardo Frei, a
Christian Democrat highly regarded in Washington.

Johnson's response to Communism in Latin America was not
appreciably different from that of Kennedy. The United States
would use force or covert means to contain its enemy. Belief in the

salutary effect of economic growth continued. But the rhetoric in Washington changed. Gone were the ringing phrases of Schlesinger and Goodwin who symbolized the commitment to liberal democracy as well as development. Thomas Mann, the new Assistant Secretary for Inter-American Affairs and Special Assistant to the President, evoked other symbols. Protection of investments seemed to be his primary concern—at least equal to anti-Communism and more important than the development of liberal democracy. So long as American interests were served, the United States would not interfere in the domestic affairs of its neighbors. Mann was Rusk's choice, as he sought someone who would work well with Johnson and reflect the views of the new President.[3]

Rusk left Latin American affairs generally to Mann, but Cuba continued to engage his energies. Contrary to his public and private approach to the major Communist powers, he opposed diplomatic or economic contacts with Cuba. Fulbright claimed Cuba was a nuisance rather than a menace. Rusk insisted it was a menace. He quarreled with the British and French who negotiated trade agreements with Havana. He succeeded in winning OAS approval for economic sanctions against Cuba because of Cuban activities against Venezuela. Rather than his usual effort to draw the enemy into the world community, Rusk persisted in advocating the isolation of Cuba. Presumably, he remained dedicated to the overthrow of the Castro regime.[4]

Why did Rusk advocate trade with Russia or Eastern Europe, but seek to isolate Cuba? The inconsistency can be rationalized. First the Cubans, like the Chinese or North Vietnamese, had to be taught a lesson, taught to behave. Once they ceased exporting revolution and began acting with civility, then contacts might be established. A much more likely reason for his policy toward Cuba was pressure from the Right. Goldwaterite attacks on the foreign policy of the Kennedy Administration had focused more often on the failure to rid the Western hemisphere of Communism than on any other alleged failing of the Democrats. Advocacy of any policy short of invading Cuba was considered moderate. The tougher the line Rusk and Johnson took short of invasion, the larger the percentage of the electorate that could be held in 1964.

Castro made overtures to the new administration, offering to end efforts elsewhere in the hemisphere in return for an end of American efforts to bring down his regime. Johnson was not interested. Rusk replied that subversion was not a subject for bargaining.[5] It would have to stop. When it did, the world would know and there would be no need to discuss it with Castro. Kind words for Castro or any bargain with the Cubans would not be an asset in the election of 1964. Johnson was enraged by the behavior of European allies who were willing to cause problems for him by selling to the Cubans. It was precisely because Cuba was a nuisance and not a menace that Johnson and Rusk could afford to subordinate policy to domestic politics.

In Brazil and Chile the stakes were larger and public awareness in the United States slight. American intelligence analysts were worried about Communist infiltration of the Brazilian Army. Little was said, but covert support was provided for Brazilian generals apprehensive about Goulart's course. If he undermined their control of the armed forces, there would be no check on him. In March, the generals launched a successful coup. From Washington came no reproach. Johnson expressed support immediately for the new regime. Overthrow of leftists was presumably part of the "democratic process." Similarly, in Chile the United States acted covertly to facilitate the victory of Frei over Allende.[6]

With Brazil and Chile secure and Cuba faced with OAS sanctions, made possible by the vote of the new regime in Rio de Janeiro, the affairs of Latin America were in perfect order for the election of Lyndon Johnson. Only one other problem existed—Panama—and the President handled it personally.

The grievance of the Panamanians was well known: they lacked control of the canal that cut across their country. The canal zone was a strip of territory ruled by and for Americans. Fulbright was among the many visitors who noted the deep antagonism between the zone and the country in which it was situated. In January, 1964, riots broke out and Americans in the zone opened fire. The President of Panama, with domestic political concerns of his own, broke relations with the United States.

Rusk had argued, early in his career, that American control of the canal was possible only with consent of the people of Panama. It was better, he thought, to use the canal with permission of friendly

Panamanians than to attempt to control it amidst a hostile populace. At some other time he likely could have persuaded Johnson to accept his judgment and give the Panamanians the treaty they wanted. But not in an election year. Johnson would not negotiate under a gun. In the Senate, Goldwaterites bristled about allowing piddling little countries to blackmail the United States. No "piss-ants" were going to blackmail Lyndon Johnson—not in an election year. He was not opposed, however, to reaching an agreement with Panama and almost succeeded in March. The Panamanian President delayed a statement Johnson expected of him and changed a word that the American leader thought critical. Johnson was furious, terminated the negotiations, and sought to make an example of the man who crossed him. Nothing more could happen until after the elections, Panamanian and U.S. Neither Communism nor any ideological quirks on the part of Mann or Rusk were involved. In this instance, the President of the United States acted alone in what he considered his own best interests.[7]

3

Events in the Congo also impinged on the election campaign of 1964. The burst of activity in response to the Congo crisis of 1961 was not sustained there or elsewhere in Africa by the Kennedy Administration. Rusk told a black audience in September, 1964, that "what happens in Dakar, Durban, and Dar-es-Salaam affects us as surely as what happens in Bonn, Bangkok, and Buenos Aires," but he, Kennedy, and Johnson chose to have the United States play a secondary role in Africa. The end of colonialism, favored by Kennedy, Johnson and all their principal advisers, was not an urgent matter, nor was it an American responsibility. Rusk asked Harriman to handle African affairs that could not be settled at the assistant secretary level—keep them away from the secretary. Let "Communist imperialism" appear, however, and the United States would be ready to move. A whiff of it appeared in the Congo again in 1964.[8]

In 1964 Chinese Communist activity in Zanzibar worried America's African experts and they were not happy about Somalia flirting with the Russians. Cyrille Adoula's Congo, however, remained their central concern. The United States had opposed both Communist influence and the neocolonial Katanga secession movement with considerable success—and major UN support—in 1961 and 1962. Now the UN force was leaving and the Adoula regime was hardly more able to govern than two years before, despite the presence of American military advisers. Lumumbists on the left and Tshombe on the right had been excluded from power, but a liberal democratic show place had not emerged. Revolt spread through the countryside, led by Lumumbists, now openly hostile to the United States. Harriman flew to the Congo in March and determined that Adoula's government needed planes and "civilian" pilots, ostensibly to train the Congolese to fly. Soon American planes, flown by Cuban exiles recruited by the CIA, were bombing and strafing Congolese rebels.[9]

The State Department was embarrassed by evidence that Cubans and other CIA recruits were participating in air raids. Rusk had been assured that the recruits would fly only training missions.[10] The CIA seemed forever to be conducting covert operations of a sort that Rusk did not approve and over which he tried in vain to gain control. But the CIA was not the only embarrassment to Rusk and his African experts. In July, Moise Tshombe replaced Adoula as Prime Minister and it was clear that the old Katanga lobbying machine had access to the White House. There were no enemies on the right.

Johnson had never shared the aversion Rusk and Kennedy felt for Tshombe. In part, this was because he had never been one to moralize with friends. If their loyalty was assured, deviations could be tolerated. In addition, he seemed to admire Tshombe's scrappiness. Tshombe was under fire from self-righteous Arabs and Indians, as well as Communists and American do-gooders. They knocked him down and he kept bouncing back. If we were in for a fight in the Congo, Tshombe seemed the kind of fighter to have on our side. Finally, the Katanga lobby contained men with whom he had worked when as a Senator from Texas he had guarded the interests of oil and gas men. Johnson did not bring Tshombe back to power, but he was certainly not embarrassed to support him.

By August the rebels controlled between a third and half of the country. Arms on a small scale were reaching them from Communist countries. One rebel leader, Pierre Mulele, had been to Peking where he had aroused the interest of Chinese authorities.[11] From the perspective of Washington, Chinese interest in the rebel cause could only intensify the determination to prop up the central government. Together with Belgium, the United States succeeded in turning the tide. Belgian officers again trained Congolese troops and the United States provided transport planes, trucks, communications equipment, military advisers, and troops to guard the planes. Tshombe recruited South African and Rhodesian mercenaries who, with air cover provided by Cuban exiles in American planes, drove back the rebel forces. Under pressure from the United States, Tshombe tried to get black Africans to help him, but could not. The Russians stepped up their aid to the rebels, but to no avail. White mercenaries and heavy Belgian and American support enabled Tshombe's government to retain control of the country.

As the rebels retreated, they took Europeans hostage and then captured several American diplomats whom they held at Stanleyville. Fearful for the safety of their nationals, Belgium and the United States combined forces for a rescue operation. Belgian paratroopers, transported by the United States Air Force, seized Stanleyville. A few hostages were killed in the fighting, but the operation succeeded. Washington was not prepared, however, for the response of the rest of Africa. Not only was the rescue mission denounced by the Communists, but by many nonaligned countries and all of black Africa but Nigeria. American embassies around the world were assaulted and the Kennedy Library in Cairo was sacked. In the UN Security Council the United States was fortunate to avoid outright condemnation. What Americans viewed as a rescue operation was viewed by much of the rest of the world as a counterrevolutionary intervention by Belgian and American imperialists.

With hindsight it is clear that there was much to be learned from the response to the Stanleyville operation. Direct American intervention in Third World affairs was likely to evoke outrage. But to Americans their ends at Stanleyville were so clearly humanitarian that the lesson was brushed aside. As sensitive an observer as Adlai Stevenson rebuked African critics of the rescue as irrational and irresponsible. Less visibly, the intervention continued.

Tshombe could not eliminate the rebels. They continued to get aid from the Russians and from several radical African states. The United States continued to send assistance, ostensibly to keep Katanga secessionists under control, but more obviously to maintain Tshombe in power against rebels who, by the end of 1964, had every reason to be hostile to the United States. Tshombe muddled on until October, 1965, when Kasavubu tried to dismiss him. Rusk told interested Senators he was doing everything possible to keep Kasavubu and Tshombe working in tandem, "the best arrangement in the Congo," but American hopes were thwarted by an old friend, Joseph Mobutu.[12] Intervening in the Kasavubu-Tshombe squabble he threw them both out, set up a military government, and named himself head of state. He was soon the proud recipient of American aid, demonstrated an unexpected capacity to govern, and kept things in the Congo reasonably quiet. In 1965 the rest of Africa seemed friendlier. Johnson and Rusk had graver crises to cope with by then.

4

The most serious problem the Johnson Administration faced was in Southeast Asia. In Laos, the Pathet Lao were on the move again, encouraged by both the North Vietnamese and the Chinese. In Vietnam, the euphoria that followed the coup against Diem faded rapidly with the realization of how little the counter-insurgency program had accomplished. The major new ingredient, however, was Lyndon Johnson. What did the new President wish to do about Vietnam? The answer was: put it on hold. In 1954 Johnson had assured Wellington Koo that the American people would support their government in a strong stand against a Communist effort to cross the partition line in Indochina.[13] In 1961 he had been second to no one in the Kennedy Administration in support for the Diem regime, second to none in determination to hold the line against the Communists. In December, 1963, Johnson had not surrendered his determination, but he had no time for careful consideration of the situation in Vietnam. He had a domestic program to carry out, and an election to win. He wanted no initiatives. If new tactics were necessary to keep things on an even keel, he wanted them carried out unostentatiously, even covertly.

The generals in Saigon, the Communist guerrillas in South Vietnam, and Barry Goldwater did not share Johnson's willingness to put Southeast Asia aside for a year or so. As the generals vied for control of the Saigon regime, the Viet Cong demonstrated increased strength. The populace was reported losing faith in the ability of the government to protect it from the Communists. In short, as the President tried to focus on the needs of the American blacks, the poor, and the campaign, the situation in Vietnam deteriorated. Increasingly, Vietnam became an issue in the campaign, with Goldwater and supporters accusing the administration of failing to do enough. Calls for invading and bombing North Vietnam began to sound more frequently. The problem would not go away.

Like Bundy and McNamara, Rusk tried to shield Johnson from pressure within the government, especially from the Pentagon, for decisive action. The President's national security advisers tried desperately to defer important decisions until the President was prepared to give them his full attention. More than the others, Rusk bore the burden of protecting the President's options with the public. Every public statement had to be prepared with the understanding that he was not merely informing the public, but containing the President's domestic enemies and signaling adversaries in Hanoi, Peking and Moscow. The effect of his words on the Saigon regime and SEATO allies had to be considered. Naturally he preferred to say little. Obliged to speak, as he so often was in 1964, he sought refuge in generalities, evading efforts by reporters to get direct answers. Determined to mislead as little as possible, he informed no more than necessary.

In his public statements Rusk gave the highest priority to warning the Vietnamese Communists and their supporters of American determination to do whatever was necessary to preserve the independence of South Vietnam. In January he reminded a Tokyo audience that "we" had demonstrated the will and ability to make the use of force "unprofitable and dangerous." A major war, our adversaries knew, would be "prohibitively destructive." "And," he added pointedly, "we intend to make certain that guerrilla aggressions, such as that to which South Vietnam is now being subjected, do not succeed." On other occasions he announced that "we are determined that Southeast Asia is not going to be taken over by the Communists" or insisted that the commitment of the United States to the security of Southeast Asia was "complete." He assured reporters, the Saigon regime, SEATO, and the enemy, that the United States was "going to see that situation through." How many American soldiers would we send, how many planes, reporters asked. "What is required will be sent there," Rusk replied. [14]

Rusk's second priority was explaining the importance of defending Vietnam to Americans in particular, and to his European allies. These statements also had to be phrased so as to persuade the Communists that the United States perceived an important stake in Southeast Asia, so as to enhance the credibility of the American commitment. In a press conference in February, he stated his basic premise. He contended that the situation in Vietnam, like earlier crises in Berlin and Cuba, was

part of a worldwide struggle over the underlying issue of our period of history, namely, what kind of world society are we going to have: the world laid out in the United Nations Charter or a world constructed around some notion of a Communist world revolution?

A month later he told the Western Political Science Association that the Korean War had taught the Communist world not to attempt to expand by "frontal assault." Now, "we and other free nations must be determined to put an end also to indirect aggression—to the filtering of men and arms across the frontiers, whether in Southeast Asia, Latin America, or anywhere else." He repeated these themes to the American Law Institute in May, insisting that the infiltration of arms and troops across "national frontiers," presumably by North Vietnamese into South Vietnam, constituted "criminal acts against neighbors." [15]

Few questioned Rusk's commitment to a world order whose norms were reflected in the UN Charter. Perhaps most men and women could appreciate the need to defend that order against a major transgressor, like Hitler's Germany or Stalin's Russia. There were, however, questions about Rusk's universalism, about whether events in far-off Vietnam really threatened the international community in which the United States functioned. Often pressed to be more specific about American interests in Vietnam, Rusk usually replied in terms of the importance of demonstrating America's will and capacity to oppose aggression as essential to prevent a third world war. In April he tried the tactic with which Acheson had successfully persuaded Congress to aid Greece and Turkey in 1947. He argued that Southeast Asia was vital to American security. It was a region of 200 million people, rich in agricultural land and mineral resources. Forcing an analogy with the Middle East, he spoke of Southeast Asia as "standing between two crossroads and two continents, . . . a region of great strategic importance, not only to all the people who live in the great arc from Karachi to Tokyo but to the free world as a whole."[16]

Rusk also paraphrased Acheson's "rotten apple" simile. If the Communists won in South Vietnam, the rest of Southeast Asia was in jeopardy and saving it would be more costly than defeating aggression in South Vietnam. The loss of Southeast Asia would bring a shift in the balance of power. Today Southeast Asia, tomorrow "the South Asian subcontinent would be flanked, and Australia would be directly threatened. Such an immense victory for the Communists might well undermine the will of free peoples on other continents to defend themselves."[17] Acheson had once remarked, apropos of educating the public, that a teacher sometimes had to tell his students "more than the truth." Rusk had learned that lesson well.

By summer it was clear that the only criticism of policy in Vietnam that might affect the election was the Goldwaterite call for vigorous prosecution of the war. Johnson and Rusk easily adopted a course to isolate Goldwater as an extremist. Amidst a television appearance in July, Rusk was asked to respond to Goldwater's charges. He argued that "we cannot solve the problems of Asia by substituting Americans for Asians in that vast mass of people." He noted that approximately two hundred Americans had been killed in Vietnam since 1961. No answer to the problems of that country would be provided by "multiplying those casualties by the tens of thousands or perhaps even by the millions." At a news conference in September he reiterated the argument that the United States could not take over the war in Vietnam and do the job for Asians. Our duty was to assist those determined to be free "so that they have the strength and the capacity to meet their problems themselves." In a speech delivered the same day, Rusk declared that the United States intended to avoid extremes. It would not withdraw or negotiate a bogus neutralization; but it would not strike out rashly into a major war. Johnson liked this approach and incorporated it into a speech of his own later that month. The message was clear. The policies Goldwater advocated would cost many more American lives and risk a major war. To that extent, the historian could hardly fault the argument.[18]

Rusk and Johnson knew, of course, that the situation in Vietnam had continued to deteriorate through the year. They knew that the holding action would not likely hold much longer. They knew that major escalation was being recommended and might prove necessary. Johnson cleared his conscience by prefacing his remarks about not substituting American boys for Asian boys with the phrase "just for the moment." The United States would not go north and drop bombs "at this stage of the game." Rusk, however, had other concerns. Not only did he believe the American people had to be prepared for a wider war; he considered it important to present the possibility of escalation as a threat to Hanoi, Peking, and Moscow. In January, he had charged that an increase in Viet Cong activities had been facilitated by "new cadres trained in North Vietnam and new supplies of weapons and ammunition from the north." A trifle obliquely he warned that "this course of action is dangerous for those who refuse to leave their neighbors alone." At a press conference in February he was asked about reports that the war might be carried to the north. Rusk insisted that the basic problems were in the south, "that no miracle in the north is going to suddenly transform or eliminate the problems in South Vietnam"—but he carefully left open the possibility that the war might be carried to North Vietnam. In his May address to the American Law Institute he warned that expansion of the war might result "if the Communists persist in their course of aggression." Finally, in July, after American forces in Vietnam had been reinforced by 4,200 men, approximately a 25% increase, he indicated that the numbers would continue to increase, if required.[19]

In September, Hilsman's successor as Assistant Secretary for Far Eastern Affairs, William P. Bundy, created a stir by restating Rusk's warning before a Japanese audience. He spoke of the importance of Vietnam to the free world and of the "unshakable" resolve of the United States. He stated clearly that the United States did not seek to overthrow the Communist regime of North Vietnam but to induce it to end the war "it directs and supports in South Vietnam." Explaining why neither negotiation nor neutralization seemed promising, he warned that "expansion of the war outside South Vietnam, while not a course we want or seek, could be forced upon us by the increased external pressures of the Communists, including a rising scale of infiltration." Speaking in Tokyo, he was certainly directing his warning toward the Communist adversary, not the American electorate. Nonetheless, newspapers in the United States picked up the statement and noted that it did not jibe with the tone of President Johnson's speeches. Bundy was upset and likely had intimations from his brother, the President's National Security Adviser, that the President was irritated. Rusk intervened, however, and assured his subordinate that there was no need for concern. Never critical of Johnson, understanding the President's political needs, Rusk conveyed to Bundy a sense that his statement reflected policy. Johnson's speeches represented something else.[20]

In fact, within the administration, Rusk was fighting a losing rearguard action against Americanization of the war. It was doomed to be a losing battle because Rusk personally remained committed to preventing South Vietnam from falling to the Communists, a goal which the people of that "nation" lacked the will and capacity to achieve on their own, even with massive American aid. Rusk kept trying to restrict the war to the south and leave it to Asian boys, but as collapse of the Saigon regime threatened, the need for more troops and an expanded war became harder to deny.

In January, 1964, the generals who overthrew Diem reassorted themselves in a coup that resulted in the regime of General Nguyen Khanh. Ambassador Lodge regarded Khanh favorably, but like the Joint Chiefs, he was persuaded that a viable government could not be built in the south until the momentum of the Viet Cong was blunted. Although American intelligence could not verify the claims, Vietnamese authorities insisted that infiltration from the north had increased greatly, that North Vietnamese regulars and even Chinese were involved in the fighting. The Americans discounted claims about Chinese and North Vietnamese regulars in the south but did find evidence of larger numbers of North Vietnamese in Laos. In Washington there was general agreement among Johnson's military and civil advisers that some way had to be found to stop the infiltration—or at least to slow it. From Khanh, Lodge, and the Joint Chiefs came calls for carrying the war to North Vietnam. It was obvious that Khanh's forces lacked the capacity to attack the north; only the United States could conduct a major campaign against the Hanoi regime.

In February, Johnson's advisers agreed that overt military operations against North Vietnam would not begin. The President did not want a wider war—at that stage. But the counsels of moderation included approval for small-scale covert operations against the north, harassing raids that the southerners could mount with minimal American assistance and no overt American involvement. Similarly, in Laos, as the Pathet Lao began their spring offensive, initially covert American air attacks were launched against the Communist forces. Confronted by Senators who had learned of the actions, Rusk called them reconaissance flights which on one or two occasions returned enemy fire.[21]

Arguments for striking at North Vietnam continued through the early months of 1964 until in May agreement was reached by Rusk, McGeorge Bundy, McNamara, and their subordinates on an eventual program of selected and gradual force applied by the United States against Hanoi. The military had argued for attacking the source of enemy strength, presumed to be in North Vietnam—or by some accounts, in China. Maxwell Taylor thought the bombing of the North would demonstrate American resolve. Lodge thought it would bolster Khanh. Eventually, but not now. The Joint Chiefs wanted to provoke North Vietnam into acts that would justify systematic bombing, but they were denied. They insisted new estimates of Viet Cong strength required additional American troops, and were given 4,200. Lodge thought nuclear weapons might be necessary, but Rusk invoked Chiang Kai-shek's opposition and the possibility of Russian retaliation. The pressures were great within and the Goldwaterites hammered away outside. Rusk led the opposition, but the principal barrier to a bombing attack on North Vietnam was Johnson's perception of his domestic political needs.

When that perception changed briefly in August and disappeared in November, neither Rusk, nor Ball nor Stevenson nor any other opponents of a wider war in Southeast Asia could rein in American military power. [22]

The critical difference between the Rusk and Ball positions was in their markedly different perceptions of the importance of Southeast Asia. Ball constantly questioned assumptions about the importance of the region, reflecting the traditional establishment focus on Western Europe or the industrial world. Vietnam was not worth what it would cost to defend. Rusk, the universalist, was arguing against specific tactics, insisting that events in Vietnam were related to broader interests of the United States. While Vietnam might be of little value to the United States, the fighting there was a symbolic confrontation with those who challenged the principles upon which the Western conception of world order was based. In March, Rusk's perception of the problem was written into NSAM 288. [23] Rusk had created an impossible dilemma for himself. If, indeed, the struggle in Vietnam was so important, how could he deny the need for a greater commitment of American aid, forces, and prestige?

Rusk's opposition to escalation in part represented an accommodation of the President's political concerns. Johnson was not ready for more vigorous action. There could not be any. Those who demanded action had to be stalled. Of greater importance were several profound concerns. If American prestige were committed to the defense of Vietnam, the United States would have to pay any cost to see the battle through to victory. Failure would be fatal to the credibility of commitments to forty other nations that depended upon American protection. The whole system might crumble. So commitment to Vietnam could not be taken lightly. If the American government determined that commitment was unavoidable, would the American people support the government to the extent necessary? In 1964, Rusk was doubtful. The kind of educational campaign that had gone into winning support for the Truman Doctrine and the Marshall Plan would be essential—and that would take time. In addition, Rusk was less optimistic than some of his colleagues about the ability of American power to accomplish miracles. He was skeptical of the viability of the Saigon regime and aware of the attractiveness of Viet Cong preachments in the countryside. He wanted to be surer of the durability of those he would save before committing his country.

In April, Rusk traveled to Saigon for the first time and spent several days with Lodge and Khanh. The Vietnamese leader and the American ambassador were eager to attack the north. Rusk held back. There would have to be evidence of North Vietnamese infiltration that would be convincing to the American people, their allies, and neutral countries. But even if such evidence were found, Rusk warned Khanh against attacking. He was adamantly opposed to risking land war with the Chinese and ruled out the use of nuclear weapons. Rusk was also skeptical about the value of air power. In the debates in Washington, an air war against the North was often proffered as less costly and less risky than a ground war. He doubted the efficacy of bombing, especially of North Vietnamese industrial targets. He argued that such attacks would have little effect on the insurgency in the south. Rusk never forgot the virtual uselessness of the bombing campaign in Korea.[24]

In Washington during May and in Honolulu in June, the debate continued, with Rusk leading the resistance to calls from Lodge and the Joint Chiefs to attack the north. He worried about instability in Saigon. He insisted, with support from McNamara and CIA chief McCone, that a Congressional resolution would be needed to authorize a wider war. He did not think the time was right to go to Congress with such a request. In the May ExCom decision to use selected and graduated force against the north *eventually*, the last piece of the puzzle is apparent. Rusk hoped force would never be necessary. He—and very likely Bundy and McNamara—hoped that evidence the United States was prepared to use force, demonstrated by deployment of troops, planes, and ships, and conveyed to Hanoi, Peking, and Moscow by every conceivable means, would be the best chance to avoid the actual use of such force. Rusk in particular saw North Vietnamese industry as a hostage for Hanoi's good behavior. The threat to bomb it might induce the desired behavior, but once bombed, there would be no further incentive for the North Vietnamese to meet American demands. The deterrent would have been expended, the "hostage" killed.[25]

But what if threats did not deter North Vietnam? The answer was all too obvious, but it had not been faced when the Tonkin Gulf incident occurred. On August 2, an American destroyer, the U.S.S. *Maddox*, was attacked by North Vietnamese torpedo boats while patrolling off the coast of North Vietnam. American intelligence analysts suggested that the attack had resulted from a mistaken assumption by the North Vietnamese that the *Maddox* was involved in clandestine operations such as the South Vietnamese had just completed in the area. The *Maddox* was ordered back to the same waters, reinforced by the presence of the U.S.S. *Turner Joy*, to demonstrate American resolve. On August 4 the North Vietnamese apparently attacked again. The attack came at night and there was uncertainty about whether it occurred, but naval authorities assured Johnson the evidence was conclusive. The President responded almost reflexively, ordering reprisals against what he called aggression on the high seas.

Rusk and Ball had opposed deployment of American destroyers to the patrol the *Maddox* had been conducting. Both men doubted the wisdom of deploying vessels so close to North Vietnam. The American ships would be in international waters, but Rusk and Ball thought their mission provocative. Nonetheless, after the second attack, Johnson called in his advisers who, he claimed, agreed unanimously "that we could not ignore this second provocation and that the attack required retaliation." Most likely, Johnson had not called these men in for advice, but to ratify his decision. One can imagine Rusk, McNamara and his deputy, Cyrus Vance, together with McCone and McGeorge Bundy, seated around the table, with the President saying something like "we've got to teach those bastards a lesson—anyone disagree?"[26]

Apart from the possibility that the President had intimidated his advisers, there were reasons for reprisal. Striking back would preempt criticism from the Goldwaterites and serve Johnson's campaign. Retaliatory attacks also provided an extraordinary opportunity to demonstrate American power and resolve, to demonstrate North Vietnamese vulnerability, without committing the United States to escalation. A reprisal was a "one-shot" affair, easily carried out, easily justified.

In selecting the targets for retaliatory attack, the Pentagon showed considerable overeagerness. Rusk, who generally tried to avoid second-guessing the military, could not refrain on this occasion. Two of the targets were unacceptable. Bombing the first would result in civilian casualties and the second was close to the Chinese border. After his experience in 1950, he was determined to give the Chinese no cause to intervene. Johnson listened to the arguments presented by Rusk and McNamara, nodded in Rusk's direction on the first, in McNamara's on the second. The Pentagon insisted that the target near China was vital. Rusk settled for half a loaf, part of a persistent pattern in which Johnson modified military demands, giving them less than they wanted, but more than they had before. Splitting the difference had proved a useful technique in the President's career on the Hill. But even then, the middle ground had not always been high ground. [27]

American intelligence analysts warned that reprisal would likely result in increased rather than decreased infiltration. By year's end that analysis appeared correct. A CIA estimate several weeks after the raids indicated that increased pressure on North Vietnam had driven it into closer partnership with China. Introduction of American forces in Vietnam was deemed to have had no effect on the Viet Cong. The Joint Chiefs and John McNaughton, Assistant Secretary of Defense for International Security Affairs, urged steps to provoke North Vietnam into actions that would justify systematic bombing by the United States, a systematic intensification of pressure to destroy the will of the North Vietnamese. Rusk fought against the recommendation. A consensus in favor of bombing was very nearly reached, but Rusk held out, demanding that every means short of bombing be exhausted. He worried about the Chinese. He warned that the Russians might retaliate by raising the tension around Berlin or in the Middle East. He prevailed at top level meetings in early September. But the prognosis for Vietnam was gloomy and Rusk agreed that Hanoi could not be allowed to win. The election was less than two months away. If there were no miracles by November, overt military action by the United States would be necessary. Opposition to an American ground war was even greater than opposition to bombing. On the eve of Johnson's election, air attacks seemed inevitable. [28]

Shortly after the attacks on the American destroyers in the Gulf of Tonkin, the President asked Congress for a resolution authorizing him to take whatever steps were necessary, including the use of force to protect any endangered state in Southeast Asia. His advisers had long agreed that such a resolution was a requisite to attacking the North, but until the incident in Tonkin Gulf, Rusk had opposed asking Congress—ostensibly on the grounds that Congress would refuse. In August the House voted 416-0 and the Senate 88-2 to give Johnson a blank check. After November 3, preparations were completed to cash it.

Early in September, after the Tonkin Gulf reprisal raids, the administration determined to retaliate against North Vietnam for specific actions directed against Americans. On November 1 the Viet Cong attacked Bien Hoa airport, destroying five bombers. On the eve of the election, the Joint Chiefs and Maxwell Taylor called for retaliation. Rusk replied, "It's out of the question." Ball, William Bundy, and McNamara agreed. So did the President.[29]

Until Johnson decided to commence air attacks on North Vietnam, Rusk led the opposition to Americanization of the war. He never surrendered his determination to defend the south, but wanted the people there to fight and win their own war. He opposed every step to carry the war to the north and almost every step toward Americanization. He knew that if the South Vietnamese could not win, the Americans could not win as their surrogates. If the South Vietnamese lacked the will and capacity—and Rusk had forebodings about the weakness of society in the south—he did not want American prestige, the creditability of the American commitment, to be fully engaged in their cause. But if the President decided to strike, Rusk, ever the good soldier, would follow. Once the war was Americanized, there would be no turning back. Then the stakes would indeed be high.

CHAPTER THIRTEEN

America Goes to War

Immediately after Johnson's landslide victory over Goldwater the Johnson Administration focused on the situation in Vietnam and the options available. A Working Group on Vietnam, chaired by William Bundy, was established. Rusk and McNamara constituted the layer between the Working Group and the President. Averell Harriman grumbled about being left out of the action.

Late in November, Rusk posed the first question: could South Vietnam be saved from the Viet Cong insurgents if the North Vietnamese were induced to withdraw their support? Conditions in the south had deteriorated in the months preceding the American election and the viability of the Khanh regime was in doubt. Before the United States considered efforts to force Hanoi out of the war, Rusk wanted to know whether success against the north would be meaningful. All through 1964 he had argued that the key to the independence of South Vietnam was in the south; that the South Vietnamese had to win their own war in their own territory. He was prepared to concede the claim that higher rates of infiltration from the north had complicated the problem, but he had reservations about the will of the Saigon regime and its adherents. Unfortunately, a conclusive argument demonstrating that Saigon would fail even if the Viet Cong were denied support from the north could not be constructed. Rusk was forced to surmise that the insurgency might be defeated if North Vietnam ended its role in the south. The fear that the regime in the south was not viable continued to gnaw at him, however, throughout the weeks that followed.[1]

Assuming that South Vietnam could be saved, should the United

States try? Most of the participants in the debate replied affirmatively. McGeorge Bundy and Forrestal of the White House staff, William Bundy for State and John McNaughton for Defense, argued that American purposes would be served even if the effort failed. By coming to the rescue of Saigon, the United States would demonstrate that it honored its commitments. They conceded that withdrawal would raise questions about the reliability of the American guarantee, but contended that a limited American effort, win or lose, would suffice to demonstrate good faith.[2]

Rusk and Ball disagreed. Both thought that if the United States attempted to save South Vietnam and failed, it would be worse off for having tried. An unsuccessful effort to defend a client state would do irreparable damage to American prestige and undermine the confidence of nations dependent on American protection. From that point their thinking diverged. Ball contended that Vietnam was not worth the gamble. He did not think the terrain was suitable for application of American power and he did not think the area was sufficiently important. Rusk, as always more concerned about the Third World, thought Southeast Asia and specifically Vietnam worth defending. But if the United States tried, it could not afford to fail. Once the war became America's war, the nation's reputation was at stake. It could not lose. Consequently, a decision to escalate the war, to Americanize it, could not be a limited commitment. The United States could not decide to do what it could up to a specified amount of money or number of troops. Once in, the United States would have to do what was necessary.[3]

In November and December, 1964, Rusk had profound doubts about stepping up American fighting in Vietnam. Covert operations against the north had carried a threat of further action, but had not involved American prestige. The bombing raids and introduction of American combat units that he heard advocated constituted a qualitative difference, a major public commitment. Rusk feared two consequences. He worried about a collapse of the Saigon regime that would leave the United States fighting alone. This he opposed. So long as the wobbliness of the South Vietnamese government was obvious, Rusk opposed escalation. He also feared that the United States would intervene but be unwilling to pay the price for victory. He suspected it would be a longer and dirtier and costlier war than its advocates would concede. Remembering the Korean War, he had doubts as to the resoluteness of Congress and the American people. If the United States intervened, then withdrew when the war became costly, it would play into the hands of de Gaulle. De Gaulle would have concrete evidence with which to question the American commitment to defend Europe and his views would spread through NATO. The very structure of the peace system, of the world order Rusk had labored so hard to create after World War II, would be threatened. The credibility of the American commitment was paramount. Should it be risked in Vietnam?

Obviously, Rusk's dilemma was compounded by the possibility that failure to do anything more in Vietnam would be construed as repudiation of a commitment. Withdrawal prior to collapse of the Saigon regime was not acceptable. Forrestal and William Sullivan of State were arguing that some action in Vietnam was necessary to contain China.[4] Rusk saw the Chinese as co-instigators of the strife in the south, was receptive to this argument, and eager to educate the People's Republic in the norms of the international community. For him, the ideal situation was one in which the Saigon regime held on, slowly improving its position with minimal increments of American assistance. William Bundy and Sullivan advocated a compatible program of restrained pressure. Throughout November, December, and January, 1965, Rusk opposed both withdrawal and escalation, hoping to muddle through. Negotiations that winter were not feasible, he thought, given the instability of Saigon. If the United States initiated talks, what little will to fight persisted in the south might disappear.[5]

The argument in favor of escalation came from McGeorge Bundy and McNamara, as well as from the Joint Chiefs. Bundy and McNamara shared Rusk's view that withdrawal was inconceivable. They were more optimistic about the ability of the United States to invigorate the Saigon regime and they shared the JCS sense of impending disaster. Unless the United States acted quickly and vigorously, they feared Viet Cong momentum would become irreversible and the Saigon regime collapse. Persuasively they insisted that there was no alternative to escalation.[6]

Johnson heard the arguments and chose not to act. Probably the principal deterrent to a policy change in December, 1964, and

January, 1965, was a political crisis in Saigon. Once again, the generals were at musical chairs. Ambassador Taylor was furious at Khanh in particular and the Vietnamese military in general. Although Taylor did not advocate bombing for military purposes, he thought a bombing campaign might be useful as a cover for American withdrawal. Bombing the north might keep the southerners fighting long enough for the United States to disengage. When he did resign himself to a bombing campaign, he saw it as a means of boosting morale in the south rather than an instrument of strategic value.

In a television interview early in January, Rusk argued against Walter Lippmann's call for withdrawal from Vietnam. Withdrawal would "open up that terrible prospect that those who are committing this aggression will feel that in success they have a confirmation of the wisdom and the possibility of their policy." He compared Vietnam to Manchuria, Ethiopia, Austria and Czechoslovakia, symbols of unopposed aggression that he implied led to world war. Equating withdrawal from Vietnam with appeasement of Germany, Italy, and Japan in the 1930s, he all but destroyed that option for the administration. Publicly he spoke of America's commitments and constructed a case for staying.[7]

In a top secret briefing of the Senate Foreign Relations Committee a few days later, Rusk protected Johnson's freedom to escalate, if the need proved inescapable. For the Senators, he began with what was becoming his standard lecture on what happened when a country was successful in its initial acts of aggression and went on to develop an argument based on the Sino-Soviet split. It was urgent for the United States to demonstrate that the militant Chinese approach would fail, that the Soviet line of peaceful coexistence was right. Otherwise, Communist nations might adopt China's belligerent approach and the Russians themselves might be forced to follow. He expressed the conviction that the Russians did not want a major struggle over Southeast Asia. He allowed Senator Frank Lausche (D-Ohio) to lead him into saying that the favorable prospects for Communism in Southeast Asia had encouraged the Indonesian Communist Party and American withdrawal would encourage Communists everywhere, especially in Latin America.[8]

Senators Fulbright and Frank Church (D-Idaho) questioned Rusk closely on the nature of the American commitment. He told Fulbright the commitment was to give the South Vietnamese "the help necessary to maintain their independence and security." He assured Church there had been no commitment to intervene with American troops. Church pursued him and Rusk replied "we have not made a commitment to put large U.S. combat forces in there and take over the war from the South Vietnamese; no sir, we have not done that." When Church then concluded that if the United States chose not to send troops, no commitment would be broken, Rusk demurred. That would depend on the circumstances, on what the north was doing. He implied that unspecified acts by the Hanoi regime might require the United States to send combat forces.[9]

Fulbright noted that Taylor had informed him there would be "no overt attacks" on North Vietnam until there was a stable government in Saigon. Rusk assured him that this remained administration policy and that the President would consult Congressional leaders if he changed his mind. Strikingly, Rusk refused to give Fulbright the requested assurance that the administration was not considering escalation because of the desperate political situation in Saigon. Fulbright asked if he would be consulted before the decision, or simply be told there would be an attack. He asked that the President check with the committee, but Rusk replied that he could merely convey the Senator's remarks to the President.[10]

Rusk shared Fulbright's discomfort about the situation in Saigon, to the point of despair. He could not condone withdrawal, but he dared not tie his country's honor to a pack of greedy warlords in Saigon. In January, 1965, the administration had thought it advisable to disclose that it had been bombing infiltration routes in Laos, but Rusk anxiously asked Taylor not to encourage the South Vietnamese leaders.[11] He considered it essential that they not be given the impression that operations in Laos were the beginning of a new campaign, a new phase in the war. Between the vagaries of the Saigon generals and his own conception of the requirements of America's honor, he was trapped in an untenable position. He hung on desperately.

By the end of January, Bundy and McNamara surrendered the hope of giving Johnson the unanimous opinion he preferred. Presenting the President with a powerful argument for commencing systematic bombing of North Vietnam, they noted that Rusk did not agree.[12] Rusk thought it imperative to make existing policy work. They thought it could not. And yet it was Rusk who brushed aside U Thant's offer to set up bilateral talks with the North Vietnamese. He did not want to bomb the north and did not see any prospect for peace on terms the United States could accept. Johnson seemed to follow his lead.

Suddenly, on February 7, Viet Cong operatives attacked an American installation in Pleiku. Seven Americans were killed and over a hundred wounded, most very seriously. Johnson responded immediately. Bombing attacks were ordered on barracks and staging areas in North Vietnam. Unlike the reprisals that followed the incidents in the Gulf of Tonkin, these were for actions by the Viet Cong, not by North Vietnamese forces. The attacks did not reflect a decision to commence a bombing campaign, but several days later, with Rusk sick and in Florida, Johnson approved the Bundy-McNamara program.

Rusk did not object to the decision, once made. That was not his mode of operation. Nor was Johnson sympathetic to those, like Stevenson, who tried to reverse decisions. Instead, Rusk tried to delay the order until the situation in Saigon was clarified and until the Anglo-Russian co-chairmen of the Geneva conference might find a way out. He won a delay of two weeks and then accepted the next round of bombings. Thereafter he concentrated on restricting targets, fighting a losing battle to limit raids to infiltration routes and staging areas. The Joint Chiefs were determined to destroy North Vietnam's capacity for war. Rusk was skeptical, continuing to believe the war would be won or lost in the South. But the Commander-in-Chief of American Forces in the Pacific, CINCPAC, had more influence over the choice of targets in the north. Rusk learned to live with that situation, too.[13]

Three days before the systematic bombing of the north began, Rusk held a news conference to explain policy and to reply to U Thant's statement that the American people would oppose further bloodshed in Vietnam if they knew the truth. Presumably, U Thant was referring to Rusk's rejection of his effort to establish bilateral talks between Washington and Hanoi in January. Without reference to U Thant's effort, which he had determined was based on erroneous assumptions about North Vietnamese interest, Rusk insisted that the American people were well informed. Patiently he repeated his standard argument for American involvement in Vietnam, stressing the right of the people of Southeast Asia to live in peace, free from aggression, and the importance of that right to over a hundred small nations around the world. More than ever before, he focused on aggression from the north, indicating negotiations would not be possible until the North Vietnamese were prepared to desist.[14]

Reporters pressed Rusk about variations in administration explanations, especially about the importance of the North Vietnamese and Chinese roles in the war. Was the United States fighting to defend South Vietnam or to resist Chinese expansion? Why after insisting that the war had to be won in the south, was he stressing Hanoi's role? If Hanoi ended support to the Viet Cong, could the United States stop aid to Saigon? Some of these questions touched Rusk's own doubts but in public that was never apparent. Defending the freedom of South Vietnam and resisting Communist aggression were one and the same. The Chinese were encouraging North Vietnam and the insurgents, providing arms and economic assistance. He suspected they influenced Hanoi's attitude. He emphasized aggression from the north now because infiltration rates had increased and changed the war. He did not reveal that he had suppressed evidence of increasing infiltration for fear its release would bring irresistible pressure for carrying the war to the north. Rusk's audience wanted to know if the United States could succeed in Vietnam. What steps would be required? Again he declared that whatever was necessary would be done. Weapons might change, he warned, but policy remained the same. The United States insisted on an independent, secure South Vietnam.[15]

A few days before Rusk spoke, General William Westmoreland, commander of American forces in Vietnam, asked for American combat units to protect the airfields from which the bombing attacks were being launched. On February 28 the bombing campaign began. On March 6 two battalions of Marines went ashore at Da Nang. On March 7, Rusk appeared on "Face The Nation." He conceded that the Marines would shoot back if shot at, but insisted that their mission was to provide security for the air base, not to kill Viet Cong. Max Frankel of the *New York Times* asked why the

United States did not send ground troops into combat. Rusk replied that the South Vietnamese did not feel they needed American combat troops and had not asked for any. Moreover, Rusk volunteered, "there is a problem about foreign troops undertaking the kind of pacification effort that is required in South Vietnam."[16]

Rusk's remark about the problem of foreign troops undertaking pacification was one of the rare occasions when he tried to preempt his opponents in an internal debate by questioning their position publicly. The Joint Chiefs thought the time had come to send massive reinforcements to Vietnam, to have American troops take over the war and mop up the Viet Cong. Westmoreland had been dubious, but his resistance was eroding. For months Rusk and Taylor had opposed a major combat role. From his experience in the China-Burma-India theater, Rusk had concluded that "white-faced" troops engendered hostility among Asians. He understood that the Vietnamese were reputed to be more xenophobic than the Chinese. He remembered the earlier Indochina wars when he had explained to Congressmen that foreign troops enabled the Communists to discredit the side on which they fought. He remembered General Marshall's argument against American intervention in China in the 1940s. As Taylor described the necessary pacification campaigns, Rusk readily agreed with the argument that Americans should not play a role. They could not distinguish between friendly and hostile villagers. The result could be disastrous.[17]

Rusk and Johnson's other civilian advisers clung to the idea that the landing of the Marines at Da Nang met a specific need at a specific time. It did not commit the United States to a land war in Vietnam. Rusk again instructed Taylor to tell the South Vietnamese leaders that although the United States would maintain pressure on Hanoi, it did not want to enlarge the struggle. Targets would be selected to avoid provocation. He expected the maximum effort to be made in South Vietnam by the South Vietnamese. Despite acquiescence in the bombing raids, Rusk remained convinced that "a real setback to Viet Cong would do more than perhaps anything else to persuade Hanoi [to] stop its aggression." Taylor gave Rusk reason for hope. He reported that South Vietnamese morale was higher and government forces more willing to fight. Eager to avoid escalations, Taylor was guilty of wishful thinking.[18]

Few in the administration shared Taylor's optimism. Most viewed the easing off of Viet Cong activity as a lull before the spring offensive. There were reports that North Vietnamese army regulars were beginning to come in—and evidence that the bombing had stiffened Hanoi's will. Debate over sending large American combat forces continued. On April 1, however, the debate over the role to be played by American forces already in Vietnam was ended by the President. One day after a public statement that no major changes in strategy were being considered, Johnson approved the use of American troops in offensive operations. Once Americans were fighting a ground war in Vietnam, could the Pentagon be denied the men and equipment it claimed necessary to win?

Several times a month, Rusk sallied forth to defend American policy to a growing number of skeptics. For a BBC audience he insisted on American reasonableness, altruism, and tenacity. Asked if Americans were willing to face something like the Korean War, he replied that the people and government of the United States were committed to South Vietnam "for the duration." "Whatever happens?" was the question. "That is the point," he replied. To the American Society of International Law he delivered an intense, emotional speech in late April, justifying the bombing he had once opposed as a means of interdicting aggression. Using Korea and Germany as analogs he insisted that "the fact that the demarcation line between North and South Viet-Nam was intended to be temporary does not make the assault on South Viet-Nam any less of an aggression." He struck out harshly against academic critics who were organizing teach-ins to mobilize opposition to the administration's policy. He professed to be troubled by "the gullibility of educated men and the stubborn disregard of plain facts by men who are supposed to be helping our young to learn—especially to learn how to think."[19]

Perhaps the intensity of Rusk's response to the critics can be explained in part by the fact that they often used arguments he had used in questioning decisions to escalate. But the views of his critics were distinguished from his own on the level of fundamental premise. They did not share his profound conviction that opposition to aggression anywhere, indirect and well as direct, was vital to the world order that guarded American interests. They did not see that the security of the United States was threatened by aggressors whose "ultimate purpose is our destruction." "Once again," he warned, "we hear expressed the views which cost the men of my generation a terrible price in World War II." They were saying Southeast Asia was faraway, that Vietnam was not important—much as men had spoken of Manchuria and Ethopia. "Surely we have learned over the past three decades that the acceptance of aggression leads only to a sure catastrophe."[20]

How could a man who had long believed that North Vietnamese support of the Viet Cong was a peripheral issue, that willingness of the people of the south to resist was central, shift the focus from counterinsurgency to resistance against aggression—and invoke all of the symbols of the 1930s to win support for bombing and combat operations he had opposed? Part of the answer rested with his conception of his role. He had lost the debate. His President had decided on the Americanization of the war. His job was to defend that policy, not to question it. But there are other, perhaps more complicated explanations possible. In Vietnam, as in Greece—the analog he preferred for understanding events in Vietnam—he saw Communist-led insurrection as indirect aggression. In both instances the insurgencies received vital external support. They were not indigenous and self-sustained. Similarly, in seeking aid for Indonesia during the Truman era, he had indicated his belief that Communist rebels invariably received aid from foreign Communists; that their activities constituted Communist aggression and imperialism. Rusk was as much aware of the independence of Tito's Yugoslavia and of the Sino-Soviet split as any observer of world affairs, but these heresies did not eliminate his wariness of Communist internationalism. Evidence of increased infiltration from North Vietnam or of the presence of units of the North Vietnamese Army had not been necessary to arouse his concern about aggression.

Aggression had to be stopped. Rusk had never doubted that. His argument within the administration had been and continued to be about means. The argument was by no means trivial. Had Rusk won, thousands of Americans, perhaps hundreds of thousands of Vietnamese, might not have died between 1965 and 1972. But Rusk wanted to make the effort, if there was any chance of success. Once the United States committed its prestige, as when it joined a test of wills by bombing the north, it had to win. To win, the American people had to be willing to support the war. Rusk's speeches were designed to persuade the people. The United States had intervened. His own doubts had to be brushed aside and the American people could not be allowed to have any, least of all his own. By the spring of 1965, he was committed to an American war in Vietnam. From then on he tirelessly evoked the symbols that stirred him, in hope of stirring his people. His people, however, had not signed on "for the duration." As he feared from the start, Americans were not willing to pay the price.

In May, 1965, the expected Viet Cong offensive began and gained in intensity as the weeks passed. The bombing program failed to have an effect on the fighting in the south. Drastically more intensive bombing was ruled out as likely to provoke Chinese intervention. Indeed, the limited bombing program was under sharp attack at home. In mid-May the administration chose to appease its critics by announcing a pause in the bombing which lasted five days. Rusk gave Dobrynin a copy of a message sent to Hanoi. On behalf of the President he indicated hope that the pause would lead to progress toward peace, but left no doubt that he meant by that a sign that Hanoi was prepared to reduce its involvement in the south.[21] He and Johnson expected no response from their adversaries and probably did not wait long enough for anything to occur. Again the situation in South Vietnam was deteriorating and harsher action was needed. Perhaps the bombing pause would satisfy critics that Johnson had made an effort, but had been rebuffed by the Communists. In fact the United States was not ready to negotiate.

Ball had never been impressed with the importance of Vietnam and thought the American cause there hopeless. In May and June he argued against wasting further resources. Accept a little humiliation and go home. William Bundy advocated a limited escalation, to perhaps 85,000 troops, to demonstrate good faith—and then a gracious exit. Rusk had not persuaded him that the effort, once begun, had to be seen through. Westmoreland and the Joint Chiefs wanted a massive build-up of American troops to go after the enemy, to conduct search-and-destroy missions. Rusk was not prominent in the discussions, although he saw the President often in this period. Alexis Johnson joined Ball in opposing the build-up, but did not advocate withdrawal. His position appears to have approximated Rusk's, but it is by no means clear that he was speaking for the secretary. The principal opponent of an American ground war was Taylor. He contended that the tactics recommended by Westmoreland and the Joint Chiefs would cost more without accomplishing more than an enclave strategy—in which fewer Americans protected a few critical areas, buying time while the South Vietnamese saved themselves. [22]

Bundy, Johnson, and Taylor, like Rusk, worried about how American troops would perform in Vietnam, fearful that they might do more harm than good. Rusk proposed integrating American and Vietnamese units, a model used in Korea, but the Army brushed the idea aside. Rusk thought Johnson gullible in following Army recommendations, remembering how deftly General Marshall had disposed of military estimates and pretensions. [23] Very likely in the debates over the use of American ground forces, Rusk held back, pressing Taylor forward. He hesitated to confront the military on military issues and had little hope of persuading Johnson to accept the State Department's view of the number of troops necessary and the appropriate means of deploying them. Taylor was easily the best stalking horse Rusk, Ball, Bundy and Alexis Johnson could find. But to no avail.

The threshold was crossed in June, 1965. On the fifth, when it was clear that Saigon's forces were reeling before the Viet Cong offensive, Johnson asked his advisers how to get what he wanted. Rusk's response demonstrated he was prepared to put his reservations aside. He was troubled by the possibility that the gradualism he had favored, the incremental increases in American strength in the south and pressures on the north, had misled Hanoi about American resolve. Now he suggested that it might be wise to send a large number of combat troops to demonstrate to "the other side" that it could not succeed without major escalation. He did not expect Hanoi to surrender its objective of taking over the south, but rather than fight a major war the Communist leaders might revert to political means. [24]

On June 7, Westmoreland cabled for more men and authority to conduct search-and-destroy operations. The debate within the administration heated up. Rusk and his subordinates at State continued to oppose this use of American troops.[25] As with covert operations and bombing raids, Rusk's willingness to send large numbers of soldiers to Vietnam did not extend to using them. He hoped they would deter the north. Using them for security purposes, in some kind of enclave strategy such as Taylor advocated, was more congenial to him. The nine American battalions in Vietnam still had base security as their mission. But Rusk knew it was a poor gamble, that in fact deployment of another 100,000 or more troops virtually assured involvement in an Asian land war. It was a risk he took because the alternative of "losing" South Vietnam was unacceptable.

Most of Johnson's civil advisers were uncomfortable, however, with the President's handling of the American public. Rusk and McGeorge Bundy, in particular, believed candor was the administration's best chance of winning support for the drastic steps taken and contemplated. Time and again Rusk explained to audiences the reasons why he thought the independence of South Vietnam important and why certain steps seemed necessary. On occasion he seemed to exaggerate. At other times he was not candid because of his concern for other audiences—as when he failed to indicate that the United States was not ready to negotiate because its position was weak. But America was going to war. American boys were going to be doing what Asian boys had failed to do for themselves. On June 8, Robert McCloskey, a State Department briefing officer, informed reporters that "American forces would be available for combat support together with Vietnamese forces when and if necessary." Questioned closely, he affirmed that the President had authorized Westmoreland to send American forces into combat in support of Vietnamese units.[26]

Johnson was enraged by what he considered an unauthorized "leak" of a secret decision. He demanded to know who was responsible. Had Rusk or Ball authorized McCloskey's statement? Get them over here. McCloskey's "ass was going to briefing people in Africa goddamn soon." It was treason. The White House denied McCloskey's statement categorically: "There has been no change in the mission of United States ground combat units in recent days or

weeks." At the Department of State, however, McCloskey's be-
heading never took place. He had apparently ferreted out the
information on his own and acted on his own, but Rusk protected
him. As in September, 1964, when William Bundy had been more
candid than the President liked, Rusk supported the target of the
President's rage—and went off to the White House to defuse its
inhabitant. McCloskey kept his job. Johnson's credibility fared less
well. [27]

Two weeks later, Rusk described the changes in American policy
and attempted to justify them in a speech to the American Foreign
Service Association. He outlined the administration's efforts to
obtain peace in Vietnam and deftly cited Fulbright's conclusion that
the Communists still hoped for victory and were uninterested in
negotiation. With no prospect of peace the United States was
sending more troops. Combat missions had been authorized by the
President at Westmoreland's discretion. The President was acting
under the power granted to the commander-in-chief by the Constitution, with authority granted by Congress in its Tonkin Gulf
resolution, and in fulfillment of the obligations of SEATO. He had
the unanimous advice of American authorities in Saigon and of his
senior civil and military advisers in Washington. If Congress did not
approve, Rusk noted that it had the constitutional power to review
and reverse policy by withholding support. [28]

Ball, encouraged by Rusk and Johnson, presented another forceful case for withdrawal July 1. He assured the President he was not
advocating abdication of American leadership in the Cold War, but
rather that the United States should choose for itself the terrain on
which to fight. South Vietnam was the worst place possible for a
stand. Ball received no support from Rusk. William Bundy persisted
with his idea of a limited additional commitment, to be followed by
withdrawal if there were no progress by the end of the summer. He
received no support from Rusk. McNamara proposed a major
military build-up, supported by McGeorge Bundy. The President
had three plans and he turned to Rusk, who told him what he
wanted to hear. [29]

Rusk responded by reading from a rare personal memorandum for
the President that he had not shown to the others before the
meeting. Very likely, Johnson had seen it in advance. Rusk con-

tended that the objective of the United States in Vietnam was to insure that North Vietnam not force its will on the south. Pointedly, he declared: "We must accomplish this objective without a general war *if possible*," but the risk would have to be taken. "The integrity of the U.S. commitment is the principal pillar of peace throughout the world," the secretary continued. He warned that if that commitment became unreliable, "the communist world would draw conclusions that would lead to our ruin and almost certainly to a catastrophic war." In the innermost councils of the administration as in public, Rusk called for willingness to fight a small war, even risk a large one, to prevent world war. His earlier skepticism and uncertainty were gone. His commitment to the principles of collective security was total: "so long as the South Vietnamese are prepared to fight for themselves, we cannot abandon them without disaster to peace and our interests throughout the world."[30]

Johnson later wrote that Rusk had touched a worry that was much on his mind: "If the Communist world finds out that we will not pursue our commitments to the end . . . I don't know where they will stay their hand." Only McNamara's prescription fitted Rusk's diagnosis. Once again, the President's three principal advisers, Rusk, McNamara, and McGeorge Bundy, were united. He was pleased and confident as thousands of American fighting men moved into the jungles and rice paddies of Vietnam. On the day the American people chose Lyndon Johnson over Barry Goldwater, fewer than 25,000 American soldiers were in Vietnam. In July, 1965, there were 75,000. A year after the election there were 165,000—and rumors that more were on the way. An interviewer asked Rusk where it would end and he replied, as before, "we have a simple commitment there . . . we will do what is required."[31]

Through the summer and fall the war went on and there were flickers of hope. South Vietnamese morale seemed high although there were signs Saigon was addicted to American bombing of the north and would waver if the raids were stopped. A new government, headed by Air Marshal Nguyen Cao Ky, seemed to reflect its young leader's aggressiveness. The People's Republic of China seemed less threatening as it suffered setbacks to its influence in Africa and Indonesia. The administration detected signals indicating Peking would not intervene if the air war in North Vietnam remained limited. Rusk reflected some optimism in secret testimony before the Senate Foreign Relations Committee in mid-October. He reported that the Saigon regime seemed much more confident and determined than in the past and that villagers were much more willing to give information about the Viet Cong. He saw these as signs the South Vietnamese people and government thought they were winning. He reported contacts with Peking, Hanoi, and Moscow in which he found the Chinese opposed to a negotiated settlement, the Russians unwilling to make any dramatic move to bring about negotiations, the North Vietnamese close to the Chinese position, but showing some flexibility. Hanoi had withdrawn its insistence on the withdrawal of American forces as a prerequisite to talks. Perhaps the American demonstration of force was having the desired effect. He assured the Senators that the war was not developing into a great land war; nor were there signs of the other side preparing for one.[32]

In late October, Llewellyn Thompson strongly recommended a bombing pause. His analysis suggested that the Russians might use their influence to bring a negotiated settlement acceptable to the United States if the aerial raids against North Vietnam stopped. Ball was an easy convert, but it was McNamara who proposed the idea to the President early in November. All three men genuinely wanted an intensive peace effort, but McNamara also thought the effort would be valuable even if it failed. If the United States stopped bombing, as requested by men of good will all over the world, and Hanoi rebuffed American calls for negotiations, the public might be receptive to increased pressure on the north.[33]

Johnson was skeptical. McGeorge Bundy was skeptical. The President called a meeting of his advisers, including Clark Clifford and General Earle G. Wheeler, Chairman of the Joint Chiefs. McNamara made his case and persuaded Bundy that the pause was worth a try. Wheeler was vehemently opposed. Clifford argued both sides and came down in opposition. Rusk was out of town, resting, but Alexis Johnson appeared in his stead, with a memorandum explicitly stating the secretary's views. Rusk argued against the bombing pause. As he had long contended privately and publicly, he saw no sign from Hanoi that the North Vietnamese were ready to respond favorably. In March, he had told a group of Congressmen that "every dangerous question that has been resolved in this postwar period has been preceded by private contacts that indicated that it could be settled." He used the Berlin Blockade of 1948 and the Korean War as texts for his lesson. The indications he sought were missing in March. They were missing in November. Rusk argued that a pause to soothe international and domestic opinion before escalating the air war would not be necessary unless the United States was preparing for extensive operations in the Hanoi-Haiphong area. Rusk opposed such bombing until the situation in the south was more favorable and therefore rejected McNamara's second point. The President decided there would not be a bombing pause. [34]

Conceivably, Rusk opposed the pause because he feared the Defense Department had picked up the idea as a means of justifying an escalation of the air war—an escalation he thought ill-advised. One of the compilers of the Pentagon Papers suggested that Rusk assumed the pause was a "card" which could only be played once. [35] The circumstances in November were not auspicious and he chose to hold the card.

In a news conference late in November, Rusk was pressed by reporters who had learned of his rejection of U Thant's efforts to set up talks with the North Vietnamese in Rangoon. Rusk replied that he had no doubt Hanoi was not prepared for peace on the basis of the agreements of 1954 and 1962. He claimed that "throughout all of last year, the general attitude of the Communist world was that they might consider some device to save the face of the United States while they themselves imposed their will on South Vietnam. Our attitude is that we are not interested in saving face but in saving Vietnam." As American casualties in Vietnam mounted, however, the number and intensity of antiwar demonstrations grew. Rusk supported the right to demonstrate, but worried about the effect of the demonstrations on the public support American policy required and on Hanoi's estimate of that support. [36]

Early in December, Dobrynin indicated to McGeorge Bundy that the Russians might be able to help if there was a bombing halt. Rusk seized this hint as the signal he had been awaiting and at a meeting on December 4 advocated a pause. At this point the top echelon of the Department—Rusk, Ball, and Alexis Johnson, and the President's other two senior advisers, McGeorge Bundy and McNamara —unanimously recommended a pause. They were opposed, however, by the President's friends, Clifford and Fortas. Johnson withheld judgment. Days passed and it seemed that the idea was dead.[37]

Rusk persisted with the fervor of a convert. Determined to find a favorable indication, he probed in all directions until he came up with something promising at the Hungarian embassy. If the United States would stop the bombing, the Hungarians would join the Russians and Poles to send a mission to Hanoi. With this information, Rusk was able to win Johnson's reluctant approval. On December 27, Rusk called McGeorge and William Bundy to his office and informed them that the President had agreed to turn a brief halt occasioned by Christmas into an extended bombing pause. It was to last 37 days during which Johnson sent Harriman, Arthur Goldberg, and Mennen Williams around the world as his messengers of peace.[38]

To the President and to Ambassador Lodge in Saigon, Rusk indicated he was not optimistic about the pause leading to a settlement. His principal concern was the American people. Their will to fulfill the nation's purpose in Vietnam was eroding. That will had to be shored up. The American people had to be prepared for what he foresaw as large-scale reinforcements of troops in Vietnam and massive increases in expenditure. "A crucial element," he cabled Lodge, "will be a clear demonstration that we have explored fully every alternative but that aggressor has left us no choice." He thought Communist propaganda on the importance of halting the bombing had to be tested and exposed. Perhaps the pause would drive a wedge between Communist powers and between Hanoi and the Communists of the south.[39]

As feared, the Russian-East European mission to Hanoi failed. Days passed without the slightest indication of North Vietnamese flexibility. The Pentagon was eager to resume bombing, fearful of allowing the enemy to resupply and regroup. Johnson, his doubts increased by Clifford and Fortas, concluded he had been mistaken to try the pause, that he had granted the enemy an advantage. At the end of January, 1966, notwithstanding passionate warnings from Ball of war with China, perhaps even with the Soviet Union, Johnson ordered a resumption of bombing.

2

The war in Vietnam was quite enough to absorb the intellectual, emotional, and physical energies of Rusk and colleagues. But there were events elsewhere in the world that demanded their attention. In May, 1965, with much of the world already alienated by the sustained bombing of North Vietnam, an insurrection in the Dominican Republic occasioned massive and unilateral intervention by the United States.

In 1961, Kennedy and Rusk had been delighted to be rid of Trujillo's repugnant regime. They had not hesitated to use their influence and the threat of force to prevent Trujillo's family from reestablishing its power on the island. Kennedy was generous in aiding the tiny Caribbean republic, hoping to transform it into a showplace for the *Alianza,* a model of liberal democracy. The administration was pleased by the results of a notably fair election in December, 1962, won by Juan Bosch, a left-speaking liberal intellectual. A contingency plan, personally approved by Kennedy, to land troops to prevent a pro-Castro or Communist regime, could be left to collect dust. The joy lasted nine months. [40]

In September, 1963, Bosch was overthrown by a right-wing coup led by General Elias Wessin y Wessin. Kennedy withheld recognition from the civilian junta, headed by Donald Reid Cabral, to which Wessin delegated authority. He ordered the cessation of aid and pressure was maintained until December when, after Kennedy's death, Lyndon Johnson reversed course. Johnson saw no point in punishing friendly regimes because of the means they used to come to power. He recognized the new Dominican government, which promised elections in 1965, and resumed economic assistance. Unrest continued, stirred primarily by supporters of Bosch, but nothing worthy of presidential attention occurred during 1964.

As time for the Dominican election neared, Reid, strongly supported by the American ambassador, W. Tapley Bennett, was eager to continue in power. His hopes and the views of the ambassador were well known. A CIA poll, however, found only 5% of the Dominicans supporting the idea. Almost everyone in local politics was ready to overthrow Reid. Even Wessin and friends wished to be rid of him. The CIA poll indicated that about a fourth of the populace favored Bosch and half preferred Joaquin Balaguer, a moderately conservative political leader. The possibility of a coup, led by Wessin or supporters of Balaguer, even those of Bosch, was in the air early in 1965. Dominican politicians scurried about, trying to align themselves with the likely power-to-be. [41]

The revolt began on April 24, led by officers sympathetic to Bosch. Ambassador Bennett was in the United States. The American chargé thought Reid would retain control. On the basis of information received in Washington that evening, neither Rusk nor the President was alerted. By the next morning it was evident that Bosch had more support in the army than anticipated. Reid was in serious trouble, a change of government seemed inevitable, and Rusk and Johnson had to decide what, if anything, the United States would do.

Rusk's desire for the Dominican Republic, like Kennedy's and, for that matter, Woodrow Wilson's, focused on the creation of a liberal democracy. [42] That vision required free elections in which the parties of Bosch and Balaguer would be the principal competitors. Balaguer would be the likely victor and Bosch relegated to the honorable position of leader of the loyal opposition. Either man was acceptable to Rusk, although he had much less confidence in Bosch than in 1962. He thought Bosch had been ineffective as President and, worse, susceptible to Communist influence. If liberal democracy was to be the end, a Communist dictatorship like Castro's Cuba was the most dreaded danger. As the insurrection developed, Rusk's concern was to determine the likelihood of a Communist takeover. If such a danger existed, there was no question but that the United States would have to act. An administration that accepted the wrath of much of the world and a growing segment of its own supporters to contain Communism in far-off Vietnam could hardly stand by while the Communists subverted a potential democracy a few hundred miles from Washington. Moreover Rusk as part of the administration that had "lost" China was not oblivious to the domestic political costs of acquiescing in the extension of Communist control to a neighboring island.

Rusk's concern for democratic institutions was widely if not universally shared by his colleagues, but the interest in the Dominican Republic that dominated their deliberations was fear of a second Cuba. The obvious function of the CIA detachment there was to report Communist activities and it did not disappoint. Increasingly, CIA and the embassy perceived growing Communist strength within the rebellion and noted that the Communists were joining in the call for Bosch's return. Evidence of Communist support for Bosch depreciated his stock rapidly on the Washington exchange. American intervention would not be designed to facilitate his resumption of office. Preventing a Communist takeover was the first priority. Anxiety about Americans whose lives were endangered by civil war was genuine and their protection was second only to national security concerns. On the 25th, the Johnson Administration accepted as inevitable the elimination of the Reid regime, opposed the return to power of Bosch, at least until the extent of Communist involvement among his supporters was clarified, and hoped for a military junta committed to elections—apparently the most likely outcome.

On the 26th, the embassy issued warnings about the inevitability of a rebel victory and Bosch's return unless the United States intervened. Neither the embassy nor anyone in Washington saw sufficient evidence of Communist influence to justify intervention. In Washington, expectation that Wessin would prevent Bosch's return reinforced prudence. Wessin struck in force on the 27th, strafing the Palace and an army camp held by Bosch supporters, "an escalation of violence unprecedented in Dominican history."[43] His tanks rumbled toward rebel-held positions in the capital city and the worst was apparently over. The rebels turned to the United States, asking for mediation, but they had no friends in high places in Washington. The Johnson Administration encouraged the Dominican military led by Wessin, asking only that it act with moderation. If the military avoided atrocities and promised to proceed with elections, it could be assured of American support.

General Wessin failed to press his advantage, however, and during the night the rebels regained the initiative. From the embassy came panicky calls for the Marines to save the Dominican Republic from the Communists and prevent a massacre of Americans. At that point, Lyndon Johnson personally took charge. The American ambassador and the Dominican military created an anti-rebel junta that asked for armed intervention by the United States to prevent a Communist takeover. Johnson instructed that the junta be informed that the United States would not intervene *unless* the junta announced it could not protect American lives. The junta seized the hint and replied that it could not. Johnson ordered the Marines, 500 strong, to land. Over 20,000 American soldiers followed. The President explained the situation to the American people with characteristic exaggeration, inventing lurid details of attacks on and threats against Americans in Santo Domingo. Rusk wanted him to say something about preserving free institutions, an oblique reference to keeping the Communists out, but the President chose the high ground of humanitarian concern.[44] Marines landing to save Americans and other foreigners from massacre, like the international expedition to save Peking from the Boxers in 1900, smelled less of gunboat diplomacy. Perhaps the fact that the United States was violating its commitment under the OAS Charter not to intervene in the internal affairs of another hemispheric state would pass unnoticed.

In retrospect no doubt remains that Johnson ordered American forces to intervene to prevent anti-rebel forces from collapsing. He was unwilling to allow pro-Bosch forces, in which the embassy was persuaded Communist influence was great, to triumph. Intervention was, in short, counterrevolutionary. There was danger to Americans, but it was never as great as the embassy claimed. The rebels were not unfriendly until it became evident that the United States was encouraging, supplying, and reinforcing anti-rebel forces. Johnson, however, did not speak of sinister influences at large on the island until after winning a cease-fire on April 30. The pattern of his explanations, repeated loyally by Rusk, undermined his credibility with the press, Congress, the American people, and world opinion.

As soon as the situation was stabilized by American forces, Johnson sent John Bartlow Martin to determine the extent of the Communist threat. A Stevenson liberal who had served as ambas-

sador to the Dominican Republic, Martin was known to be partial to
Bosch and skeptical about allegations of Castroite influence on the
rebels. Nonetheless, he reported that Colonel Francisco Caamaño
Deñó, the rebel leader, was a potential Castro and that at least one
of his closest advisers was probably a Communist agent. On the basis
of this confirmation of embassy and CIA fears, Johnson was more
determined to support the military-backed junta, now led by Antonio Imbert Barrera. On May 2 the President announced that the
Communists had taken over the revolution.

American journalists and foreign analysts were skeptical about
Communist involvement in the Bosch movement. The embassy and
CIA could produce but scanty evidence. There were indeed a few
Communists in the country and a few of these had been involved in
the insurrection, but there was no proof that any of these were
linked to Caamaño or other rebel leaders. Quickly, the administration was on the defensive and on May 8, Rusk declared that the
"danger of a Communist takeover was established beyond question." In support of Johnson's claim he told an Associated Press
reporter that "what began in the Dominican Republic as a democratic revolution was taken over by Communist conspirators who
had been trained for, and had carefully planned, that operation."
His statement, supporting the President's, was false, but it is
possible that the information available to him at the time was
misleading.[45]

After another week, it was clear to Rusk and ultimately to the
President that the embassy had greatly overestimated the Communist danger. Getting out of the Dominican Republic now became
Johnson's primary concern. He was eager to have OAS forces
relieve Americans and to have provision made for restitution of
constitutional government. He was eager to salvage what remained
of his country's good name. American officials in the Dominican
Republic were ordered to cease support of Imbert. They did not
approve his offensive in violation of the cease-fire on May 13, and
acted to restrain him. Once it was clear that the country was not
in danger of becoming a second Cuba, most of Johnson's advisers,
Rusk included, were willing to see Bosch return, if such an arrangement could be reached peacefully. In a secret briefing on May 21,
Rusk informed the Senate Foreign Relations Committee that the

Communist danger had passed and a moderate government was needed. He conceded the unacceptability of Imbert, but spoke contemptuously of both Caamaño and Wessin. Rusk wanted a regime somewhere between the extremes of Trujilloism and Castroism, and Johnson sent McGeorge Bundy, Cyrus Vance, and Tom Mann to Santo Domingo to work out the arrangements.[46]

The mission was divided from the start. Bundy and Vance, consistent with Rusk's views, were prepared to find a place for Bosch and supporters. In a coalition government Bundy was even willing to accept a few who were ideologically questionable. Mann, however, was implacably hostile to the Bosch movement, considering all Bosch supporters dangerous. While Bundy and Vance remained, trying to twist Imbert's arm, Mann returned to Washington where he persuaded Johnson not to accept the arrangements. Imbert could be brought into line only if Washington was prepared to exert pressure. Neither Mann nor Johnson was.[47]

Bundy's efforts were taken over by the OAS which devised a formula not very different from his. OAS forces relieved American troops. Hector Garcia Godoy, a liberal democrat who had served in the Bosch government as foreign minister, became provisional president. Imbert, whose civil and military payrolls were being met in Washington, was put under heavy pressure and accepted the plan. Johnson's attention had long since moved elsewhere. In June, 1966, another fair election was held. The results resembled the CIA poll of 1965 with Balaguer the victor and Bosch the gracious runner-up. The crushing poverty of the country was not relieved, but for the second time in the decade of the 1960s there was decent government and a modicum of hope.

Both the danger of a Communist coup and of a massacre of American and other foreigners in the Dominican Republic in April, 1965, appear to have been grossly exaggerated. The reporting of the rebellion by the CIA and the American embassy was poor, misleading the President and his advisers, profoundly absorbed by events in Vietnam. Rusk might well have moved more cautiously, despite the panic at the embassy, but the President seized the reins himself, responding with characteristic vigor. Most observers have argued that he overracted. But neither Rusk nor any of the President's other advisers was willing to risk the success of a

Communist-dominated rebellion in the Dominican Republic. Foreign observers and a later generation of Americans may wonder what possible danger another tiny Communist country could have posed to the United States. In 1965 such a question was irrelevant, if for no other reason than that it would have been politically suicidal. It was an era of reflexive response.

Johnson's least excusable failing in the Dominican crisis was of explication. Assuming that he believed a Communist takeover was imminent, a statement to that effect would have alienated few Americans or members of the OAS. When he discovered the threat was slight, a frank statement was in order. Had he left the task of explaining to Rusk or Bundy, the administration's credibility might have survived. Instead, leaders of opinion in the United States and abroad saw their worst misgivings confirmed. The President appeared to resemble that other "damned cowboy" in the White House, to be an old-fashioned trigger-happy imperialist like Theodore Roosevelt—and a liar, to boot. Men like Fulbright came to doubt everything Johnson and Rusk told them and became adversaries. The cost in international esteem and confidence in American leadership was deemed by a Council on Foreign Relations publication to be "incalculable."[48] Intervention in the Dominican Republic, reinforced by doubt over escalation in Vietnam, probably cost the Johnson Administration the vital support of the foreign policy establishment.

CHAPTER FOURTEEN

Vietnam, A Billion Chinese—and Six Days in the Sinai

Rusk was committed to the war in Vietnam for the duration and Johnson was determined to win, but elsewhere in America opposition grew. Even men who shared Rusk's estimate of the importance of Southeast Asia and of the importance of demonstrating the seriousness with which the United States regarded its commitments wondered if the cost was not too great. Every week scores, sometimes hundreds, of Americans and thousands of Vietnamese died. Billions of dollars that might have been spent on the Johnson-Rusk vision of a Great Society were drained away for Vietnam-related expenditures. Slowly the fabric of American society strained, threatened to unravel, and was rent apart as the President and his advisers concentrated time, energy, and the nation's resources on the war. Abroad, the Western Alliance was a shambles and European liberals viewed the United States with a contempt hitherto reserved for Chiang Kai-shek, Franco, and Stalin. America the liberator, the protector was gone, replaced by the brutal oppressor of tiny Vietnam. Crises elsewhere in the world, as in the Middle East, exhausted American leaders already taut with tensions in Vietnam and at home. Further movement toward detente with Khrushchev's successors in the Kremlin would have to wait.

Between January 28 and February 18, 1966, the Senate Foreign Relations Committee held six televised hearings on the war. Rusk appeared twice to explain and defend the administration's policy. He spoke at great length, politely, clearly, remaining calm under

269

intense cross-examination. He opened his testimony by invoking the Truman Doctrine. Before he was through, critics charged that he had in fact created the "Rusk Doctrine," committing the United States to oppose Communist aggression, direct or indirect, all along the periphery of the Communist world. The *New Republic* quoted James Reston of the *New York Times* approvingly when he suggested that the Rusk Doctrine "makes the Monroe Doctrine or the Truman Doctrine seem rather cheap."[1]

Throughout his testimony and specifically at the conclusion of his opening remarks during his second appearance, Rusk offered the committee and the television audience the articles of his faith. He insisted that the "war in Viet-Nam is as much an act of outside aggression as though the Hanoi regime had sent an army across the 17th parallel rather than infiltrating armed forces by stealth." The United States had "commitments to assist South Vietnam to repel this aggression." Patiently he explained that these commitments had not been made "in isolation but are part of a systematic effort in the postwar period to assure a stable peace." Because of the worldwide scope of American commitments, the issue in Southeast Asia became world-wide: "we must make clear that the United States keeps its word wherever it is pledged." He staunchly repeated the American desire for peace, which could come very quickly "if the armed attack against South Vietnam is brought to an end."[2]

Maxwell Taylor and David E. Bell, AID Administrator, also spoke in defense of the administration's policies. But perhaps of greatest consequence were the appearances of General James M. Gavin and George Kennan as critics. Kennan, in particular, consistent with his low regard for the importance of underdeveloped countries, left no doubt that he believed increasing involvement in Vietnam was foolish and might well, in the end, lead to a disastrous war with China. He had no doubt that withdrawal would be tolerable. The televised hearings, revealing the reservations of prominent and highly regarded observers, assured millions of Americans of the respectability of dissent.[3] A few days later, Robert Kennedy added his voice to those critical of the administration. Intimates of his brother rallied around him, supporting his suggestion that the risk of a coalition with the NLF was less than the risk of trying to exclude the Front from the Saigon government. Few people were less likely to persuade Johnson to change course than the late President's brother. Ideas coming from what Johnson perceived as the enemy camp were to be proven wrong, not accepted. Criticism mounted, but Johnson was a stubborn man.

The war went on. More American boys died fighting a war "our" Asian boys could not win for themselves. Many more Vietnamese—men, women, and children—died. On June 27, 1966, Rusk told a SEATO conference: "I see no prospect of peace at the present time." Two days later the air war was extended as the Pentagon was at long last granted permission to carry out attacks on petroleum storage areas in the Hanoi-Haiphong area, a major escalation. Two weeks later, after Rusk returned to the United States, he told reporters "we are not over the hump yet. We haven't begun to see the end of this thing yet."[4]

Privately, Rusk's role did not change. He continued to believe success depended upon events in the south, upon the ability of the Saigon regime to win the support of its people and pacify areas dominated by the Viet Cong. At a high-level meeting in Honolulu in February, 1966, he argued that weakness in the south was responsible for the unwillingness of the Hanoi regime to negotiate. If the government of South Vietnam built an "indestructible" society, Hanoi would be more responsive. The south had to demonstrate confidence and momentum before Hanoi would "stop this aggression." Troop increases by the United States, and acquiescence to military demands for more bombing targets struck Rusk as the wrong way to fight. As long as the North Vietnamese were persuaded that the south lacked the will and capacity to defend itself, lacked a viable society, they would keep coming. Jockeying among the Saigon generals and trouble between the regime and the Buddhists angered Rusk. In March, he evidenced frustration in a cable to Lodge. He warned that if bickering within the South Vietnamese government did not stop, if the government did not start focusing on the Viet Cong, the southerners would have no country to quarrel about. The United States, he contended, could not succeed "except in support of the South Vietnamese." Unless they were able to join ranks, Rusk thought the prospects "grim."[5]

Rusk's role in the decision to escalate the air war by striking at petroleum storage areas near Hanoi and Haiphong is ambiguous. It is clear that he opposed the decision, advocated forcefully by McNamara. But he had framed his opposition in terms of a request for delay pending a Canadian effort to see if Hanoi would consider negotiations. McNamara was skeptical, but Rusk warned of "general international revulsion" if the Canadian mission was sabotaged by new raids. The Secretary of State was clearly concerned about the ramifications of undermining a mission undertaken with American approval, but insisted that it was also urgent to determine whether Hanoi's "thus far harsh and unyielding attitude" had changed, precluding the need for a new escalation. Johnson accepted Rusk's argument. Attacks were delayed until conclusion of the Canadian mission to Hanoi. Rusk had slowed the devastation of the north by two or three weeks, nothing more.[6]

Rusk's hope had been to prevent the escalation, but he had no leverage in the contest with McNamara. In the spring of 1966, Johnson still had enormous admiration for the Secretary of Defense. McNamara, who never hesitated to rein in the military when he thought it necessary, now argued on behalf of the request to hit the petroleum tanks. With absolute confidence, statistical evidence and impressive logic, he explained how such attacks would cripple the north's logistical support for the war in the south and decrease infiltration. The attacks would turn the war around. Rusk was dubious, but the Canadian mission was the only card he had to play. There was no way to prove in advance that McNamara and the Joint Chiefs were wrong. Rusk was not as ready to accede to military demands as was the President, but no less reluctant to deny them operations they claimed could save American lives and accomplish American purposes. He could and did talk of the failure of strategic bombing in the Korean War, but he could not play that tune forever. His only hope in June, 1966, was for delay—and the success of the Canadian mission. When it failed, he could no longer object to bombing. This was, after all, a war of whose importance he was profoundly convinced.

The escalation, like those before it, failed. An appraisal of its effects was provided by CIA and the Defense Department's own intelligence analysts after eleven weeks of attacking the new targets. There was no evidence that the bombing had affected significantly

North Vietnamese morale or ability to send men and materials. In fact, Hanoi was able to obtain aid from other Communist countries that more than compensated for the damage American planes were inflicting. After eleven weeks of increased death and destruction in the north and increased casualties to American pilots, the enemy's capacity to wage war in the south may well have improved. Intelligence analysts could find nothing to suggest that increased, less restrained bombing, such as advocated by CINCPAC, would help.[7]

Rusk did not have to force the obvious conclusion on McNamara. At last he, too, questioned the value of escalations of the air war. He was greatly disturbed by the inaccuracy of air force and navy predictions and increasingly at odds with the Joint Chiefs. The latter were angered by McNamara's pessimism, objected to his desire to limit the number of American soldiers in Vietnam and draw the line against increased bombing or new targets. They kept the President informed of their own views. Through the fall of 1966, McNamara, supported by his civilian aides, prevailed. But the war and the dying went on. McNamara saw no way to end it. In the war for the hearts and minds of the people, "the important war," he concluded "we find ourselves . . . no better, and if anything, worse off."[8]

Lodge, in Saigon, remained optimistic. In August he insisted "we are not losing . . . never have things been going better; indeed never have things been going so well. We are 'on the track' with regard to almost every aspect of the war and we are winning in several." In November, General Wheeler told the President the war was going well, "in a very favorable fashion." He insisted that the initiative was Westmoreland's, who "in every operation to date has managed to defeat the enemy." These were the kind of reports the President, quite naturally, wanted to hear. The White House staff, headed now by Walt Rostow, was optimistic. In December, amidst a Polish peace effort and while Rusk was abroad, the bombing of North Vietnam intensified. Targets close to Hanoi were struck, with heavy and confirmed damage to civilian areas.[9]

Johnson was determined to win. Clifford and Fortas urged him on. Rostow was confident. Rusk was troubled, but could see no alternative. McGeorge Bundy and Ball were gone. McNamara's doubts were beginning to irritate the President. In January, 1967, McNamara told a joint session of the Senate Armed Forces and

Appropriations Committees that the bombing had failed and no bombing program he could contemplate "would significantly reduce [the] actual flow of men and material to the South."[10] He was merely offering, almost verbatim, the estimate of American intelligence experts, but the President was furious. As McNamara's doubts increased, his influence declined. His statements before the Senate committees ended his importance among the President's advisers. Only Rusk, who was "in for the duration," retained his stature. Increasingly, Johnson turned to General Wheeler for the advice he wanted from the Pentagon. Slowly, Rostow's aggressiveness and determination drew him into the inner circle. But it was a circle of "yea-sayers," of boosters, of "can-dooers."

The international demand that the United States stop bombing intensified, especially after New York Times editor Harrison Salisbury confirmed Hanoi's claims that nonmilitary targets were being hit. The North Vietnamese demanded that the bombing stop. Rusk insisted that the bombing constituted only half the war and demanded that Hanoi promise a reciprocal deescalation of its own war effort.[11] The North Vietnamese refused and the bombing continued. In January, 1967, however, despite the opposition of the Joint Chiefs, agreement was reached for a bombing halt over the Tet or lunar New Year holidays. The impending lull in the fighting corresponded coincidentally to a visit to London scheduled by Soviet Premier Alexsei Kosygin. Johnson agreed to an attempt by British Prime Minister Harold Wilson to gain Soviet support for a peace conference.

The Wilson-Kosygin talks very nearly produced a major Soviet effort to bring North Vietnam to the peace table. On January 28 the North Vietnamese foreign minister gave an interview in which he appeared to indicate that talks were possible following an unconditional bombing halt. On February 2, Johnson in a televised press conference declared himself willing to meet the Communists more than halfway. If they were ready to talk, he was willing to discuss almost anything at almost any place. At the same time the idea for a letter from Johnson to Ho Chi Minh had taken hold in Washington. Rusk was doubtful, but Rostow was, as always, determined. Chester Cooper, a special assistant to Harriman, was shown several drafts of the Johnson-Ho letter before he left for London to brief Wilson.

Cooper assumed the President and his advisers were prepared to proceed on the basis of what had come to be known as the "Phase A—Phase B" formula. The United States was prepared to stop bombing North Vietnam, announcing what appeared to be an unconditional halt. It would do so upon receipt of secret assurance that Hanoi would stop sending troops south shortly after the bombing stopped, whereupon the United States would stop the augmentation of its troops. Cooper recommended that Wilson propose this formula to Kosygin. After the first day of talks between Wilson and Kosygin, Cooper received instructions from "Washington"— probably from Harriman—to ask Wilson to emphasize the Phase A—Phase B arrangement and drop the idea of a Geneva Conference. [12]

On February 8, the day the Tet pause began, Kosygin spoke in London, paraphrasing the North Vietnamese foreign minister. There would have to be an unconditional bombing halt before talks were possible. Later that day, Rusk told Congressional leaders that he was "convinced that the Soviet Union would be prepared to see this matter settled on the basis of the 17th parallel and the status quo ante." The Russians seemed willing to help. Rusk was persuaded they would be satisfied with terms that were acceptable to the United States. On the following day Kosygin expressed interest in the Phase A—Phase B formula and asked to see it. Cooper helped prepare a draft, a copy of which was cabled to Washington for approval. Approval never came. After more than twenty-four hours without response from Washington, Cooper and Wilson chose to interpret silence as consent. They believed they were following an outline prepared in consultation with the President, Rusk and Rostow, among others. The message was passed on to Kosygin. [13]

On the evening of February 10, after Cooper's draft had been passed to Kosygin, Cooper received a call from Rostow at the White House. A new version of the message to Kosygin was on the way. When it arrived, Cooper and Wilson were shattered. The Phase A—Phase B formula had been dropped and the United States had reverted to its demand that the infiltration stop before the United States stopped bombing. It was, as Kosygin noted, a very different proposition, which Hanoi had rejected countless times. Wilson, Cooper, and Kosygin fell back on an effort to extend the pause in exchange for a promise by the North Vietnamese to keep their forces north of the 17th parallel, but accomplished nothing. On February 14 the bombing resumed. [14]

The decision to withdraw the Phase A—Phase B proposal was, of course, Johnson's. The message to Kosygin was drafted by Rusk at the White House—at the direction of the President. The principal reason for the decision appears to have been the President's mistrust of the North Vietnamese. He was convinced he had been misled the previous year, when he had agreed to an extended bombing pause. Clifford, Fortas, and Rostow argued that the North Vietnamese had deceived him into thinking there was a chance for peace and had used the time to improve their military position. Now, in 1967, it was evident that the North Vietnamese had been poised for a massive resupply operation on the eve of the Tet cease-fire. The President would not make that mistake again. Rusk might argue that the Russians were desirous of ending the war in Vietnam and getting on with steps toward detente, but Rostow could point to the enormous quantities of men and material moving south. Cooper also recalled that Johnson and Rostow were unenthusiastic about Wilson's role, suspecting him of "grandstanding." If peace talks did begin, the President wanted them to come as the result of his own efforts. The Nobel Peace Prize for an Englishman was not the President's idea of an appropriate end to America's war in Vietnam. [15]

In the months that followed, a struggle developed in which Rusk, McNamara and most of their subordinates were aligned against the military. The Joint Chiefs, Westmoreland and Admiral Ulysses G. Sharp, CINCPAC, demanded freedom from restraint on bombing targets and an increase in American forces in Vietnam, already numbering 436,000 by the beginning of May, 1967. Rusk had never been a proponent of strategic bombing. McNamara had lost confidence in it. On May 4, McGeorge Bundy, an early advocate of the bombing, joined his brother in opposition. Johnson was presented with a proposal to stop the bombing above the 20th parallel. The Secretaries of State and Defense supported the proposal which, in effect, ended strategic bombing while continuing the harassment of North Vietnamese forces and supply operations near the demilitarized zone. Johnson appeared interested. The military opposed strenuously. Johnson decided to authorize one more target that the Joint Chiefs of Staff contended was critical: Hanoi's thermal power plant. Attacks on the plant began May 19, took months to accomplish their purpose, and devastated nearby civilian areas. Rusk offered the idea again in June, on the eve of Johnson's meeting with Kosygin at Glassboro, but the President had lost interest.[16]

By May, 1967, McNamara had reached the point where he could contemplate withdrawal from Vietnam on grounds that might once have appealed to Rusk. He argued that the only American commitment to South Vietnam was to assure its people an opportunity to determine their own future. If that country ceased to help itself, the commitment ended. But McNamara also argued that the larger objective of containing China had already been accomplished. This Rusk did not believe. The Chinese had not demonstrated that they had learned the necessary lesson. William Bundy also argued that withdrawal or a feigned peace would have an adverse effect on Asians who, he contended, saw Vietnam as a test case of American resolve in their part of the world.[17]

For Rusk and those who thought like him, the dilemma remained. They could not contemplate withdrawal, yet there seemed no way to accomplish their ends by force. In late May the CIA reported that "short of a major invasion or nuclear attack, there is probably no level of air or naval actions against North Vietnam which Hanoi has determined in advance would be so intolerable that the war had to be stopped." The Communist regime remained confident of victory and the popular mood was described as "resolute stoicism with a considerable reservoir of endurance still untapped." A few days later another CIA analysis conceded that the goal of interdicting supplies between north and south was beyond attainment. Rusk and Bundy had always believed that the war had to be won in the south, but Westmoreland was talking of needing 565,000 men to win in three years, 665,000 if he was expected to win in two. And over at the Pentagon, Alain Enthoven, Assistant Secretary of Defense, director of Systems Analysis, contended that Westmoreland's analysis was spurious, that more American troops would do little good and great harm, especially to the economy of South Vietnam.[18]

There seemed nowhere to go. Victory remained illusory. Defeat was inconceivable. Frustration with the war was growing in the country. But after his meeting with Kosygin in June, Johnson was confident there was no danger of American persistence in Vietnam leading to a larger war. The Chinese were enmeshed in their Cultural Revolution and had signaled their intention not to intervene long before. At Glassboro, Kosygin left Johnson assured that the Soviet Union would not allow the war in Vietnam to lead to a confrontation. Johnson decided to hold course. Westmoreland would get a few more men, but not as many as he wanted. The bombers would get a few more targets, but not all they demanded.

In July, Newark and Detroit erupted with riots. Scores were killed, thousands arrested, millions of dollars in property damage registered. The anger of the black ghettoes was not directly related to the war in Vietnam, but the riots added to the sense of a society breaking apart. Some critics of administration policy in Vietnam demanded that funds bringing death to Southeast Asia be diverted to saving lives at home, to the war on poverty. As Rusk dreamt of saving the world community, the community at home verged on disintegration.

Both in the United States and abroad, the demand to stop the bombing intensified in the summer of 1967. The military continued to insist that decisive results could be obtained if target restraints were removed. They took their case to the Senate Preparedness Subcommittee, notoriously sympathetic to the desires of the armed forces. Finally, McNamara testified. He insisted that North Vietnam could not be "bombed to the negotiating table," and argued against escalation of the air war. The committee disregarded his arguments and urged Johnson to listen to his uniformed advisers. The President held back and he and Rusk used the pressure from the military to defend their course before the country. Rusk expressed confidence that the overwhelming majority of Americans would reject both alternatives, withdrawing or fighting a larger war.[19]

On September 29 at San Antonio the President stated that the United States would stop bombing North Vietnam "when this will lead promptly to productive discussions." He assumed that "while discussions proceed, North Vietnam would not take advantage of the bombing cessation or limitation." Johnson appeared to be taking a new position, indicating the United States would stop bombing without the cessation of infiltration if Hanoi would not use the opportunity to increase its operations. The North Vietnamese were not interested. Support for administration policy was dwindling and Hanoi knew it. Eugene McCarthy had stepped forward as a peace candidate, determined to challenge Johnson for the Democratic nomination, and even the Pope was calling for suspension of the bombing. Domestic pressure on Johnson might force further concessions. The Communist leaders misjudged their man. Before the year had ended, Johnson nominated McNamara to head the World Bank. The President named Clifford, who shared his own resolve, to replace the faltering Secretary of Defense. Brushing aside the objections of Rusk as well as those of McNamara, Johnson authorized the military to bomb the targets his top civil advisers had counseled against hitting. Rusk was more successful in thwarting the military desire to conduct operations in Cambodia, prevailing on Johnson to send Bowles to Cambodia to work out arrangements with Prince Sihanouk.[20]

Johnson began the new year with a new team, on which there were no doubters apparent. Rostow was as confident and determined as Wheeler, Westmoreland and CINCPAC. Clifford had generally favored a more aggressive course than had Rusk. And the Secretary of State was still determined to do whatever was necessary.

In the waning hours of 1967 the North Vietnamese foreign minister stated categorically that Hanoi would negotiate if the United States stopped bombing. The North Vietnamese did not modify their goals. Nonetheless, the foreign minister's statement was the first unequivocal assurance that talks were possible. The United States had halted the bombing for a New Year's truce, but resumed the raids on January 2. Rusk was not ignoring the North Vietnamese overture. He seemed haunted, however, by recollections of the Korean War, of talks that went on for two years while fighting continued. He tried to find out what Hanoi had in mind, while his allies in Saigon warned against a unilateral American decision to negotiate.[21]

As the days passed, evidence accumulated of a massive Communist build-up, especially in the area around Khe Sanh. It appeared as if the North Vietnamese might have reverted to the model of their campaign against the French, seeking a decisive victory along the order of Dienbienphu. Westmoreland cancelled the Tet truce in the vicinity of Khe Sanh. He was ready to show his adversaries the difference between the United States and France. On January 30, the Communist offensive came, but not at Khe Sanh. Instead the Viet Cong struck at the major cities of South Vietnam. In Saigon they penetrated the American embassy, an incredible sight for millions of Americans who watched it on their television sets. So much for negotiation, so much for victory.

2

In October, 1967, pressed by reporters to explain why he deemed the security of the United States to be at stake in Southeast Asia, Rusk replied with reference to "a billion Chinese, armed with nuclear weapons." Critics of the administration seized the phrase and charged that Rusk was evoking fear of a "Yellow peril," or that he had an irrational hatred of the Chinese that explained the irrational policies he had advocated toward Vietnam. Among some members of the White House staff and even among subordinates at the Department of State, Rusk had a reputation for intense hostility toward the Chinese Communists, the roots of which were usually traced to the Korean War. His notorious "Slavic Manchukuo" speech seemed ample evidence.[22]

As indicated earlier, that speech did not derive from hatred of the Chinese Communists, irrational or otherwise. The address was a carefully conceived, deliberate device for accomplishing two purposes of the Truman Administration. First, it was designed to goad non-Stalinist Chinese Communists to act more like Chinese nationalists, to continue administration efforts to drive a wedge between China and the Soviet Union. Second, it was to protect the administration from rightist attacks amidst the investigations following MacArthur's recall from Korea. It was an ill-considered speech, served neither purpose, and misled the American people—and perhaps the rest of the world. It was not, however, the result of one man's rage.

In the 1950s, Rusk's ideas about China and American policy toward China approximated the view prevalent among academic liberals. He wanted accommodation with the People's Republic, wanted China to be brought into the international community, bound into the fabric, to learn its norms. He shared none of the fears of a barbarous China, used none of the rhetoric of his friend Dulles. Unlike a number of leading liberals, Senators Paul Douglas, Jacob Javits, and Hubert Humphrey among them, Rusk thought the People's Republic belonged in the United Nations. Like Bowles and perhaps most other liberals, by 1960, Rusk hoped for a two Chinas approach to the UN question and perhaps, ultimately, to recognition.

As Secretary of State, Rusk was allowed no opportunity for initiatives toward China. Kennedy rejected the proposals Rusk and Bowles brought to him. He may have feared the so-called "China Lobby," whose influence Rusk thought exaggerated in the 1960s. More likely, Kennedy's decision on approaches to Mao reflected hostility toward the Chinese Communists—or support for Chiang. His advisers did not think domestic political exigencies required his secret promise in 1961 to use the veto if the People's Republic were admitted to the UN. Certainly fear of the China lobby did not necessitate Kennedy's decision in 1962 to cooperate with Chiang in covert operations against the People's Republic.

After Kennedy's death, Hilsman's two Chinas initiative was allowed. Johnson was generally considered more flexible than Kennedy about China. Nonetheless, American policy toward the People's Republic, official rhetoric, and Rusk's attitude hardened. The explanation for this change, after the promising moment of Hilsman's speech, will be found less in Rusk's psyche than in Chinese behavior. The Kennedy years had been a time in which Chinese policy had stressed militant anti-imperialism and support of national liberation movements. By 1964, Chinese efforts seemed productive in Southeast Asia and Africa. By 1964, also, improved relations with the Soviet Union freed the United States to focus more on East Asia and Chinese activities.

Some government and many academic specialists argued that

China was engaging in defensive rhetoric and need not be feared. Rusk gave more credence to what the Russians were telling him. Dobrynin explained the Sino-Soviet split in terms of Chinese militancy and blamed the problems of Southeast Asia and other areas on China. Khrushchev accused the Chinese of pursuing "an openly expansionist program with far-reaching pretensions" and exhibited a Chinese textbook showing that China claimed most of South Asia. The Russians persuaded Rusk they were operating in good faith in Laos, that it was the Chinese who were responsible for refusal of the Pathet Lao and the North Vietnamese to abide by the 1962 agreement. Had the same charges come from American rightists, Rusk would have been more skeptical. But the Russians, instead of condemning the United States, accused their Chinese comrades of being the gravest threat to world peace—and Rusk found this source impossible to ignore.[23]

Having progressed toward rapprochement with the Soviet Union in 1963, Rusk and other Americans wanted to know, in 1964, if peaceful coexistence with the Chinese was possible. The Sino-Soviet split had its disadvantages. Gains won with Moscow were more likely to be debits than assets in Peking. Could the People's Republic be brought into the international community and persuaded to live by its norms?

In January, after France had disregarded American sentiment and recognized the People's Republic, Rusk catalogued his concerns for a Tokyo audience. "Peiping" still insisted on the surrender of Formosa, abandonment of 12 million people there, as the sine qua non for improving Sino-American relations. "Peiping" had violated the 1954 and 1962 Geneva agreements: "it incites and actively supports aggression in Southeast Asia." "Peiping" was attempting to "extend its tactics of terror and subversion into Latin America and Africa." "Peiping" had "nothing but contempt for the most elementary condition for peace": it would not leave its neighbors alone. Referring obliquely to France, Rusk argued that "free nations must not reward the militancy of Peiping or give Communists anywhere any ground for hope of profit from the use or threat of force." His argument emerged clearly. The Chinese had to learn that deviations from acceptable norms of international behavior would not be tolerated. De Gaulle was confusing the message. The United States would not. When Rusk visited Chiang a few months later, he assured him that the new President would honor Kennedy's promise to use the veto to keep the People's Republic out of the UN—and would continue to cooperate in operations against the mainland.[24]

Early in February, McNamara told a joint session of the Senate Armed Services Committee and the Subcommittee on Department of Defense Appropriations that the Chinese armed forces were having supply problems as a result of the Sino-Soviet split. He did not think they would undertake a major campaign against India, South Korea or Formosa within the next year. "However," he warned, "there is always the danger that, as a result of another agricultural disaster, the Chinese Communists may, as an act of desperation, attempt to overrun Southeast Asia—which is normally a food surplus area." Perhaps he could not appear too sanguine when he was trying to get money for his Department.[25]

Later in the month, Robert Komer, an aide to McGeorge Bundy, recommended "a harder Chicom line in general, designed to support and help validate our effort to scare off Hanoi on Vietnam, stem a GRC rout [protect Taiwan's seat in the UN], box in the Japs, convince the Indians (and Paks) we still mean business, etc." The implication was that for tactical reasons, in support of other policies, it would be useful to appear more hostile to the People's Republic. Komer did not seem fearful of the Chinese. But in October, the People's Republic exploded its first atomic bomb. By December, Ray Cline, Deputy Director of CIA, warned Bundy that the Chinese intended to break through the American policy of containment worldwide.[26]

The election behind them, Johnson and advisers faced the situation in East Asia. Concern about a militant China armed with nuclear weapons was fundamental in their decision-making. One observer feared that China's nuclear capability "placed an awesome new weapon in the hands of a government that had shown notorious contempt for human life and for accepted standards of international ethics, even Communist ethics."[27] Rusk in particular was concerned about Chinese rhetoric and behavior. The idea that American interests would be served best by a world living according to generally accepted rules of behavior was the central element of his faith. In 1964 and 1965 the People's Republic was the one major state that stood outside that order and openly condemned it. Even the Russians at their worst paid lip service to the UN Charter and its principles. The Chinese championed a different world order and a militant behavior that Rusk feared would mean chaos, war, and, in a nuclear world, the destruction of civilization. He saw an analogy between what Mao was doing and what Hitler had done. When the Indonesians left the United Nations, apparently throwing their lot in with the Chinese, Rusk was badly shaken by the precedent. It was a major success for forces that sought to undermine all that had been accomplished by winning the Second World War. Peking, like a Siren, was luring mankind to destruction. It was essential to demonstrate to the world that Mao was wrong, that rejection of civilized behavior did not pay. Rusk understood as well as Ball that Vietnam was a poor place to make his stand, but no better terrain seemed available. If Communist militancy could be defeated in Vietnam, under the best possible circumstances for the Communists, there could be no doubt as to the lesson.

French recognition of the People's Republic continued to sting Rusk. In January, 1965, he explained his view that trade, recognition, or admission to the United Nations would encourage the Chinese to believe their policy was "paying dividends." Reinforcing their behavior was "not in the interests of getting peace established in the Pacific area."[28] Increasingly, the frustrations of the war in Vietnam came to be attributed to Chinese militancy. Simultaneously, Rusk equated winning the war with winning a battle for the principles of the UN Charter over the apocalyptic alternative the Chinese posed. He became hostile to the Chinese to a degree not apparent in the 1950s. A conflict seemed to emerge in his mind between the desire to draw China into the international community and a fear that the Chinese would mistake amity for weakness, for evidence that militance brought reward. Early in Johnson's presidency, in 1964 or early 1965, he concluded that China would have to be taught a lesson before Mao could be expected to play a salutary role in world affairs, before the "little threads" would serve any purpose.

In February, 1965, Ball and Rusk took turns briefing Congressmen on Vietnam. Ball referred to "the fact that behind the government of Ho Chi Minh is the very large specter of an expansionist Red China." Asked about a de Gaulle suggestion for an international conference, Rusk brushed the idea aside by saying that the free world knew what had to be done "if this course of aggression by Peking is to be slowed up." In June, Rusk told the Foreign Service Association that the Chinese were looking beyond Vietnam "to the hope of domination in all of Southeast Asia—and indeed beyond." The CIA was reporting expansion of Chinese influence in Africa, especially in the Congo (Brazzaville), Mali, Ghana, and Tanzania. Rusk was intensely apprehensive. They had to be stopped. [29]

In August, Rusk tried to assure the Chinese they had nothing to fear from the United States. He argued that there was "nothing in the conduct of the last 15 or 20 years to give any support" to the idea that the United States might attack China. Operations in the vicinity of the Yalu in 1950 and years of subsequent covert operations were not noted. But his purpose was apparently to signal Peking. He insisted that the purpose of confrontation in Vietnam was not to destroy the regime in "Peiping." If the Chinese wanted to test America's purpose, let them live in peace with their neighbors "and they would find out that the United States is not aggressive with respect to mainland China." [30]

There is no indication of how reassured Mao and his colleagues in "Peiping" were, but late summer and fall brought evidence that the Chinese threat might be receding. The Indian defeat of Pakistan, failure of the Communist coup in Indonesia, and Chou En-lai's inability to resurrect the Algiers conference of Afro-Asian nations were seen as defeats for the People's Republic. Nonetheless, fear that the Chinese would intervene in Vietnam in response to the massive American escalation of the war remained strong until early 1966. In October, Rusk branded the Chinese as "blatant advocates of violence "and compared Lin Piao's "Long Live the Victory of People's War" with Hitler's *Mein Kampf*. Little wonder that public opinion polls found most Americans more worried about China as a threat to the peace than the Soviet Union. [31]

There were other currents in the administration and in the country. In the White House, James C. Thomson of Bundy's staff kept pressing for action to reach out to the Chinese. Like many academic students of Chinese affairs, Thomson did not share Rusk's view of China as a potential aggressor. William Bundy found his own staff trying to soften his words when he spoke of China. Even Rusk, though his position had stiffened, could speak of Chinese prudence. In a secret meeting with the Senate Foreign Relations Committee in October, 1965, he spoke of the enormous stake of the United States in persuading the People's Republic it was on the wrong course. But he conceded that the Chinese were showing "an extraordinary amount of caution in the Southeast Asia problem." A year earlier, he confessed, he would not have believed the United States could put so many men into the south and bomb so much of the north without a Chinese reaction. He wanted to keep the Chinese out of the UN, but expected them to be there when peace came to Southeast Asia. Arms limitation talks were another matter. Rusk had not changed his mind: the Chinese should participate. At year's end, in a private conversation with Cyrus Sulzberger of the *New York Times,* he described the Chinese as realistic people and predicted that common sense would prevail in their Southeast Asian policy. It was important not to push them into a corner. However grudgingly, he acquiesced in a program designed to establish contact with the Chinese. Containment "without isolation," had after all been a policy to which he had been committed years before.[32]

In March, 1966, Senator Fulbright held hearings on American policy toward China in which "containment without isolation," voiced by Vice President Hubert Humphrey, received endorsement from most of the authorities who testified. Rusk spoke at length and, as had become customary, under pressure from critics. He did not expect the Chinese to commit direct aggression; they had been cautious. But, he warned, "if the costs and risks of a greater use of force were reduced by, for example, our unilateral withdrawal from the region, Peiping might well feel freer to use its power to intimidate or overwhelm a recalcitrant opponent or to aid directly insurgent forces." The United States had to use its power to keep China cautious. Although he conceded that Lin Piao's call for revolution had stressed that the people of each country would have to rely on themselves, not China, comparisons of Chinese leaders with Hitler crept back into his testimony. He could not resist the urge to lecture on the need to contain aggression in Asia as in

Europe, nor would he back away from strictures against appeasement. His concluding remarks were milder. As soon as the People's Republic stopped using force and gave up its strategy for achieving revolution, "we would welcome an era of good relations." The United States would not attack China. Without jeopardizing other American interests, the administration would continue to seek possibilities for unofficial contact with the People's Republic.[33]

In a press conference a few days later Rusk argued that much of China's isolation was "self-imposed." Interviewed not long afterward he returned to the theme, outlining unsuccessful American efforts to enter discussions. He stressed his conception of Chinese leaders as prudent and rational, although it was important to be sure they did not underestimate American determination in Southeast Asia. He was confident the Chinese would mellow as a result of world resistance to their revolutionary militance. Curiously he stressed Hanoi's responsibility for escalating the war and seemed to absolve the Chinese. The purpose was ambiguous, but very likely he was trying to assuage American fear that escalation in Vietnam would lead to war with China—a fear fanned by some of the testimony at Fulbright's hearings.[34]

Before long the significance of the Great Proletarian Cultural Revolution in China impressed itself on the outside world. By midsummer, 1966, it was apparent the Chinese were turning inward, that Mao was bent on tearing apart his own society, hoping to bring it closer to his vision. Chinese influence in world affairs was soon negligible. Some apprehension that the Cultural Revolution would burst over China's borders was stimulated by Red Guard incidents in Macao in November and December, but after a few more months, it was clear that scattered incidents throughout the world merely decreased China's prestige without constituting any threat.

With China racked by the Cultural Revolution, the Johnson Administration concluded that American bombers could approach closer to the Chinese border, bombing with impunity. The attitude of the Peking government could be ignored. But in its rhetoric, and its treatment of foreigners, the People's Republic was more violent than ever, displaying, according to one sober observer, "a total lack of inhibition in violating the ordinary decencies of international behavior." Rusk remained worried by China's ideological antipathy. He was offended by China's behavior. What would happen after the Cultural Revolution? Among his concerns was the one he voiced in October, 1967. What would happen if "a billion Chinese, armed with nuclear weapons," emerged from the Cultural Revolution united, stronger, determined to implement Mao's words? He explained, sensibly, that Americans had a stake in a peaceful Asia and in redirecting "the interests of people in mainland China to the pragmatic requirements of their own people and away from a doctrinaire and ideological adventurism abroad." In the context of any discussion other than a defense of American action in Vietnam, Rusk's remarks were unexceptional. When a reporter asked if the "net objective" of American policy was containment of the Chinese Communist military, the reply was predictable: "No, the central objective is an organized and stable peace."[35]

In January, 1968, Rusk offered his last major statement on China. China was not the "real" enemy in Vietnam, but Chinese attitudes and positions were "not unrelated" to Hanoi's policies. He contended that "by advocating and abetting the violent overthrow of legally constituted governments, there is little doubt that Peking has in practical terms designated itself as a state antagonistic to what we and virtually every other state in the world see as the rule of law and order in international relations." For those who would follow him that far, Rusk asked that they understand that "if Hanoi were to take over South Viet-Nam by force, the effect would be to stimulate the expansionist ambitions of Communist China." The linkage was rarely as apparent to others as it was to Rusk. China was hostile to the world order embodied in the UN Charter. To fail to meet the threat of aggression in Vietnam, "advocated and abetted" by the Chinese, would encourage China to continue on a course that would surely end in nuclear holocaust.[36]

Years later William Bundy asked himself if perhaps China had been less threatening than it had appeared in 1964 and 1965? Could a different assessment of China have been made "with a resulting different sense of the importance of seeing the Vietnam struggle through at great cost?"[37] Bundy did not know. Perhaps no one can. For Rusk, it appeared that the assessment of China's power was less important than what China might become, "a billion Chinese, armed with nuclear weapons." China's strength troubled him less than the public commitment to destroy the world order to which he was committed. The Chinese had to be converted, had to be tamed, before they became a great power. For Rusk, Chinese rhetoric, combined with de Gaulle's taunts about the credibility of American commitments in a nuclear world, required staying in "for the duration."

3

The problems of East Asia all but consumed Rusk and his colleagues; nonetheless, in 1967 still another crisis demanded attention. The Arabs and Israelis maneuvered themselves into another confrontation. In Washington, the will—and probably the capacity—to act vigorously in the Middle East did not exist.

Tension between Israel and its Arab neighbors rose and ebbed, but never disappeared. In 1964, there had been a moment of danger when the Arabs threatened to divert the headwaters of the Jordan, and Israel indicated it would fight to retain access to that vital resource. Khrushchev had stirred trouble by an address in Egypt in which he accused Israel, stooge of the imperialists, of robbing the Arabs of their water. Rusk had Alexis Johnson warn all nations of the Middle East that the United States would aid the victim of aggression. The United States was neutral, but opposed the use of force. The Arabs were angered by the American position which Nasser interpreted as a threat. As cool to Nasser as Rusk was, he thought it worthwhile to soothe the Egyptian leader. The United States urged the International Monetary Fund to lend money to the Egyptians—money Congress would never appropriate in an election year.[38]

Early in 1965, American relations with Egypt deteriorated as a result of Belgian-American operations in the Congo. Nasser spoke harshly against the United States and a mob burned down the Kennedy Memorial Library in Cairo. Johnson reacted sharply to such anti-Americanism and would gladly have cut off aid to Egypt. The House passed legislation to block such aid. Rusk, however, asked the Senate Foreign Relations Committee to allow the administration some discretion. He agreed that it was useful for the authorities in Cairo to be aware of Congressional sentiment, but he needed a "sweetener," a carrot of some sort to use in negotiations. Nasser had been responsive at times. A failure by the United States to meet its promises on the delivery of food might lead to irrational action that would climax in the need for American troops. Rusk's prescription for the treatment of Nasser generally seemed to come from a handbook on adolescent psychology. And it seemed to work. In October he returned to the committee to report an improvement in Nasser's behavior and suggest some thought be given to another short-term aid program.[39]

As Nasser tended his own garden in 1965, 1966, early 1967—even extricating himself from Yemen—the Syrian-Israeli border became a more likely trouble spot. The revolutionary regime in Syria seemed receptive to both Soviet influence and the requirements of the Palestinian Liberation Organization (PLO) created in 1964. A United Nations Expeditionary Force in the Sinai since 1956 had prevented guerrilla raids, but the Palestinians were able to operate from Lebanon, Jordan, and increasingly from Syria. The Syrian government was under internal pressure to facilitate the raids. In Israel, the relatively pacific regime of Levi Eshkol faced intense domestic pressure for reprisals. In 1966 the Israelis responded to a terrorist attack by destroying the Jordanian village of Es Samu, an act that Arthur Goldberg, the American ambassador to the UN, deplored.

Early in May, 1967, rumor circulated in the Middle East of Israeli preparation for an attack on Syria. The rumor was believed to have been planted by Soviet operatives, conceivably without authorization from Kosygin or Brezhnev. A UN investigation found no evidence to substantiate it. The Arab world remained alarmed, however, and Nasser apparently felt obliged to act. The Syrians, the PLO and other Arab radicals had been critical of his passive role in the struggle against Zionism. On May 14, he warned Israel that if Syria were attacked, Egypt would come to its defense. He ordered mobilization of the Egyptian army to give credence to his threat. Sensitive to charges that he hid behind the skirts of the UN Expeditionary Force, he demanded that the UN withdraw its troops. To the chagrin of most neutral observers, perhaps to Nasser as well, the Secretary-General complied with the request immediately. There is no question but that U Thant could have delayed a few days with the possibility that the affair would end. He did not and the removal of the UN buffer allowed, and conceivably forced, Nasser to move troops to Sharm El-sheik, from whence they could and did close the Strait of Tiran (Gulf of Aqaba) to vessels headed for the Israeli port of Elath.

Nasser's intentions are not known. Some observers have speculated that he was bluffing; others have suggested that what began as a bluff became an ambitious operation as he concluded that the United States would not act and that the Eshkol government did not want to use force. Whatever his original purpose, the decision to close the Strait on May 22 precipitated a crisis. Unfortunately for Johnson and Rusk, President Eisenhower had committed the United States to keep the Strait open in return for Israeli withdrawal from the Sinai after the war in 1956. As the Israeli public demanded action and the Arab peoples responded with elation, the Israelis asked the United States to honor Eisenhower's commitment.

Johnson announced that the United States considered the Gulf of Aqaba an international waterway and the blockade illegal. The Sixth Fleet was ordered into the Eastern Mediterranean. When Rusk and McNamara met with Congressional leaders, however, they found them overwhelmingly opposed to intervention, whatever Eisenhower had promised. Rusk was surprised. He tried to gain time to calm both sides. Through the "hot line" he and Johnson tried for Russian support. He believed Kosygin eager to prevent war. Rusk contacted both sides, trying to play the same role he had played in 1948, talking to first one and then another ambassador, seeking ground on which a confrontation could be avoided.[40]

While Rusk worked with the Russians, Israelis and Arabs, the Johnson Administration pressed another idea, suggested by the British. Eugene Rostow, undersecretary of state, tried to put together an international armada that would force the blockade and open the Straits. Rusk was dubious, as were other Department officials, but Walt Rostow and the President tried to get European support. Rusk was supposed to keep the Israelis from fighting until the multinational fleet assembled. The CIA was confident the Israelis could take an attack on all three fronts, throw it back and win. Rusk was not so sure; nor was he foolish enough to think he could convince the Israelis to hold back on the basis of such an estimate. Nonetheless, he counseled patience and thought he had Israeli assurances that they would give the United States a little more time to find a peaceful solution.[41]

On May 30, Jordan and Egypt signed an agreement to join their military forces. Other Arab states began to send units to the confrontation states. Pressure on Eshkol became unbearable. On June 1, he was forced to surrender the defense ministry to a political enemy, the militant Moshe Dayan. On June 4, Iraq adhered to the Jordanian-Egyptian agreement and Egyptian equipment and officers were flown into Jordan in an all-day airlift. Reports of the movement of troops from Algeria, Libya and the Sudan toward the Egyptian front reached Israel and the United States. On the morning of June 6, Israeli forces went into action. Without warning Israeli fighter bombers struck Egyptian airfields and Israeli armor drove across the border into the Sinai. In a few hours Israel was at war on three fronts, as the Syrians and Jordanians attacked. In six days, Israeli forces that were outnumbered and outweighed in the quantity and quality of their equipment ravaged the armies of their Arab enemies, conquered the Sinai, the Golan Heights, the West bank of the Jordan. Superbly led, they won what appeared to be a decisive victory, sparing their American friends the embarrassment of breaching a promise to protect Israel's interests in the Gulf of Aqaba. The principal American contribution was a tactic to delay a cease-fire order by the UN until the Israelis could complete their operations.

Although appreciative of Israeli concerns, Rusk was irritated by their unwillingness to give him and the Russians time. During the fighting he and Johnson retained contact with Moscow, exchanging assurances that a great power confrontation was not desired. Much would depend, however, on the behavior of their surrogates. The rapid Israeli victory helped prevent explosive tensions in the United States and the Soviet Union. With war's end, the United States joined in the call for Israel's withdrawal from the conquered territories, but thwarted moves in the United Nations that were obviously anti-Israel.

In Israel and in the United States the Israeli victory was a source of joy. Some Americans, in and out of Washington, saw the result as a victory for the West in the Cold War. The celebration was short-lived, however. Quickly the Russians rearmed Egypt and Syria and expanded their influence in both countries. Any hope that the Israelis had of peace was dashed when the Arab League met in September, 1967, and agreed there would be no negotiations with Israel, no peace, no recognition. As months passed, it was clear that Israel had gained territories the Arabs would never concede, like Jerusalem, as sacred to Arab as to Jew, like the West Bank and the Gaza strip already heavily populated by Arabs, or the Golan Heights which were as important strategically to the Syrians as to the Israelis. Determined as many Americans might be to preserve the State of Israel, few had any commitment to the borders to which Israel now pretended. How long could the Israeli government bask in the glory of those six days in June? Long enough, at least, for Rusk, Johnson and Rostow to return their attention to Vietnam.

CHAPTER FIFTEEN

Toward Detente in Europe, Peace in Vietnam

Few people remembered, during the years of America's war in Vietnam, that the central confrontation of the Cold War was with the Soviet Union—that Europe was the area of most interest for both principal antagonists. The Russians were remarkably quiescent during the Johnson presidency. Europe was in ferment and some of the brew was bitter to the American palate. Nonetheless, there was nothing to rival the Berlin crises of earlier years. Sensing no threat, there was a tendency for the Western allies to relax. Rusk tried stoutly to arouse NATO to the danger, but met little success. Indeed, privately, he was also persuaded that the bear had been tamed and wanted only to keep the whip visible to guarantee future good behavior.

Toward Europe, Johnson and Rusk sought policies that would keep friends satisfied with American leadership while the United States improved relations with the Soviet Union. The Soviet-American rapprochement of 1963 caught the NATO allies by surprise and caused some uneasiness, especially in Bonn. West Germany posed the principal obstacle to a European settlement. Adenauer and successors demanded reunification of Germany and refused to accept boundaries agreed to by East Germany and the Soviet Union. The Russians feared German "revanchism"—and were apprehensive about Bonn's insistence on access to nuclear weapons. Somehow the United States had to satisfy German aspirations without threatening the Russians. Somehow, Soviet-American differences in Europe had to be resolved without alienating the Germans.

At Kennedy's direction Rusk had labored to encourage pluralism in Eastern Europe. The Johnson Administration continued to cultivate contacts with the smaller Communist countries, with the hope of letting a hundred Titos bloom. These policies, too, created complications. Was support for the independence of Eastern European states compatible with the desire for improved relations with the Soviet Union? Certainly the Russians had doubts. Extolling nationalism in Eastern Europe also posed problems in Western Europe, where Rusk, profoundly antagonistic to de Gaulle's independent policies, stressed interdependence. His commitment to polycentrism in the 1960s was genuine, but limited to the breakup of the enemy camp. It was hardly calculated to comfort the Russians.

Rusk's attitude toward Communism in Europe as in Asia was unambiguous. Millions of non-Catholics around the world had looked upon Pope John with deep affection as a man who had nudged the Church toward the twentieth century. Rusk saw him as a man whose tolerance of Communism allowed 500,000 Italian women to vote for Communists. He was relieved when Paul succeeded John, apparently expecting the new Pope to put the fear of God back in the *signoras*.[1] William F. Buckley would hardly have disagreed.

In February, 1964, Rusk delivered an address acknowledging the administration's awareness that Communism was not monolithic. "The Communist world," he maintained, was "no longer a single flock of sheep following blindly behind one leader." He declared that the first object of American policy toward the Communist world was to stop Communist imperialism. The United States would stop the expansion of the Communist domain, whatever Communists were involved. Some countries deserved different treatment, however, because they were more responsive to the aspirations of their own people than to international Communism. As its second object, the United States would reach out to these countries, encourage their evolution toward national independence, peaceful cooperation, and open societies. Finally, in relations with all Communist countries, the United States sought agreement to reduce the danger of war. In a variety of ways, Rusk expressed this three-part formula throughout the year: containment, reduction of tension, reinforcement of nationalism in what was once the Sino-Soviet bloc. Johnson was surprised at the absence of outcry from the right in response to Rusk's disposal of the myth of a Communist monolith, and ready to intensify efforts to build bridges—after the election.[2]

In May 1964 Rusk was in Europe, talking to his NATO allies. To them he spoke of the continued threat of Communism to the free world. Russian leaders had not renounced their aim of world revolution. True, vigilance had deflected "somewhat" the threat to Europe, but it existed in "more diversified and more sophisticated forms." Communists were seeking to expand in other parts of the world. The need for a strong NATO alliance remained. The quest for independent national policies so praiseworthy in Eastern Europe, he found "almost" incomprehensible in the West; "For compelling and practical reasons the notion of national independence each day gives more ground to the principle of interdependence . . . we almost cannot understand the revival of the notion of independence in dealing with the affairs of the free world, because we have almost none of it ourselves." De Gaulle was not impressed.[3]

Similarly, in an address to the foreign ministers of the OAS countries in July he stressed the continued danger of "international communism." He saw it at work everywhere, "constantly probing and testing for weak spots." He saw it "in modern dress", marching "in the guise of diplomatic relations, trade missions, and cultural exchanges, and peace movements, and youth organizations and the like." "No one," he begged, "should be deceived." Rusk's rhetoric with the OAS group was incredible for a man presumably interested in building bridges to Eastern Europe. But his address was designed to move his audience to condemn and isolate Cuba, not to enter into trade relations with European Communists. Obviously Rusk believed the United States had the strength and sophistication to increase contacts with the Communists, but not the Latin-Americans—and probably not the Europeans.[4]

Perhaps as well as anyone, Rusk understood the problem of multiple audiences for foreign policy statements. Nonetheless, he apparently thought the risk of contradictory signals worth taking. Perhaps he assured Dobrynin, prior to or immediately after each of his Cassandra calls, that he was really talking about the Chinese, that he had confidence in the course of Soviet-American relations. It is more difficult to imagine how he expected to persuade Congress to accept additional Soviet consulates around the United States, or additional trade and cultural relations with the Russians or other Communist countries. Apprehensive Congressmen hardly needed J. Edgar Hoover's nightmares when they could quote the Secretary of State. And yet it is clear from remarks in closed sessions or in private, that he did not find the Soviet Union threatening—even after the replacement of Khrushchev by Kosygin and Brezhnev. He was convinced that the strong American response to Stalinism had persuaded the Russians to behave in a more civilized fashion. He feared, as he remarked in June, 1966, subsequent to the French decision to withdraw forces from NATO, that "the surest way to lose the peace is to destroy or weaken the instruments that are preserving the peace."[5]

One area in which Rusk's colleagues sought agreement to reduce tensions with the Russians was arms control. The limited test-ban treaty had inspired hope of progress, but little of consequence followed. In the spring of 1964, to provide an illusion of momentum, Johnson and Khrushchev announced reduction in the production of fissionable materials. Increasingly, American officials concerned with arms control worried about the proliferation of nuclear weapons. After the Chinese demonstrated their device in 1964, concern with nonproliferation became an obsession. The Russians were equally interested in such an arrangement, primarily to prevent West Germany from becoming a nuclear power. For the Russians, nonproliferation provided an extra dividend, the possible disruption of NATO. They informed American negotiators that abandonment of the MLF concept was a requisite to any treaty to stop the spread of nuclear weapon technology.

Rusk was not convinced the Russians feared MLF.[6] The idea was never more than an elaborate charade to provide the Bonn government with a sense of control over NATO's nuclear power—without allowing any such control. Unable to take MLF seriously, he did not believe the Russians did. There is no question, however, but that the nonproliferation treaty was easier to negotiate once the idea of a multi-lateral force was put aside.

After Kennedy's death, Ball and the "theologians" resumed their effort to advance the MLF. In April, 1964, they succeeded in having Johnson study the concept briefly and won his approval. The President was sensitive to the argument that without some such plan a thwarted Germany might go it alone in a decade, reverting to militarism. In June the first mixed-manned vessel, the *Biddle*, put to sea. Naval officers the world over—and especially in the British Admiralty—were apoplectic in their contempt for the idea. Rusk and McGeorge Bundy urged the President to discuss MLF with Congressional leaders but Johnson had other priorities in the summer of 1964.[7]

Most of the NATO allies were skeptical about MLF. De Gaulle was intensely hostile, warning the West Germans that it would disrupt Franco-German relations. He withdrew French naval officers from NATO commands even before the voyage of the *Biddle*. Other than the Germans, only the Italians and the Dutch evidenced interest. But it was December, 1964, after the election and on the eve of a visit from Prime Minister Wilson, before Johnson reviewed MLF carefully. Ball had gone to Europe, to press Wilson and other European leaders. In Washington Bundy alerted the President to Congressional opposition and, perhaps of greater importance, to the reluctance of most of Europe to accept Ball's plans. Bundy had concluded that it was a mistake to continue the pressure, that it would be best to drop the idea. Rusk knew of Bundy's opposition, but neglected to warn Ball. He was content to have the steamroller stalled.[8]

When Wilson reached Washington, he was delighted to find that Johnson was not insisting on the MLF and was receptive to Britain's ideas for an Allied Naval Force (ANF) that appeared to threaten no one. Johnson had endorsed Bundy's argument. He would not use his capital to win Congressional support for an idea which the Europeans were considering largely because of American pressure. Let MLF float, alongside ANF, or anything else the Europeans had to offer. Rusk suggested that he return the idea to London and Bonn, to let them derive a formula with which they would be content. Johnson liked Rusk's approach, particularly if the British and the Germans could save a place for France. He was not prepared to read France out of the Atlantic Community.[9]

Later, Rusk and McNamara attended a NATO meeting in Europe at which France, Belgium, and Norway opposed the MLF concept. One recurring French argument against MLF was that it would prevent reunification of Germany. Rusk defended MLF as an offer made by the United States in good faith, a response to European desires for increased participation in decisions about nuclear weapons. Rusk was not insistent, reflecting the flexibility of Johnson and Bundy rather than the dogmatism of Ball. The American position in 1965 was a sharp departure from Ball's approach. The Europeans were assured of American interest in MLF should they agree on a specific proposal, but the United States would not insist on one. Ball and like-minded colleagues might continue their efforts, but they were enjoined from threats. Whatever Ball's ego involvement, American prestige would not be enmeshed in the proposal. Ball pushed as hard as he could, but the idea was dead by 1966 and Ball left the Department of State before the year was out. In Germany, the rise of Willy Brandt, who became foreign minister in 1966, meant a decline in German insistence on a nuclear role. The tempest passed.[10]

Rusk's behavior in the MLF controversy frustrated a number of colleagues, both supporters and opponents of the concept. As was often the case, they were not sure what he was telling the President. Most knew he was skeptical, and wondered why he allowed Ball to press so hard. If he did not support the idea, why did he let it float so long? Why did he allow so much energy to be expended? At one level the answer is obvious. Rusk thought MLF was useful as a basis for discussion among the NATO allies. It could be used to block more dangerous alternatives, such as German insistence on an independent nuclear weapon. The allies wanted something. Let them discuss MLF, see how complicated and costly the proposals were, and turn them down. The United States would not be denying European aspirations and the whole problem might fade away, as it did. Rusk did not expect MLF to be implemented. He did not expect his Presidents to insist on it and was perfectly satisfied by the results. On another level, Rusk was loath to say "no" to Ball and Henry Owen, men for whom he had a high regard. Perhaps unwisely, he thought it would do no harm to let them go ahead. They were able men who might come up with something of great value. But Rusk seems to have underestimated the momentum Ball could generate. Before long, Rusk had to protect MLF to spare his own people from embarrassment and Bundy's intercession may have been necessary to rein Ball in. The management procedures appear questionable, but the policy results, however divinely achieved, may be judged benign.

Regardless of the disposition of the MLF concept, the troubles within the NATO alliance could not be brushed aside. DeGaulle continued to plague Rusk and his colleagues. He withdrew French troops from NATO commands and in March, 1966, ordered NATO to remove its installations and forces from French soil. Rusk was outraged, as were Ball, Acheson, and most other advocates of an Atlantic community. Johnson could not have been pleased, but he did prevent the Atlanticists from accepting the challenge. At his direction the reply to de Gaulle was toned down, transformed from an argument to a polite response, including the sentence, "as our old friend and ally, her place will await France whenever she decides to resume her leading role." Perhaps as a result of advice from men like Bundy and Bohlen, his ambassador to France, Johnson was uncharacteristically tactful in all of his dealings with the French President.[11]

As their prospective blocs showed a marked lack of cohesion, the United States and the Soviet Union became less bristly in their bilateral relations. Despite Americanization of the war in Vietnam and large-scale Soviet assistance to the North Vietnamese, the principal Cold War adversaries stepped mincingly toward detente. In December, 1966, both countries made important concessions that permitted them to agree to a treaty banning nuclear weapons in outer space. In March, 1967, Johnson overcame strong opposition from conservatives, abetted by FBI Director J. Edgar Hoover, to win Senate consent to a Soviet-American Consular Convention signed almost three years earlier. The Russians waited fourteen months for a more propitious moment before ratifying the convention, and then another "little thread" was secured. In the autumn of 1966, Soviet and American arms control negotiators came close to agreement on a nuclear nonproliferation treaty. Rusk delayed the signing until the Russians withdrew language he considered designed to offend American allies. By December, 1966, Rusk was sufficiently satisfied with Soviet concessions to take the treaty to a NATO meeting. He wanted the treaty and thought it important, but not so important that he would alienate the Bonn government to get it. A variety of complications, especially the war in Vietnam, delayed ratification. In July, 1968, when Hanoi and Washington were negotiating, the United States and the Soviet Union, joined by scores of other nations, signed the treaty in New York, at the UN. The next step was to work for limits on strategic arms. Johnson and Rusk pressed hard, eager to cap their public careers with so important an agreement. The Russians were intensely interested and on August 19, 1968, agreed to begin negotiation. Unfortunately, on August 20 the Soviet Union led Warsaw pact forces in an invasion of Czechoslovakia. SALT talks would have to wait.[12]

Rusk unquestionably perceived and reciprocated the Soviet desire for detente. In his last years in office he spoke openly, even to Catholic War Veterans, about the new "prudence" in Soviet-American relations. Accommodation had to be sought. The world was too dangerous for "a policy of hostility across the board," he declared in June, 1968. But he was persuaded that the Russians could still be dangerous. They remained committed to world revolution, wars of national liberation—to what Rusk considered a policy of using force to impose their will on others, contrary to norms of international behavior. They were stepping up the pace of their ICBM deployments. They continued to spend on arms and military research—such as the antiballistic missile system. Nonetheless, he was impressed with their restraint in the Middle East crisis, with Kosygin's conciliatory posture at Glassboro, with the Soviets' "rather phlegmatic" response to the intensified bombing of North Vietnam in August, 1967. There were many signs that the Soviet Union placed rapprochement with the United States high on its priorities—short of accepting strategic inferiority or tolerating defections from the Warsaw Pact. And short of contributing to the erosion of support for the foreign aid program, American spending for research and development of military systems, NATO or the war in Vietnam, Rusk publicly took cognizance of the new phase in Soviet-American relations.[13]

The Russians had indicated that the war in Vietnam, however distasteful, need not affect bilateral relations with the United States.

Apparently they believed the United States would respond comparably if they were forced to take action Americans might find distasteful. On the eve of President Johnson's intended announcement of SALT talks, the Soviet Union ended the Czech "spring", perhaps the most exciting experiment in the history of Communism: a regime that respected human rights. Throughout the spring and early summer, men and women of goodwill throughout the world rejoiced over the liberalization of Czechoslovakia and marveled at the courage of Alexander Dubcek and his colleagues as they resisted Soviet pressure. Dubcek assured the Russians that Czechoslovakia would not withdraw from the Warsaw Pact, but to no avail. The Czech effort to create "Marxism with a human face" deviated too far from the Soviet model. Prague's interest in normalizing relations with West Germany aroused apprehension in East Germany as well as in Moscow. The warmth of Czech relations with Rumania and Yugoslavia may have evoked premonitions of a dissident socialist bloc. The tanks came, the Czechs were crushed, and all mankind took a step backward.

As tension increased in July, Rusk indicated that the United States would not intervene.[14] There would be no repetition of the immoral calls to arms of 1956 that led Hungarian "freedom fighters" to expect American support. Czechoslovakia was in a zone that the Soviet Union considered vital to its security. Intervention might well mean world war, in a region in which the United States would be at a disadvantage under the best of circumstances. With 535,000 American fighting men in Vietnam and the strategic reserve decimated, circumstances were not the best. The United States would not fight for "socialism with a human face" in Czechoslovakia—and Rusk wanted to be sure Dubcek was warned. Unfortunately the Russians also were assured they had a free hand.

In October, Rusk spoke eloquently before the General Assembly. He was critical of the invasion of Czechoslovakia and warned that such actions threatened progress toward detente. He noted signs that Moscow had been allowing Eastern Europe a measure of independence, that the Russians had shown interest in arms control and were allowing their people some contact with the outside world. There had been rising hope—and now the subjugation of Czechoslovakia. Pointedly, Rusk advised his audience: "Let us say very plainly to the Soviet Union: The road to detente is the road of the Charter."[15]

SALT talks were delayed and the United States feared the Soviet Union would attack Rumania next. Dobrynin had gone to Rusk's house on the evening of August 31 to assure Rusk that rumors of Soviet troop movements toward Rumania were false, but Rusk sounded a public warning nonetheless.[16] The attack did not occur. The teeth of the Brezhnev Doctrine, having been bared, seemed threat enough. The momentum toward detente was lost. Time ran out on Rusk and Johnson. The kudos went to their successors, men with fewer scruples about human rights for Eastern Europe.

2

The epitaph for the Johnson Administration was written, of course, in Vietnam. As Westmoreland prepared to reverse the decision of Dienbienphu at Khe Sanh, the Viet Cong struck at most of the major towns and cities in their Tet offensive. Communist losses were enormous and Westmoreland, Johnson and Rusk claimed victory. Rusk insisted that Viet Cong hopes of triggering an uprising against the Saigon regime had been shattered.[17] The Communists failed to hold any of the provincial capitals they overran or to demonstrate popular support. But Hué remained in Communist hands for almost four weeks, despite heavy attacks by American troops as well as South Vietnamese regulars. The Communist forces, allegedly facing defeat, demonstrated ability to launch simultaneous surprise attacks against more than a hundred population centers throughout the country.

In the United States, not only the public but the government evidenced profound shock at the demonstration of Viet Cong capability and American and South Vietnamese failing. The ability of the Saigon regime to recover from the onslaught, to capitalize on its "victory," was widely doubted. Support for the American war effort eroded not only among the people, but within the establishment, among the "in and outers" to whom Presidents and Cabinet officers were most responsive. The Communists had won the psychological victory they sought. Johnson could not hold course. There would have to be changes in American policy. Westmoreland, prompted by Wheeler, asked for 206,000 more men to apply the coup de grace to the enemy. Even Johnson was not prepared for that tack. He appointed a committee, headed by the incoming Secretary of Defense, Clifford, to study the proposal while he sought to hold a consensus in favor of continuing the fight.

Although on February 8 the North Vietnamese foreign minister reiterated willingness to commence negotiations following an unconditional bombing halt, Rusk argued that the North Vietnamese were not serious. They did not respond on the battlefield to American restraint and had rejected all American terms for peace. "We are not interested," he declared, "in propaganda gestures whose purpose is to mislead and confuse." Johnson, Rostow, and the Joint Chiefs wanted to resume bombing in the Haiphong area. Rusk had consistently opposed such operations, but acquiesced once again.[18]

On March 3, Clifford was sworn in as Secretary of Defense and the *New York Times* reported joy in the Pentagon. The Joint Chiefs were relieved to be rid of McNamara and expected Clifford to continue to support their aspirations, and be less responsive to the civilian staff McNamara had assembled. His first pronouncement did not disappoint them. He rejected McNamara's argument that attainment of nuclear parity by the Soviet Union would be stabilizing and announced he would maintain superiority. The next day his task force gave the President its recommendation in response to the Westmoreland-Wheeler troop request. As widely anticipated, Clifford recommended giving the military a fraction of the men they wanted. He had listened to arguments from Nitze, Deputy Secretary, and from Paul Warnke, Assistant Secretary for International Security Affairs, on the need to change policy, but his principal concern was to meet Westmoreland's needs. Nitze and Warnke persisted and Enthoven, Assistant Secretary for Systems Analysis, provided supporting data. Philip G. Goulding, Assistant Secretary for Public Affairs, stressed the likelihood of negative public response to anything but denial of Westmoreland's requests and announcement of a new startegy. But all were willing to send Westmoreland 25,000 men. This did not satisfy Westmoreland, the Joint Chiefs, or CINCPAC, who wanted more forces, more aggressive tactics, fewer restraints. But the military had rarely been satisfied. Here at least was another slice, another compromise. Business as usual, on this, the fifth consecutive week that 400 or more Americans were killed in Vietnam.[19]

Nonetheless an important point had been reached. Clifford had not been won over to the side of those who argued the price of success in Vietnam was too high for America to pay. But he had been shaken a little. He was no longer the irresponsible advocate of a more aggressive war. Doubt had been planted. He had heard new questions. Shrewd, less committed to the war than the men who had been on board for the "duration," he was responsive to new ideas. As the ides of March approached he continued to be buffeted by his subordinates until he was converted by Nitze's willingness to resign rather than defend further troop deployments before the Senate Foreign Relations Committee.[20]

In the days between the recommendation of Clifford's task force and Nitze's threatened resignation, Rusk began to lobby for a bombing pause. He had never approved the strategic bombing of the North and had tried in the summer of 1967 to persuade Johnson to restrict bombing to interdiction of infiltration. After the Tet offensive, as he gauged the public response, he was convinced that policy in Vietnam would have to change. He did not surrender his conviction that Southeast Asia was important to the United States, that aggression had to be stopped in Vietnam. He concluded, however, that the strategic bombing of the north, which he knew to be both ineffective and repugnant to many Americans, as well as to much of the rest of the world, had to be stopped. Like Nitze he concluded that commitments elsewhere precluded deploying additional troops to Vietnam. A way out had to be found, but it could not be a surrender, could not be a retreat from the American commitment.

With McNamara and Bundy gone, replaced by two men who were staunch believers in strategic bombing, there was no easy way to wean the President from the Joint Chiefs. Johnson's intense sensitivity to what he considered disloyalty created a situation analogous to that among Japanese cabinet ministers who in 1945 were afraid to admit to each other that they favored surrender. It was difficult to solicit support, difficult to be sure where one's colleagues stood. Knowing his President, Rusk knew he could not risk Johnson's suspicion if he was to succeed in winning a change. The task was difficult, the risk of losing the President's confidence great, but the stakes too high to forgo the effort. Rusk feared that the American people were not only turning against the war, but against collective security, responsibilities of world leadership, and the machinery for peace he and like-minded men had constructed after World War II. There had to be a change. The ebbing of public support had to halt.

Rusk's strategy was obvious. He forwarded to the President an article by Barbara Ward and other British intellectuals outlining an approach that included a bombing halt, reinforcements in Vietnam, and a peace offensive. On March 4, when the report of the Clifford task force was discussed, Rusk advised that most of the bombing of the north could be stopped during the monsoon season without significant risk. Perhaps because the proposal came from Rusk, the President was receptive. On the following day, Rusk read a rare personal memorandum at lunch. He proposed an unconditional but partial bombing halt and rejected the idea of additional troops to Vietnam. He reminded the Joint Chiefs that weather conditions over North Vietnam would limit sorties in any event. For the President as well as the Joint Chiefs, he explicitly stated that the bombing halt was necessary to appease public opposition to the war. He conceded that he had little hope of favorable response from North Vietnam, but it was worth a try. The bombing could always be resumed, he assured his audience. But he deftly indicated only two conditions that would provoke resumption of bombing of the north: a major attack at Khe Sanh or a second attempt to take the cities of South Vietnam—neither of which was likely given the losses sustained by the Communists during the Tet offensive. Rusk did not want a complete bombing halt. As in the past, tactical air attacks, limited to battlefield related areas, won his approval. The bombing should continue in the vicinity of the demilitarized zone.[21]

General Wheeler was skeptical, but he could live with Rusk's proposals. Failure of Hanoi to respond might lead to fewer restraints on the military in the future. Johnson was also skeptical. He had tried bombing pauses without result. Indeed, Clifford had argued he had been greatly mistaken to do so. On March 5, however,

Clifford acquiesced in Rusk's proposal, except for insisting that the halt be conditional, that the North Vietnamese be told explicitly what the United States expected in return. Rusk reminded those present of Hanoi's refusal to consider conditions, any demand for reciprocity. The meeting ended without decision, but Rusk and William Bundy tried to force one by drafting a cable describing Rusk's proposal for the American ambassador in Saigon. Johnson ruled against sending the cable. The President was not ready.[22]

For many months, Senator Fulbright had been trying to get Rusk to testify publicly about the war in Vietnam. Johnson instructed his Secretary of State not to do so. In March, however, Rusk overcame the President's objections. The public debate was going badly and the administration's case had to be made. On March 11, Rusk began what proved to be ten and a half hours of testimony. The *New York Times* conceded that he had scored more points than his critics, but complained that "despite all his eloquence, Mr. Rusk's performance at times seemed like a television rerun of an old movie." He repeated all of his explanations for America's role in Vietnam, defended past actions, and gave no inkling of the ferment at the White House for which he was providing much of the yeast. When the President made up his mind, *he* would tell the people, including Fulbright, what they needed to know.[23]

On March 12 the domestic political context in which Lyndon Johnson would act began to change radically. On that day, Eugene McCarthy, the quixotic peace candidate for the Democratic nomination, received a stunning 40% of the votes in the New Hampshire primary, very nearly defeating an incumbent President. On March 16 after McCarthy demonstrated Johnson's vulnerability, Robert Kennedy reassessed his own chances and declared his candidacy. The President's political advisers knew he was in political trouble. These events, as much as Nitze's threatened resignation, may have led to Clifford's conversion.

On the eve of Kennedy's announcement Rusk moved on two fronts, with help from Henry H. Fowler, the Secretary of the Treasury, and Arthur Goldberg, the ambassador to the United Nations. Using Treasury data, Rusk argued against deployment of troops to Vietnam. He feared the effect of reserve call-ups and overseas deployments on American monetary problems. Unless there was a tax increase, difficult to obtain in an election year, there would be serious inflation in the United States, panic in Europe, and possibly a collapse of the international monetary system. Using Goldberg's proposal for an unconditional and complete halt to the bombing of North Vietnam, he persuaded the President to allow him to take steps that led to adoption of his own "more modest" plan. On March 16, Johnson authorized Rusk to describe the Goldberg and Rusk proposals to Ambassador Bunker to determine which could be sold to the Saigon regime. Rusk never had doubt as to how Bunker would reply. Once Johnson approved the cable, he was confident the President would adopt his plan for an unconditional partial halt without stipulation for reciprocity.[24]

Clifford was not aware of Rusk's activities or of Rusk's purpose. The two men were not at ease with each other, despite ties going back to the Truman era. Clifford and Warnke, upon whose advice the new secretary leaned increasingly, suspected that Rusk was merely trying to manipulate public opinion. Unaware of his attitude toward strategic bombing, unable to penetrate his reserve, they believed Rusk opposed negotiation and was preparing the public for more intensive bombing. They apparently equated his thinking with that of the Joint Chiefs. Rusk's style and conception of his role as the President's adviser inadvertently contributed to their deception. Clifford and Rusk appear to have been working toward the same end without Clifford ever knowing.[25]

The problem both men faced was to find a way to persuade Johnson to change strategy. They shared responsibility for the President's conviction that he had to win in Vietnam, that he could win in Vietnam. Clifford had urged the course he had taken and Rusk, however much he dragged anchor, had gone along for the ride. Circumstances dictated a new direction, but the President did not like being forced off course. In the past, efforts to turn him about had resulted in loss of influence or banishment. Clifford, once converted, was direct and prodded the President. Johnson was irritated and distance between the two men grew. Rusk moved with characteristic tact and indirection, crediting opposition arguments, anticipating them, and gently moving the President over, a degree at a time. Instinctively, he appreciated the value of Clifford's approach or Goldberg's which enabled him to seize the middle ground, where the President was always most comfortable. Johnson's later statement that "Rusk had the best understanding of the way I wished to move" very likely had validity beyond the President's comprehension.[26]

On March 20 and 22, Johnson met with his advisers, Goldberg, McGeorge Bundy, and Vice President Humphrey, to discuss a speech he intended to give on Vietnam. Rusk insisted a bombing halt would be the essential of any proposal for negotiation with Hanoi. He continued to argue for stopping without conditions. Clifford did not believe Rusk's approach would lead to negotiation nor was he persuaded in the least that Rusk genuinely wanted negotiation. He proposed a series of cutbacks on bombing, a series of deescalatory steps, to be pursued contingent upon North Vietnamese responses, until an agreement on negotiation could be reached. Warnke had convinced him that Hanoi had already accepted the "San Antonio formula" and would not "take advantage" of American deescalation. Goldberg apparently agreed. Rusk did not, and his position was supported by Bundy. No one present at these meetings was optimistic that a reduction in bombing, such as both Rusk and Clifford advocated, would induce Hanoi to negotiate. No one present was confident that a bombing halt would not endanger American soldiers near the demilitarized zone. Johnson did not indicate the direction of his thoughts, although he asked that the section on a possible peace initiative be separated from the rest of the speech. Clifford was discouraged, assuming there would be no steps toward peace.[27]

Clifford's next move was to assemble the so-called "Wise Men," or "in-and-outers," a group of highly prominent former government officials. Only a few months earlier most of these men had supported the President's policy. Clifford had learned that several of them had reservations. With the President's approval, Clifford invited Acheson, Ball, Omar Bradley, McGeorge Bundy, Arthur Dean, Dillon, Fortas, Goldberg, Lodge, McCloy, Robert Murphy, Ridgway, Taylor, and Vance to a meeting on March 25. After a dinner with Rusk, Harriman, Nicholas Katzenbach, William Bundy, Clifford, Nitze, Wheeler, Rostow and Richard Helms, Director of the CIA, the group received briefings from Philip Habib for State, Major General William E. DePuy for the Pentagon, and George

Carver for CIA. The next day Wheeler and General Creighton Abrams, Westmoreland's deputy, briefed the "Wise Men" on the military situation. Then the group reported to the President.

With exception of Fortas, Murphy, and Taylor the mood was pessimistic. Acheson, Ball, Dean, and Dillon, Atlanticists all, thought Vietnam was absorbing too much energy, too many resources. Bradley, Lodge, Ridgway and Vance opposed troop increases and urged a scaling down of the American effort and objectives, Vietnamization of the war. Ball and Goldberg insisted on a bombing halt. The President perceived that all these men were profoundly troubled by the divisions in American society and most had concluded that the time had come to find a way out. There seems to be no doubt that he was shaken by the group's response, that neither he nor Rusk nor Rostow had anticipated so radical a change of attitude. Nor can there be any doubt that the group was more pessimistic than Rusk thought justified. [28]

Rusk was afraid that pressure was building to yield too much. He agreed with those who insisted tactical changes were necessary. He was delighted to have support for his own opposition to the strategic bombing of North Vietnam and for his desire to stress the military role of South Vietnamese forces. But he wanted to move slowly, for fear of a stampede. There was no need to surrender American objectives in Vietnam. He remembered far darker days in Korea, when the Chinese had hurled American forces back and MacArthur had despaired. He and Kennan had stemmed defeatism in Washington and brave men had held the line in Korea. It could be done again. There was still time, if the support of the American people could be maintained. If the people would stand behind the administration, an acceptable settlement might come. He had few illusions about how urgent it was to get the North Vietnamese to the conference table before the war was lost in America. The hour, however, was later than he knew. [29]

On March 28, Clifford, Rostow, William Bundy, and presidential speech writer Harry McPherson met with Rusk at his office to prepare a revised draft of the address Johnson intended to deliver. Clifford had been kept at arms' length for several days and could not fathom the President's mind; nor had he come any closer to understanding Rusk's tactics. He was appalled by the draft he saw, believing it too aggressive, inconsistent with the mood of the country. Unhesitatingly, he urged softening the speech, stressing peace, not war. He argued in favor of announcing a partial bombing halt. To his surprise Rusk was most agreeable. The changes in tone Clifford sought were adopted and Rusk dictated a paragraph embodying his own original proposal for a bombing halt north of the 20th parallel. Rusk also instructed Bundy to draft a cable notifying Bunker that the President had approved the partial bombing halt. Not ever Rostow objected. Clifford left the meeting with a sense of having redirected the President's speech—and perhaps the course of the war.[30]

Without denigrating Clifford's role, which had been and continued to be important, it is clear that by March 28 his powers of persuasion and eloquence were no longer essential. Rusk and Rostow were aware that the President would accept the bombing-halt proposal. That evening Clifford, Rostow and Rusk met Johnson and presented him with a draft speech prepared in the Defense Department, incorporating Rusk's proposal in tones reflecting the views of Clifford, Warnke and Goulding. At the close of the meeting Johnson called Rusk into his office and, after brief discussion, authorized him to send the cable to Bunker. The President's speech would include an announcement that bombing would stop north of the 20th parallel.[31] On March 31 the President addressed the American people.

Johnson spoke of his efforts to achieve peace in the past and announced the unilateral cessation of attacks on North Vietnam except for staging areas just north of the demilitarized zone. Even the attacks on staging areas would be stopped if Hanoi indicated restraint. He spoke of no conditions for the halt and said nothing of circumstances that might require resumption of bombing. Then he shifted suddenly to a discussion of the accomplishments of his presidency and to his concern for national unity. Insisting that the stakes were too great to allow the presidency to become involved in election-year partisanship, he declared, dramatically: "I shall not seek, and I will not accept, the nomination of my Party for another term as your President." A more striking means of bidding for national unity and of seeking to persuade Hanoi of the sincerity of his peace initiative is not easily imagined.

Three days later the government of North Vietnam offered to begin negotiations. Visions of peace danced before many eyes, but Christmas was still many years away.

3

The day after Johnson announced the North Vietnamese expression of willingness to meet his representatives, Martin Luther King, Jr., was murdered. Hours later parts of Washington were in flames. Riots spread across the country, north, south, east and west. The Great Society, Fulbright once said, had become a sick society. Two months later Robert Kennedy was murdered. Neither killing was directly related to Vietnam. Perhaps Kennedy's death at the hands of a Jordanian immigrant was unrelated to American problems. But no one could deny that the country was in the midst of a crisis, that tension caused by the war in Vietnam and by racism at home had infected almost every aspect of American society. Nerves were taut, and international affairs had to be conducted in this atmosphere. Johnson and his advisers were pitted against the sweep of the hour hand. Could they find an acceptable peace in Vietnam before the bell tolled for America?

Clifford sensed that the administration had less time than Johnson and Rusk realized. Rusk was determined to see North Vietnamese restraint before agreeing to a total bombing halt—and not satisfied with what he saw in April and May. He feared the North Vietnamese were maneuvering to end American attacks on them while they fought on, relentlessly. A month passed before agreement could be reached on a site for negotiations, as Rusk, remembering Panmunjom, was determined to find a place where American negotiators could not be intimidated. Finally the North Vietnamese suggested Paris and Rusk advised Johnson to accept immediately. He recommended Harriman and Llewellyn Thompson as negotiators, but Johnson substituted Vance for Thompson. On May 13 the first formal session was held. That week 562 Americans were killed in Vietnam, the highest weekly total of the war. Hanoi demanded a complete cessation of the bombing. Rusk insisted there was no evidence of restraint. Clifford was frustrated, but could not dispute the evidence. Nonetheless in his public appearances he made every effort to make the partial bombing halt and the ceiling on American forces in Vietnam permanent. Momentum toward peace could not be reversed.[32]

In May and early June, Communist forces in South Vietnam launched a second series of attacks on the cities. It was not nearly as dramatic as the Tet offensive, nor was it an indication of the reciprocity Rusk demanded. The North Vietnamese negotiators were informed that the reduction in their activities requisite to a complete end to the bombing included cessation of attacks on southern cities. But although Rusk had specified attacks on the cities as one of the conditions for resuming bombing north of the 20th parallel, he continued to support the "pause." When Johnson asked if continuing the pause would make ultimate resumption more difficult, Clifford disingenuously insisted it would not. Rusk, more honest with the President, said "yes," it would be harder to resume bombing later, but urged continuing the pause nonetheless.[33]

In July, American intelligence estimates showed a reduction in North Vietnamese activity in the south. Vance reported indications that the lull was meaningful. Johnson asked for another report in about two weeks. At the end of July, Harriman and Vance cabled their conviction that the lull had political significance. Five weeks had passed since the last rocket attack on Saigon. They asked the President to consider a complete bombing halt on assumption that the cutback in North Vietnamese activities would continue. Rusk was amenable to the Harriman-Vance proposal, but the President rejected it angrily. He was persuaded, apparently by Rostow, perhaps by Fortas, that the North Vietnamese were preparing another offensive. On July 30, Rusk publicly conceded the lull in the fighting and reported that Hanoi had dropped its demands for full adherence to the program of the National Liberation Front. But he insisted he saw no signs of reciprocity, that infiltration had increased. The American position seemed to be stiffening and an important opportunity for progress toward peace, as seen by Harriman and Vance, slipped away.[34]

One problem over which the negotiations faltered was participation of the National Liberation Front. The NLF and the Saigon regime deserved places at the peace table, but Nguyen Van Thieu,

President of South Vietnam, refused to negotiate with the NLF. By late August, supporters of Richard M. Nixon, Republican presidential candidate, had led Thieu to hope for better terms if peace came after the election—assuming their man won. Saigon became increasingly recalcitrant.[35]

In October, Vance returned from Paris to inform Johnson that he and Harriman were persuaded there was a chance for a breakthrough. He asked the President for permission to advise the North Vietnamese negotiators that the United States held certain assumptions about what was going to happen, to tell what these assumptions were, what was expected, and what would happen if the Communists did not act in accord with American assumptions. He and Harriman were trying to circumvent the semantic obstacle of reciprocity, upon which the United States had insisted and which Hanoi had persistently refused to accept. Johnson gave approval, provided Rusk agreed. To his delight and great relief, Vance found that Rusk agreed with the proposed course. Together Vance and Rusk worked out the language of the formula Vance and Harriman would present in Paris. The agreement they sought provided for an expanded meeting including the NLF and Thieu's representatives, an end to rocket attacks on major cities, an end to infiltration of troops or supplies, a cessation of firing across or massing troops on either side of the demilitarized zone, and, of course, an end of all American bombing of North Vietnam.[36]

Vance and Harriman achieved agreement with astonishing speed—and the help of the Soviet Union. Rusk worked with Dobrynin in Washington and Vance with a member of the Soviet embassy in Paris. The Russians took it upon themselves to make sure the Vietnamese knew what was expected of them—and apparently pressed them toward agreement on precisely the terms Rusk had demanded for years. But the initial agreement proved unacceptable to Rusk because the North Vietnamese would not specify the date on which negotiations would commence following a complete bombing halt. Again, Rusk remembered the lessons of the Korean negotiations. As the learned scholar, Henry A. Kissinger, had argued, when military pressure on the enemy was relieved, the enemy lost the incentive to negotiate or to conclude negotiations. This time Rusk determined to maintain as much pressure as possible until the negotiations began—and to continue with maximum allowable pressure until negotiations concluded.[37]

On October 27 the North Vietnamese offered a date. If the United States would end the bombing of the north, expanded negotiations and the rest of American assumptions would be realized within a week. Rusk and William Bundy wanted to notify Thieu immediately and let the Vietnamese leader know the United States would proceed unilaterally if Saigon refused to participate. Johnson hesitated. He wanted to consult Creighton Abrams, who had replaced Westmoreland in Vietnam, and wanted time to think about it. While he delayed, Thieu was persuaded that Nixon would win and the new administration would demand better terms than those Johnson and Rusk would accept. As the hours passed, Johnson found all his advisers ready to go ahead without Thieu. He cleared the decision with Congressional leaders, with Humphrey and Nixon, and on October 31, 1968, ordered cessation of all air, naval, and artillery bombardment of North Vietnam.[38]

On November 1, Rusk held a news conference to explain the decision. He brushed aside suspicions that Johnson was trying to influence the election and insisted that the bombing had been ended because of developments in Paris. His remaining remarks indicated his objectives had not changed and he was prepared to announce victory. Peace would not come to Southeast Asia until North Vietnamese troops were withdrawn from both South Vietnam and Laos. He attributed Hanoi's willingness to negotiate to heavy losses the Communists had suffered in 1968. He thought "it must finally be dawning upon the people in Hanoi that they cannot succeed in their military effort." Asked if the United States was still unwilling to compromise, he insisted that withdrawal of North Vietnamese from the south was part of a compromise. In return the United States would bring its troops home.[39]

Rusk's remarks were probably not intended to implement a suggestion once made by Senator George F. Aiken of Vermont—that the United States declare that it had won and go home. More likely he was trying once more to rally public opinion behind the American effort to preserve a non-Communist Vietnam. The North Vietnamese were willing to negotiate because they were hurting. If they would go home, leave their neighbors alone, then strategic bombing was certainly expendable. American troops could be brought home rapidly and the war turned over to the South Vietnamese to fight among themselves. American purposes would have been served. Aggression would have been repelled, the fallacy of the Chinese model demonstrated, and the norms of the international community upheld. If eventually a corrupt Thieu regime fell to an indigenous Communist revolt, with no evidence of outside intervention, perhaps he could live with that, too. Whatever Rusk's fantasies on November 1, he must have returned to reality the next day when Thieu announced the Saigon regime would not participate in the meetings if the NLF attended as a separate delegation.

The Johnson Administration agreed on efforts to force Saigon to attend the Paris meeting scheduled for November 6. Clifford favored threats and Rusk characteristically preferred indirection, but to no avail.[40] Thieu preferred to gamble on a Nixon victory. After the election it became clear the Saigon regime could not be budged. Thieu continued to insist that the Johnson Administration had acted unilaterally to betray his interests. Nixon's victory had the opposite effect on the North Vietnamese, who were suddenly eager to reach a settlement before facing the Republican Administration. Concessions by Hanoi allowed the negotiators to agree on a formula satisfactory to Saigon for the expanded talks, but Thieu would allow nothing of substance to be decided. Time ran out on Johnson and Rusk and the war went on—and on.

4

On December 9, 1968, a White House driver appeared at the Rusk house with a message for Mrs. Rusk. To her, the President wrote: "The man who has served me most intelligently, faithfully and nobly is Dean Rusk."[41] There could hardly be a better way to sum up the Rusk-Johnson relationship. Alone of his senior advisers, Rusk served Johnson with the loyalty the President expected—although there was much upon which they did not agree. Early in the Johnson presidency McNamara was probably more influential. In 1968 there were times when the President was more comfortable with the tune Rostow played. But in their five years together the

President and his Secretary of State enjoyed an uninterruptedly warm relationship based on trust. Perhaps it was two Southern poor boys, back to back against an unappreciative, sometimes hostile world. Perhaps they needed each other—and certainly found they could rely on each other in adversity.

The foreign policy of the Johnson Administration will inevitably and appropriately be judged in light of the war in Vietnam. Little else that happened in the world can be blamed or credited to their account. Rusk and Johnson exploited Soviet interest in detente, but almost certainly would have progressed more rapidly were it not for American actions in Vietnam. During their tenure, the margin of American strategic superiority over the Russians declined. Thoughtful analysts considered Soviet parity with the United States inevitable—and salutary. The Russians determined to have "peaceful coexistence" between equals and the Johnson Administration proved receptive. The Chinese spent most of the Johnson years in the throes of the Cultural Revolution and were little affected by American policy. Until Mao was satisfied with conditions at home, it is difficult to imagine that any useful Sino-American dialogue was possible. The Sino-Soviet split doubtless enhanced American security. The United States, however, had nothing to do with its origins and found an independent China more threatening than a "Slavic Manchukuo."

Similarly, the problems that wracked the Western Alliance did not reflect responses to the policies of the Johnson Administration. Turkey and Greece had differences over Cyprus for which the United States bore no responsibility. De Gaulle's aspirations for France and suspicions of Great Britain and the United States derived from experiences in World War II, if not from his mother's milk. The general European resistance to American hegemony had begun with recovery in the 1950s. Events in Vietnam, however, did nothing to relieve European anxieties about the quality of American leadership.

In the Middle East, Africa, and South Asia, many people fought and died over local issues in which the United States was rarely more than peripherally involved. The issues antedated the Johnson years and were the sources of more fighting and more suffering for some time after Johnson and Rusk were in retirement. Israel and its

Arab foes, Indians and Pakistanis, rival tribes in Africa manipulated the superpowers as best they could, paying heed only to their own judgments and interests.

Latin America, specifically the Dominican Republic, was an exception to the general portrait of limited American power. In 1965 the United States used its power to suppress an insurrection in the Dominican Republic. The results, far from glorious, seemed benign—at least for those who would wish a liberal democracy for the local people. But the Dominican intervention, like the Americanization of the war in Vietnam, had an effect not restricted to the area in which force was used. The widely perceived abuse of power, the resort to old-fashioned "gunboat" diplomacy, depreciated American currency all through Latin America, Western Europe, and the unaligned states. American intervention in the Dominican Republic was precisely the evidence of which hostile propagandists dreamt.

And then, inescapably, there was Lyndon Johnson's war in Vietnam, overshadowing his impressive achievements in domestic affairs and everything else he did in international affairs. True, he inherited the war from Kennedy—and the war was going badly. The men who had advised Kennedy to escalate advised Johnson to escalate. Nonetheless, there was nothing inevitable or inexorable about the decisions to bomb North Vietnam or to send hundreds of thousands of Americans to fight on the Asian mainland. Indeed, Rusk advised against such an Americanization of the war. But men seek advisers who will tell them what they want to hear—and until 1968, Johnson sought out Bundy, McNamara, Clifford, Fortas, Rostow, Wheeler, men who assured him he could win and advised him to escalate. The slaughter in Vietnam brought America the contempt of decent people everywhere and alienated an important segment of the American people from their government. America had been shamed. If the war in Vietnam was an example of the responsibilities of world leadership, increasing numbers of Americans were prepared to abandon that role.

In general, over a five-year period, Rusk's advice to Johnson was better than most of what the President heard. He did not serve as the check he might have been on the President's impetuous action in the Dominican Republic. His advice for getting tough with de Gaulle was inferior to that the President received from Bundy and Bohlen. There were issues that he could not give the attention they deserved because of preoccupation with Vietnam. But he handled Soviet affairs well and his record on Vietnam compares favorably with that of all senior officials except Ball. He tried to prevent the Americanization of the war in 1965, and in 1968 he was the key figure in maneuvering Johnson into accepting the bombing halt that led to negotiations. Having remained loyal despite being disregarded in 1965, having held tenaciously to his conception of his role as the President's servant, he retained sufficient credibility to sway Johnson when a stubborn refusal to yield to his critics hindered the President's perception of the need for a change. Rusk was not one of his critics. There was no threat of betrayal. If the loyal Rusk thought the time had come, the President would act.

But if Rusk's advice on Vietnam was better than most, it was not nearly as good as Ball's. Ball simply did not believe Southeast Asia was worth the struggle and had advocated withdrawal before the stakes became too high. Rusk mistrusted Ball's premises. He believed Southeast Asia important to the United States and was convinced that the principles of the Charter had to be fought for there as anywhere else. He did not want to bomb North Vietnam and he did not want to send American combat troops to South Vietnam. But he did not want to withdraw until a non-Communist regime was secure in the south. Given the end upon which he insisted, he could never give the President the kind of advice that might prevent him from sinking ever deeper into the quagmire. So Lyndon Johnson's war in Vietnam was unquestionably Dean Rusk's as well. Rusk would not have had it any other way.

CONCLUSION

Dean Rusk, American Liberalism, and the War in Vietnam

In January, 1969, Dean Rusk left Foggy Bottom after eight years as Secretary of State. He had endured the office longer than any man in the nation's history, save Cordell Hull. Inevitably, he will be remembered as the man who defended the long and unpopular war in Vietnam.

Disowned by many, perhaps most American liberals in the course of the 1960s, Rusk was unquestionably one of them. In 1960 the *New Republic* quite rightly approved his credentials and classed him with Chester Bowles and Adlai Stevenson. These men shared an ideology that separated them from fellow Democrats like Dean Acheson as well as from conservative Republicans like Barry Goldwater. Perhaps Americans were all Wilsonians representative of the liberal consensus scholars have found in America, but there were important differences. Rusk's cohort was intensely anticolonial, more deeply committed to liberal democracy at home and abroad than were men like Acheson and Goldwater. The Rusk group was universalist whereas Acheson's followers were Atlanticists, generally contemptuous of developing countries. Rusk, Bowles, and Stevenson were committed to principles of international behavior embodied in the United Nations Charter which probably transcended Goldwater's comprehension. Only in their anti-Communism did all of these men come together. In a majoritarian political system, where disparate groups must be joined to gain sufficient support for policy, the necessary common denominator was anti-Communism. In the 1960s, all foreign policy was at least

320

nominally anti-Communist, as were all policy makers. Whatever men wanted to do abroad was done in the guise of containing Communism. When there was debate, other issues were involved.

Rusk's universalism appears to derive from his experiences in the rural South of his boyhood, in Europe in the 1930s and in Asia in the 1940s. He concluded, simply enough, that men and women everywhere were alike in their needs and aspirations. As Franklin D. Roosevelt had perceived during World War II, people everywhere demanded freedom from want and from fear. And they required peace. Nothing Rusk observed in government service or his years with the Rockefeller Foundation caused him to modify that sense of human desires. Moreover, this son of a Presbyterian minister, who had once considered the ministry for himself, believed that people everywhere, Africans and Asians as well as Americans and Europeans, were entitled to the gratification of their needs. Very likely because he was a Southern liberal he was intensely sensitive to any slighting of colored people around the world.

Like most Americans, Rusk was convinced that liberal democracy, the American *ideal*, was the political system likely to meet the aspirations of mankind. He had studied other societies and observed some at firsthand; none equaled the system that had rewarded him so well. At home he worked for reforms to bring reality closer to the American dream. In foreign affairs Rusk, like Wilson, wished to extend the blessings of democracy. Perhaps most of all he wanted the United States to serve as the model and the beacon for democratic revolutions.

Wilson's quest for an international organization to oversee universal adherence to agreed principles of international behavior also affected Rusk. The issue of whether the United States should join the League of Nations engaged Rusk's interest as a teenager. At Oxford, he was attracted to the ideas of British supporters of the League and won a prize named after one of the most articulate of them, Lord Cecil. He studied and came to appreciate the structure of agreements, rules, and restraints accepted by Europeans as essential to the preservation of peace. And he witnessed the dismantling of that structure by Germany, Italy, and Japan. The failure of the United States to come in from the periphery of the international community and stop aggression in the 1930s, to support the peace system, was probably the defining experience of his life. Never again.

At the conclusion of World War II, Rusk was an ardent supporter of the United Nations and collective security. His ultimate commitment, however, was not to the organization, which could be corrupted—or even to the idea of collective security. Both were *means* of upholding the principles of international behavior he deemed essential to protection of the weak, to peace, and to the gratification of human aspirations. These principles were embodied in the Charter of the United Nations. For Rusk the Charter, particularly its first two articles, was as meaningful as the Ten Commandments were to Moses. Violators had to be stopped—collectively if possible, through the UN, if possible, or unilaterally by the United States, if necessary. The alternative to the law was war—and with the next world war would come the holocaust, the end of man and his aspirations.

Rusk's anti-Communism followed naturally from his universalism, his anti-colonialism, his faith in liberal democracy and his commitment to the Charter. After World War II, he saw Stalin's Russia playing the role Hitler's Germany had played in the 1930s. Unquestionably, there were flaws in the analogy, in the conception Americans had of "red fascism." But Stalin suppressed human rights in the Soviet Union and wherever the Red Army marched. Stalin would not be bound by the principles of the Charter. Stalin and the men who called themselves Communists denied basic human needs and refused to abide by the norms of the international community, endangering peace. The struggle for the world that Wilson, Cecil, and Rusk envisaged went on—and the Communists were the adversaries.

Rusk was also hostile to rightist regimes that oppressed their people, like those of Trujillo, Franco, and Salazar. These regimes posed less of a threat to Rusk's world, however. They were anachronisms; no one had illusions about such political systems providing blueprints for the future. He was convinced they would wither and democracy might establish itself in their place. Where Communists seized power, with the strength and resources of the Soviet Union behind them, there could be no more hope for human rights.

In the Dominican Republic, Portugal, and Spain, democracy remained a prospect. However unsavory such governments might be, they were preferable to Communism; they preserved the opportunity for democratic institutions.

In his years with the Truman Administration Rusk dealt at length with many of the problems he had to face in the 1960s, particularly those of the Middle East and of Asia, problems involving the expansion of Communism and questions of colonialism. It was President Truman, of course, who directed the course of American policy—and Marshall and Acheson who were his principal navigators. Rusk accepted the decisions of his superiors, but as an assistant secretary he was quite ready to advocate openly directions with which neither his superiors nor his peers were in sympathy.

On three issues in particular, Rusk's differences with colleagues in the Department of State reflected values of the liberal community. He fought consistently for more serious efforts by the United States to work through the United Nations, irritating Kennan and occasionally Acheson as well. In the early months of 1948 he appeared alone among senior officers of the Department in support of the partition of Palestine and the creation of a Jewish state, driving Kennan and James Forrestal to near distraction. Finally, he worked with Jessup to finesse the Atlanticists on behalf of the independence of Indonesia. On all of these issues Rusk and the liberals chose a higher moral ground than that offered by Kennan's "realism."

Rusk's views on policy toward China suggested the ambivalence of liberals toward Mao. He shared the liberal aversion to Chiang Kai-shek, but having served in the China-Burma-India Theater, he was more sympathetic than most to the plight of Chinese fleeing from the Communists. If Communism was bad for Europeans, a point on which there seemed widespread agreement in the United States, it was bad for Asians. Rusk was very much aware of Acheson's condescension toward Asians and his relative indifference to Asia. He was not comfortable with Acheson's approach, with the Truman Administration's apparent willingness to follow Kennan's advice to write off the Asian mainland. Unwilling to associate the United States with Chiang, Rusk nonetheless sought alternatives to Communism for the people on Taiwan. Unwilling to facilitate

Chiang's return to the mainland, he remained interested in other anti-Communist groups that might have survived there. The quest for a liberal democratic alternative to Chiang and Mao was not easily abandoned.

Late in 1949 and throughout 1950, the Truman Administration grudgingly extended its containment policy to Asia. Rusk was one of the architects of this new policy and he was far less reluctant to undertake it than was Acheson. In part the difference is explicable in Rusk's attitude toward China. But it was really his universalism that distinguished his attitude toward East Asian policy from that of Acheson and Kennan. Kennan had been sharply critical of the apparent universalism of the Truman Doctrine. Acheson had not intended to apply the policy to Asia. Rusk, however, was dissatisfied with a policy that would protect the weak of Europe, but not those of Asia. He understood as well as Kennan the greater importance to American interests of preserving industrial states and accepted Kennan's priorities, but believed it was wrong to abandon Asians to the oppressions of Communism. Rusk's distaste for Chiang was the principal barrier to a closer association with respectable elements of the China bloc like Paul Douglas and Walter Judd. For men like Rusk, concerned with human rights, there proved no happy choice for China.

In 1961, with Rusk as Secretary of State, Bowles as undersecretary, and Stevenson at the United Nations, the three most respected liberals of the foreign affairs establishment seemed extraordinarily well-placed to influence policy. They confronted, however, a President who had strong views, markedly less liberal, and strong competitors for his ear in the persons of McGeorge Bundy and McNamara. The Bay of Pigs operation, with which Rusk, Bowles and Stevenson were decidedly unhappy, provided early evidence of the limit of the liberals' power and skill. Bowles was exiled soon thereafter and Stevenson never penetrated the President's inner circle. Rusk as Secretary of State was infinitely less open an advocate than he had been as assistant secretary in the 1940s. Nonetheless it is clear that the President heard his voice and that in the highest echelons of government he was the principal supporter of views espoused by the liberal community.

The area in which the most important liberal-conservative

dichotomy emerged was Africa. Rusk did not have to persuade Kennedy or Bundy or McNamara of the value of restoring America's image as an opponent of imperialism and a supporter of nationalist revolution or alert them to the opportunity. Through Mennen Williams the Kennedy Administration quickly identified itself with the aspirations of African nationalists, to the delight of American liberals—and the chagrin of the Portuguese, as well as American conservatives. But the crisis Kennedy inherited in the Congo soon forced the administration to do more than posture. Rusk found himself in the happy situation of being able to advocate a policy that incorporated most of his values and violated none. American support of the UN effort to strengthen the central government of the Republic of the Congo strengthened the UN, blocked Communist influence, provided the hope of a liberal democratic government, and thwarted the plans of European imperialists. American conservatives, less interested in the UN and its Charter, liberal democracy in the Congo or anywhere else, or anti-imperialism, demanded support for Tshombe and his mercenaries—the Union Minière du Haut Katanga's hired bastions against Communism. Insisting that theirs was the better way to keep Communism out of central Africa, Rusk and the other liberals prevailed. Had Rusk not been Secretary of State, the outcome might have been different.

The parameters of the Cold War changed in the 1960s and Rusk's analysis of the new situation was both idiosyncratic and of consequence. After the apparent taming of Khrushchev during the missile crisis, he focused on the Sino-Soviet split and de Gaulle's effect on the Western alliance. His bêtes noires became the People's Republic of China and France. China rejected his concept of behavior among nations. The Chinese were contemptuous of the UN and its Charter, remained committed to world revolution, and advocated wars of national liberation. De Gaulle questioned the commitment of the United States to the principles of international behavior incorporated in the Charter. He questioned the willingness of the United States to endanger itself, to pay any price, to maintain the rules, conventions and treaties upon which the weak depended for their protection. By the time Lyndon Johnson succeeded Kennedy, Rusk's highest priority was to demonstrate to Mao and to de Gaulle the integrity of the American commitment to the Charter and to those nations it had volunteered to protect against transgressors. In Rusk's mind, the war in Vietnam was transformed into a test of his principles, a means of realizing abstractions like "collective security" and "peace system." Vietnam would be a lesson for the Chinese. Perseverence there would demonstrate to France, Europe, and the rest of the world American willingness to shoulder the burden of maintaining peace.

In the early 1960s, when it became apparent to Rusk and his colleagues that the Saigon regime was in trouble, they did not doubt that it had to be helped to defend itself against the Communist insurgents. To Rusk at least, a Communist-led rebellion was invariably a form of indirect aggression because outside Communists contributed aid. He was wary of Communist internationalism despite Yugoslav independence and mounting evidence of the reality of the Sino-Soviet split. South Vietnam had to be defended. The weak had to be protected and only the United States could undertake the task.

Rusk wanted the American effort in Vietnam to be a selfless crusade on behalf of a people whose yearning for freedom was in danger of being frustrated by the Communists. He was aware that Diem and successors and the course of the war itself flawed that imagery—and he was filled with doubts. But after the spring of 1965, when Johnson committed himself to the Americanization of the war, when American prestige was committed, there was no longer room for doubt. Rusk brushed aside his own and tried to prevent any from developing among the American people. He evoked the symbols that stirred him in hope of inspiring them.

There were, however, skeptics in high places in the Johnson Administration, notably Ball and Warnke. Had one of them been Secretary of State, he might have served more effectively as a brake on the President, but not likely. For reasons of his own Johnson needed to win in Vietnam and there were always people like Clifford to urge him on. Ball and Warnke differed from Rusk primarily over the price to be paid for the defense of South Vietnam. Ball, the Atlanticist and investment banker, saw little of worth in Southeast Asia and wanted to withdraw from the area before cost exceeded the value. Rusk's universalism drove him to a different conclusion, to a deeper involvement in Vietnam than a Ball or an

Acheson would likely have risked. Warnke and other younger liberals were appalled by the devastation and the drain on American resources. But because the principles he held dearest, the principles of the Charter, seemed at stake, Rusk was willing to pay a higher price.

By 1968, Rusk realized that he had failed to persuade the American people of the importance of the task in Vietnam. He realized he had overestimated the ability as well as the will of Americans to pay the price. He suspected that Americanization of the war, which he had opposed, had shattered the fragile hold of the Saigon regime on its people. The cohesiveness of society in South Vietnam had been destroyed. It was time to change course, if matters of transcendent importance were to be salvaged. Fear that disillusionment with Vietnam was alienating the American people from all their commitments, from the hard-won lessons of World War II, led Rusk to agree that the limit of intervention had been reached.

Vietnam was for Rusk what Suez had been for Anthony Eden. The ultimate concern of both men was preservation of the peace system, of principles of international behavior whose acceptance would prevent world war. Both were profoundly influenced by the thought of Lord Cecil and men like him. They had witnessed the failure of collective security in the 1930s—and the results of failure. They were determined that there would not be another failure of nerve. Aggressors would be crushed. Deviants from the norms of the international community would not go unpunished. When Nasser seized the Suez Canal in 1956, Eden saw visions of Hitler, of a new pattern of violations of law that would lead to world war. Chinese and Vietnamese advocacy of wars of national liberation evoked comparable visions for Rusk. Eden and Rusk both failed to appreciate the extent to which a national liberation movement differs from the aggression of a great power; that the "aggression" of a national liberation movement is much more complicated morally and much harder to cope with politically or militarily. Suez brought Eden's downfall. Rusk's reputation was damaged by Vietnam—the more tragically because he was a more liberal man, far more concerned for the weak and the poor than was Eden, far less tolerant of imperialism.

Rusk was committed to what the historian Gordon Levin has

called the idea of American "liberal exceptionalism." He was a patriot who believed the United States had demonstrated its uniqueness and decency by refusing to exploit its power in 1945. The United States had failed the international community after the First World War, but not after the Second. Like so many liberal internationalists, he wanted the United States to protect the weak and meet the demands of what came to be called the "revolution of rising expectations." Americans could afford to be relatively selfless and disinterested. His adversaries at home were those who would reject responsibility to the world community, the isolationists of the past or the unilateralists of the postwar era, and those who would exploit or ignore weaker nations.

As the war escalated in Vietnam and the suffering of the people of that benighted nation became apparent to most of the world, Rusk did not face what was going on there. He had to believe that what the United States was doing in Southeast Asia was right. The image of America, protector of the weak, had to be preserved. Least of all was he prepared to see himself as an accomplice to the destruction of that image, of that vision of his country of which he was proudest. However painful the effort, he saw the war as an instrument of international progress, as an American contribution to a peaceful world order in which democracy prevailed in competition against Communism. Rusk was an extremely moral man, but his acquiescence in the killing of Vietnamese as a demonstration to Mao, de Gaulle, and any who would question the integrity of America's commitments might well have come from an Orwell plot.

Perhaps better than his nongovernmental critics, Rusk understood that force had to be used to demonstrate American power. He had fewer illusions about an international order in which American power was not a variable. But ultimately of greater consequence was his failure to comprehend before 1968, as many of his critics had long before, that the price of power in Vietnam was greater than either American society or the Vietnamese people could afford.

America's tragic war in Vietnam was facilitated by the liberals' concern for the developing nations as well as by anti-Communism. Men like Acheson, Ball, and Kennan were anti-Communist, but the strategy they chose for America might have avoided the agonies of Vietnam. Few Americans were tolerant of Communism, but memories of how Acheson was pilloried in the McCarthy era, of how Nitze's career was hampered, should suffice to demonstrate that there were important differences as to how Communism should be combatted. Acheson, Ball, and Kennan advocated an enclave strategy. American power was limited and could be used only sparingly. In the struggle against Communism, the United States would protect the sources of industrial power in Europe, the Middle East, and Japan. Let the Communists feed the hungry millions or billions of the Afro-Asian world. They echoed Mao's call, aligning the cities of the world against the countryside.

The enclave strategy was rejected on moral grounds by Americans both left and right. Conservatives wanted to oppose Communism everywhere because their wealth and power, as well as their principles, were being threatened. To the left, liberals, even many who considered themselves socialists, were offended by a strategy that seemed to abandon the developing nations, the weak and the poor. They were not hostile to Communism as an economic system. It was not a matter of keeping the Lowell girls off Brook Farm. Like Rusk, they were concerned about the rights to which they believed men and women everywhere were entitled. Africans and Asians too were worthy of the blessings of democracy. In the 1960s, a conservative-liberal consensus was reached on the notion that the Third World constituted the new arena of the Cold War. George Kennan was left outside, to continue his sermons against universalism and moralism in American policy. Liberal messianism eased the path to Vietnam.

Dean Rusk, Secretary of State to John F. Kennedy and Lyndon Baines Johnson, generally gave his Presidents good advice. When it was not heeded, he served his superiors as best he could. The record for the Truman years is full and clear. He spoke his leaders' words even when he questioned their wisdom. The record for the 1960s is clear enough. He was a better man, a wiser, more decent, humane, and moral man than either of the Presidents he served. Nonetheless, he gave unending support to them and to a war being fought by means of which he did not approve—and of which he was not always aware—and by men whose purposes were not always his. In choosing to defend decisions of questionable morality, in serving as an instrument for converting the phrase "The Yanks are coming" from one that elicited joy and the hope of deliverance to one bringing fear and hatred and visions of horrible death, he remained too long the good soldier.

In the mid-1960s, some liberals shed their universalism and recognized the irrelevance of liberal democracy and a Eurocentric peace system for much of Asia and Africa. They concluded, as more radical thinkers had long before, that anti-Communism was senseless when Communism might be the best alternative offered a people. Rusk, however, remained loyal to his President and to an earlier vision. He thus betrayed his own better instincts, the interests of his country, the principles of the UN. Much may be said in mitigation, but never enough.

Notes

CHAPTER ONE

1. "Notes on the Establishment in America," *American Scholar*, XXX (1961), 489-95.
2. J. Robert Moskin, "Dean Rusk: Cool Man in a Hot World," *Look*, XXX (September 6, 1966), 14-21. See also Michael J. O'Neill, "The Quiet Diplomat: Dean Rusk," in Lester Tanzer (ed.), *The Kennedy Circle* (Washington, D.C.: Robert B. Luce, Inc., 1961), 109-38.
3. General Charles H. Bonesteel, III to author, July 29, 1975; David M. French to author, July 3, 1975.
4. *Ibid.*
5. Recollection of Parks Rusk, *New York Times*, December 13, 1960, 18; interview with Dean Rusk, April 9, 1977.
6. Moskin, "Dean Rusk;" *New York Times*, December 10, 1944, 2.
7. Bonesteel to author; interview with John P. Davies, July 22, 1976. I am unable to identify my source on Rusk as a "ladies' man."
8. Bonesteel to author; interview with Ernest Gross, March 26, 1976; Rusk to G. Bernard Noble, July 12, 1950, Department of State, *Foreign Relations of the United States* (hereafter FRUS), *1945, VI: The British Commonwealth, The Far East* (Washington, D.C., Government Printing Office, 1969), 1039.
9. Alger Hiss to James F. Byrnes, March 22, 1946, *FRUS, 1946, I: General, The United Nations* (1972), 19 (see also 764-66).
10. Interview with Gross, March 26, 1976; interview with Harding Bancroft, October 14, 1976.

CHAPTER TWO

1. Rusk, Office Assignment Sheet, April 1, 1947, Department of State decimal file (hereafter SD) 111.73/4-147, National Archives (NA). See also *FRUS, 1947, I: General, The United Nations* (1973), 3 note 1.
2. George F. Kennan, *Memoirs (1925-1950)* (New York: Bantam Books, 1969), 517, 522; interviews with Harding Bancroft, October 14, 1976, Dorothy Fosdick, November 17, 1976, and Louis Henkin, October 14, 1976.

3. Rusk to Merriam, August 3, 1948, "Palestine Reference Book of Dean Rusk," August 1-October 31, 1948, NA.

4. Rusk memorandum, May 3, 1946, *FRUS, 1946, I: General, UN*, 783-85.

5. Secretary of War to Secretary of State, February 7, 1947, *FRUS, 1947, I: General, UN*, 401-4.

6. Joseph M. Jones, *The Fifteen Weeks* (New York: Viking, 1955), 154-55, 160-61.

7. *Ibid.*, 179-82; Rusk to Acheson, March 18, 1947 and Acheson to Rusk, March 19, 1947, *FRUS, 1947, V: The Near East and Africa* (1971), 124-27.

8. Rusk memorandum, July 23, 1947, Kennan memorandum, August 7, 1947, Minutes of Fourth Meeting of US Delegation to the General Assembly, September 13, 1947, *FRUS, 1947, I: General, UN*, 567-68, 170-73.

9. Minutes of Fifteenth Meeting of US Delegation to the General Assembly, October 3, 1947, *ibid*, 675-78; Rusk memorandum, January 22, 1948, SD 501/1-2248, NA.

10. "Summary of Discussion on Problems of Relief, Rehabilitation, and Reconstruction of Europe," May 29, 1947, *FRUS, 1947, III: The British Commonwealth, Europe* (1972).

11. Rusk memorandum, July 23, 1947, minutes of SWNCC meeting, September 8, 1947, *FRUS, 1947, I: General, UN*, 570, 628-31; minutes of meeting, April 2, 1948, *FRUS, 1948, I: General, United Nations (part 1)* (1975), 318-22.

12. Minutes of Ninth Meeting of US Delegation to the General Assembly, September 30, 1948, *FRUS, 1948, I.* 440-42.

13. Rusk memorandum, August 30, 1947, SD 711F.1914/8-3047, NA.

14. Philip C. Jessup, *The Birth of Nations* (New York and London: Columbia University Press, 1974), 83-87.

15. *Ibid.*, 215-16, 219-20.

16. *Ibid.*, 220-24; memorandum, April 8, 1949, Acheson Papers, Box 64, Harry S. Truman Library, Independence, Missouri.

17. Rusk and Henderson for Secretary of State, November 18, 1947, *FRUS, 1947, V: Near East and Africa* (1971), 1264-66.

18. McClintock memorandum of Rusk telephone conversation, November 19, 1947, Palestine Reference Book of Dean Rusk, NA; Matthew J. Connally for President Truman, Papers of Harry S. Truman, Office file Box 773, HST Library.

19. Rusk memorandum, January 26, 1948, *FRUS, 1948, V: Near East and Africa (part 2)* (1976), 556-62.

20. Kennan memorandum, January 29, 1948 and Henderson memorandum, *ibid.*, 573-81, 600-3.

21. PPS memorandum, February 11, 1948, *ibid.*, 619-25.

22. *Ibid.*, 631-33, 645.

23. *Ibid.*, 664-65.

24. Memorandum March 8, 1948, *ibid.*, 690-96.

25. Austin statement, *ibid.*, 742-44. See also editorial note 744-46.

26. Rusk memorandum, March 22, 1948, *ibid.*, 750-51 (see also copy with penciled notes in Papers of Clark M. Clifford, Box 13, HST Library); Truman statement, *ibid.*, 759-60.

27. *Ibid.*, 759-60, 797-98; Walter Millis (ed.), *The Forrestal Diaries* (New York: Viking Press, 1951), 410-11.

28. Memorandum of conversation between Rusk and Mahmoud Fawzi Bey, April 20, 1948 and Rusk to Lovett, April 29, 1948, Palestine Reference Book of Dean Rusk,

NA; memorandum of conversation between Rusk and Truman, April 30, 1948, *FRUS, 1948, V (part 2),* 877-79.

29. Rusk memorandum, May 6, 1948 and Marshall to Bevin, May 8, 1948, *FRUS, 1948, V (part 2),* 920-23, 940-41; Rusk memorandum, May 8, 1948, Palestine Reference Book, NA.

30. Memorandum of conversation with Rusk, May 8, 1948, Clifford Papers, Box 13, HST Library; *FRUS, 1948, V (part 2),* 972-76.

31. For Clifford arrangement with Epstein see *FRUS, 1948, V (part 2),* 989n; Lovett memorandum, May 17, 1948, 1005-7.

32. Rusk to Department of State Historical Office, June 13, 1974, *ibid.,* 993.

33. *Ibid.,* 1020-22.

34. *Ibid.,* 1027-28.

35. Rusk draft of letter, Marshall to Forrestal, July 28, 1948 and Rusk to Marshall, August 26, 1948, Palestine Reference Book, NA; NSC 27/1, Papers of Harry S. Truman, PSF/NSC meetings, Box 204, HST Library.

36. Memorandum by Clifford June 17, 1948 and memoranda by Lovett, June 22 and June 28, 1948, Rusk to Lovett, November 26, 1948, *FRUS, 1948, V (part 2),* 1117-19, 1131-32, 1151-52, 1629-30.

37. Rusk to Lovett, October 2, 1948, *ibid.,* 1448-49; Lovett to Clifford, October 13, 1948, Clifford Papers, Box 13, HST Library.

38. Memoranda for Truman, August 19, 1948 and for Lovett, August 20, 1948, *FRUS, 1948, V (part 2),* 1324-26, 1331-32; McClintock to Lovett, August 27, 1948, Palestine Reference Book, NA.

39. Rusk for Webb, March 3,1949, 501.BB Palestine/3-349, Rusk for Acheson, March 29, 1949 and memorandum of conversation between Rusk and Israeli mission, June 17, 1949, Palestine Reference Book, NA.

CHAPTER THREE

1. This paragraph and following discussion based on my interviews with Harding Bancroft, October 14, 1976, John P. Davies, July 22, 1976, Dorothy Fosdick, November 17, 1976, Ernest Gross, March 26, 1976, Louis Henkin, October 14, 1976, and Philip C. Jessup, October 1, 1976.

2. Rusk for Acheson and Webb, March 10, 1949, 501.BB Palestine/3-1049; Rusk for Acheson, March 22, 1949, 860 H. 50/3-2249; Rusk for Acheson, December 20, 1949, 501.BB Palestine/12-2049, NA.

3. Jessup to James Gifford, August 17, 1948, Papers of Philip C. Jessup, Box 49, Library of Congress (LC); interview with Gross and Jessup.

4. U.S. Congress, Senate, Committee on Foreign Relations, "Nomination of Dr. [sic] Dean Rusk to be Assistant Secretary of State," February 2, 1949.

5. Interview with Jessup.

6. Rusk memorandum of conversations, 868.00/5-1649, NA.

7. Rusk to Acheson, April 11, 1949, 501.BB Balkan/4-1149, NA.

8. *New York Times,* April 1, 1949, 13; record of roundtable discussion, Truman Papers, WHCF, Confidential file, Box 36, HST Library.

9. *Department of State Bulletin* (DSB), 21 (October 24, 1949), 630-33, 22 (April 3, 1950), 526-32.

10. Record of roundtable discussion, above.

11. *DSB*, 21 (October 31, 1949), 652-57.

12. *Ibid.*, 22 (April 3, 1950), 526-32.

13. Memorandum by R. Gordon Arneson, August 2, 1949, *FRUS, 1949, I: National Security Affairs, Foreign Economic Policy* (1976), 506-7; minutes of meeting of PPS attended by Acheson and Rusk, *ibid.*, 573-85.

14. *New York Times,* March 13, 1949, 46; Rusk memorandum, December 27, 1949, 852.00/12-2749, NA.

15. See my essay "The Department of State and China, 1949-1950" prepared for the Conference on the Cause of the Cold War and Sino-American Relations, June 1978 (to be published by Columbia University Press).

16. "Evolution of Letter of Transmittal in China White Paper," September 26, 1951, Jessup Papers, Box 45, LC.

17. Ogburn memorandum, November 2, 1949, *FRUS, 1949, IX Far East: China* (1974), 160-62.

18. Record of roundtable discussion, above.

19. Notes of conversation with Rusk, August 26, 1949, Papers of Wellington Koo, Box 130, Columbia University.

20. See notes of conversations with Dulles, Koo Papers, Box 180, Columbia.

21. Acheson memorandum of meeting with JCS, December 29, 1949, *FRUS, 1949, IX,* 463-67.

22. *Ibid.*

23. Rusk to Major General James H. Burns, March 7, 1950, US Congress, House, Committee on Armed Services, *United States-Vietnam Relations 1945-1967* (hereafter *Pentagon Papers*), Book I, IV.A.2, 8.

24. Acheson, *Present at the Creation* (New York: Signet, 1970), 560.

CHAPTER FOUR

1. *New York Times,* March 28, 1950, 4.

2. Notes of conversation with Griffith, June 3, 1950, Koo Papers, Box 180, Columbia.

3. Interview with Rusk, April 9, 1977; Rusk memorandum, July 16, 1949, 890.00/7-1649, NA; "Discussion of Far Eastern Affairs in Preparation for Conversation with Mr. Bevin," September 13, 1949, 890.00/9-1349, NA.

4. Memorandum by W. Park Armstrong, May 31, 1950, *FRUS, 1950, VI: East Asia and the Pacific* (1978), 347-51; diary entry for June 4, 1950, Box 217, Koo Papers, Columbia.

5. Notes on conversation with Dulles, June 12, 1950 and inter-office memorandum by Ch'en Chih-mai, June 15, 1950, Koo Papers, Box 180, Columbia.

6. Diary entry, April 20, 1950, Koo Papers, Box 217, Columbia.

7. Notes on conversation with Rusk, April 20, 1950, Koo Papers, Box 180.

8. Diary entry, June 4, 1950, Koo Papers, Box 217.

9. US Congress, Senate, Committee on Foreign Relations, Committee on Armed Services, Historical Series, June 8, 1950, 254-55, 263-69; US Congress, House, Committee on International Relations, Selected Executive Sessions, 1943-50, VIII, part 2, June 20, 1950, 466-79, 485-89, 505.

10. US Congress, Senate, Committees on Foreign Relations and Armed Services, Historical Series, June 8, 1950, 279-91.

11. US Congress, House, Committee on International Relations, Selected Executive Sessions, June 20, 1950, 506.

12. US Congress, Senate Committees on Foreign Relations and Armed Services, Historical series, June 8, 1950, 263-69.

13. *Ibid.*, 254-55.

14. Interview with Davies.

15. Rusk memorandum, May 24, 1949, 740.00119 Control (Korea)/5-2449, NA; US Congress, House, Committee on International Relations, Selected Executive Sessions, June 20, 1950, 464.

16. Glenn D. Paige, *The Korean Decision* (New York: Free Press, 1968), 284, and Ernest R. May, *"Lessons" of the Past* (New York: Oxford, 1973), 72. I agree with the argument of David S. McLellan, *Dean Acheson, The State Department Years* (New York: Dodd, Mead and Company, 1976), 275.

17. Paige, *Korean Decision*, 125-27.

18. Memorandum, "Korean Situation," June 26, 1950, Papers of Dean Acheson, Box 65, HST Library.

19. Memoranda of conversations with Rusk, July 3 and July 7, 1950, Koo Papers, Box 180.

20. Memorandum of conversation with Louis Johnson, June 30, 1950, Box 180; diary entry, July 25, 1950, Box 218; memorandum of conversation with Rusk, July 25, 1950, Box 180, Koo Papers.

21. Memorandum of conversation with Rusk, August 31, 1950, Box 180, Koo Papers.

22. "Fundamentals of Far Eastern Policy," *DSB*, 23 (September 18, 1950), 465-68.

23. Memorandum of conversation with Rusk, July 25, 1950, Box 180, Koo Papers.

24. Memorandum of conversation with Rusk, September 19, 1950, Box 180, Koo Papers.

25. Memorandum of meeting with Truman, October 9, 1950, Acheson Papers, Box 65, HST Library.

26. Gaddis Smith, *Dean Acheson* in Robert H. Ferrell (ed.), *The American Secretaries of State*, XVI (New York: Cooper Square Publishers, 1972), 215-16.

27. *DSB*, 23 (December 4, 1950), 889-94; see Allen S. Whiting, *China Crosses the Yalu* (New York: Macmillan, 1960), 44 and Robert R. Simmons, *The Strained Alliance* (New York: Free Press, 1975), 118.

28. *DSB*, 24 (February 12, 1951), 262.

29. Memorandum of conversation with Rusk, November 29, 1950, Box 180, Koo papers.

30. Smith, *Dean Acheson*, 227-29; Acheson, *Present at the Creation*, 615.

31. Harry S. Truman, *Memoirs: Years of Trial and Hope, 1946-1952* (Garden City: Doubleday, 1956), 407-8; memorandum of conversation with Dulles, December 19, 1950, Box 180, Koo papers.

32. Interview with Davies; *DSB*, 24 (January 8, 1951), 64-65.

33. Diary entries, December 5, 1950, February 9, 1951, February 14, March 15, March 23, 1951, Box 218; memoranda of conversations with Rusk, January 18 and March 23, 1951, Box 184, Koo papers.

34. *Pentagon Papers*, Book 8, V.B.2, 426-37.

35. DSB, 24 (May 28, 1951), 846-48; *New York Times*, May 19, 1951, 1.

36. *New York Times,* May 19, 1951, 1, 14: May 20, 1951, IV, 8; May 21, 1951, 1, 4; May 23, 1951, 1; May 24, 1951, 34 (Krock column).

37. *Ibid.,* May 24, 1951, 1; May 26, 1951, 16; *Time,* 57 (June 4, 1951), 20; *Newsweek,* 37 (June 4, 1951), 22.

38. *Time* and *Newsweek,* above; *US News and World Report,* 30 (June 1, 1951), 36-37.

39. Diary entries, May 19, 21, and 31, 1951, Box 218; Ch'en Chih-mai memorandum, May 25, 1951, Box 119, Koo papers.

40. Memorandum of conversation with Truman, May 21, 1951, Acheson Papers, Box 66, HST Library.

41. *New York Times,* May 21, 1951, 4.

42. US Congress, Senate, Committee on Foreign Relations, Historical series, July 2, 1951, 536-43.

43. *Ibid.,* 548.

44. *Ibid.,* 556-57; *New York Times,* July 3, 1951, 1.

45. Princeton Seminar, March 14, 1954, Acheson Papers, HST Library.

46. *Ibid.,* interview of Dean Rusk, Dulles Oral History Collection (OHC), Princeton.

47. Memoranda of conversations with Dulles, May 31 and June 2, 1951, with Rusk, June 6 and August 9, 1951, with Dulles and Rusk, June 15 and 19, 1951, Box 184, Koo papers.

48. Diary entry, August 14, 1951, Box 218, Koo papers.

49. Memoranda of conversation with Rusk, November 2, 1951, Box 184, Koo papers.

50. Princeton Seminar, March 14, 1954, 1503, Acheson papers.

51. *New York Times,* August 14, 1950, 1, 5; Jessup, *Birth of Nations,* 193; *New York Times,* November 28, 1950, 6; interview with Harland Cleveland, October 11, 1976.

52. US Congress, Senate, Committees on Foreign Relations and Armed Services, July 7, 1951, 533.

53. US Congress, House, Committee on Foreign Affairs, July 23, 1951, 888-94.

54. *Ibid.,* 915.

55. *DSB,* 26 (November 19, 1951), 821-25.

56. *New York Times,* November 30, 1951, 4; December 7, 1951, 17, 26.

57. Truman Papers, PPF 6035, HST Library.

CHAPTER FIVE

1. Dulles to Rusk, January 29, 1948, Papers of John Foster Dulles, Princeton.

2. Dulles to Rusk, October 16, 1951 and Rusk to Dulles, October 22, 1951, Dulles Papers.

3. Rusk to Dulles, November 11, 1951, Dulles Papers.

4. Rusk to Feis, December 18, 1951, Papers of Herbert Feis, Box 25, LC; Rusk to Jessup, December 31, 1951, Jessup Papers, Box 61, LC.

5. Interview with Flora M. Rhind, Columbia OHC, 1023, 1050-51, 1060-61, 1070, 1287.

6. *Ibid.*, 1023-27, 1066-67, 1073; interview with Rusk, April 9, 1977.

7. Rhind interview, 962.

8. *Ibid.*, 973, 1066; interview with Davies.

9. Rhind interview, 1023, 1030, 1044, 1053, 1071-72, 1514.

10. Rusk memorandum, November 29, 1955; Dean Rusk Diary, March 6, 1957, Rockefeller Archives Center.

11. *New York Times*, December 28, 1959, 1; Rhind interview, 1302.

12. Dean Rusk Diary, October 10, 1956, Rockefeller Archives.

13. Princeton Seminar, March 14, 1954, Acheson Papers.

14. Rusk to Dulles, March 11, 1952, Dulles Papers.

15. *New York Times*, April 29, 1952, 2.

16. Interview with Rusk, April 9, 1977.

17. Rusk to Bowles, December 4, 1959, Chester Bowles Collection, Box 215, Yale University.

18. DR, "Thoughts While Shaving," June 8, 1960, Jessup Papers, Box 11 (second series), LC.

19. Rusk to Dulles, March 11, 1952, Dulles Papers.

20. *New York Times*, September 30, 1953, 3; January 6, 1958, 18.

21. (New York: Harper and Row, 1956); *New York Times*, May 23, 1956, 17; Rusk to Dulles, April 19, 1953, Dulles Papers.

22. A. A. Berle, *Navigating the Rapids, 1918-1971* (New York: Harcourt, Brace, Jovanovich, 1973), 755.

23. *Prospect For America* (Garden City: Doubleday, 1961), 5-7, 11.

24. *Ibid.*, 15; *New York Times*, July 15, 1960, 10.

25. *Prospect for America*, 24.

26. *Ibid.*, 39-43.

27. *Ibid.*, 42, 46-48.

28. *Ibid.*, 53-58.

29. *Ibid.*, 65-75.

30. Acheson to Jessup, March 5, 1958, Jessup papers, Box 5 (second series), LC; "The President," *Foreign Affairs*, XXXVIII (April 1960), 353-69.

CHAPTER SIX

1. Interview with George F. Kennan, 34, John F. Kennedy OHC, John F. Kennedy Library.

2. *New York Times*, December 13, 1960, 18, 22; December 18, 1960, IV, 3; *Businessweek*, December 17, 1960, 23-24; *Newsweek*, 57 (February 6, 1961), 19-22.

3. *Businessweek*, above; "The New Team at State," *New Republic*, 143 (December 19, 1960), 3-5; Chester Bowles, *Promises to Keep: My Years in Public Life, 1961-1969* (New York: Harper and Row, 1971), 299-300; interview with Rusk, April 9, 1977; *Time*, 76 (December 26, 1960), 8-11.

4. *Businessweek*, above; *New Republic*, 143 (November 14, 1960), 5.

5. *New York Times*, December 13, 1960, 30.

6. Interview with Rusk, April 9, 1977.

7. *Ibid.*; interview with Chester Bowles, Kennedy OHC; Philip D. Sprouse to

author, August 13, 1976; Roger Hilsman, *To Move a Nation* (Garden City: Doubleday, 1967), 15.

8. Interviews with Roger W. Jones, 19, 49 and Benjamin H. Read, Kennedy OHC; my interview with George Ball, June 12, 1976 and with Lucius D. Battle, November 9, 1976.

9. Interview with Henry Owen, November 15, 1976 and with Roger Hilsman, September 28, 1976; telephone conversation with Thomas L. Hughes, November 15, 1976.

10. Interviews with Battle and with Rusk.

11. *New York Times*, February 24, 1961, 28.

12. Interview with Battle.

13. Quotation is from Theodore C. Sorensen, *Kennedy* (New York: Harper and Row, 1965), 270.

14. Rusk and McGeorge Bundy both assure me that Rusk was always informed of such communications. Interview with Rusk, November 5, 1977 and with Bundy, June 12, 1978.

15. Interviews with Ball, Chester Bowles, July 26, 1976, Battle, November 23, 1976, Hilsman, Philips Talbot, October 4, 1976, William Tyler, November 11, 1976.

16. Rusk informs me that he rarely asked for and was never denied private access.

17. Kennedy to Rusk, February, 1961, Papers of John F. Kennedy, WHCF, Box 122, JFK Library; interview with Rusk, April 9, 1977.

18. *New York Times*, May 7, 1961, IV, I; May 19, 30; May 28, IV, 5; June 18, IV, 8.

19. "Disarray at State," *New Republic*, 145 (July 24, 1961), 3-4; *New York Times*, July 19, 1961, 28.

20. Rusk memorandum, undated [July, 1961?], Kennedy Papers, POF, Box 88, JFK Library.

21. *Harpers*, 223 (November 1961), 43-50.

22. Arthur M. Schlesinger, Jr., *A Thousand Days* (New York: Fawcett, 1967), 404.

CHAPTER SEVEN

1. Interviews with Cleveland, J. William Fulbright, November 16, 1976, Paul H. Nitze, November 9, 1976, Owen, Benjamin H. Read, November 10, 1976, and Talbot.

2. U.S. Congress, Senate, Committee on Foreign Relations, Executive Session, September 16, 1958, 77-78; *DSB* 46 (February 12, 1962), 241-44.

3. *DSB* 44 (February 27, 1961), 296-309.

4. US Congress, Senate, Committee on Foreign Relations, Executive Session, February 28, 1961, 10-12.

5. *Ibid.*, 64-65.

6. *DSB*, 44 (April 10, 1961), 515-19; (March 27, 1961), 439-44.

7. *Ibid.*, (May 22, 1961), 747-50.

8. Rusk memorandum for Kennedy, February 24, 1961, Kennedy Papers, POF, Box 114A, JFK Library; Schlesinger, *A Thousand Days*, 235; interview with Richard Bissell, Kennedy OHC.

9. Bissell interview; Harold Macmillan, *Pointing the Way* (New York: Harper and Row, 1972), 353-54; Schlesinger, *A Thousand Days*, 255-56.

10. Interview with Rusk, April 9, 1977; Schlesinger, *A Thousand Days*, 236; Sorensen, *Kennedy*, 296.

11. Stephan R. Weissman, *American Foreign Policy in the Congo, 1960-64* (Ithaca: Cornell University Press, 1974) is my source unless otherwise indicated.

12. Rusk memoranda for Kennedy, February 1 and 2, 1961, *Declassified Documents Reference System (DDRS)*, 1975, 281D and quarterly catalogue, I.

13. US Congress, Senate, Committee on Foreign Relations, Executive Session, February 28, 1961.

14. Interview with Rusk, April 9, 1977.

15. Rusk memorandum for Kennedy, August 3, 1961, *DDRS*, 1975, 283B.

16. Brian Urquhart, *Hammarskjold* (New York: Knopf, 1972), 575.

17. US Congress, Senate, Committee on Foreign Relations, Executive Session, September 20, 1961, 8-9; Rusk memorandum, 770g.00/11-1161 and enclosure, "Congo Policy." Obtained from Department of State by invoking Freedom of Information Act.

18. Rusk for Kennedy, December 9, 1961, *DDRS*, 1975, 289A; Council on Foreign Relations, *Documents on American Foreign Relations, 1961* (New York: Harper and Row, 1962), 352-53.

19. Memorandum of telephone conversation, December 13, 1961, abstract in DDRS quarterly catalogue, I; Macmillan, *Pointing the Way*, 456-57.

20. US Congress, Senate, Committee on Foreign Relations, Subcommittee on African Affairs, Executive Session, January 18, 1962, 4-30.

21. Clifford memorandum dated September 29, 1967 (!) of meeting January 19, 1961. *Pentagon Papers*, Book 10, V.B.3, 1362-63.

22. "Ambassador Brown's Call, February 3, 10:30 AM," Kennedy Papers, POF, Box 120, JFK Library; Hilsman, *To Move A Nation*, 128.

23. US Congress, Senate, Committee on Foreign Relations, Executive Session, February 28, 1961, 14-18.

24. *Ibid.*, 19-20.

25. *DSB*, 44 (April 17, 1961), 547-49.

26. Stanley Karnow, "Dean Rusk's Debut," *Reporter*, 24 (April 27, 1961), 37-38.

27. Macmillan, *Pointing the Way*, 344-45.

28. *Pentagon Papers*, Book 11, V.B.3, 62-66.

29. *New York Times*, May 14, 1961, I, 1, IV, 1; May 16, 1; interview with Harriman, Kennedy OHC, JFK Library.

30. *New York Times*, May 18, 1961, 1, 4; May 28, IV, 4; Richard Stebbins (ed.), *Documents on American Foreign Relations 1961* (New York: Harper and Row, 1962), 311-18.

31. Interview with Harriman, Columbia OHC; interview with Rusk, April 9, 1977; SNIE 10-2-61, June 27, 1961, *DDRS*, 1977, 24D.

CHAPTER EIGHT

1. Interview with David E. Bell, Kennedy OHC; Thompson cable, January 19, 1961, Kennedy Papers, POF Box 127, JFK Library; Bohlen draft of approach to

Khrushchev, June 1, 1961 and Kennan cable, June 2, 1961, Kennedy Papers, POF Box 126, JFK Library.

2. Rusk to Kennedy, Kennedy Papers, POF Box 117 and February 2, 1961, POF Box 116A, JFK Library.

3. Alexander L. George and Richard Smoke, *Deterrence in American Foreign Policy* (New York: Columbia, 1974), 414.

4. Cyrus Sulzberger, *Last of the Giants* (New York: Macmillan, 1970), 860.

5. Jack M. Schick, *The Berlin Crisis, 1958-1962* (Philadelphia: University of Pennsylvania Press, 1971), 144-47.

6. Seyom Brown, *Faces of Power* (New York: Columbia, 1968), 248-51; Schlesinger, *A Thousand Days*, 362, 370-71.

7. Robert M. Slusser, *The Berlin Crisis of 1961* (Baltimore: Johns Hopkins University Press, 1973), 77-79.

8. Interview with Owen; interview with Rusk, April 9, 1977; Schlesinger, *A Thousand Days*, 370-71; interview with senior adviser, not for attribution.

9. Schick, *Berlin Crisis*, 160.

10. "Sigh of relief" claim is by Jean Edward Smith, *The Defense of Berlin* (Baltimore: Johns Hopkins University Press, 1963), 277-78; see also Schick, *Berlin Crisis*, 167; US Congress, Senate, Committee on Foreign Relations, Executive Session, September 20, 1961, 17.

11. Interview with Rusk, April 9, 1977; Slusser, *Berlin Crisis*, 149-50.

12. Slusser, *Berlin Crisis*, 207-9, 251.

13. US Congress, Senate, Committee on Foreign Relations, Executive Session, September 20, 1961, 12-37.

14. Interview with Rusk, April 9, 1977; Schick, *Berlin Crisis*, 181.

15. Schick, *Berlin Crisis*, 182-84; *New York Times*, October 17, 1961, 2; Berle, *Navigating the Rapids*, 755.

16. Sorensen, *Kennedy*, 599.

17. Slusser, *Berlin Crisis*, 430, 440-41.

18. Schick, *Berlin Crisis*, 194-96.

19. US Congress, Senate, Committee on Foreign Relations, Executive Session, March 29, 1962, 11-16.

20. *Ibid.*, 17.

21. *Ibid.*

22. Sulzberger, *Last of the Giants*, 908-9.

23. Rusk for Kennedy, undated (October 17, 1962), obtained from Department of State through FOI.

24. Rusk was aware of only one discussion of an assassination plot in which his representative, Llewellyn Thompson, rejected the idea. He knew of no assassination attempts. Interview, April 9, 1977.

25. *Ibid.*

26. *DSB*, 47 (October 22, 1962), 595-98.

27. Elie Abel, *The Missile Crisis* (Philadelphia and New York: J. B. Lippincott Company, 1966), 52-58.

28. *Ibid.*, 69-70; Graham T. Allison, *Essence of Decision* (Boston: Little, Brown, 1971), 199-200.

29. *Ibid.*

30. Abel, *Missile Crisis*, 77; Allison, *Essence of Decision*, 201.

31. Abel, *Missile Crisis*, 80, 83, 89-90.

32. *Ibid.*, 93; interview with Rusk, November 5, 1977.
33. Interview with Rusk, April 9, 1977.
34. Sorensen, *Kennedy*, 706; interview with Edwin M. Martin, Kennedy OHC.
35. Allison, *Essence of Decision*, 198, 218-30.
36. Abel, *Missile Crisis*, 179; Hilsman, *To Move A Nation*, 218.
37. Abel, *Missile Crisis*, 179.
38. *Ibid.*, 180, 184, 207.
39. *Ibid.*, 191.
40. Rusk contends the idea originated with Thompson. Interview November 5, 1977.
41. Rostow and Nitze, quoted in Allison, *Essence of Decision*, 62.
42. *DSB*, 47 (December 17, 1962), 907-17.
43. Interview with Thompson, Kennedy OHC; US Congress, Senate, Committee on Foreign Relations, Executive Sessions, July 23 and August 28, 1963; *DSB*, 49 (November 11, 1963), 726-31.
44. *DSB*, 49 (October 28, 1963), 654-58; (November 11, 1963), 726-31; 48 (April 1, 1963), 467-75.

CHAPTER NINE

1. *The United States and China*, a reprint of Dean Rusk's speech of May 18, 1951 by the Committee of One Million, undated.
2. Interview with Rusk, April 9, 1977; W. W. Kulski, *The Soviet Union in World Affairs* (Syracuse: Syracuse University Press, 1973), 353-54.
3. Interview with Rusk, April 9, 1977; Schlesinger, *A Thousand Days*, 443.
4. Hilsman, *To Move a Nation*, 303-4; US Congress, Senate, Committee on Foreign Relations, Executive Session, February 28, 1961.
5. Interview with Cleveland; Bowles, *Promises to Keep*, 401.
6. Memoranda for Kennedy, undated and unsigned (May 24, 1961), Box 114, and "Chinese Representation," July 31, 1961, Box 113A, POF, Kennedy Papers.
7. Interview with McGeorge Bundy, October 5, 1976.
8. *New York Times*, March 4, 1961, 3.
9. George H. Gallup, *The Gallup Poll* (New York: Random House, 1972), III, 1881.
10. US Congress, Senate, Committee on Foreign Relations, Executive Session, February 28, 1961; *New York Times*, July 7, 1961, 6.
11. *DSB*, 45 (July 31, 1961), 175-79, (June 11, 1962), 931-36.
12. Unpublished manuscript by William P. Bundy; Hilsman, *To Move a Nation*, 314-15; Richard P. Stebbins, *United States in World Affairs, 1962* (New York: Harper and Row, 1963), 211.
13. Interview with Rusk, April 9, 1977; Thompson interview, Kennedy OHC.
14. *DSB*, 48 (April 29, 1963), 641-43; 49 (July 1, 1963), 19-26.
15. Read interview, Kennedy OHC; Kennedy Papers, National Security File, NSC meetings 1963, meeting of July 31, 1963 (including SNIE 13-4-63), JFK Library.
16. Stebbins, *US in World Affairs, 1963*.
17. Thomson, "On the Making of U.S. China Policy, 1961-1969: A Study in Bureaucratic Politics," *China Quarterly* 50 (April/June 1972), 220-43.

18. Hilsman, *To Move a Nation*, 355; interview with Hilsman, September 28, 1976.

19. *Pentagon Papers*, Book 9, V.B.3, 206-11.

20. *Ibid.*, 306, 362, 479, 482.

21. *Ibid.*, Book 10, 1077-80.

22. *Ibid.*, 1083, 1088, 1131.

23. *Ibid.*, 1298-1301.

24. McGeorge Bundy to McNamara, Rusk and Allen Dulles, January 27, 1961, *DDRS* 1975, 328A; Rostow memorandum, January 30, 1961, *DDRS*, 1975, 328C.

25. *Pentagon Papers*, Book 9, V.B.3, 555-57.

26. Stebbins (ed.), *Documents on American Foreign Relations, 1961*, 318-20; *Pentagon Papers*, Book 11, V.B.4, 67.

27. *DSB* 44 (May 22, 1961), 756-63.

28. *Pentagon Papers*, Book 11, V.B.4, 245-46.

29. *Ibid.*, 258-59, 291-96.

30. *Ibid.*, Book 2, IV.B.1, 118.

31. *Ibid.*, 125-33.

32. *DSB*, 45 (December 25, 1961), 1053-59.

33. *Ibid.*, 46 (March 19, 1962), 448-54.

34. *Pentagon Papers*, Book 12, V.B.4, 488.

35. *DSB*, 48 (March 11, 1963), 361-68; (April 29, 1963), 641-43, 664-71.

36. *Pentagon Papers*, Book 12, V.B.4, 524.

37. US Congress, Senate, Committee on Foreign Relations, Executive Session, March 9, 1962, 12-13; Sulzberger, *Last of the Giants*, 861-62; DSB, 48 (May 6, 1963), 698-703.

38. *DSB*, 48 (May 13, 1963), 727-35.

39. Schlesinger, *A Thousand Days*, 901; Hilsman, *To Move a Nation*, 478.

40. Hilsman, *To Move a Nation*, 488.

41. *Ibid.*, 488-92.

42. *Pentagon Papers*, Book 3, IV.B.5, 14-19, 22-23; interview with Rusk, November 5, 1977.

43. *Pentagon Papers*, Book 12, V.B.4, 540-44.

44. *Ibid.*, Book 3, IV.B.5, 64, Book 12, V.B.4, 579ff, Book 3, IV.B.4, 24.

CHAPTER TEN

1. Interviews with a former assistant secretary of state, with Rusk, April 9, 1977, and with Ball.

2. Russell F. Weigley, *The American Way of War* (New York: Macmillan, 1973), 410-40.

3. *Ibid.*, 410-11, 438-39; Brown, *Faces of Power*, 161-62.

4. Brown, *Faces of Power*, 161-62, 171-72; interview with Adrian Fisher, November 16, 1976.

5. Sulzberger, *Last of the Giants*, 15, 826, 876.

6. *New York Times*, May 14, 1961, IV, 1.

7. *Ibid.*, May 8, 1961, 34, May 12, 28.

8. Stebbins, *US in World Affairs, 1962*, 134, 26-27; Brown, *Faces of Power*, 182-84.

9. Rusk to Kennedy and Ball, June 23, 1962, Kennedy Papers, POF Box 88; Read interview, Kennedy OHC; interview with Owen; Stebbins, *US in World Affairs, 1962.*

10. Stebbins, *US in World Affairs, 1962,* 150; Morton H. Halperin, "Why Bureaucrats Play Games," *Foreign Policy,* 2 (1971), 70-90.

11. Schlesinger, *A Thousand Days,* 785; Sorensen, *Kennedy,* 565; interview with Ball.

12. Schlesinger, *A Thousand Days,* 789; Stebbins, *US in World Affairs, 1962,* 152; interview with Rusk, April 9, 1977.

13. Interview with Adam Yarmolinsky, Kennedy OHC; Brown, *Faces of Power,* 186-87.

14. Brown, *Faces of Power,* 305; interviews with Rusk, April 9, 1977, with Nitze, and with Owen; Merchant memorandum of conversation with Rusk, March 21, 1963, FOI; Stebbins, *US in World Affairs, 1963,* 116.

15. Rusk argues that rejection of de Gaulle's proposal was central to tensions that developed between Washington and Paris. Interview with Rusk, November 5, 1977.

16. Rusk for Kennedy, August 24, 1961, enclosures, 739.00/8-2461, FOI.

17. Stebbins, *US in World Affairs, 1962,* 285.

18. *Ibid.,* 290-91; Schlesinger, *A Thousand Days,* 712.

19. *New York Times,* May 17, 1961, 1, 4; Rusk for Kennedy, September 1, 1961, Kennedy papers, POF Box 120.

20. Stebbins, *US in World Affairs, 1963,* 213-14.

21. Interviews with McGeorge Bundy and Philips Talbot; Bowles interview, Kennedy OHC, 68-70.

22. Talbot interview; US Congress, Senate, Committee on Foreign Relations, Executive Session, September 17, 1958; note to Bundy, unsigned, May 9, 1963, Kennedy Papers, National Security File, NSC Meetings, 1963; Bowles interview, Kennedy OHC.

23. Stebbins, *US in World Affairs, 1961,* 216, 347ff; *US in World Affairs, 1962,* 331; Schlesinger, *A Thousand Days,* 486.

24. Stebbins, *US in World Affairs, 1962,* 205-209; Schlesinger, *A Thousand Days,* 492-94; Harriman interview, Kennedy-OHC.

25. Rusk for Kennedy, April 3, 1961, National Security File/W. New Guinea and Rusk for Kennedy, September 9, 1961, POF Box 119, Kennedy Papers.

26. Johnson for Rostow, October 13, 1961, National Security File/W. New Guinea, Kennedy Papers.

27. Bundy for Kennedy, July 26, 1962, POF Box 119, Kennedy Papers.

28. Rusk for Kennedy, September 11, 1961, National Security File/NSC/NSAM 89, Bundy notes for record, December 18, 1961 (meeting December 5), National Security File, NSC meetings 1961, Kennedy Papers.

29. Interview with Talbot.

30. Interview with Rusk, November 5, 1977.

31. *New York Times,* April 28, 1961, 3.

CHAPTER ELEVEN

1. Schlesinger, *A Thousand Days,* 927.

2. Rusk interview, November 5, 1977.

3. Interview with Robert Komer, November 16, 1976.

4. Interview with William P. Bundy, October 6, 1976.

5. See White House Central File, FG 105, Lyndon B. Johnson Library, Austin, Texas.

6. Interviews with Benjamin H. Read, Kennedy OHC and Johnson OHC; interview with Arthur Krock, Johnson OHC.

7. "The Enigma of Dean Rusk," *Harper's*, 231 (July 1965), 100-3; *Atlantic*, 214 (November 1964), 10; *Newsweek*, 65 (May 17, 1965), 32; Milton Viorst, "Incidentally, Who *is* Dean Rusk?" *Esquire*, 69 (April 1968), 98-101.

8. Rusk interview, April 9, 1977. Confirmed by several senior officials on "not for attribution" basis.

CHAPTER TWELVE

1. *DSB*, 51 (August 10, 1964), 174-79.

2. *Ibid.*, 50 (March 16, 1964), 390-96.

3. Philip Geyelin, *LBJ and the World* (New York: Praeger, 1966), 96-97.

4. *Ibid.*, 90-92.

5. Jules Davids, *US in World Affairs, 1964* (New York: Harper and Row, 1965), 225.

6. Geyelin, *LBJ and the World*, 120-22; US Congress, Senate, Committee on Foreign Relations, Executive Session, June 18, 1964, 28-32.

7. Geyelin, *LBJ and the World*, 104-9.

8. *DSB*, 51 (October 12, 1964), 498-503; interview with Rusk, April 9, 1977; Papers of Lyndon B. Johnson, National Security File/State Department, volume I, memorandum for the record, February 4, 1964, LBJ Library.

9. Davids, *US in World Affairs, 1964*, 224-25; Weissman, *American Policy in the Congo*, 245.

10. US Congress, Senate, Committee on Foreign Relations, Executive Session, June 18, 1964, 18.

11. Peter Van Ness, *Revolution and Chinese Foreign Policy* (Berkeley: University of California Press, 1970), 61; Weissman, *American Foreign Policy in the Congo*, 214-20.

12. US Congress, Senate, Committee on Foreign Relations, Executive Session, October 13, 1965, 26.

13. Memorandum of conversation with Johnson, July 16, 1954, Box 191, Koo Papers.

14. *DSB*, 50 (February 17, 1964), 230-34; (March 2, 1964), 330-36; 51 (August 17, 1964), 221-28.

15. *Ibid.*, 50 (February 24, 1964), 275; (April 6, 1964), 530-35; (June 8, 1964), 886-91.

16. *Ibid.*, (May 11, 1964), 732-37.

17. *Ibid.*

18. *Ibid.*, 51 (August 17, 1964), 231-37; (October 5, 1964), 463-72.

19. *Ibid.*, 50 (February 10, 1964), 190-95; (March 16, 1964), 403-9; (June 8, 1964), 886-91; 51 (August 17, 1964), 221-28.

20. Department of State, *American Foreign Policy: Current Documents, 1964*

(Washington: Government Printing Office, 1967), 824-34; interview with William P. Bundy, 36-37, Johnson OHC.

21. US Congress, Senate, Committee on Foreign Relations, Executive Session, June 15, 1964, 59-60.

22. *Pentagon Papers*, Book 3, IV.C.2, 21-22, 25-26, 30, 33; IV.C.1, 67.

23. *Ibid.*, IV.C.1, 46-47.

24. *Ibid.*, 65-68, IV.C.2, 18.

25. Sulzberger, *An Age of Mediocrity* (New York: Macmillan, 1973), 89; *Pentagon Papers*, Book 3, IV.C.2., 18, 21, 25-26, 31-32.

26. Read interview, Johnson OHC; Lyndon B. Johnson, *The Vantage Point* (New York: Holt, Rinehart and Winston, 1971), 114.

27. Geyelin, *LBJ and the World*, 191.

28. CIA Weekly Report, August 5, 1964, *DDRS*, 1975, 248D; CIA Weekly Report, September 9, 1964, *DDRS*, 1975, 27C; *Pentagon Papers*, Book 4, IV.C.2.(b), 26, 34, 41; Johnson, *Vantage Point*, 119-20.

29. William P. Bundy interview, Johnson OHC.

CHAPTER THIRTEEN

1. *Pentagon Papers*, Book 4, IV.C.2 (c), 39.

2. *Ibid.*, 40; Bundy manuscript, chapter XVIII.

3. *Ibid.*

4. *Pentagon Papers*, Book 4, IV.C.2 (c), 14-15.

5. McGeorge Bundy, quoted in Johnson, *Vantage Point*, 123; Bundy manuscript, chapters XVII and XXII.

6. Johnson, *Vantage Point*, 122-23.

7. *DSB*, 52 (January 18, 1965), 62-74.

8. US Congress, Senate, Committee on Foreign Relations, Executive Session, January 8, 1965, 82-86, 120-29.

9. *Ibid.*, 125, 147-48.

10. *Ibid.*, 165-68.

11. *Pentagon Papers*, Book 4, IV.C.2 (c), 80.

12. Johnson, *Vantage Point*, 122-23. See also Leslie Gelb, "The Pentagon Papers and *The Vantage Point*," *Foreign Policy*, 6 (1972), 25-41.

13. *Pentagon Papers*, Book 4, IV.C.3, 58; interview with Rusk, April 9, 1977.

14. *DSB*, 52 (March 15, 1965), 362-71.

15. *Ibid.*

16. *Ibid.* (March 29, 1965), 442-48.

17. Haynes Johnson, "The Irreconcilable Conflict Between Press and Government: 'Whose Side Are You On?' " in Thomas M. Frank and Edward Weisband (ed.), *Secrecy and Foreign Policy* (New York: Oxford University Press, 1974), 171; *Pentagon Papers*, Book 4, IV.C.4, 2-3.

18. *Pentagon Papers*, Book 4, IV.C.4, 1, IV.C.3, 72-73; IV.C.5, 42-43, 114.

19. *DSB*, 52 (April 19. 1965), 569-71; (May 10, 1965), 694-701.

20. *Ibid.*, (May 10, 1965), 699.

21. *Pentagon Papers*, Book 4, IV.C.3, 115.

22. *Ibid.*, IV.C.5, 67, 104-6.

23. Interview with Rusk, April 9, 1977.

24. Bundy manuscript, chapter XXVI; interview with Rusk, April 9, 1977.

25. *Pentagon Papers*, Book 4, IV.C.5, 94.

26. *Ibid.*, 81.

27. David Halberstam, *The Best and the Brightest* (Greenwich, Conn.: Fawcett Crest, 1973), 712-13.

28. *DSB*, 53 (July 12, 1965), 50-55.

29. Interview with Ball; Bundy manuscript, chapter XXVII: *Pentagon Papers*, Book 6, IV.C.7 (a), 7-9.

30. *Pentagon Papers*, Book 6, IV.C.7(a), 8.

31. Johnson, *Vantage Point*, 147; *DSB*, 53 (August 2, 1965), 186.

32. U.S. Congress, Senate, Committee on Foreign Relations, Executive Session, October 13, 1965.

33. Bundy manuscript, chapter XXXIII.

34. *Ibid.*; *Pentagon Papers*, Book 6, IV.C.7(c), 23; Congressional briefing, March 11, 1965, 10, LBJ Library.

35. *Pentagon Papers*, Book 6, IV.C.7(c), 23.

36. *DSB*, 53 (December 13, 1965), 930-39.

37. Bundy manuscript, chapter XXXVII.

38. *Ibid.*; Johnson, *Vantage Point*, 234-36; Bundy interview, 16-24, Johnson OHC.

39. *Pentagon Papers*, Book 6, IV.C. 7(a), 30.

40. Abraham F. Lowenthal, *The Dominican Intervention* (Cambridge, Mass.: Harvard University Press, 1972), 26. I have relied heavily on Lowenthal's account.

41. *Ibid.*, 44–49.

42. US Congress, Senate, Committee on Foreign Relations, Executive Session, May 21, 1965, 50; interview with Rusk, April 9, 1977.

43. Lowenthal, *Dominican Intervention*, 77.

44. *Ibid.*, 105.

45. *DSB*, 52 (May 31, 1965), 842-44.

46. US Congress, Senate, Committee on Foreign Relations, Executive Session, May 21, 1965.

47. Stebbins, *US in World Affairs, 1965*, 97-98; interviews with Cyrus Vance and Thomas C. Mann, Johnson OHC.

48. Stebbins, *US in World Affairs, 1965*, 101.

CHAPTER FOURTEEN

1. "The Rusk Doctrine," *New Republic*, 154 (March 5, 1966), 5-7.

2. *DSB*, 54 (March 7, 1966), 346-56.

3. *The Vietnam Hearings* (New York: Vintage Books, 1966).

4. *Pentagon Papers*, Book 6, IV.C.7(a), 111; *DSB* 55 (August 1, 1966), 162-68.

5. *Pentagon Papers*, Book 6, IV.C.8, 38, IV.C.7(a), 89; John B. Henry II and William Espinosa, "The Tragedy of Dean Rusk," *Foreign Policy*, 8 (1972), 187.

6. *Pentagon Papers*, Book 6, IV.C.7(a), 124.

7. *Ibid.*, Book 5, IV.C.6(a), 90-91.

8. *Ibid.*, Book 6, 144-45, 166-68; Book 5, IV.C.6(a), 82.

9. *Ibid.*, Book 5, IV.C.6(a), 56, 103; Chester L. Cooper, *The Lost Crusade* (New York: Dodd, Mead and Co., 1970), 342.

10. *Pentagon Papers*, Book 6, IV.C.7(a), 145.

11. *DSB*, 56 (January 23, 1967), 126-32.

12. Cooper, *Lost Crusade*, 35-57.

13. Congressional briefing, February 8, 1967, LBJ Library; Cooper, *Lost Crusade*, 357-60.

14. Harold Wilson, *A Personal Record* (Boston: Little, Brown, 1971), 355-59.

15. Bundy interview, Johnson OHC; Cooper, *Lost Crusade*, 355-56.

16. *Pentagon Papers*, Book 6, IV.C.7(b), 21-27; Cooper, *Lost Crusade*, 375-76.

17. *Pentagon Papers*, Book 6, IV.C.7(b), 49-50, 60.

18. *Ibid.*, 58, 62-63, Book 5, IV.C.6(c), 25-36.

19. Townsend Hoopes, *The Limits of Intervention* (New York: David McKay, 1969), 87; *DSB*, 57 (September 25, 1967), 383-90.

20. Hoopes, *Limits of Intervention*, 123; Bowles, *Promises to Keep*, 577.

21. Stebbins, *US in World Affairs*, 1967, 78; *New York Times*, January 7, 1968, IV.

22. *DSB* 57 (October 30, 1967), 555-64; Rusk's hostility to Chinese was mentioned frequently by his associates. All were surprised by evidence to the contrary.

23. Interview with Rusk, April 9, 1977; Jules Davids, *US in World Affairs*, 1964, 122-23.

24. *DSB*, 50 (February 17, 1964), 230-34; Ralph Clough to Department of State, April 27, 1964, Johnson Papers, National Security File/China, LBJ Library.

25. *DDRS*, 1975, 151B.

26. *Ibid.*, 327E and 1977, 6F.

27. Stebbins, *US in World Affairs, 1965*, 148.

28. *DSB*, 52 (January 18, 1965), 62-74; Rusk presented similar arguments to a host of foreign diplomats from 1964-1966. See State Department file UN 6 CHI COM. FOI.

29. Congressional briefings by Ball, February 9, 1965, by Rusk, February 16, 1965, LBJ Library; *DSB*, 53 (July 12, 1965), 50-55; *DDRS*, 1977, 7A.

30. *DSB*, 53 (September 13, 1965), 431-44.

31. *Ibid.* (November 1, 1965), 690-99; Gallup, *Gallup Poll*, III, 1881; *Public Opinion* (October, 1971), no. 6.

32. Thomson to Bundy, September 2, 1965, Johnson Papers, National Security File/China, LBJ Library; Bundy manuscript, Chapters XVI, XXXII; US Congress, Senate, Committee on Foreign Relations, Executive Session, October 13, 1965, 58-69.

33. Geyelin, *LBJ and the World*, 276; *DSB*, 54 (May 2, 1966), 686-95.

34. *Ibid.* (April 11, 1966), 557-64, (May 16, 1966), 772-75.

35. *Ibid.*, 57 (October 30, 1967), 555-64.

36. *Ibid.*, 58 (February 12, 1968), 206-9.

37. Bundy manuscript, chapter XXXII.

38. Davids, *US in World Affairs, 1964*, 247.

39. US Congress, Senate, Committee on Foreign Relations, Executive Session, January 27, 1965 and October 13, 1965, 28-31.

40. Interviews with Rusk, April 9, 1977, with Battle, November 23, 1976, with Read, November 10, 1976.

41. *Ibid.*; Sulzberger, *Age of Mediocrity*, 346.

CHAPTER FIFTEEN

1. Sulzberger, *Age of Mediocrity*, 54.

2. *DSB*, 50 (March 16, 1964), 390-96, Brown, *Faces of Power*, 317.

3. *DSB*, 50 (May 25, 1964), 810-15.

4. *Ibid.*, 51 (August 10, 1964), 174-79.

5. *Ibid.*, 55 (July 11, 1966), 44-49.

6. W. W. Rostow, *Diffusion of Power* (New York: Macmillan, 1972), 391.

7. Geyelin, *LBJ and the World*, 161-71; Bundy for Johnson, June 15, 1964 covering Rusk memorandum, Johnson Papers, Confidential File FG 105 (1964), LBJ Library.

8. Wilson, *A Personal Record*, 46; Geyelin, *LBJ and the World*, 172.

9. Wilson, *A Personal Record*, 50-51; Geyelin, *LBJ and the World*, 173-76.

10. Davids, *US in World Affairs, 1964*, 49; Bundy for Johnson, January 28, 1966, Johnson Papers, Confidential File, FG 105 (Department of State) January-June 1966; Geyelin, *LBJ and the World*, 180.

11. Bundy for Johnson, November 16, 1965, Johnson Papers, WHCF (Confidential File) CO81 France (1964-1965), LBJ Library; interview with Charles Bohlen, Johnson OHC; interview with John M. Leddy, Johnson OHC.

12. Johnson, *Vantage Point*, 478-79, 487-89; interview with Rusk, April 9, 1977.

13. *DSB*, 57 (August 28, 1967), 251-55; 59 (July 8, 1968), 33-38; Sulzberger, *Age of Mediocrity*, 348; Stebbins, *US in World Affairs, 1967*, 164.

14. *New York Times*, July 28, 1968, IV, 3.

15. *DSB*, 59 (October 21, 1968), 405-10.

16. James R. Jones memorandum of Rusk telephone call, August 31, 1968, Johnson Papers, WHCF, FG 105, LBJ Library; *DSB*, 59 (December 23, 1968), 645-50.

17. *DSB*, 58 (February 26, 1968), 261-72.

18. *New York Times*, February 18, 1968, IV, 1; Johnson, *Vantage Point*, 387.

19. *New York Times*, March 3, 1968, IV, 3; Johnson, *Vantage Point*, 398; Hoopes, *Limits of Intervention*, 173-75; *Pentagon Papers*, Book 5, IV.C.6(c), 32.

20. Interview with Paul Warnke, Johnson OHC; interview with Paul H. Nitze, November 9, 1976.

21. Johnson, *Vantage Point*, 399-400; Herbert Y. Schandler, *The Unmaking of a President* (Princeton: Princeton U. Press, 1977), 185-88; *Pentagon Papers*, Book 6, IV.C.7(b), 180-81.

22. Schandler, *Unmaking of a President*, 188, 190-92.

23. "TRB," *New Republic*, 158 (March 16, 1968), 4; *New York Times*, March 17, 1968, IV, 2.

24. Schandler, *Unmaking of a President*, 237-40; Johnson, *Vantage Point*, 407-10; Harry McPherson, *A Political Education* (Boston: Little, Brown, 1972), 432.

25. Hoopes, "LBJ's Account of March, 1968," *New Republic*, 162 (March 14, 1970), 17-19; Schandler, *Unmaking of a President*, 192.

26. Johnson, *Vantage Point*, 410.

27. Schandler, *Unmaking of a President*, 250-54; Johnson, *Vantage Point*, 412-13; Hoopes, *Limits of Intervention*, 211.

28. Schandler, *Unmaking of a President*, 262-64.

29. Johnson, *Vantage Point*, 419; interviews with Nitze and William Bundy.

30. McPherson, *Political Education*, 435-36; Hoopes, *Limits of Intervention*, 219-20; interview with Clark M. Clifford, Johnson OHC.

31. Schandler, *Unmaking of a President*, 276; Johnson, *Vantage Point*, 421.

32. Schandler, *Unmaking of a President*, 306, 311-12; Johnson, *Vantage Point* 499-505; McPherson, *Political Education*, 441.

33. Bundy interview, Johnson OHC; Johnson, *Vantage Point*, 509.

34. Bundy and Vance interviews, Johnson OHC; *DSB* 59 (August 19, 1968), 185-92; interview with W. Averell Harriman, Johnson OHC.

35. Johnson, *Vantage Point*, 522.

36. Vance interview, Johnson OHC.

37. *Ibid.*, Bundy interview, Johnson OHC.

38. Bundy interview, Johnson OHC; Johnson, *Vantage Point*, 522-27.

39. *DSB*, 59 (November 18, 1968), 520-25.

40. Read interview, Johnson OHC.

41. Johnson Papers, WHCF, Dean Rusk, LBJ Library.

Bibliographical Essay

Although the bulk of documents pertinent to foreign policy during Rusk's career remain classified, an unusually large number are accessible, thanks to the *Pentagon Papers* and the Freedom of Information Act. Documents obtained by any scholar through FOI or mandatory review requests are available to all at the relevant presidential library or the National Archives. The *Declassified Documents Reference System* remains the most efficient means of using such material. At my request, Senator Sparkman used FOI procedures to have a large number of executive sessions of the Committee on Foreign Relations declassified. The transcripts may be read at the Archives.

Oral history interviews in the collections at Columbia and the presidential libraries can be of extraordinary value, used in accordance with rules of evidence. Of those I read, the following were helpful:

Columbia

Chester Bowles

Eleanor L. Dulles

Ernest A. Gross

W. Averell Harriman

Flora M. Rhind

Eric Severeid

Dulles Collection, Princeton

Dean Rusk

Truman Library

Loy Henderson

Philip D. Sprouse

Kennedy Library

John S. Badeau
Charles Baldwin
David E. Bell
Richard Bissell
Chester Bowles
Juan Bosch
Winthrop G. Brown
Charles W. Cole
Chester Cooper
Frederick C. Dutton
Adrian Fisher
William Gaud
W. Averell Harriman
U. Alexis Johnson

Roger W. Jones
George F. Kennan
Peter Lisagor
Robert A. Lovett
Edwin E. Martin
Thomas C. Mann
George C. McGhee
Thruston Morton
Benjamin H. Read
George A. Smathers
Theodore C. Sorensen
Llewellyn Thompson
Adam Yarmolinsky

Johnson Library

Charles Bohlen
Chester Bowles
David Bruce
William P. Bundy
George E. Christian
Clark M. Clifford
Douglas Dillon
Ralph Dungan
Adrian Fisher
W. Averell Harriman

Arthur Krock
John M. Leddy
Thomas C. Mann
William B. Macomber
John J. McCloy
George C. McGhee
Henry Owen
Benjamin H. Read
Cyrus Vance
Paul Warnke

I interviewed the following people on the dates indicated:
George Ball, June 12, 1976
Harding Bancroft, October 14, 1976
Lucius D. Battle, November 9 and 23, 1976
Chester Bowles, July 26, 1976
McGeorge Bundy, October 5, 1976 and June 12, 1978
William P. Bundy, November 5, 1975 and October 6, 1976
Harlan Cleveland, October 11, 1976
Clark M. Clifford, November 15, 1976
O. Edmund Clubb, October 12, 1976

John P. Davies, July 22, 1976
Adrian Fisher, November 16, 1976
Dorothy Fosdick, November 17, 1976
J. William Fulbright, November 16, 1976
Leslie Gelb, November 19, 1976
Roswell Gilpatric, October 6, 1976
Ernest A. Gross, March 26, 1976
Louis Henkin, October 14, 1976
Roger Hilsman, September 28, 1976
Thomas L. Hughes, November 15, 1976 (telephone)
Philip C. Jessup, October 1, 1976
Robert Komer, November 16, 1976
George C. McGhee, November 11, 1976
Paul H. Nitze, November 9, 1976
Henry Owen, November 15, 1976
Benjamin H. Read, November 10, 1976
W. W. Rostow, December 9, 1976
Dean Rusk, April 9 and November 5, 1977
Phillips Talbot, October 4, 1976
William R. Tyler, November 11, 1976

I obtained valuable information and insights in letters from the following men, as dated:
General Charles H. Bonesteel, III, June 29, 1975
David M. French, July 3, 1975
Martin J. Hillenbrand, April 27, 1977
James K. Penfield, April 26, 1976
Philip D. Sprouse, August 13, 1976
Of the manuscript materials I used, the papers of V. K. Wellington Koo, Columbia, were most fascinating. They provide rare insights into the workings of a foreign government and extraordinary evidence of intrigue between officials of the American government, including a Secretary of Defense, and Chiang Kai-shek's government. I also found material of value in the following collections:
Dean Acheson, Truman Library
Chester Bowles, Yale
Clark M. Clifford, Truman Library
John Foster Dulles, Princeton
Herbert Feis, Library of Congress

Philip C. Jessup, Library of Congress
Lyndon B. Johnson, Johnson Library
John F. Kennedy, Kennedy Library
James C. Thomson, Kennedy Library
Harry S. Truman, Truman Library

The Rockefeller Foundation allowed me to read Dean Rusk's Diary as President of the Foundation and a few selected papers. William P. Bundy permitted me to read an unpublished manuscript in his possession, which he wrote from his own papers and from information provided by other participants. The Bundy manuscript is a valuable supplement to the Pentagon Papers.

The most useful published documents were the volumes of the Department of State's *Foreign Relations of the United States* series, 1945-1950 and *Bulletin*, 1947-1968, the *Pentagon Papers*, and the historical series of the Senate Committee on Foreign Relations and the House Committee on International Relations.

The *New York Times* and the various periodicals indexed in the *Reader's Guide to Periodic Literature* contain a wealth of comment on Rusk and the foreign affairs with which he was concerned throughout his career. My notes for each chapter indicate articles of particular value.

The following published works were used. Most are cited in the notes.

Abel, Elie, *The Missile Crisis* (Philadelphia: J.B. Lippincott, 1966)

Acheson, Dean G., *Present at the Creation* (New York: Signet, 1970)

Allison, Graham T., *Essence of Decision* (Boston: Little, Brown, 1971)

Alsop, Stuart, "The Trouble with the State Department," *Saturday Evening Post*, 235 (March 3, 1962), 11-15

———, "Mr. Dove and Mr. Hawk," *Saturday Evening Post*, 239 (June 18, 1966), 18

Berle, A.A. *Navigating the Rapids, 1918-1971* (New York: Harcourt, Brace, Jovanovich, 1973)

Bohlen, Charles E., *Witness to History, 1929-1969* (New York: W. W. Norton, 1973)

Borg, Dorothy and Heinrichs, Waldo (eds.), *Uncertain Years: Chinese-American Relations, 1947-1950* (New York: Columbia University Press, 1980)

Bowles, Chester, *Promises to Keep: My Years in Public Life, 1961-1969* (New York: Harper and Row, 1971)

Brown, Seyom, *Faces of Power* (New York: Columbia, 1968)

Campbell, Alex, "The Mild Mr. Rusk: You Don't Fight a Storm, You Ride It Out," *New Republic*, 150 (April 11, 1964), 13-16

Clifford, Clark M., "A Viet Nam Appraisal," *Foreign Affairs*, 47 (July 1969), 601-22

Cooper, Chester, *The Lost Crusade* (New York: Dodd, Mead, 1970)

Davids, Jules, *The United States in World Affairs, 1964* (New York: Harper and Row, 1965)

FitzSimons, Louise, *The Kennedy Doctrine* (New York: Random House, 1972)

Frankel, Max, "The President's 'Just-a-Minute' Man," *New York Times Magazine* (September 12, 1965), 48-49

Gallup, George H., *The Gallup Polls*, 3 vols. (New York: Random House, 1972)

Gelb, Leslie, "The Pentagon Papers and *The Vantage Point*," *Foreign Policy*, 6 (1972), 25-41.

George, Alexander L. and Smoke, Richard, *Deterrence in American Foreign Policy* (New York: Columbia, 1974)

Geyelin, Philip, *LBJ and the World* (New York: Praeger, 1966)

Goldman, Eric F., *The Tragedy of Lyndon Johnson* (New York: Dell, 1969)

Goodman, Allen E., *The Lost Peace: America's Search for a Negotiated Settlement of the Vietnam War* (Stanford: Hoover Institution Press, 1978)

Graff, Henry F., *The Tuesday Cabinet* (Englewood, N.J.: Prentice-Hall, 1970)

Halberstam, David, *The Best and the Brightest* (Greenwich, Conn.: Fawcett Crest, 1973)

Halperin, Morton H., "Why Bureaucrats Play Games," *Foreign Policy*, 2 (1971), 70-90

Henry, John B., II and Espinosa, William, "The Tragedy of Dean Rusk," *Foreign Policy*, 8 (1972), 166-89

Hilsman, Roger, *To Move a Nation* (Garden City: Doubleday, 1967)

Home, Alec Douglas, *The Way the Wind Blows* (London: William Collins, 1976)

Hoopes, Townsend, "LBJ's Account of March 1968," *New Republic*, 162 (March 14, 1970), 17-19

———, *The Limits of Intervention* (New York: David McKay, 1969)

Hughes, Thomas H., "The Power to Speak and the Power to Listen: Reflections on Bureaucratic Politics and a Recommendation on Information Flows," in Thomas M. Frank and Edward Weisband (eds.), *Secrecy and Foreign Policy* (New York: Oxford, 1974)

Jessup, Philip C., *The Birth of Nations* (New York: Columbia, 1974)

Johnson, Haynes, "The Irreconcilable Conflict Between Press and Government: Whose Side Are You On?" in Thomas M. Frank and Edward Weisband (eds.), *Secrecy and Foreign Policy* (New York: Oxford, 1974)

Johnson, Lyndon B., *The Vantage Point* (New York: Holt, Rinehart and Winston, 1971)

Jones, Joseph M., *The Fifteen Weeks* (New York: Viking, 1955)

Karnow, Stanley, "Dean Rusk's Debut," *Reporter*, 24 (April 27, 1961), 37-38

Kennan, George F., *Memoirs 1925-1950* (New York: Bantam, 1969)

———, *Memoirs 1950-1963* (Boston: Little, Brown, 1972)

Kraft, Joseph, "The Comeback of the State Department," *Harper's*, 223 (November 1961), 43-50

———, "Enigma of Dean Rusk," *Harper's*, 231 (July 1965), 100-3

Kulski, W. W., *The Soviet Union in World Affairs* (Syracuse: Syracuse University Press, 1973)

Lash, Joseph P., *Dag Hammarskjold* (Garden City: Doubleday, 1961)

Lowenthal, Abraham F., *The Dominican Intervention* (Cambridge: Harvard, 1972)

Macmillan, Harold, *At the End of the Day* (London: Macmillan, 1973)

———, *Pointing the Way* (New York: Harper and Row, 1972)

Masters, Roger D., "Rusk's Francophobia," *Commonweal*, 84 (July 8, 1966), 431-33

May, Ernest R., *"Lessons" of the Past* (New York: Oxford, 1973)

McLellan, David S., *Dean Acheson: The State Department Years* (New York: Dodd, Mead, 1976)

McPherson, Harry, *A Political Education* (Boston: Little, Brown, 1972)

Millis, Walter (ed.), *The Forrestal Diaries* (New York: Viking, 1951)

Moskin, J. Robert, "Dean Rusk: Cool Man in a Hot World," *Look*, 30 (September 6, 1966), 14-21

O'Neill, Michael J., "The Quiet Diplomat: Dean Rusk," in Lester Tanzer (ed.), *The Kennedy Circle* (Washington: Robert B. Bruce, 1961)

Paige, Glenn D., *The Korean Decision* (New York: Free Press, 1968)

Prospect for America: The Rockefeller Panel Reports (Garden City: Doubleday, 1961)

Radványi, János, *Delusion and Reality: Gambits, Hoaxes, and Diplomatic One-Upmanship in Vietnam* (South Bend, Ind.: Gateway Editions, 1978)

Richardson, James L., *Germany and the Atlantic Alliance* (Cambridge:Harvard, 1966)

Rostow, W. W., *Diffusion of Power* (New York: Macmillan, 1972)

Rovere, Richard, "Notes on the Establishment in America," *American Scholar*, 30 (1961), 489-95

Rusk, Dean, "The President," *Foreign Affairs*, 38 (April 1960), 353-69

Schandler, Herbert Y., *The Unmaking of a President* (Princeton: Princeton University Press, 1977)

Schick, Jack M., *The Berlin Crisis, 1958-1962* (Philadelphia: University of Pennsylvania Press, 1971)

Schlesinger, Arthur M., Jr., *A Thousand Days* (New York: Fawcett, 1967)

―――, *Robert Kennedy and His Times* (New York: Houghton Mifflin, 1978)

Shannon, William V., "Dean Rusk and the President," *Commonweal*, 78 (March 26, 1963), 5-6

Simmons, Robert M., *The Strained Alliance* (New York: Free Press, 1975)

Simpson, Smith, "Who Runs the State Department? The Rusk Enigma," *Nation*, 204 (March 6, 1967), 294-99

Slusser, Robert M., *The Berlin Crisis of 1961* (Baltimore: Johns Hopkins University Press, 1973)

―――, "America, China, and the Hydra-Headed Opposition," in P. H. Juviler and H. W. Morton (eds.), *Soviet Policy-making* (New York: Praeger, 1967)

Smith, Gaddis, *Dean Acheson* in Robert H. Ferrell (ed.), *The American Secretaries of State and Their Diplomacy*, XVI (New York: Cooper Square, 1972)

Smith, Jean Edward, *The Defense of Berlin* (Baltimore: Johns Hopkins University Press, 1963)

Snetsinger, John, *Truman, The Jewish Vote, and the Creation of Israel* (Stanford: Hoover Institution, 1974)

Sorensen, Theodore C., *Kennedy* (New York: Harper and Row, 1965)

Stebbins, Richard P., *The United States in World Affairs, 1961* (New York: Harper and Row, 1962)

———, *The United States in World Affairs, 1962* (New York: Harper and Row, 1963)

———, *The United States in World Affairs, 1963* (New York: Harper and Row, 1964)

———, *The United States in World Affairs, 1965* (New York: Harper and Row, 1966)

———, *The United States in World Affairs, 1966* (New York: Harper and Row, 1967)

———, *The United States in World Affairs, 1967* (New York: Harper and Row, 1968)

Stillman, Edmund, "Dean Rusk: In the American Grain," *Commentary*, 45 (May 1968)

Sulzberger, Cyrus, *Age of Mediocrity* (New York: Macmillan, 1973)

———, *Last of the Giants* (New York: Macmillian, 1970)

Thomson, James C., "On the Making of U.S. China Policy, 1961-1969: A Study in Bureaucratic Politics," *China Quarterly*, 50 (1972), 220-43

Truman, Harry S., *Memoirs: Years of Trial and Hope, 1946-1952* (Garden City: Doubleday, 1956)

Urquhart, Brian, *Hammarskjold* (New York: Knopf, 1972)

Van Ness, Peter, *Revolution and Chinese Foreign Policy* (Berkeley: University of California Press, 1970)

Viorst, Milton, "Incidentally, Who is Dean Rusk?" *Esquire*, 69 (April 1968), 98-101

Walton, Richard J., *Cold War and Counter-Revolution* (Baltimore: Penguin, 1973)

Weigley, Russell F., *The American Way of War* (New York: Macmillan, 1973)

Weissman, Stephan R., *American Foreign Policy in the Congo, 1960-1964* (Ithaca: Cornell University Press, 1974)

Whiting, Allen S., *China Crosses the Yalu* (New York: Macmillan, 1960)

Wicker, Tom, *JFK and LBJ* (Baltimore: Penguin, 1970)

Wilson, Harold, *A Personal Record* (Boston: Little, Brown, 1971)

Windsor, Philip, *City on Leave* (London: Chatto and Windus, 1963)

Index

Abdullah ibn Hussein, King of Jordan, 25
Abrams, General Creighton, 310, 315
Acheson, Dean G., 5, 31, 110, 168, 214; attitude toward UN, 7–11, 52, 84; assessment of Soviet Union, 10; and Truman Doctrine, 10–11; on Marshall Plan, 13; succeeded by Lovett, 13; on colonialism, 15; and Jessup, 15, 34; on complainers and whiners, 27; becomes secretary of state, 31–2; contempt for Congressmen, 35; on atomic weapons, 38; memoir, 39; and Chinese revolution, 39–44; and "White Paper," 39–40; on Formosa, 41–4, 52–3, 164; and Chinese intervention in Korea, 57–9; and "Slavic Manchukuo" speech, 63–5; forced to aid Chiang, 65; and Korean cease-fire, 67–9; accepts containment in Asia, 72; on summit conferences, 91; recommends Rusk for secretary of state, 93; Kennan and Kennedy on, 94; as Atlanticist, 109, 134; critical of Kennedy (1954), 126; and Berlin crisis, 138–9; on McCarthyites, 165; on aid to French in Indochina, 173; on "massive retaliation," 195; meeting of "Wise Men," 309–10; contrasted with Rusk, 320, 323–4,

Acheson, Dean G. *continued*
326–7; conception of Cold War strategy, 328–9
Acheson family, 1
Adenauer, Konrad, and Berlin crisis, 138, 141–9; and Rusk, 194, 198; and de Gaulle, 196, 198; and MLF, 201; suspicion of Soviet-American rapprochement, 294
Adoula, Cyrille, elected premier of Congo, 120–21; negotiates with Tshombe, 122; survives vote on censure, 124; replaced by Tshombe, 230
Aiken, Senator George F., 315
Algeria, 292
Algerian National Liberation Front, 118
Allende, Salvador, 226, 228
Alliance for Progress, 204–5, 217, 262
Allied Naval Force (ANF), 298
American Committee for Aid to Katanga Freedom Fighters, 122
American Friends Service Committee, 3
Angola, 202
Arab refugees, 30–31
Armstrong, Hamilton Fish, 36, 87
atomic energy control, 13–4
Attlee, Clement, 59
Austin, Warren, 22–3, 26

Balaguer, Joaquin, 263, 267

359